FA Carling
PREMIERSHIP

POCKET ANNUAL 1994-95

Editor: Bruce Smith
Phil Heady

2nd Year of Publication

FA Carling Premiership Annual 1994/95

ISBN: 1-898351-06-6

First published in 1994 by
Words on Sport

Typeset by Bruce Smith Books Ltd

All photographs:
Empics Photo Agency

Words on Sport Ltd
PO Box 382
St. Albans
Herts, AL2 3JD

Registered Office:
Worplesdon Chase, Worplesdon,
Guildford, Surrey, GU3 3LA
Reg. No.: 2917013

Printed and bound in Great Britain by
Ashford Colour Press, Gosport

Disclaimer

In a book of this type it is inevitable that some errors will creep in. While every effort has been made to ensure that the details given in this annual are correct at the time of going to press, neither the editor nor the publishers can accept any responsibility for errors within.

CONTENTS

FA Carling Premiership Club Directory 1994-95

Transfers Involving FA Premier League Clubs 1993-94

A-Z of FA Premier League Players 1994-95

The A-Z of Ex-FA Premier League Players

Bruce Smith's View...

For the majority of supporters it was a fabulous season – great games, great entertainment, and magnificent triumphs that had many on the edge of their seats whether it be in the superb new stadia being unveiled or in the comfort of home with Sky Sports in full flow. But for every joy there is despair and, relegations apart, there was a thunderbolt for Tottenham and the demise of the national side. But as always there's hope and Spurs' appeal was partly successful and Terry Venables' England side has shown a touch of panache – although we wait to see if it can produce the goods on the world stage.

Having taken some 25 years to build on early title success in 1992-93, Manchester United continued to carry the flag and achieved only the fourth double this century. They also came as close as anyone to achieving an unprecedented treble by reaching the Coca-Cola Cup final only to be out-witted by Ron Atkinson's Aston Villa. It shouldn't be forgotten that United also started the season with a Charity Shield win as well. To complete the honours at Old Trafford, Alex Ferguson took the Manager of the Year award for good measure. That particular award now seems to be devalued by simply awarding it to the manager of the Championship side – true Ferguson in completing the double was a worthy winner, but surely the real manager of the year was Joe Kinnear who achieved wonders on a fraction of what money is available at United. And don't be fooled – forget that kick and run image of old – Wimbledon produced some highly entertaining games last season. Watch them if you can – don't become stereo-typed like the rest – form your own opinion and you might be pleasantly surprised!

Magnificent Arsenal. The Pet Shop Boys' 'Go West' will never quite be the same again but their achievement in just not winning, but in getting to the Cup-Winners' Cup final was truly a fine achievement. They will be joined there this year by Chelsea and don't be surprised if the Gunners become the first team to retain that particular pot.

Much has already been written about England's exit from the World Cup by R.Koeman esq. This is history but what everyone seemed to forget is that Frank Rijkaard had a perfectly good goal disallowed before that and, as the World Cup Final, showed – who's to say 10 men wouldn't have faired better than England's 11? Things do look brighter now though, but then they have done in the past – time will tell. I hope Terry Venables is a lucky England Coach.

There was sadness at the loss of two great names, Tottenham's Danny Blanchflower and Manchester United's Sir Matt Busby – they were not the first and they will not be the last but like the rest they will not be forgotten.

In Europe, Manchester United got their wish and were awarded a place directly in the Champions' League – that should ensure them of six matches and with the top two sides going into the knockout quarter-final stage they should be able to progress. Newcastle United's magnificent first season back

5

at the top was rewarded with a UEFA Cup spot where they join Blackburn Rovers and Aston Villa.

As always there was plenty of controversy last season, none more so than the succession of dismissals that plagued Manchester United. Goalkeepers got their fair share of marching orders at all levels of the game and for most I have no sympathy. Peter Schmeichel's red card in the FA Cup tie with Charlton was indicative of many keepers' receive. Goalkeepers must remember that when they leave their penalty area they are no longer a goalkeeper in the rules of the game but a defender. As such they must act like one. How many times have you seen the likes of a Gary Pallister or a Tony Adams go it with a two footed tackle and arms flaying in the air? If the handball didn't get them dismissed, the two-footed tackled would. So why should keepers be any different?

The 1994-95 season promises to be another intriguing one. The Premiership will take a reduction in size at the end of it with four clubs being relegated and only two being promoted. The Football League Division 1 champions will be promoted and the four clubs below them will play-off for the second spot.

1994-95 also sees the first season of all-seater stadia in the Premiership. Many of the grounds are magnificent and in my view better than most of what the continent has to offer. Indeed with the exception of a few grounds in Italy and Spain they are now the best.

The Taylor Report, the FA Premiership – the last two years have seen phenomenal changes. They have been worth it – let's all reap the benefits by supporting the game in the best way possible.

List of Acknowledgments
Many thanks to everyone who has contributed to this year's Annual – not least the following, with apologies to those I may have missed: Phil Heady (Players), John Kelly (Club reviews), Tim Healey (Football Information Services), Peter Fitzpatrick, Mark Webb, Susan Fakes and Martin Ritchie.

Manchester United FC 1993-94 – Double Winners

The Coca-Cola Cup

WINNERS
1993 / 94

The Coca-Cola Cup

Aston Villa FC

Arsenal FC – European Cup-Winners' Cup Winners 1993-94

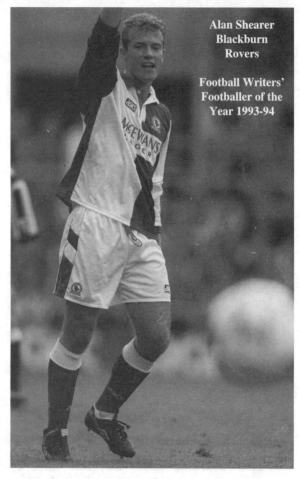

Alan Shearer
Blackburn
Rovers

Football Writers'
Footballer of the
Year 1993-94

August

The English close season saw more progression off the pitch or more literally around the pitch, as the improvements and renovations instigated as part of the Taylor Report continued to move stadia in England forward. All Premiership and first division grounds had just one season left to become all-seater. Many games during the course of the season were be played in eerie atmospheres as clubs such as Manchester United and Blackburn Rovers to name but two demolished old and rebuilt new stands.

Pre and early season transfers saw a number of high value moves. Top of these was the £3.75 million signing by Manchester United of relegated Nottingham Forest midfielder Roy Keane. Other obscene sums included the £2.7 million paid by Sheffield Wednesday for QPR's Andy Sinton where he joined Des Walker, newly arrived from Sampdoria. Leeds United bought Brian Deane from Sheffield United for a similar amount, Sheffield replaced him with Jostein Flo from Norwegian club Sogndal. Liverpool paid £2 million for Nigel Clough, Jason Dozzell moved from Ipswich to Tottenham and in a surprise move Newcastle United welcomed back Peter Beardsley from Everton.

The season kicked off with Manchester United still celebrating their first championship title in 26 years and already installed as favourites to retain the title. They faced double cup-winners Arsenal in the traditional curtain raiser – the FA Charity Shield – at Wembley and, after an exciting 1-1 draw, captured the trophy in a penalty shoot-out.

The Premiership season got underway with the three newcomers – Newcastle United, West Ham United and Swindon Town – all suffering defeats. England international Carlton Palmer became the first player to be sent off, just 13 minutes into the new campaign as Sheffield Wednesday went down 2-0 at Anfield. In London Arsenal – opening their new all-seater North Bank stand – were on the end of the shock of the day, losing 3-0 at home to Coventry for whom Mick Quinn got the season's first hat-trick. Manchester United meanwhile recorded a 2-0 win at Norwich City who started the season contemplating European competition for the first time in their history. As ever, Wimbledon were not far from the headlines with club chairman, Sam Hammam reported to the FA for scribbling obscenities on the dressing room wall at West Ham where his team had won 2-0.

Peter Swales, the controversial Manchester City chairman, handed over the day-to-day running of the club to newly appointed general manager, John Maddock who in turn sacked player-manager Peter Reid and his assistant, Sam Ellis, just four games into the new season. Manchester City's poor start – one point from those four games – was cited as the cause. Reid was the eleventh manager at Maine Road since Peter Swales took over as chairman in 1973, and police were called in to quell an angry demonstration against Swales by more than 1,000 City fans. Brian Horton, ex-manager of Oxford United, was announced as Reid's successor, bringing with him his assistant, David Moss from the first division side.

At Elland Road there were calls for Howard Wilkinson's resignation after Leeds were defeated by two goals at Liverpool. There was slightly better news for Swindon Town though as the end of the month arrived, gaining their first Premiership point in a 0-0 draw at Norwich City. It was their fifth game. Likewise there was call for celebration in the Sheffield Wednesday camp when they scored their first goal of the season – after 371 minutes play – in a 1-1 draw at Chelsea.

September

September saw the national side beat Poland 3-0 at Wembley in a World Cup qualifying encounter. England played their hearts out and played Poland off the pitch with a display full of skill, understanding and application. Stuart Pearce returned as captain and scored into the bargain.

Manchester United continued to increase their lead at the top but suffered their first defeat of the season and their first league defeat in six months losing 1-0 at Chelsea. On the other side of the city the fans didn't know whether to boo or cheer. Manchester City won 3-0 over QPR but there was a protest after the game by 10,000 fans calling for the resignation of chairman Peter Swales. Former player and multi-millionaire Francis Lee was the favourite to take over. Leeds gained their first away win, 2-0 at Southampton, since they won the championship two seasons before.

The first round of European competition saw a clean bill of health for all English clubs. Manchester United saw off Honved; Arsenal recovered from an own goal to beat Odense in the Cup-Winners' Cup; in the UEFA Cup Aston Villa disposed of Slovan Bratislava; Norwich City eased past Vitesse.

Norwich City's Euro form finally rubbed off in the league as Efan Ekoku scored four goals – a record for the Premiership – in their 5-1 win at Goodison Park. It was Everton's heaviest home defeat in years. Across Stanley Park Liverpool completed a month with no league goals and no league points and speculation started about the future of manager Graeme Souness.

October

October saw the Premiership sides enter the second round of the Coca-Cola (League) Cup. With a few exceptions all came through unscathed. The exceptions were Sheffield United deposed by second division Blackpool, Leeds who were beaten by first division Sunderland (1973 and all that) whilst third division Shrewsbury pulled off the biggest upset humiliating Southampton. Liverpool's Robbie Fowler scored all five as Fulham came unstuck at Anfield and there were hat-tricks for Newcastle's Cole and Queens Park Rangers' Allen.

Internationally, England's brief revival faltered leaving qualification only a slim possibility. A 2-0 defeat in Rotterdam was surrounded in controversy not least because of Ronald Koeman's man-handling of David Platt when clear through on goal.

There were also mixed results in the second round of European competitions. Manchester United threw away a 2-0 lead before scrapping a 3-3 home draw with Galatasaray. Arsenal faired better with a 3-0 win over Standard Liege while, in only their third European game ever, Norwich City managed what no other English team had accomplished – victory in Germany against three times European champions, Bayern Munich. Norwich's victory overshadowed Aston Villa's success in holding in-form Spanish side Deportivo La Coruna to a 1-1 draw in Spain, a game which saw Mark Bosnich save an early penalty.

As the month drew to a close Bobby Gould resigned as manager of Coventry City after watching his side lose 5-1 to in-form QPR. In the third round of the Coca-Cola Cup first division Nottingham Forest knocked-out struggling Eastenders West Ham but they were the only lower division side to succeed over higher opposition. Meanwhile Manchester United extended their lead to 11 points as the chasing pack dropped points in a series of draws.

While it was good news in the league it was bad new in the Champions' Cup for United as November dawned. A disappointing 0-0 draw in Istanbul which ended controversially saw them miss out on the lucrative Champions' League stage. It was also bad news in Birmingham where Aston Villa lost 1-0 to a formidable Deportivo La Coruna side to go out of the UEFA Cup. Better news came from East Anglia though as Norwich completed their mini demolition of Bayern Munich in Norfolk's biggest night in football. In the Cup-Winners' Cup Arsenal, without a goal in their previous four league games, dropped top scorer Ian Wright and travelled to Liege to defend a 3-0 first leg lead. They won 7-0 to confound all their critics with a superb display of attacking football.

Blackburn Rovers continued their sweeping up of top players by breaking the British record for a goalkeeper, spending £2.4 million on Southampton's Tim Flowers. Arsenal's scoring glut looked to have rubbed off in the league when they scored their first league goal in seven hours and 33 minutes of football but they conceded two to lose at home to Aston Villa! Sheffield Wednesday recorded their first away win of the season – 4-1 at Ipswich.

There was uproar when Sepp Blatter, FIFA General Secretary, accused British football of being 30 years behind the times. In response the FA unveiled a range of plans aimed at helping youth soccer in this country. It didn't help the national side though. It was Goodbye, USA as Holland won in Poland and England failed to do the business against San Marino, suffering the humiliation of going behind to the amateurs after just nine seconds of play. As if to amplify Blatter's thoughts a major shake-up of the British game from the way it is coached, played and administrated was called for from all quarters. Many remained sceptical and as expected England manager Graham Taylor resigned from the post and Terry Venables was installed as favourite to take over the FA's hot seat. Things also looked bleak for Norwich City in the UEFA Cup as they lost at home to Internazionale through a goal from Dennis Bergkamp.

After four weeks as caretaker manager, Phil Neal was confirmed as Coventry City's new boss. There was further controversy for Wimbledon as Tottenham's Gary Mabbutt was stretchered off with a fractured skull after a collision with John Fashanu's elbow. The subsequent FA inquiry cleared Fashanu of intent. Bottom placed Swindon's 16th Premiership match saw their first victory in the top flight – 1-0 over QPR. Manchester United stretched their lead at the top to 14 points and City's Peter Swales resigned and was replaced by Francis Lee.

In the fourth round of the Coca-Cola Cup, holders Arsenal lost their first cup tie in 25 games, 1-0 at home to Aston Villa. First division Tranmere Rovers toppled Oldham 3-0 and Manchester United marched on with a win 2-0 at Everton.

December

December started with another resignation. After Everton beat Southampton 1-0 in front of their smallest ever Premiership crowd manager Howard Kendall announced his decision. As expected Norwich bowed out of the UEFA Cup with their pride intact and their reputation enhanced. As the fourth round of the Coca-Cola Cup progressed Wimbledon beat Liverpool on penalties after a 2-2 draw and Manchester City lost their replay 2-1 at home to Nottingham Forest.

The FA Carling Premiership reached its halfway stage and showed Manchester United as leaders having taken 52 from a possible 63 points, the latest three coming from a 3-1 win over Aston Villa. In the first games after the Christmas festivities it needed a last minute equaliser to rescue United from a first home defeat of the season at the hands of chasers Blackburn Rovers. Chelsea – without a win in 12 games – defeated high flying Newcastle United which continued their habit of only claiming prize scalps, their other victims being QPR, Liverpool and Manchester United.

January

The New Year began with new faces in new jobs. Troubled Everton poached a disillusioned Mike Walker from Norwich City for whom John Deehan stepped up. Ian Branfoot left Southampton and the fans' choice, Alan Ball, took over. Terry Venables was finally announced as England coach after months of FA dithering. Graeme Souness stepped down as Liverpool boss after his team's first defeat in 13 games – a 1-0 shocker at Anfield to Bristol City which put the Reds out of the FA Cup. Promotion from within saw long time boot-room 'boy' Roy Evans take charge.

Manchester United cleared the often difficult Christmas hurdle without losing although a few too many draws put Blackburn in contention albeit at a distance. One of United's draws was a 3-3 thriller at Anfield which saw them surrender a 3-0 lead built in just 25 minutes. United also marched on in the third round of the FA Cup succeeding where they failed the previous season – 1-0 victory at Sheffield United. Queens Park Rangers fell to second division Stockport County, Everton stumbled at home to Bolton of the first. Non-League Kidderminster captured the headlines though winning at troubled Birmingham City.

A replay win at Portsmouth saw Manchester United through to the semi-finals of the Coca-Cola Cup where they were joined by Sheffield Wednesday, Villa and Tranmere Rovers.

As the month drew to a close the FA Cup fourth round saw Manchester City bow out to second division strugglers Cardiff City but most other games followed form or ended in draws. Kidderminster Harriers made the last 16 by beating Preston North End.

The nation was saddened by the news of Sir Matt Busby's death at the age of 84 just days before the European Championship draw was held in Manchester.

February

As the dust settled on the hectic cup month of January the talk was of Manchester United's possibilities of winning an unprecedented 'Treble'. Odds of 4-1 were aided by the performances of possible contenders in the FA Cup as holders Arsenal tumbled to first division Bolton Wanderers in extra time of a replay at Highbury. Other clubs to fall by the wayside included Newcastle United, Leeds United, Blackburn Rovers and Aston Villa. Indeed just seven Premiership sides played in the fifth round but that saw West Ham finish off non-league Kidderminster Harriers' cup dreams. In the Coca Cola Cup semi-finals Aston Villa inched out Tranmere Rovers to clinch a place at Wembley.

In the League only Blackburn remained as a possible threat to Manchester United's lead as the chasing pack shed points. Tottenham Hotspur set an unwanted club record as they slumped to seven consecutive league defeats leaving manager Osvaldo Ardiles under a cloud of mounting pressure.

March

As March dawned Chelsea remained the only team to have beaten Manchester United in the league and they proceeded to make it a double with a win at Old Trafford with Peacock again grabbing the only goal. At the same time Tottenham scraped a 1-1 home draw with Villa to earn their first league point of the year and Wimbledon ended Norwich's sequence of six straight draws with a 3-1 win. John Deehan was finally appointed manager at Norwich and he immediately recorded a 3-0 over previous manager Mike Walker's Everton side.

New England coach, Terry Venables, picked his first international squad to play Denmark. He close 18 'elite' players, most of whom the media had been citing for inclusion in World Cup squads: Matthew Le Tissier, Graeme Le Saux, Darren Anderton, Peter Beardsley and Alan Shearer. England won 1-0 playing with considerable panache. Not surprisingly Terry Venables was accorded an ovation by the Wembley crowd and the talk was of what might have been...

Back in the real world the Premiership teams asserted themselves in the FA Cup. United disposed of Charlton, 3-1, despite the dismissal of 'keeper Peter Schmeichel, and Oldham overcame the first division's Cup heroes, Bolton Wanderers, 1-0. Chelsea had no difficulties beating Wolves 1-0 and it was left to Luton Town to fly the minnows' flag. They held West Ham to a goalless draw at Upton Park and took the replay 3-2 thanks to a hat-trick from Scott Oakes.

Eric Cantona started to make the back page headlines for all the wrong reasons. Sent off at Swindon he followed that up with a dismissal at Highbury where United were fortunate to gain a point in a 2-2 draw. Cantona had some good news though as he was voted the Professional Footballers' Player of the Year. The Football Writer's Association award went to Alan Shearer.

Dreams of Trebles were finally dashed as, without suspended Schmeichel, United lost a thrilling Coca-Cola Cup final at Wembley 1-3 to Aston Villa. United's woe was completed by the sending off of Andrei Kanchelskis at the very end of play for deliberate handball. He became the fourth United player to be sent off in five games.

April

The penultimate month of the league season saw Blackburn Rovers draw level on points with United at the top of the Premiership as the Manchester club faltered. They lost 2-0 at Ewood Park with Alan Shearer bagging both goals in spectacular fashion.

In the FA Cup semi-finals, controversially held at Wembley, Chelsea put paid to the first division dreams, disposing of a below par Luton Town. The following day Oldham and Manchester United needed extra time before a Latic goal materialised. But United forced a replay inside the last minute thanks to a superb Mark Hughes goal. In the replay there was only one team in it as United showed the style of football which won them so many plaudits during the season.

Arsenal continued to fly the flag in Europe as they got through to the final of the Cup-Winners' Cup proving too strong over two legs for the French league leaders, Paris St Germain. Arsenal drew 1-1 in Paris and won 1-0 at Highbury. It was bad news though as a second booking meant they would be without striker Ian Wright in the final and a week later an injury to John Jensen playing for Denmark against Hungary ruled him out of the final against holders Parma.

The noise of protest also continued unabated at Loftus Road where QPR supporters staged another sit-down protest following a 4-0 drubbing by Leeds United. QPR were in equally charitable mood when they played Swindon handing the Wiltshire club their first away win of the season. It did Swindon no good as they had already been relegated. In the first division Crystal Palace were crowned as champions with Nottingham Forest claiming the second automatic promotion place.

May

Coventry City's defeat of Blackburn Rovers at Highfield Road meant that the Premiership title went to Manchester United for the second year running. It was the first successful title defence since the 1986-87 season. Blackburn though were assured of their UEFA Cup place for next season, having made sure of the runners-up spot. Newcastle United took third place and (in June) were granted a UEFA Cup place. Arsenal produced another magnificent performance to lift the Cup-Winners' Cup. Without four key players Alan Smith rifled in the only goal of the game in Copenhagen.

Throughout the Premiership clubs have said their farewells to their famous terraces as standing room only gives way to all-seater stadia. Most famous of all, Liverpool's Kop watched as Norwich City spoiled the party and highlighted the deficiencies of the current side compared with the great teams of the past. Tottenham and Manchester City scraped together enough points to assure themselves of continued life in the Premiership. The final Saturday of the season saw any two from Oldham, Everton, Ipswich Town, Sheffield United and Southampton facing relegation alongside Swindon. Oldham failed to make the cut drawing 1-1 at Norwich. Everton looked set to say farewell to

18

40 years of football in the top flight as they fell 2-0 behind at home to Wimbledon but recovered strongly to win 3-2 and saved their skins. Ipswich and Southampton did just enough by drawing 0-0 at Blackburn and 3-3 at West Ham respectively. That left Sheffield United. They were 2-1 up with a quarter of an hour left to play at Cup finalists Chelsea when they conceded another goal to make the game 2-2. That would have still been just enough but a Chelsea goal in the 90th minute condemned them to the first division.

FA Cup Final day arrived with the usual fanfare and Chelsea took to the Wembley pitch knowing that they would be playing in the next season's Cup-Winners' Cup whatever the result thanks to Manchester United's Champions' Cup commitments. Fortune favoured the Reds however. Despite dominating the first two-thirds of the game and rattling the United crossbar, Chelsea were beaten 4-0. The first two United goals were penalties leaving a rueful Glenn Hoddle to reflect after the game that United's first clear chance was their third goal.

The result crowned a wonderful season for Manchester United. They became only the fourth team this century to complete the double of league championship and FA Cup. They joined an exclusive list of the greatest English league teams: Tottenham Hotspur (1961), Arsenal (1971) and Liverpool (1986).

National optimism continued as England thrashed World Cup qualifiers Greece 5-0 at Wembley, but arch-rivals Norway spoiled the final party of the season by keeping England at bay in a goalless draw. In prospect was a nervous summer for Tottenham Hotspur though as they looked certain to be investigated on multiple charges of financial irregularities with the possibility of relegation from the Premiership. The FA took the unprecedented step of announcing that Sheffield United would remain in the Premiership should Tottenham be demoted.

On the field, the Play-offs continued and it was third time lucky for Leicester City who beat Derby County with a last minute goal to clinch the final promotion place.

June

Tottenham were found guilty of illegal payments by the FA and were given record breaking punishments and fine including suspension from the FA Cup for the 94-95 season, deduction of 12 Premiership points for the 94-95 season and a £600,000 fine. This was later increased to £1.5 million at the reduction of 6 Premiership points on appeal.

19

FINAL TABLES 1993-94

FA Carling Premiership

		HOME					AWAY					
	P	W	D	L	F	A	W	D	L	F	A	Pts
Manchester United	42	14	6	1	39	13	13	5	3	41	25	92
Blackburn Rovers	42	14	5	2	31	11	11	4	6	32	25	84
Newcastle United	42	14	4	3	51	14	9	4	8	31	27	77
Arsenal	42	10	8	3	25	15	8	9	4	28	13	71
Leeds United	42	13	6	2	37	18	5	10	6	28	21	70
Wimbledon	42	12	5	4	35	21	6	6	9	21	32	65
Sheffield Wednesday	42	10	7	4	48	24	6	9	6	28	30	64
Liverpool	42	12	4	5	33	23	5	5	11	26	32	60
Queens Park Rangers	42	8	7	6	32	29	8	3	8	30	32	60
Aston Villa	42	8	5	8	23	18	7	7	7	23	32	57
Coventry City	42	9	7	5	23	17	5	7	9	20	28	56
Norwich City	42	4	9	8	26	29	8	8	5	39	32	53
West Ham United	42	6	7	8	26	31	7	6	8	21	27	52
Chelsea	42	11	5	5	31	20	2	7	12	18	33	51
Tottenham Hotspur	42	4	8	9	29	33	7	4	10	25	26	45
Manchester City	42	6	10	5	24	22	3	8	10	14	27	45
Everton	42	8	4	9	26	30	4	4	13	16	33	44
Southampton	42	9	2	10	30	31	3	5	13	19	35	43
Ipswich Town	42	5	8	8	21	32	4	8	9	14	26	43
Sheffield United	42	6	10	5	24	23	2	8	11	18	37	42
Oldham Athletic	42	5	8	8	24	33	4	5	12	18	35	40
Swindon Town	42	4	7	10	25	45	1	8	12	22	55	30

Endsleigh League Division 1

		HOME					AWAY					
	P	W	D	L	F	A	W	D	L	F	A	Pts
Crystal Palace	46	16	4	3	39	18	11	5	7	34	28	90
Nottingham Forest	46	12	9	2	38	22	11	5	7	36	27	83
Millwall	46	14	8	1	36	17	5	9	9	22	32	74
Leicester City	46	11	9	3	45	30	8	7	8	27	29	73
Tranmere Rovers	46	15	3	5	48	23	6	6	11	21	30	72
Derby County	46	15	3	5	44	25	5	8	10	29	43	71
Notts County	46	16	3	4	43	26	4	5	14	22	43	68
Wolverhampton Wanderers	46	10	10	3	34	19	7	7	9	26	28	68
Middlesbrough	46	12	6	5	40	19	6	7	10	26	35	67
Stoke City	46	14	4	5	35	19	4	9	10	22	40	67
Charlton Athletic	46	14	3	6	39	22	5	5	13	22	36	65
Sunderland	46	14	2	7	35	22	5	6	12	19	35	65
Bristol City	46	11	7	5	27	18	5	9	9	20	32	64
Bolton Wanderers	46	10	8	5	40	31	5	6	12	23	33	59

	P	W	D	L	F	A	W	D	L	F	A	Pts
Southend	46	10	5	8	34	28	7	3	13	29	39	59
Grimsby Town	46	7	14	2	26	16	6	6	11	26	31	59
Portsmouth	46	10	6	7	29	22	5	7	11	23	36	58
Barnsley	46	9	3	11	25	26	7	4	12	30	41	55
Watford	46	10	5	8	39	35	4	5	14	27	45	54
Luton	46	12	4	7	38	25	2	7	14	18	35	53
West Bromwich Albion	46	9	7	7	38	31	4	5	14	22	38	51
Birmingham City	46	9	7	7	28	29	4	5	14	24	40	51
Oxford	46	10	5	8	33	33	3	5	15	21	42	49
Peterborough United	46	6	9	8	31	30	2	4	17	17	46	37

Endsleigh League Division 2

		HOME					AWAY					
	P	W	D	L	F	A	W	D	L	F	A	Pts
Reading	46	15	6	2	40	16	11	5	7	41	28	89
Port Vale	46	16	6	1	46	18	10	4	9	33	28	88
Plymouth	46	16	4	3	46	26	9	6	8	42	30	85
Stockport	46	15	3	5	50	22	9	10	4	24	22	85
York	46	12	7	4	33	13	9	5	9	31	27	75
Burnley	46	17	4	2	55	18	4	6	13	24	40	73
Bradford	46	13	5	5	34	20	6	8	9	27	33	70
Bristol Rovers	46	10	8	5	33	26	10	2	11	27	33	70
Hull	46	9	9	5	33	20	9	5	9	29	34	68
Cambridge	46	11	5	7	38	29	8	4	11	41	44	66
Huddersfield	46	9	8	6	27	26	8	6	9	31	35	65
Wrexham	46	13	4	6	45	33	4	7	12	21	44	62
Swansea	46	12	7	4	37	20	4	5	14	19	38	60
Brighton	46	10	7	6	38	29	5	7	11	22	38	59
Rotherham	46	11	4	8	42	30	4	9	10	21	30	58
Brentford	46	7	10	6	30	28	6	9	8	27	27	58
Bournemouth	46	8	7	8	26	27	6	8	9	25	32	57
Orient	46	11	9	3	38	26	3	5	15	19	45	56
Cardiff	46	10	7	6	39	33	3	8	12	27	46	54
Blackpool	46	12	2	9	41	36	4	3	16	22	38	53
Fulham	46	7	6	10	20	23	4	12	30	40	52
Exeter	46	8	7	8	38	37	3	5	15	14	46	45
Hartlepool	46	8	3	12	28	40	1	6	16	12	47	36
Barnet	46	4	6	13	22	32	1	7	15	19	54	28

Endsleigh League Division 3

		HOME					AWAY					
	P	W	D	L	F	A	W	D	L	F	A	Pts
Shrewsbury	42	10	8	3	28	17	12	5	4	35	22	79
Chester	42	13	5	3	35	18	8	6	7	34	28	74
Crewe	42	12	4	5	45	30	9	6	6	35	31	73
Wycombe	42	11	6	4	34	21	8	7	6	33	32	70
Preston	42	13	5	3	46	23	5	8	8	33	37	67
Torquay	42	8	10	3	30	24	9	6	6	34	32	67

		W	D	L	F	A	W	D	L	F	A	
Carlisle	42	10	4	7	35	23	8	6	7	22	19	64
Chesterfield	42	8	8	5	32	22	8	6	7	23	26	62
Rochdale	42	10	5	6	38	22	6	7	8	25	29	60
Walsall	42	7	5	9	28	26	10	4	7	20	27	60
Scunthorpe	42	9	7	5	40	26	6	7	8	24	30	59
Mansfield	42	9	3	9	28	30	6	7	8	25	32	55
Bury	42	9	6	6	33	22	5	5	11	22	34	53
Scarborough	42	8	4	9	29	28	7	4	10	26	33	53
Doncaster	42	8	6	7	24	26	6	4	11	20	31	52
Gillingham	42	8	8	5	27	23	4	7	10	17	28	51
Colchester	42	8	4	9	31	33	5	6	10	25	38	49
Lincoln	42	7	4	10	26	29	5	7	9	26	34	47
Wigan	42	6	7	8	33	33	5	5	11	18	37	45
Hereford	42	6	4	11	34	33	6	2	13	26	46	42
Darlington	42	7	5	9	24	28	3	6	12	18	36	41
Northampton	42	6	7	8	25	23	3	4	14	19	43	38

FA Carling Premiership
Promotions and Relegations

1993-94	Promoted	Crystal Palace	Champions
		Nottingham Forest	Runners-up
		Leicester City	Play-off winners (4th)
	Relegated	Sheffield United	20th
		Oldham Athletic	21st
		Swindon Town	22nd
1992-93	Promoted	Newcastle United	Champions
		West Ham United	Runners-up
		Swindon Town	Play-off winners (5th)
	Relegated	Crystal Palace	20th
		Middlesborough	21st
		Nottingham Forest	22nd

Eric Cantona
Manchester United
PFA Footballer of
the Year 1993-94

FA PREMIER LEAGUE

	Arsenal	Aston Villa	Blackburn R	Chelsea	Coventry City	Everton	Ipswich Town	Liverpool	Leeds United	Man City	Man Utd
Arsenal	•	1-2	1-0	1-0	0-3	2-0	4-0	1-0	2-1	0-0	0-0
Aston Villa	1-2	•	0-1	1-0	0-0	0-0	0-1	2-1	1-0	0-0	1-2
Blackburn Rovers	1-1	1-0	•	2-0	2-1	0-0	0-0	2-0	2-1	2-0	2-0
Chelsea	0-2	1-1	1-2	•	1-2	4-2	1-1	1-0	1-1	0-0	1-0
Coventry City	1-0	0-1	2-1	1-1	•	2-1	1-0	2-0	0-2	4-0	0-1
Everton	1-1	1-2	0-3	4-2	0-0	•	0-0	2-0	1-1	1-0	0-1
Ipswich Town	1-5	2-0	1-0	1-0	0-2	0-0	•	1-2	0-0	2-2	1-2
Leeds United	2-1	2-1	3-3	4-1	1-0	2-0	0-0	2-0	•	3-2	0-2
Liverpool	0-0	2-1	0-1	2-1	1-0	3-0	1-0	•	2-0	2-1	3-3
Manchester City	1-0	3-0	0-2	2-2	1-1	2-1	2-1	1-1	1-1	•	2-3
Manchester United	2-0	3-1	1-1	0-1	0-0	1-0	0-0	1-0	0-0	2-0	•
Newcastle United	1-1	5-1	1-1	0-0	4-0	1-0	2-0	3-0	1-1	2-0	1-1
Norwich City	0-0	1-2	2-2	1-1	1-0	3-0	1-0	2-2	2-1	1-1	0-2
Oldham Athletic	1-1	1-1	1-2	2-1	3-3	0-1	0-3	0-3	0-4	0-0	2-5
Queens Park Rangers	1-1	2-2	1-0	1-0	5-1	3-0	3-0	1-3	2-2	1-1	2-3
Sheffield United	1-1	1-2	1-2	3-1	0-0	1-1	1-1	0-0	3-3	0-1	0-3
Sheffield Wednesday	0-1	0-0	3-1	1-1	1-0	2-0	5-0	3-1	0-2	1-1	2-3
Southampton	0-4	4-1	1-3	3-1	3-1	5-1	0-1	4-2	0-5	1-3	1-3
Swindon Town	0-4	1-2	0-2	1-3	1-2	0-2	2-2	0-5	1-1	1-0	2-2
Tottenham Hotspur	0-1	1-1	1-1	1-1	3-2	3-2	1-1	3-3	0-1	1-0	0-1
West Ham United	0-0	0-0	1-2	1-0	0-1	0-1	2-1	1-2	1-0	3-1	2-2
Wimbledon	0-3	2-2	4-1	1-1	1-2	1-1	0-2	1-1		1-0	1-0

RESULTS 1993-94

	Newcastle Utd	Norwich City	Oldham Ath.	QPR	Sheffield Utd	Sheffield Wed	Southampton	Swindon	Tottenham Hot	West Ham Utd	Wimbledon
Arsenal	2-1	0-0	1-1	0-0	3-0	1-0	1-0	1-1	1-1	0-2	1-1
Aston Villa	0-2	0-0	1-2	4-1	1-0	2-2	0-2	5-0	1-0	3-1	0-1
Blackburn Rovers	1-0	2-3	1-0	1-1	0-0	1-1	2-0	3-1	0-0	0-2	3-0
Chelsea	0-0	1-2	0-1	2-0	3-2	1-1	2-0	1-1	4-3	2-0	2-0
Coventry City	2-1	2-1	1-1	0-1	0-0	1-1	1-1	1-1	1-0	1-1	1-2
Everton	0-2	1-5	2-1	0-3	4-2	0-2	1-0	6-2	0-1	0-1	3-2
Ipswich Town	1-1	2-1	0-0	1-3	3-2	1-4	1-0	1-1	2-2	1-1	0-0
Leeds United	1-1	0-4	1-0	1-1	2-1	2-1	0-0	3-0	2-0	1-0	4-0
Liverpool	0-2	0-1	2-1	3-2	1-2	2-0	4-2	2-2	1-2	2-0	1-1
Manchester City	2-1	1-1	1-0	3-0	1-2	1-3	1-1	2-1	0-2	0-0	0-1
Manchester United	2-1	2-2	2-1	2-1	3-0	5-0	2-0	4-2	0-1	3-0	3-1
Newcastle United	•	3-0	3-2	1-2	4-0	4-2	1-2	7-1	1-2	2-0	4-0
Norwich City	1-2	•	3-2	3-4	0-1	1-1	4-5	0-0	0-2	0-0	0-1
Oldham Athletic	1-3	2-1	•	4-1	1-1	0-0	2-1	2-1	1-1	1-2	1-1
Queens Park Rangers	1-2	2-2	2-0	•	0-1	1-2	2-1	1-3	2-2	0-0	1-0
Sheffield United	2-0	1-2	2-1	1-1	•	1-1	0-0	3-1	1-0	3-2	2-1
Sheffield Wednesday	0-1	3-3	3-0	3-1	3-1	•	2-0	3-3	1-0	5-0	2-2
Southampton	2-1	0-1	1-3	3-1	3-3	1-1	•	5-1	2-1	0-2	1-0
Swindon Town	2-2	3-3	0-1	1-0	0-0	0-1	2-1	•	2-1	1-1	2-4
Tottenham Hotspur	3-3	1-3	5-0	1-2	2-2	1-3	3-0	1-1	•	1-4	1-1
West Ham United	2-4	3-3	2-0	0-4	0-0	2-0	3-3	0-0	1-3	•	0-2
Wimbledon	4-2	3-1	3-0	1-1	2-0	2-1	1-0	3-0	2-1	1-2	•

FA PREMIER LEAGUE

	Arsenal	Aston Villa	Blackburn R	Chelsea	Coventry City	Everton	Ipswich Town	Leeds United	Liverpool	Man City	Man Utd
Arsenal	•	31,773	35,030	34,314	24,897	29,063	28,563	29,042	35,556	29,567	36,203
Aston Villa	31,580	•	40,903	29,706	31,181	36,044	23,732	26,919	45,347	19,254	39,624
Blackburn Rovers	14,051	19,287	•	15,736	15,136	21,462	20,633	16,938	20,831	18,741	20,866
Chelsea	26,839	18,341	29,189	•	8,923	18,338	12,508	18,544	31,271	10,128	37,064
Coventry City	12,722	14,325	16,653	13,660	•	15,662	11,265	13,934	16,740	11,735	17,020
Everton	19,891	24,022	27,427	18,821	23,217	•	19,588	17,066	38,157	26,036	35,430
Ipswich Town	18,656	16,617	14,582	17,582	12,633	15,078	•	17,548	22,355	13,099	22,559
Leeds United	37,515	33,120	37,827	35,022	30,023	35,487	31,317	•	40,053	33,821	41,125
Liverpool	42,750	38,484	37,355	38,629	38,547	44,281	30,485	44,068	•	41,872	42,795
Manchester City	25,642	26,075	25,185	33,594	21,537	20,513	28,188	32,366	30,403	•	35,155
Manchester United	44,009	44,499	44,511	44,745	44,717	44,750	43,300	44,724	44,751	44,333	•
Newcastle United	32,216	32,216	34,272	32,216	32,216	34,833	32,216	36,388	36,374	35,658	36,388
Norwich City	17,667	20,650	15,193	19,472	16,239	16,432	19,189	16,586	19,746	16,626	19,705
Oldham Athletic	12,105	12,836	13,887	12,022	10,817	13,666	12,182	11,136	14,573	16,464	16,708
Queens Park Rangers	11,442	14,915	17,636	15,735	12,999	13,330	13,292	11,366	19,635	13,474	21,267
Sheffield United	20,019	18,402	19,124	16,119	15,394	15,135	17,932	19,425	22,932	20,067	26,744
Sheffield Wednesday	26,023	28,450	24,699	20,433	23,379	24,096	23,457	31,892	32,177	33,773	34,548
Southampton	16,790	19,003	19,105	14,221	12,397	14,051	9,028	13,511	18,306	16,377	16,189
Swindon	17,651	16,530	15,224	16,456	14,640	14,414	13,343	17,539	17,017	14,300	18,102
Tottenham Hotspur	28,355	17,452	30,236	27,567	26,015	27,487	26,653	31,275	31,394	24,535	31,343
West Ham United	20,279	20,425	22,186	18,917	17,243	20,243	18,307	20,468	26,096	16,605	28,832
Wimbledon	16,584	7,533	10,537	11,083	4,739	6,934	7,756	9,035	13,819	8,481	28,553

ATTENDANCES 1993-94

	Newcastle U.	Norwich City	Oldham Ath.	QPR	Sheffield Utd	Sheffield We.	Southampton	Swindon	Tottenham HC	West Ham Ut.	Wimbledon
Arsenal	36,091	30,516	26,524	34,935	27,035	22,026	26,902	31,634	35,669	33,701	21,292
Aston Villa	37,336	25,416	21,214	32,944	24,686	20,304	16,180	26,637	32,498	28,869	17,940
Blackburn Rovers	21,269	14,236	13,731	19,313	13,505	13,917	16,666	20,046	16,849	13,943	16,215
Chelsea	22,133	16,923	15,372	20,191	21,782	16,652	19,801	11,180	16,807	19,545	11,903
Coventry City	15,760	13,514	11,800	12,107	10,429	13,013	9,984	15,825	14,491	12,909	11,290
Everton	25,189	20,531	18,837	17,089	24,169	16,777	13,660	20,546	23,580	19,579	31,297
Ipswich Town	19,102	19,498	12,004	15,182	10,747	15,070	14,569	14,934	19,411	21,024	12,372
Leeds United	40,005	32,008	28,717	39,106	33,892	33,806	30,890	32,630	33,658	34,588	30,020
Liverpool	44,601	44,339	32,661	36,642	44,004	34,004	32,818	32,739	42,456	42,254	32,232
Manchester City	33,774	28,020	21,401	24,561	25,448	23,416	24,712	26,360	21,566	29,118	23,981
Manchester United	41,829	44,694	44,686	44,663	41,949	43,669	44,705	44,583	44,655	44,613	44,748
Newcastle United	•	32,216	32,216	33,926	35,101	33,890	32,129	32,216	35,216	34,336	33,392
Norwich City	19,564	•	20,394	16,499	18,474	18,311	17,150	17,614	21,181		14,851
Oldham Athletic	13,821	10,198	•	10,440	14,779	12,967	9,982	9,771	14,283	11,669	9,633
Queens Park Rangers	15,774	13,359	13,218	•	11,113	16,858	10,613	9,875	17,694	10,850	11,368
Sheffield United	29,013	18,254	17,066	14,183	•	30,044	19,522	20,904	21,325	13,646	15,555
Sheffield Wednesday	33,224	25,175	18,509	22,437	34,959	•	22,503	30,570	32,514	26,350	21,752
Southampton	13,804	16,556	14,101	11,946	11,619	16,391	•	12,581	16,017	13,258	14,790
Swindon Town	15,015	15,405	11,970	14,147	12,734	13,727	13,284	•	16,563	14,924	12,237
Tottenham Hotspur	30,780	33,130	24,614	26,105	25,741	23,078	25,959	31,394	•	31,502	17,744
West Ham United	23,132	20,738	17,251	18,084	20,365	19,441	26,952	15,777	20,787	•	20,363
Wimbledon	13,358	7,206	6,766	9,478	6,728	5,536	6,036	7,758	20,875	10,903	•

27

FA PREMIER LEAGUE RECORDS 1993-94

SCORERS

Top Scorers All Competitions

Player	Club	L	F	C	E	O	Total
Andy COLE	Newcastle United	34	1	6	0	0	41
Alan SHEARER	Blackburn Rovers	31	2	1	0	0	34
Ian WRIGHT	Arsenal	23	1	6	4	0	34
Chris SUTTON	Norwich City	25	2	1	0	0	28
Mark STEIN	Chelsea	21	1	4	0	1	27
Matt Le TISSIER	Southampton	25	0	0	0	0	25
Mick McCARTHY	Oldham Athletic	18	0	7	0	0	25
Peter BEARDSLEY	Newcastle United	21	2	1	0	0	24
Dean HOLDSWORTH	Wimbledon	17	3	4	0	0	24
Mark BRIGHT	Sheffield Wednesday	10	2	2	0	0	23

L=League, F=FA Cup, C=Coca-Cola Cup, E=Europe O=Other

FA Carling Premiership Top Scorers

Player	Club	Goals	All-time Total
Andy COLE	Newcastle United	34	34
Alan SHEARER	Blackburn Rovers	31	47
Chris SUTTON	Norwich City	25	33
Matt Le TISSIER	Southampton	25	40
Ian WRIGHT	Arsenal	23	38
Peter BEARDLSEY	Newcastle United	21	31
Mark BRIGHT	Sheffield Wednesday	19	31
Eric CANTONA	Manchester United	18	33
Les FERNINAND	QPR	17	36
Dean HOLDSWORTH	Wimbledon	17	36
Rod WALLACE	Leeds United	17	24
Tony COTTEE	Everton	16	28
Kevin CAMPBELL	Arsenal	14	18
Ian RUSH	Liverpool	14	28
Teddy SHERINGHAM	Tottenham Hotspur	14	36
Ryan GIGGS	Manchester United	13	22
Trevor MORLEY	West Ham United	13	13
Mark STEIN	Chelsea	13	13
Efan EKOKU	Norwich City	12	15

Robbie FOWLER	Liverpool	12	34
Mark HUGHES	Manchester United	12	27
Gordon WATSON	Sheffield Wednesday	12	12
John FASHANU	Wimbledon	11	17
Peter NDLOVU	Coventry City	11	18
Ian MARSHALL	Ipswich Town	10	12
Dean SAUNDERS	Aston Villa	10	24

FA Carling Premiership Top Scorers by Club

Club	Scorers
Arsenal	Wright 23, Campbell 14, Merson 8
Aston Villa	Saunders 10, Atkinson 8, Richardson 5
Blackburn Rovers	Shearer 31, Gallagher 7, Newell 6, Wilcox 6
Chelsea	Stein 13, Peacock 8, Shipperley 4
Coventry City	Ndlovu 11, Quinn 8, Wegerle 6
Everton	Cottee 16, Rideout 6, Ebbrell 4
Ipswich Town	Marshall 10, Kiwomya 5
Leeds United	Rod Wallace 17, Deane 11, McAllister 9
Liverpool	Rush 14, Fowler 12, Clough 7
Manchester City	Sheron 6, Quinn 5
Manchester United	Cantona 18, Giggs 13, Hughes 12
Newcastle United	Cole 34, Beardsley 21, Lee 7
Norwich City	Sutton 25, Ekoku 12
QPR	Ferdinand 17, White 8, Penrice 8
Sheffield Wednesday	Bright 19, Watson 12
Southampton	Le Tissier 25, Dowie 5
Tottenham Hotspur	Sheringham 14, Dozzell 8, Anderton 6
West Ham United	Morley 13, Allen M 7, Chapman 7
Wimbledon	Holdsworth 17, Fashanu 11, Earle 9

FA Carling Premiership Hat-tricks

Player	Match	Date
Mick QUINN	Arsenal v COVENTRY CITY (0-3)	14/08/93
Tony COTTEE	EVERTON v Sheffield United (4-2)	18/08/93
Kevin CAMPBELL	ARSENAL v Ipswich Town (4-0)	11/09/93
Efan EKOKU*	Everton v NORWICH CITY (1-5)	25/09/93
Alan SHEARER	Leeds United v BLACKBURN RVRS (3-3)	23/10/93
Robbie FOWLER	LIVERPOOL v Southampton (4-2)	30/10/93
Peter BEARDSLEY	NEWCASTLE UNITED v Wimbledon (4-0)	30/10/93
Bradley ALLEN	Everton v QUEENS PARK RANGERS (0-3)	20/11/93
Andy COLE	NEWCASTLE UNITED v Liverpool (3-0)	21/11/93
Kevin CAMPBELL	Swindon Town v ARSENAL (0-4)	27/12/93
Tony COTTEE	EVERTON v Swindon Town (6-2)	15/01/94
J FJORTOFT	SWINDON TOWN v Coventry (3-1)	05/02/94
Dean SAUNDERS	ASTON VILLA v Swindon Town (5-0)	12/02/94

Matt LE TISSIER	SOUTHAMPTON v Liverpool (4-2)	14/02/94
Andy COLE	NEWCASTLE UNITED v Coventry (4-0)	23/02/94
Ian WRIGHT	Ipswich Town v ARSENAL (1-5)	05/02/94
Ian WRIGHT	Southampton v ARSENAL (0-4)	19/03/94
Matt LE TISSIER	Norwich City v SOUTHAMPTON (4-5)	09/04/94
D HOLDSWORTH	WIMBLEDON v Oldham Athletic (3-0)	26/04/94

4 goals, Premiership record

ATTENDANCES

Attendance Summaries by Club

Club	Total	Ave
Arsenal	640,333	30,492
Aston Villa	608,314	28,967
Blackburn Rovers	363,371	17,303
Chelsea	403,434	19,211
Coventry City	284,838	13,564
Everton	480,909	22,900
Ipswich Town	344,622	16,411
Leeds United	724,630	34,506
Liverpool	808,573	38,503
Manchester City	560,899	26,709
Manchester United	929,133	44,244
Newcastle United	709,631	33,792
Norwich City	381,754	18,179
Oldham Athletic	263,939	12,569
Queens Park Rangers	296,792	14,133
Sheffield United	410,805	19,562
Sheffield Wednesday	570,920	27,187
Southampton	310,041	14,764
Swindon	315,222	15,011
Tottenham Hotspur	572,359	27,255
West Ham United	432,491	20,595
Wimbledon	219,698	10,462
Total	10,632,708	24,110

Top Attendances by Number

Club	Posn	Total	Ave
Manchester United	1st	929,133	44,244
Liverpool	8th	808,573	38,503
Leeds United	5th	724,630	34,506
Newcastle United	3rd	709,631	33,792

Arsenal	4th	640,333	30,492
Aston Villa	10th	608,314	28,967
Tottenham Hotspur	15th	572,359	27,255
Sheffield Wednesday	7th	570,920	27,187
Manchester City	16th	560,899	26,709
Everton	17th	480,909	22,900
West Ham United	13th	432,491	20,595
Sheffield United	20th	410,805	19,562
Chelsea	14th	403,434	19,211
Norwich City	12th	381,754	18,179
Blackburn Rovers	2nd	363,371	17,303
Ipswich Town	19th	344,622	16,411
Swindon Town	22nd	315,222	15,011
Southampton	18th	310,041	14,764
Queens Park Rangers	9th	296,792	14,133
Coventry City	11th	284,838	13,564
Oldham Athletic	21st	263,939	12,569
Wimbledon	6th	219,698	10,462

SCORES

Highest Aggregate Scores (8)

4-5	Norwich City v Southampton	09/04/94
7-1	Newcastle United v Swindon Town	12/03/94
6-2	Everton v Swindon Town	15/01/94

Biggest Home Win

7-1	Newcastle United v Swindon Town	12/03/94

Biggest Away Wins

0-5	Swindon Town v Liverpool	22/08/94
0-5	Swindon Town v Leeds United	07/05/94

Highest Score Draws

3-3	Liverpool v Manchester United	04/01/94
	Tottenham Hotspur v Liverpool	18/12/93
	Leeds United v Blackburn Rovers	23/10/93
	Oldham Athletic v Coventry City	24/08/93
	Sheffield Wednesday v Leeds United	30/10/93
	Sheffield Wednesday v Norwich City	01/09/93
	Sheffield Wednesday v Swindon Town	29/12/93

Southampton v Sheffield United	02/10/93
Swindon Town v Norwich City	19/02/93
West Ham United v Norwich City	24/01/93
West Ham United v Southampton	07/05/93

Score Frequencies 1993-94

Home Win		*Away Win*		*Draws*	
Score	*Total No.*	*Score*	*Total No.*	*Score*	*Total No.*
1-0	51	0-1	32	0-0	43
2-0	32	0-2	22	1-1	67
3-0	16	0-3	7	2-2	21
4-0	6	0-4	5	3-3	11
5-0	5	0-5	2		
2-1	38	1-2	35		
3-1	16	1-3	12		
4-1	5	1-4	2		
5-1	4	1-5	2		
7-1	1	2-3	4		
3-2	10	2-4	2		
4-2	8	2-5	1		
6-2	1	3-4	1		
4-3	1	4-5	1		
Total	**194**	**Total**	**128**	**Total**	**142**

TRANSFERS of £500,000+

Transfers involving FA Carling Premiership Clubs

Player	*From*	*To*	*Fee*
Roy Keane	Nottingham Forest	Manchester Utd	£3,750,000
Brian Deane	Sheffield Utd	Leeds Utd	£2,900,000
Darren Peacock	QPR	Newcastle	£2,750,000
David Batty	Leeds Utd	Blackburn	£2,750,000
Andy Sinton	QPR	Sheffield Wed	£2,700,000
Des Walker	Sampdoria	Sheffield Wed	£2,700,000
Paul Warhurst	Sheff Wed	Blackburn	£2,700,000
Neil Ruddock	Tottenham	Liverpool	£2,500,000
Tim Flowers	Southampton	Blackburn	£2,400,000
Nigel Clough	Nottingham Forest	Liverpool	£2,275,000
Ruel Fox	Norwich	Newcastle	£2,250,000
Andy Townsend	Chelsea	Aston Villa	£2,100,000
Jason Dozzell	Ipswich	Tottenham	£1,750,000

Alan Kernaghan	Middlesbrough	Man City	£1,600,000
Anders Limpar	Arsenal	Everton	£1,600,000
Mark Stein	Stoke	Chelsea	£1,500,000
Peter Beardsley	Everton	Newcastle	£1,400,000
Colin Calderwood	Swindon	Tottenham	£1,250,000
Gavin Peacock	Newcastle	Chelsea	£1,200,000
Gordon Durie	Tottenham	Rangers	£1,200,000
Peter Beagrie	Everton	Man City	£1,100,000
Eddie McGoldrick	Crystal Palace	Arsenal	£1,000,000
Kevin Scott	Newcastle	Tottenham	£850,000
Graham Stuart	Chelsea	Everton	£850,000
Joe Parkinson	Bournemouth	Everton	£800,000
Dale Gordon	Rangers	West Ham Utd	£750,000
Ian Marshall	Oldham	Ipswich	£750,000
Trevor Sinclair	Blackpool	QPR	£750,000
Steve Yates	Bristol Rovers	QPR	£750,000
Stuart Slater	Celtic	Ipswich	£750,000
Jim Magilton	Oxford	Southampton	£650,000
Paul Allen	Tottenham	Southampton	£550,000
Mike Hooper	Liverpool	Newcastle	£550,000
Roger Nilsson	V Stavanger	Sheff Utd	£550,000
Simon Webster	Charlton	West Ham Utd	£525,000
Brett Angell	Southend	Everton	£500,000
Jan-Aage Fjortoft	Rapid Vienna	Swindon	£500,000
Carl Griffiths	Shrewsbury	Man City	£500,000
Alphonse Groenendijk	Ajax	Man City	£500,000
Sean McCarthy	Bradford	Oldham	£500,000
Andy Pearce	Coventry	Sheffield Wed	£500,000
Tore Pedersen	FK Brann	Oldham	£500,000
David White	Man City	Leeds Utd.	*swap
David Rocastle	Leeds Utd	Man City	*swap
Mike Marsh	Liverpool	West Ham	†swap
David Burrows	Liverpool	West Ham	†swap
Julian Dicks	West Ham	Liverpool	†swap

* valued at £2,000,000   † valued at £1,600,000

A full list of transfers and loans on a month-by-month basis can be found later in this Annual.

BOOKINGS & DISMISSALS

Players Sent Off

Player	Match	Date	Official
Carlton PALMER	Liverpool v SHEFFIELD WED	14/08/93	G Ashby
Pavel SRNICEK	Coventry v NEWCASTLE UTD	18/08/93	J Borrett
David LEE	CHELSEA v Sheffield Wed	28/08/93	K Morton
Rob JONES	Coventry City v LIVERPOOL	01/09/93	K Burge
C CALDERWOOD	Ipswich v TOTTENHAM H	26/09/93	G Ashby
David TUTTLE	Southampton v SHEFF UTD	02/10/93	G Poll
Dennis WISE	West Ham v CHELSEA	02/10/93	R Hart
Rick HOLDEN	OLDHAM ATH v Arsenal	23/10/93	M Reed
Chris MAKIN	West Ham v OLDHAM ATH	20/11/93	D Allison
David SEAMAN	West Ham v ARSENAL	24/11/93	P Durkin
Chris MAKIN	OLDHAM ATH v Norwich	27/11/93	P Don
Simon BARKER	Liverpool v QPR	08/12/93	V Callow
Les FERDINAND	Liverpool v QPR	08/12/93	V Callow
Karl READY	Southampton v QPR	11/12/93	K Barrett
Lee POWER	Ipswich v NORWICH CITY	18/12/93	M Reed
Andy MUTCH	Everton v SWINDON TOWN	15/01/94	G Ashby
Alan CORK	SHEFFIELD UTD v Blackburn	15/01/94	P Foakes
Carl BRADSHAW	SHEFFIELD UTD v Blackburn	15/01/94	P Foakes
Bryan GUNN	NORWICH CITY v Liverpool	05/02/94	D Gallagher
John POLSTON	NORWICH CITY v Blackburn	22/02/94	K Barratt
Graeme SHARP	Everton v OLDHAM ATH	05/03/94	D Elleray
Andy PEARCE	SHEFFIELD WED v Newcastle	05/03/94	P Durkin
Eric CANTONA	Swindon v MAN UTD	19/03/94	B Hill
Eric CANTONA	Arsenal v MAN UTD	22/03/94	V Callow
Simon TRACEY	Oldham v SHEFFIELD UTD	03/05/94	A Wilkie

Referees by Number of Bookings Issued

32 referees have officiated in the 93-94 Premiership season. The table below demonstrates how many matches they have each officiated and gives a count of the number of yellow and red cards that have been shown.

The Bookings/Match column gives a rough illustration of which referees are more likely to reach for the paperwork. Equally it gives an indication of which referees have officiated at the toughest games. How much it reflects either situation is a matter for debate. In either case it can only be a rough estimation. Mr D Crick for instance, tops this particular league with a Bookings/Match ratio of four bookings per game. However, as he only officiated at one Premiership game this season the statistic is hardly significant. In the Bookings/Match column a sending off is calculated as being equivalent to two bookings.

Matches	Referee	Y	R	Bookings/match
22	A Gunn (Sussex)	24	–	1.09
21	J Worrall (Warrington)	8	–	0.38
20	G Ashby (Worcester)	35	3	2.05
20	A Wilkie (Chester-le-Street)	26	1	1.30
20	K Morton (Bury St Edmunds)	22	1	1.20
19	K Cooper (Pontypridd)	38	–	2.00
19	V Callow (Solihull)	27	3	1.74
18	P Durkin (Portland, Dorset)	27	2	1.72
18	P Don (Hanworth Park, Middx)	28	1	1.67
17	K Burge (Mid-Glamorgan)	26	1	1.65
17	R Hart (Darlington)	17	1	1.11
17	D Allison (Lancaster)	13	1	0.88
17	K Hackett (Sheffield)	14	–	0.82
16	D Elleray (Harrow)	31	1	2.06
16	S Lodge (Barnsley)	26	–	1.62
16	D Gallagher (Banbury)	19	1	1.31
16	M Bodenham (Looe, Cornwall)	17	–	1.06
16	R Milford (Bristol)	16	–	1.00
15	M Reed (Birmingham)	29	2	2.20
13	K Barratt (Coventry)	26	2	2.31
13	J Borrett (Great Yarmouth)	19	1	1.61
13	R Gifford (Mid-Glamorgan)	10	–	0.77
12	P Foakes (Clacton, Essex)	14	2	1.50
12	T Holbrook (Walsall)	3	–	0.25
11	G Poll (Berkhamsted)	19	1	1.91
10	D Frampton (Poole)	25	–	2.50
10	B Hill (Kettering)	12	1	1.40
10	R Dilkes (Mossley)	14	–	1.40
9	J Lloyd (Wrexham)	4	–	0.44
4	L Dilkes (Mossley)	2	–	0.50
3	H King (Merthyr Tydfil)	4	–	1.33
1	D Crick (London)	4	–	4.00

THE MANAGERS

Premiership Managers by Length of Tenure

Club	Manager	Arrived
Arsenal	George Graham	May '86
Manchester United	Alex Ferguson	November '86

Leeds United	Howard Wilkinson	October '88
West Ham United	Billy Bonds	February '90
Wimbledon	Joe Kinnear	January '91
Leicester City	Brian Little	May '91
Queens Park Rangers	Gerry Francis	May '91
Aston Villa	Ron Atkinson	June '91
Sheffield Wednesday	Trevor Francis	June '91
Blackburn Rovers	Kenny Dalglish	October '91
Newcastle United	Kevin Keegan	February '92
Ipswich Town	Mick McGiven	July '92
Crystal Palace	Alan Smith	June '93
Nottingham Forest	Frank Clark	June '93
Tottenham Hotspur	Osvaldo Ardiles	June '93
Chelsea	Glenn Hoddle	June '93
Manchester City	Brian Horton	September '93
Coventry City	Phil Neal	November '93
Southampton	Alan Ball	January '94
Norwich City	John Deehan	January '94
Liverpool	Roy Evans	January '94
Everton	Mike Walker	January '94

FA PREMIER LEAGUE ALL-TIME RECORDS

All-Time Record FAPL Attendances by Club

Club	Att	Opponents	Date
Arsenal	36,203	Manchester United	22/03/94
Aston Villa	45,347	Liverpool	07/05/94
Blackburn Rovers	21,462	Everton	29/12/93
Chelsea	37,064	Manchester United	11/09/93
Coventry City	24,410	Manchester United	12/04/94
Crystal Palace	30,115	Manchester United	21/04/93
Everton	38,157	Liverpool	18/09/93
Ipswich Town	22,559	Manchester United	01/05/94
Leeds United	41,125	Manchester United	27/04/94
Liverpool	44,619	Everton	20/03/93
Manchester City	37,136	Manchester United	20/03/93

Manchester Utd	44,751	Liverpool	04/01/94
Norwich City	21,181	Tottenham Hotspur	
Nottingham Forest	26,752	Sheffield United	01/05/93
Queens Park Rangers	21,267	Manchester United	05/02/94
Sheffield United	30,044	Sheffield Wednesday	23/10/93
Sheffield Wednesday	38,668	Sheffield United	13/03/93
Southampton	19,654	Tottenham Hotspur	15/08/92
Tottenham Hotspur	33,709	Arsenal	12/12/92
Wimbledon	30,115	Manchester United	08/05/93

All-Time Top 10 FAPL Attendances

All ten top attendances were set during the 93-94 season. All were (marginally) larger than the previous season's record of 44,619 between Liverpool and Everton.

Psn	Att	Match	Date
1	45,347	Aston Villa v Liverpool	07/05/94
2	44,751	Manchester United v Liverpool	30/03/94
3	44,750	Manchester United v Everton	22/01/94
4	44,748	Manchester United v Wimbledon	20/11/93
5	44,745	Manchester United v Chelsea	05/02/94
6	44,724	Manchester United v Leeds United	01/01/94
7	44,717	Manchester United v Coventry City	08/05/94
8	44,705	Manchester United v Southampton	04/05/94
9	44,694	Manchester United v Norwich City	04/12/93
10	44,686	Manchester United v Oldham Athletic	04/04/94

All-time FAPL Lowest Attendances by Club

Club	Att	Opponents	Date
Arsenal	18,253	Wimbledon	10/02/92
Aston Villa	16,180	Southampton	24/11/93
Blackburn Rovers	13,505	Sheffield Utd	18/10/93
Chelsea	8,923	Coventry City	04/05/94
Coventry City	9,984	Southampton	16/10/93
Crystal Palace	11,224	Oldham Athletic	12/09/92
Everton	13,660	Southampton	04/12/93
Ipswich Town	10,747	Sheffield United	21/08/93
Leeds United	25,774	Wimbledon	15/08/92
Liverpool	24,561	QPR	08/12/93
Manchester City	20,513	Everton	08/12/93
Manchester United	29,736	Crystal Palace	02/09/92
Norwich City	12,452	Southampton	05/09/92
Nottingham Forest	17,553	Arsenal	17/10/92
Oldham Athletic	9,633	Wimbledon	28/08/93
Queens Park Rangers	9,875	Swindon Town	30/04/94

Sheffield United	13,646	West Ham Utd	28/03/94
Sheffield Wednesday	18,509	Oldham Athletic	24/11/93
Southampton	9,028	Ipswich Town	08/12/93
Tottenham Hotspur	17,452	Aston Villa	02/03/94
Wimbledon	3,039	Everton	26/01/93

All Time Lowest FAPL Attendances

Psn	Att	Match	Date
1	3,039	Wimbledon v Everton	26/01/93
2	3,386	Wimbledon v Oldham Athletic	12/12/92
3	3,759	Wimbledon v Coventry City	22/08/92
4	3,979	Wimbledon v Sheffield United	20/02/93
5	4,534	Wimbledon v Southampton	06/03/93
6	4,714	Wimbledon v Manchester City	01/09/92
7	4,739	Wimbledon v Coventry City	26/12/92
8	4,954	Wimbledon v Ipswich Town	18/08/92
9	5,536	Wimbledon v Sheffield Wednesday	15/01/94
10	5,740	Wimbledon v Sheffield Wednesday	28/11/92

All-Time Biggest Home Wins

7-1	Blackburn Rovers v Norwich City	02/10/92
7-1	Newcastle United v Swindon Town	12/03/94
6-0	Sheffield United v Tottenham Hotspur	02/03/93

All-Time Biggest Away Wins

| 0-5 | Swindon Town v Liverpool | 22/08/93 |
| 0-5 | Swindon Town v Leeds United | 07/05/94 |

All-Time Highest Score Draws

3-3	Crystal Palace v Blackburn Rovers	15/08/92
	Sheffield Wednesday v Manchester United	26/12/92
	West Ham United v Norwich City	24/01/93
	Swindon Town v Norwich City	19/02/93
	West Ham United v Southampton	07/05/93
	Coventry City v Leeds United	08/05/93
	Middlesbrough v Norwich City	08/05/93
	Oldham Athletic v Coventry City	24/08/93
	Sheffield Wednesday v Norwich City	01/09/93
	Southampton v Sheffield United	02/10/93
	Leeds United v Blackburn Rovers	23/10/93
	Sheffield Wednesday v Leeds United	30/10/93
	Tottenham v Liverpool	18/12/93
	Sheffield Wednesday v Swindon Town	29/12/93
	Liverpool v Manchester United	04/01/94

General Records

Most Goals Scored in a Season	Newcastle United	84	1993-94	†
Fewest Goals Scored in a Season	Ipswich Town	35	1993-94	†
Most Goals Conceded in a Season	Swindon Town	100	1993-94	†
Fewest Goals Conceded in a Season	Arsenal	28	1993-94	†
Most Points in a Season	Manchester United	92	1993-94	†
Fewest Points in a Season	Swindon Town	30	1993-94	†
Most Wins in a Season	Manchester United	27	1993-94	†
Fewest Wins in a Season	Swindon Town	5	1993-94	†
Fewest Defeats in a Season	Manchester United	4	1993-94	†
Most Defeats in a Season	Nottingham Forest	22	1992-93	†
	Swindon Town	22	1993-94	†
Most Draws in a Season	Manchester City	18	1993-94	†
	Sheffield United	18	1993-94	†

† 42 games

FA CHALLENGE CUP
1993-94

Third Round – 8th January 1994

Barnet	v	Chelsea	0-0	23,200
Birmingham City	v	Kidderminster Harriers	1-2	19,666
Blackburn Rovers	v	Portsmouth	3-3	17,219
Bolton Wanderers	v	Everton	1-1	21,702
Bristol City	v	Liverpool	1-1	20,617

(match abandoned after 65 minutes due to floodlight failure)

Bromsgrove Rovers	v	Barnsley	1-2	4,893
Cardiff City	v	Middlesbrough	2-2	13,750
Charlton Athletic	v	Burnley	3-0	8,336
Exeter City	v	Aston Villa	0-1	10,570
Grimsby Town	v	Wigan Athletic	1-0	4,488
Leeds United	v	Crewe Alexandra	3-1	23,475
Luton Town	v	Southend United	1-0	7,955
Manchester City	v	Leicester City	4-1	22,613
Millwall	v	Arsenal	0-1	20,093
Newcastle United	v	Coventry City	2-0	35,444
Notts County	v	Sutton United	3-2	6,805
Oldham Athletic	v	Derby County	2-1	12,810
Oxford United	v	Tranmere Rovers	2-0	5,283
Peterborough United	v	Tottenham Hotspur	1-1	19,169
Plymouth Argyle	v	Chester City	1-0	9,170
Preston North End	v	Bournemouth	2-1	8,457
Sheffield United	v	Manchester United	0-1	22,019
Sheffield Wednesday	v	Nottingham Forest	1-1	32,488
Southampton	v	Port Vale	1-1	11,086
Stockport County	v	Queens Park Rangers	2-1	7,569
Stoke City	v	Bath City	0-0	14,159
Sunderland	v	Carlisle United	1-1	23,587
Swindon Town	v	Ipswich Town	1-1	12,105
West Ham United	v	Watford	2-1	19,802
Wimbledon	v	Scunthorpe	3-0	4,944
Wolves	v	Crystal Palace	1-0	25,047
Wycombe Wanderers	v	Norwich City	0-2	7,802

Third Round Rematch

Liverpool	v	Bristol City	1-1	21,718

Third Round Replays

Chelsea	v	Barnet	4-0	16,209
Portsmouth	v	Blackburn Rovers	1-3	23,035
Everton	v	Bolton Wanderers	2-3†	34,642
Bristol City	v	Liverpool	1-0	36,720
Middlesbrough	v	Cardiff City	1-2	10,789
Tottenham Hotspur	v	Peterborough United	1-1†	24,893
(Tottenham won 5-4 on penalties)				
Nottingham Forest	v	Sheffield Wednesday	0-2	25,268
Port Vale	v	Southampton	1-0	12,042
Bath City	v	Stoke City	1-4	6,213
Carlisle United	v	Sunderland	0-1	12,771
Ipswich Town	v	Swindon Town	2-1	12,796

Fourth Round – 29th January 1994

Bolton Wanderers	v	Arsenal	2-2	18,891
Cardiff City	v	Manchester City	1-0	20,486
Charlton Athletic	v	Blackburn Rovers	0-0	8,352
Chelsea	v	Sheffield Wednesday	1-1	26,094
Grimsby	v	Aston Villa	1-2	15,771
Ipswich Town	v	Tottenham Hotspur	3-0	22,539
Kidderminster Harriers	v	Preston North End	1-0	7,000
Newcastle United	v	Luton Town	1-1	32,216
Norwich City	v	Manchester Utd	0-2	21,060
Notts County	v	West Ham Utd	1-1	14,952
Oldham Athletic	v	Stoke City	0-0	14,465
Oxford United	v	Leeds United	2-2	11,029
Plymouth Argyle	v	Barnsley	2-2	12,760
Port Vale	v	Wolverhampton Wdrs	0-2	21,999
Stockport County	v	Bristol City	0-4	7,691
Wimbledon	v	Sunderland	2-1	10,477

Fourth Round Replays

Arsenal	v	Bolton Wanderers	1-3	33,863
Blackburn Rovers	v	Charlton Athletic	0-1	15,438
Sheffield Wednesday	v	Chelsea	1-3	26,114
Luton Town	v	Newcastle United	2-0	12,503
West Ham Utd	v	Notts County	1-0	23,375
Stoke City	v	Oldham Athletic	0-1	19,871
Leeds United	v	Oxford United	2-3	22,167
Barnsley	v	Plymouth Argyle	1-0	10,912

Fifth Round – 19th February 1994

Bolton Wanderers	v	Aston Villa	1-0	18,817
Bristol City	v	Charlton Athletic	1-1	20,416
Cardiff City	v	Luton Town	1-2	17,296
Kidderminster Harriers	v	West Ham Utd	0-1	7,850
Oldham Athletic	v	Barnsley	1-0	15,685
Oxford United	v	Chelsea	1-2	10,787
Wimbledon	v	Manchester Utd	0-3	27,511
Wolverhampton Wdrs	v	Ipswich Town	1-1	28,234

Fifth Round Replays

Charlton Athletic	v	Bristol City	2-0	8,205
Ipswich Town	v	Wolverhampton Wdrs	1-2	19,385

Sixth Round – 12th March 1994

Bolton Wanderers	v	Oldham Athletic	0-1	20,321
Chelsea	v	Wolverhampton Wdrs	1-0	29,340
Manchester United	v	Charlton	3-1	44,347
West Ham United	v	Luton Town	0-0	27,311

Sixth Round Replays

Luton Town	v	West Ham United	3-2	13,166

Semi Finals

Chelsea	v	Luton Town	2-0	59,989

(Wembley Stadium, 9th April 94)

Manchester United	v	Oldham Athletic	1-1†	56,399

(Wembley Stadium, 10th April 94)

Semi Final Replay

Oldham Athletic	v	Manchester United	1-4	32,211

(Maine Road, 13th April 94)

Final – 14th May 1994 at Wembley Stadium

Manchester United	v	Chelsea	4-0	79,634

Cantona (pen) 60, (pen) 66,
Hughes 69, McClair 90

Manchester United: Schmeichel, Parker, Irwin (Sharpe 84), Bruce, Pallister, Cantona, Ince, Giggs, Kanchelskis (McClair 84), Keane, Hughes

Chelsea: Kharin, Clarke, Johnsen, Kjeldbjerg, Sinclair, Burley (Hoddle 68), Newton, Spencer, Peacock, Stein (Cascarino 78), Wise

Referee: Mr D Elleray (Harrow)

† after extra time

FA CHALLENGE CUP
FINALS 1872-1994

Year	Winners	Runners-up	Score
1872	The Wanderers	Royal Engineers	1-0
1873	The Wanderers	Oxford University	2-0
1874	Oxford University	Royal Engineers	2-0
1875	Royal Engineers	Old Etonians	1-1
	Royal Engineers	Old Etonians	2-0
1876	The Wanderers	Old Etonians	1-1 †
	The Wanderers	Old Etonians	3-0
1877	The Wanderers	Oxford University	2-1 †
1878	The Wanderers*	Royal Engineers	3-1
1879	Old Etonians	Clapham Rovers	1-0
1880	Clapham Rovers	Oxford University	1-0
1881	Old Carthusians	Old Etonians	3-0
1882	Old Etonians	Blackburn Rovers	1-0
1883	Blackburn Olympic	Old Etonians	2-1 †
1884	Blackburn Rovers	Queen's Park, Glasgow	2-1
1885	Blackburn Rovers	Queen's Park, Glasgow	2-0
1886	Blackburn Rovers**	West Bromwich Albion	0-0
	Blackburn Rovers**	West Bromwich Albion	2-0
1887	Aston Villa	West Bromwich Albion	2-0
1888	West Bromwich Albion	Preston North End	2-1
1889	Preston North End	Wolverhampton Wanderers	3-0
1890	Blackburn Rovers	Sheffield Wednesday	6-1
1891	Blackburn Rovers	Notts County	3-1
1892	West Bromwich Albion	Aston Villa	3-0
1893	Wolverhampton Wanderers	Everton	1-0
1894	Notts County	Bolton Wanderers	4-1
1895	Aston Villa	West Bromwich Albion	1-0
1896	Sheffield Wednesday	Wolverhampton Wanderers	2-1
1897	Aston Villa	Everton	3-2
1898	Nottingham Forest	Derby County	3-1
1899	Sheffield United	Derby County	4-1
1900	Bury	Southampton	4-0
1901	Tottenham Hotspur	Sheffield United	2-2
	Tottenham Hotspur	Sheffield United	3-1

Year	Winners	Runners-up	Score
1902	Sheffield United	Southampton	1-1
	Sheffield United	Southampton	2-1
1903	Bury	Derby County	6-0
1904	Manchester City	Bolton Wanderers	1-0
1905	Aston Villa	Newcastle United	2-0
1906	Everton	Newcastle United	1-0
1907	Sheffield Wednesday	Everton	2-1
1908	Wolverhampton Wanderers	Newcastle United	3-1
1909	Manchester United	Bristol City	1-0
1910	Newcastle United	Barnsley	1-1
	Newcastle United	Barnsley	2-0
1911	Bradford City	Newcastle United	0-0
	Bradford City	Newcastle United	1-0
1912	Barnsley	West Bromwich Albion	0-0 †
	Barnsley	West Bromwich Albion	1-0
1913	Aston Villa	Sunderland	1-0
1914	Burnley	Liverpool	1-0
1915	Sheffield United	Chelsea	3-0
1920	Aston Villa	Huddersfield Town	1-0 †
1921	Tottenham Hotspur	Wolverhampton Wanderers	1-0
1922	Huddersfield Town	Preston North End	1-0
1923	Bolton Wanderers	West Ham United	2-0
1924	Newcastle United	Aston Villa	2-0
1925	Sheffield United	Cardiff City	1-0
1926	Bolton Wanderers	Manchester City	1-0
1927	Cardiff City	Arsenal	1-0
1928	Blackburn Rovers	Huddersfield Town	3-1
1929	Bolton Wanderers	Portsmouth	2-0
1930	Arsenal	Huddersfield Town	2-0
1931	West Bromwich Albion	Birmingham	2-1
1932	Newcastle United	Arsenal	2-1
1933	Everton	Manchester City	3-0
1934	Manchester City	Portsmouth	2-1
1935	Sheffield Wednesday	West Bromwich Albion	4-2
1936	Arsenal	Sheffield United	1-0
1937	Sunderland	Preston North End	3-1
1938	Preston North End	Huddersfield Town	1-0 †
1939	Portsmouth	Wolverhampton Wanderers	4-1
1946	Derby County	Charlton Athletic	4-1 †

Year	Winners	Runners-up	Score
1947	Charlton Athletic	Burnley	1-0 †
1948	Manchester United	Blackpool	4-2
1949	Wolverhampton Wanderers	Leicester City	3-1
1950	Arsenal	Liverpool	2-0
1951	Newcastle United	Blackpool	2-0
1952	Newcastle United	Arsenal	1-0
1953	Blackpool	Bolton Wanderers	4-3
1954	West Bromwich Albion	Preston North End	3-2
1955	Newcastle United	Manchester City	3-1
1956	Manchester City	Birmingham City	3-1
1957	Aston Villa	Manchester United	2-1
1958	Bolton Wanderers	Manchester United	2-0
1959	Nottingham Forest	Luton Town	2-1
1960	Wolverhampton Wanderers	Blackburn Rovers	3-0
1961	Tottenham Hotspur	Leicester City	2-0
1962	Tottenham Hotspur	Burnley	3-1
1963	Manchester United	Leicester City	3-1
1964	West Ham United	Preston North End	3-2
1965	Liverpool	Leeds United	2-1 †
1966	Everton	Sheffield Wednesday	3-2
1967	Tottenham Hotspur	Chelsea	2-1
1968	West Bromwich Albion	Everton	1-0 †
1969	Manchester City	Leicester City	1-0
1970	Chelsea	Leeds United	2-2 †
	Chelsea	Leeds United	2-1 †
1971	Arsenal	Liverpool	2-1 †
1972	Leeds United	Arsenal	1-0
1973	Sunderland	Leeds United	1-0
1974	Liverpool	Newcastle United	3-0
1975	West Ham United	Fulham	2-0
1976	Southampton	Manchester United	1-0
1977	Manchester United	Liverpool	2-1
1978	Ipswich Town	Arsenal	1-0
1979	Arsenal	Manchester United	3-2
1980	West Ham United	Arsenal	1-0
1981	Tottenham Hotspur	Manchester City	1-1 †
	Tottenham Hotspur	Manchester City	3-2
1982	Tottenham Hotspur	Queens Park Rangers	1-1 †
	Tottenham Hotspur	Queens Park Rangers	1-0

45

Year	Winners	Runners-up	Score
1983	Manchester United	Brighton & Hove Albion	2-2
	Manchester United	Brighton & Hove Albion	4-0
1984	Everton	Watford	2-0
1985	Manchester United	Everton	1-0 †
1986	Liverpool	Everton	3- 1
1987	Coventry City	Tottenham Hotspur	3-2 †
1988	Wimbledon	Liverpool	1-0
1989	Liverpool	Everton	3-2 †
1990	Manchester United	Crystal Palace	3-3 †
	Manchester United	Crystal Palace	1-0
1991	Tottenham Hotspur	Nottingham Forest	2-1 †
1992	Liverpool	Sunderland	2-0
1993	Arsenal	Sheffield Wednesday	1-1 †
	Arsenal	Sheffield Wednesday	2-1 †
1994	Manchester United	Chelsea	4-0

Final Venues

1872	Kennington Oval
1873	Lillie Bridge
1874-92	Kennington Oval
1893	Fallowfield, Manchester
1894	Everton
1895-1914	Crystal Palace
1915	Old Trafford
1920-22	Stamford Bridge
1923 –1994	Wembley

Replay Venues

1886	Derby
1901	Bolton
1910	Everton
1911	Old Trafford
1912	Bramall Lane
1970	Old Trafford
1981	Wembley
1982	Wembley
1983	Wembley
1990	Wembley
1993	Wembley

* Trophy won outright by The Wanderers, but restored to the FA.

** Special trophy awarded for a third consecutive win.

† after extra time.

FA CHALLENGE CUP WINS BY CLUB

Manchester United	1909, 1948, 1963, 1977, 1983, 1985, 1990, 1994
Tottenham Hotspur	1901, 1921, 1961, 1962, 1967, 1981, 1982, 1991
Aston Villa	1887, 1895, 1897, 1905, 1913, 1920, 1957
Arsenal	1930, 1936, 1950, 1971, 1979, 1993
Blackburn Rovers	1884, 1885, 1886, 1890, 1891, 1928
Newcastle United	1910, 1924, 1932, 1951, 1952, 1955
Liverpool	1965, 1974, 1986, 1989, 1992
The Wanderers	1872, 1873, 1876, 1877, 1878
West Bromwich Albion	1888, 1892, 1931, 1954, 1968
Bolton	1923, 1926, 1929, 1958
Everton	1894, 1906, 1933, 1966
Manchester City	1904, 1934, 1956, 1969
Sheffield United	1899, 1902, 1915, 1925
Wolverhampton Wanderers	1893, 1908, 1949, 1960
Sheffield Wednesday	1896, 1907, 1935
West Ham United	1964, 1975, 1980
Bury	1900, 1903
Nottingham Forest	1898, 1959
Old Etonians	1879, 1882
Preston North End	1889, 1938
Sunderland	1937, 1973

Barnsley	1912	Ipswich Town	1978
Blackburn Olympic	1883	Leeds United	1972
Blackpool	1953	Notts County	1894
Bradford City	1911	Old Carthusians	1881
Burnley	1914	Oxford University	1874
Cardiff City	1927	Portsmouth	1939
Charlton Athletic	1947	Royal Engineers	1875
Chelsea	1970	Southampton	1976
Clapham Rovers	1880	Wimbledon	1988
Coventry City	1987		
Derby County	1946		
Huddersfield Town	1922		

FA CHARITY SHIELD
WINNERS 1908-93

1908	Manchester United v Queens Park Rangers	4-0
	after 1-1 draw	
1909	Newcastle United v Northampton Town	2-0
1910	Brighton & Hove Albion v Aston Villa	1-0
1911	Manchester United v Swindon Town	8-4
1912	Blackburn Rovers v Queens Park Rangers	2-1
1913	Professionals v Amateurs	7-2
1919	West Bromwich Albion v Tottenham Hotspur	2-0
1920	Tottenham Hotspur v Burnley	2-0
1921	Huddersfield Town v Liverpool	1-0
1922	Not Played	
1923	Professionals v Amateurs	2-0
1924	Professionals v Amateurs	3-1
1925	Amateurs v Professionals	6-1
1926	Amateurs v Professionals	6-3
1927	Cardiff City v Corinthians	2-1
1928	Everton v Blackburn Rovers	2-1
1929	Professionals v Amateurs	3-0
1930	Arsenal v Sheffield Wednesday	2-1
1931	Arsenal v West Bromwich Albion	1-0
1932	Everton v Newcastle United	5-3
1933	Arsenal v Everton	3-0
1934	Arsenal v Manchester City	4-0
1935	Sheffield Wednesday v Arsenal	1-0
1936	Sunderland v Arsenal	2-1
1937	Manchester City v Sunderland	2-0
1938	Arsenal v Preston North End	2-1
1948	Arsenal v Manchester United	4-3
1949	Portsmouth v Wolverhampton Wanderes	† 1-1
1950	World Cup Team v Canadian Touring Team	4-2
1951	Tottenham Hotspur v Newcastle United	2-1
1952	Manchester United v Newcastle United	4-2
1953	Arsenal v Blackpool	† 3-1
1954	Wolverhampton Wanderers v West Bromwich Albion	† 4-4
1955	Chelsea v Newcastle United	3-0
1956	Manchester United v Manchester City	1-0

1957	Manchester United v Aston Villa	4-0
1958	Bolton Wanderers v Wolverhampton Wanderers	4-1
1959	Wolverhampton Wanderers v Nottingham Forest	3-1
1960	Burnley v Wolverhampton Wanderers	† 2-2
1961	Tottenham Hotspur v FA XI	3-2
1962	Tottenham Hotspur v Ipswich Town	5-1
1963	Everton v Manchester United	4-0
1964	Liverpool v West Ham United	† 2-2
1965	Manchester United v Liverpool	† 2-2
1966	Liverpool v Everton	1-0
1967	Manchester United v Tottenham Hotspur	† 3-3
1968	Manchester City v West Bromwich Albion	6-1
1969	Leeds United v Manchester City	2-1
1970	Everton v Chelsea	2-1
1971	Leicester City v Liverpool	1-0
1972	Manchester City v Aston Villa	1-0
1973	Burnley v Manchester City	1-0
1974	Liverpool v Leeds United	1-1
	Liverpool won on penalties	
1975	Derby County v West Ham United	2-0
1976	Liverpool v Southampton	1-0
1977	Liverpool v Manchester United	† 0-0
1978	Nottingham Forest v Ipswich Town	5-0
1979	Liverpool v Arsenal	3-1
1980	Liverpool v West Ham United	1-0
1981	Aston Villa v Tottenham Hotspur	† 2-2
1982	Liverpool v Tottenham Hotspur	1-0
1983	Manchester United v Liverpool	2-0
1984	Everton v Liverpool	1-0
1985	Everton v Manchester United	2-0
1986	Everton v Liverpool	† 1-1
1987	Everton v Coventry City	1-0
1988	Liverpool v Wimbledon	2-1
1989	Liverpool v Arsenal	1-0
1990	Liverpool v Manchester United	† 1-1
1991	Arsenal v Tottenham Hotspur	† 0-0
1992	Leeds United v Liverpool	4-3
1993	Manchester United v Arsenal	1-1
	Manchester United won on penalties	

† *Each club retained Shield for six months*

FOOTBALL LEAGUE COCA-COLA CUP 93-94

First Round – two legs

			1st Leg	2nd Leg	Agg
Birmingham	v	Plymouth	3-0	0-2	3-2
Bolton	v	Bury	0-2	2-0†	2-2
(Bolton won 3-0 on penalties)					
Bournemouth	v	Cardiff	3-1	1-1	4-2
Brentford	v	Watford	2-2	1-3	3-5
Bristol Rovers	v	West Brom	1-4	0-0	1-4
Cambridge	v	Luton	1-0	1-0	2-0
Chesterfield	v	Carlisle	3-1	1-1	4-2
Crewe	v	Wrexham	0-1	3-3	3-4
Darlington	v	Bradford	1-5	0-6	1-11
Doncaster	v	Blackpool	0-1	3-3	3-4
Fulham	v	Colchester	2-1	2-1	4-2
Gillingham	v	Brighton	1-0	0-2	1-2
Hereford	v	Torquay	0-2	2-0†	2-2
(Hereford won 4-3 on penalties)					
Huddersfield	v	Scarborough	0-0	3-0	3-0
Leyton Orient	v	Wycombe	0-0	0-1	0-1
Notts County	v	Hull	2-0	1-3†	3-3
(Notts County won on away goals)					
Port Vale	v	Lincoln	2-2	0-0†	2-2
(Lincoln won on away goals)					
Preston	v	Burnley	1-2	1-4	2-6
Reading	v	Northampton	3-0	2-0	5-0
Rochdale	v	York	2-0	0-0	2-0
Shrewsbury	v	Scunthorpe	1-0	1-1	2-1
Southend	v	Barnet	0-2	1-1	1-3
Stockport	v	Hartlepool	1-1	1-2	2-3
Stoke	v	Mansfield	2-2	3-1	5-3
Sunderland	v	Chester	3-1	0-0	3-1
Swansea	v	Bristol City	0-1	2-0	2-1
Walsall	v	Exeter	0-0	1-2	1-2
Wigan	v	Rotherham	0-1	2-4	2-5

Second Round – two legs

			1st Leg	2nd Leg	Agg
Barnet	v	QPR	1-2	0-4	1-6
Birmingham	v	Aston Villa	0-1	0-1	0-2
Blackburn	v	Bournemouth	1-0	0-0	1-0
Blackpool	v	Sheffield United	3-0	0-2	3-2
Bolton	v	Sheffield Wednesday	1-1	0-1	1-2
Bradford	v	Norwich	2-1	0-3	2-4
Burnley	v	Tottenham	0-0	1-3	1-3
Coventry	v	Wycombe	3-0	2-4	5-4
Fulham	v	Liverpool	1-3	0-5	1-8
Hereford	v	Wimbledon	0-1	1-4	1-5
Huddersfield	v	Arsenal	0-5	1-1	1-6
Ipswich	v	Cambridge	2-1	2-0	4-1
Lincoln	v	Everton	3-4	2-4	5-8
Manchester City	v	Reading	1-1	2-1	3-2
Newcastle	v	Notts County	4-1	7-1	11-2
Southampton	v	Shrewsbury	1-0	0-2	1-2
Stoke	v	Manchester Utd	2-1	0-2	2-3
Sunderland	v	Leeds Utd	2-1	2-1	4-2
Swansea	v	Oldham	2-1	0-2	2-3
Swindon	v	Wolves	2-0	1-2	3-2
WBA	v	Chelsea	1-1	1-2	2-3
West Ham	v	Chesterfield	5-1	2-0	7-1
Wrexham	v	Nottingham Forest	3-3	1-3	4-7

Third Round

				Replay
Arsenal	v	Norwich	1-1	3-0
Blackpool	v	Peterborough	2-2	1-2
Blackburn	v	Shrewsbury	0-0	4-3
Derby	v	Tottenham	0-1	
Everton	v	Crystal Palace	2-2	4-1
Liverpool	v	Ipswich	3-2	
Man City	v	Chelsea	1-0	
Manchester Utd	v	Leicester City	5-1	
Middlesbrough	v	Sheffield Wednesday	1-1	1-2
Nottingham Forest	v	West Ham	2-1	
Oldham	v	Coventry	2-0	
QPR	v	Millwall	3-0	
Sunderland	v	Aston Villa	1-4	
Swindon	v	Portsmouth	2-0	
Wimbledon	v	Newcastle	2-1	

Fourth Round

Arsenal	v	Aston Villa	0-1	26,453
Everton	v	Manchester United	0-2	34,052
Liverpool	v	Wimbledon	1-1	19,290
Nottingham Forest	v	Manchester City	0-0	22,195
Peterborough	v	Portsmouth	0-0	6,141
Queens Park Rangers	v	Sheffield Wednesday	1-2	13,253
Tottenham	v	Blackburn	1-0	22,295
Tranmere Rovers	v	Oldham Athletic	3-0	9,477

Fourth Round Replays

Wimbledon	v	Liverpool	2-2†	11,393

(Wimbledon won 4-3 on penalties)

Manchester City	v	Nottingham Forest	1-2	14,117
Portsmouth	v	Peterborough	1-0†	9,634

Fifth Round

Manchester United	v	Portsmouth	2-2	43,794
Nottingham Forest	v	Tranmere Rovers	1-1	20,066
Tottenham Hotspur	v	Aston Villa	1-2	31,408
Wimbledon	v	Sheffield Wednesday	1-2	8,784

Fifth Round Replays

Portsmouth	v	Manchester United	0-1	24,950
Tranmere Rovers	v	Nottingham Forest	2-0	12,578

Semi-Finals – first leg

Tranmere Rovers	v	Aston Villa	3-1	17,140
Manchester United	v	Sheffield Wednesday	1-0	43,294

Semi-Finals – second leg

Aston Villa	v	Tranmere Rovers	3-1	40,593

(4-4 on aggregate, level on away goals rule, Villa win 5-4 on penalties)

Sheffield Wednesday	v	Manchester United	1-4	34,878

(Manchester United win 5-1 on aggregate)

Final – 27th March 1994 at Wembley Stadium

Aston Villa	v	Manchester United	3-1	77,231

Atkinson 25,
Saunders 75, 90 (pen)

Hughes 82

Aston Villa: Bosnich, Barrett, McGrath, Teale, Staunton (Cox 79), Atkinson, Fenton, Richardson, Townsend, Daley, Saunders.
Manchester United: Sealey, Parker, Bruce (McClair 83), Pallister, Irwin, Kanchelskis, Keane, Ince, Giggs (Sharpe 68), Cantona, Hughes.

FOOTBALL LEAGUE CUP
FINALS 1961-1994

Year	Winners	Runners-up	1st	2nd	Agg
1961	Aston Villa	Rotherham United	0-2†	3-0	3-2
1962	Norwich City	Rochdale	3-0	1-0	4-0
1963	Birmingham City	Aston Villa	3-1	0-0	3-1
1964	Leicester City	Stoke City	1-1	3-2	4-3
1965	Chelsea	Leicester City	3-2	0-0	3-2
1966	West Bromwich Albion	West Ham United	1-2	4-1	5-3
1967	Queens Park Rangers	West Bromwich Albion	3-2		
1968	Leeds United	Arsenal	1-0		
1969	Swindon Town	Arsenal	† 3-1		
1970	Manchester City	West Bromwich Albion	2-1		
1971	Tottenham Hotspur	Aston Villa	† 2-0		
1972	Stoke City	Chelsea	2-1		
1973	Tottenham Hotspur	Norwich City	1-0		
1974	Wolverhampton W	Manchester City	2-1		
1975	Aston Villa	Norwich City	1-0		
1976	Manchester City	Newcastle United	2-1		
1977	Aston Villa	Everton	† 3-2		
	after 0-0 draw and 1-1 draw aet				
1978	Nottingham Forest	Liverpool	1-0		
	after 0-0 draw aet				
1979	Nottingham Forest	Southampton	3-2		
1980	Wolverhampton W	Nottingham Forest	1-0		
1981	Liverpool	West Ham United	2-1		
	after 1-1 draw aet				

Milk Cup

1982	Liverpool	Tottenham Hotspur	† 3-1		
1983	Liverpool	Manchester United	† 2-1		
1984	Liverpool	Everton	1-0		
	after 0-0 draw aet				
1985	Norwich City	Sunderland	1-0		
1986	Oxford United	Queens Park Rangers	3-0		

Littlewoods Cup

1987	Arsenal	Liverpool	2-1
1988	Luton Town	Arsenal	3-2
1989	Nottingham Forest	Luton Town	3-1
1990	Nottingham Forest	Oldham Athletic	1-0

Rumbelows League Cup

| 1991 | Sheffield Wednesday | Manchester United | 1-0 |
| 1992 | Manchester United | Nottingham Forest | 1-0 |

Coca–Cola Cup

| 1993 | Arsenal | Sheffield Wednesday | 2-1 |
| 1994 | Aston Villa | Manchester United | 3-1 |

FOOTBALL LEAGUE CUP WINS BY CLUB

Liverpool	1981, 1982, 1983, 1984
Nottingham Forest	1978, 1979, 1989, 1990
Aston Villa	1961, 1975, 1977, 1994
Arsenal	1987, 1993
Manchester City	1970, 1976
Tottenham Hotspur	1971, 1973
Norwich City	1962, 1985
Wolverhampton Wanderers	1974, 1980
Birmingham City	1963
Leicester City	1964
Chelsea	1965
WBA	1966
QPR	1967
Leeds United	1968
Swindon Town	1969
Stoke City	1972
Oxford United	1986
Luton Town	1988
Sheffield Wednesday	1991
Manchester United	1992

FA PREMIER LEAGUE CLUBS IN EUROPE 93-94

Cup-Winners' Cup – Arsenal

1st Round

Odense Boldklub Keown (18 og)	**Arsenal** Wright (35), Merson (68)	1-2	9,580
Arsenal Campbell (52)	**Odense Boldklub** A Nielsen (86)	1-1	25,689

Arsenal win 3-2 on aggregate

2nd Round

Arsenal Wright (39, 64), Merson (51)	**Standard Liege**	3-0	25,258
Standard Liege	**Arsenal** Smith (2), Selley (20), Adams (37), Campbell (41, 79), Merson (71), McGoldrick (81)	0-7	15,000

Arsenal win 10-0 on aggregate

Quarter-Finals

Torino	**Arsenal**	0-0	32,480
Arsenal Adams (66)	**Torino**	1-0	34,678

Arsenal win 1-0 on aggregate

Semi-Finals

Paris St Germain Ginola (50)	**Arsenal** Wright (35)	1-1	46,000
Arsenal Campbell (7)	**Paris St Germain**	1-0	34,212

Arsenal win 2-1 on aggregate

Final – 4th May 1994, Copenhagen

Arsenal Smith (20)	**Parma**	1-0	33,765

Arsenal: Seaman, Dixon, Winterburn, Bould, Adams, Morrow, Davis, Merson (McGoldrick), Selley, Smith, Campbell

Champions' Cup – Manchester United

1st Round

Honved Szabados (39), Stefanov (68)	**Manchester United** Keane (9, 42), Cantona (44)	2-3	10,000
Manchester United Bruce (55, 64)	**Honved**	2-0	35,781

Manchester United win 5-2 on aggregate

2nd Round

Manchester United Robson (3), Hakan (13 og), Cantona (81)	**Galatasaray** Arif (16), Kubilay (31, 63)	3-3	39,396
Galatasaray	**Manchester United**	0-0	40,000

Galatasaray win on away goals rule

UEFA Cup – Norwich City, Aston Villa

1st Round

Slovan Bratislava	**Aston Villa**	0-0	10,886
Aston Villa Atkinson (15), Townsend (22)	**Slovan Bratislava** Tittel (86)	2-1	24,461

Aston Villa win 2-1 on aggregate

Norwich City Ekoku (50), Goss (67), Polston (71)	**Vitesse Arnhem**	3-0	16,818
Vitesse Arnhem	**Norwich City**	0-0	18,000

Norwich City win 3-0 on aggregate

2nd Round

Deportivo La Coruna Riesco (87)	**Aston Villa** Saunders (78)	1-1	22,000
Aston Villa	**Deportivo La Coruna** Manjarin (36)	0-1	26,737

Deportivo La Coruna win 2-1 on aggregate

Bayern Munich Nerlinger (41)	**Norwich City** Goss (12), Bowen (30)	1-2	18,000
Norwich City Goss (50)	**Bayern Munich** Valencia (5)	1-1	20,829

Norwich City win 3-2 on aggregate

3rd Round

Norwich City	**Internazionale**	**0-1**	**20,805**
	Bergkamp (80, pen)		
Internazionale	**Norwich City**	**1-0**	**30,000**
Bergkamp (88)			

Internazionale win 2-0 on aggregate

Scorers by Club

Arsenal – Cup-Winners' Cup

4	Campbell
4	Wright
3	Merson
2	Adams
2	Smith
1	McGoldrick
1	Selley

Manchester United – Champions' Cup

2	Bruce, Cantona, Keane
1	Robson

Aston Villa – UEFA Cup

1	Atkinson, Saunders, Townsend

Norwich City – UEFA Cup

3	Goss
1	Bowen, Ekoku, Polston

ENGLAND 1993-94

Wembley, September 8th 1993 – World Cup European Qualifying Group 2

ENGLAND   **POLAND**   **3-0**   **71,220**

Ferdinand (5), Gascoigne (48),
Pearce (52)

England: Seaman, R. Jones, Pearce, Sharpe, Adams, Pallister, Platt,
Gascoigne, Ferdinand, Wright, Ince

Rotterdam, October 13th 1993 – World Cup European Qualifying Group 2

HOLLAND   **ENGLAND**   **2-0**   **48,000**

Koeman (62), Bergkamp (68)

England: Seaman, Parker, Dorigo, Adams, Pallister, Palmer (Sinton 45),
Platt, Ince, Sharpe, Shearer, Merson (Wright 68)

Bologna, November 17th 1993 – World Cup European Qualifying Group 2

SAN MARINO   **ENGLAND**   **1-7**   **2,378**

Gualtieri (1)   Ince (21, 73), Wright (34, 46, 78, 90),
                  Ferdinand (38)

England: Seaman, Dixon, Pallister, Walker, Pearce, Ripley, Ince, Platt,
Sinton, Ferdinand, Wright

Wembley, March 9th 1994 – Friendly

ENGLAND   **DENMARK**   **1-0**   **71,970**

Platt (16)

England: Seaman, Parker, Le Saux, Ince (Le Tissier 66), Adams, Pallister,
Platt, Gascoigne (Batty 66), Shearer, Beardsley, Anderton

Wembley, May 17th 1994 – Friendly

ENGLAND   **GREECE**   **5-0**   **23,659**

Anderton (24), Beardsley (37),
Platt (45 pen, 55), Shearer 65

England: Flowers, R. Jones (Pearce 81), Bould, Adams, Le Saux, Anderton
(Le Tissier 68), Richardson, Merson, Platt, Beardsley (Wright 70), Shearer

Wembley, May 22nd 1994 – Friendly

ENGLAND   **NORWAY**   **0-0**

England: Seaman, R. Jones, Bould, Adams, Le Saux, Anderton (Wright 76),
Ince (Le Tissier 76), Wise, Platt, Beardsley, Shearer

England Record 93-94

P	W	D	L	F	A
6	4	1	1	16	3

Appearance and Goalscorers Summary 1993-94

Player	Club	Apps	Sub	Goals
Tony ADAMS	Arsenal	5	–	–
Darren ANDERTON	Tottenham Hotspur	3	–	1
David BATTY	Leeds United	–	1	–
Peter BEARDSLEY	Newcastle United	3	–	1
Steve BOULD	Arsenal	4	–	–
Lee DIXON	Arsenal	1	–	–
Tony DORIGO	Leeds United	1	–	–
Les FERDINAND	QPR	2	–	2
Tim FLOWERS	Blackburn Rovers	1	–	–
Paul GASCOIGNE	Lazio	2	–	1
Paul INCE	Manchester United	5	–	2
Rob JONES	Liverpool	3	–	–
Graeme LE SAUX	Blackburn Rovers	3	–	–
Matthew LE TISSIER	Southampton	–	3	–
Paul MERSON	Arsenal	2	–	–
Gary PALLISTER	Manchester United	4	–	–
Carlton PALMER	Sheffield Wednesday	1	–	–
Paul PARKER	Manchester United	2	–	–
Stuart PEARCE	Nottingham Forest	2	1	1
David PLATT	Sampdoria	5	–	3
Kevin RICHARDSON	Aston Villa	1	–	–
Stuart RIPLEY	Blackburn Rovers	1	–	–
David SEAMAN	Arsenal	4	–	–
Lee SHARPE	Manchester United	2	–	–
Alan SHEARER	Blackburn Rovers	4	–	1
Andy SINTON	QPR	1	1	–
Des WALKER	Sheffield Wednesday	1	–	–
Ian WRIGHT	Arsenal	2	3	4
Dennis WISE	Chelsea	1	–	–

1993-94 APPEARANCE CHART

	Poland	Holland	San Marino	Denmark	Greece	Norway
ADAMS	•	•	–	•	•	•
ANDERTON	–	–	–	–	•	•
BATTY	–	–	–	66	–	–
BEARDSLEY	–	–	–	•	–	•
BOULD	–	–	–	–	•	•
DIXON	–	–	•	–	–	–
DORIGO	–	•	–	–	–	–
FERDINAND	•	–	•	–	–	–
FLOWERS	–	–	–	–	•	–
GASCOIGNE	•	–	–	•	–	–
INCE	•	•	•	–	•	–
JONES	•	–	–	–	•	•
LE SAUX	–	–	–	•	•	•
LE TISSIER	–	–	–	66	68	76
MERSON	–	•	•	–	•	–
PALLISTER	•	•	•	•	–	–
PALMER	–	•	•	–	–	–
PARKER	–	•	–	•	–	–
PEARCE	•	–	•	–	81	–
PLATT	•	•	•	•	•	•
RICHARDSON	–	–	–	–	•	–
RIPLEY	–	–	•	–	–	–
SEAMAN	•	•	•	•	–	•
SHARPE	•	•	–	•	–	–
SHEARER	–	•	–	•	•	•
SINTON	–	45	•	–	–	–
WALKER	–	–	•	–	–	–
WRIGHT	•	68	•	–	70	76
WISE	–	–	–	–	–	•

• Started match. – No appearance. A number indicates an appearance as substitute, the number relating the minute the player entered the match.

CLUB DIRECTORY
1994-95

Arsenal

Formed as Dial Square, a workshop in Woolwich Arsenal with a sundial over the entrance, in October 1886, becoming Royal Arsenal, the 'Royal' possibly from a local public house, later the same year. Turned professional and became Woolwich Arsenal in 1891. Selected for an expanded Football League Division Two in 1893, the first southern team to join.

Moved from the Manor Ground, Plumstead south-east London, to Highbury, north London, in 1913 changing name again at the same time. Elected from fifth in Division Two to the expanded First Division for the 1919-20 season and never relegated. Premier League founder members 1992.

Ground: Arsenal Stadium, Highbury, London N5.
Phone: 071-226 0304   **Nickname:** Gunners
Colours: Red/White sleeves, White, Red
Change: Yellow, Navy Blue, Yellow
Capacity: 39,497   **Pitch:** 110 yds x 71 yds
Directions: *From North:* M1, J2 follow sign for City. After Holloway Rd station (c 6 miles) take third left into Drayton Park. Then right into Aubert Park after ¼ mile and 2nd left into Avenell Rd. *From South:* Signs for Bank of England then Angel from London Bridge. Right at traffic lights towards Highbury roundabout. Follow Holloway Rd then third right into Drayton Pk, thereafter as above. *From West:* A40(M) to A501 ring road. Left at Angel to Highbury roundabout, then as above.
Rail: Drayton Park/Finsbury Park   **Tube** (Piccadilly line): Arsenal

Chairman: P.D. Hill-Wood   **Vice-Chairman:** D. Dein
Managing Director: K.J. Friar   **Secretary:** K.J. Friar
Manager: George Graham   **Assistant/Coach:** Stewart Houston
Physio: Gary Lewin

Record FAPL Win: 5-1 v Ipswich Town 5/02/94
Record FAPL Defeat: 0-3 v Leeds United, 21/11/92 and
                          0-3 v Coventry City 14/08/93
Record FL Win: 12-0 v Loughborough Town, Division 2, 12/3/1900
Record FL Defeat: 0-8 v Loughborough T, Division 2, 12/12/1896
Record Cup Win: 11-1 v Darwen, FA Cup R3, 9/1/32
Record Fee Received: £1.5m from Liverpool for Michael Thomas, 11/1991
Record Fee Paid: £2.5m to Crystal Palace for Ian Wright, 9/1991
Most FAPL Appearances: David Seaman, 78,1992-94
Most FL Appearances: David O'Leary, 547, 1975-92

Record Attendance (all-time): 73,295 v Sunderland, Division 1, 9/3/35
Record Attendance (FAPL): 36,203 v Manchester United, 22/03/94
Highest Scorer in FAPL Season: Ian Wright, 30, 1992-93
Most FAPL Goals in season: 53, 1993-94
Most FAPL Points in season: 71, 1993-94
Most Capped Player: Kenny Sansom, England: 77 out of 86

Season 1993-94
Biggest Home Win: 4-0 v Ipswich Town, 11/09/93
Biggest Home Defeat: 0-3 v Coventry City, 14/08/93
Biggest Away Win: 5-1 v Ipswich Town, 05/02/94
Biggest Away Defeat: 0-2 v Newcastle United, 27/11/93
Biggest Home Attendance: 36,203 v Manchester United, 22/03/94
Smallest Home Attendance: 21,292 v Wimbledon, 19/04/94
Average Attendance: 30,492 (+25.0%)
Last Season: *FAPL:* 4th *FA Cup:* 4th Round *Coca-Cola Cup:* 4th Round,
            European Cup Winners' Cup: Winners
Leading Scorer: Ian Wright (23)

League History: 1893 Elected to Division 2; 1904-13 Division 1; 1913-19 Division 2; 1919-92 Division 1; 1992 – FA Premier League.
Honours: Football League: Division 1 – Champions 1930-31, 1932-33, 1933-34, 1934-35, 1937-38, 1947-48, 1952-53, 1970-71, 1988-89, 1990-91; Runners-up 1925-26, 1931-32, 1972-73; Division 2 – Runners-up 1903-04. FA Cup: Winners 1929-30, 1935-36, 1949-50, 1970-71, 1978-79, 1992-93; Runners-up 1926-27, 1931-32, 1951-52, 1971-72, 1977-78, 1979-80. Football League Cup: Winners 1986-87, 1992-93; Runners-up 1967-68, 1968-69, 1987-88. League-Cup Double Performed: 1970-71. Cup-Cup Double Performed: 1992-93
European Competitions: European Cup: 1971-72, 1991-92; European Cup-Winners' Cup: 1979-80 (runners-up), 1993-94 (winners); European Fairs Cup: 1963-64, 1969-70 (winners), 1970-71; UEFA Cup: 1978-79, 1981-82, 1982-83.
Managers (and Secretary-managers): Sam Hollis 1894-97, Tom Mitchell 1897-98, George Elcoat 1898-99, Harry Bradshaw 1899-1904, Phil Kelso 1904-08, George Morrell 1908-15, Leslie Knighton 1919-25, Herbert Chapman 1925-34, George Allison 1934-47, Tom Whittaker 1947-56, Jack Crayston 1956-58, George Swindin 1958-62, Billy Wright 1962-66, Bertie Mee 1966-76, Terry Neill 1976-83, Don Howe 1984-86, George Graham May, 1986-.

5-Year League Record

	Div.	P	W	D	L	F	A	Pts	Pos	FAC	FLC
89-90	1	38	18	8	12	54	38	62	4	4	4
90-91	1	38	24	13	1	74	18	83*	1	SF	4
91-92	1	42	19	15	8	81	46	72	4	3	3
92-93	PL	42	15	11	16	40	38	56	10	W	W
93-94	PL	42	18	17	7	53	28	71	4	4	4

*2 points deducted

Summary of Appearances and Goals 1993-94

Player	A	G	B	Player	A	G	B
Adams	35		1	Linighan	20(1)		
Bould	23(2)	1	2	McGoldrick	23(3)		1
Campbell	28(9)	14		Merson	24(9)	8	1
Davis	21(1)		2	Miller	3(1)		
Dickov	(1)			Morrow	7(4)		1
Dixon	32(1)		2	Parlour	24(3)	2	1
Flatts	2(1)			Seaman	39		(1)
Heaney	1			Selley	16(2)		3
Hillier	11(4)		1	Smith	21(4)	3	
Jensen	27		1	Winterburn	34		3
Keown	23(9)		4	Wright	39	23	6
Limpar	9(1)		3				

A=Appearances (as Sub)   G=Goals   B=Bookings (Sent Off)

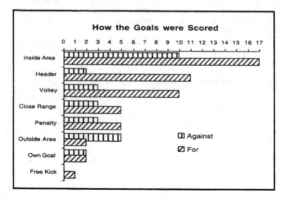

Euro Success for Golden Graham

The double Cup-winners got off to a bad start in 1993-94, but as the season went on they steadily got better and better. August opened with the Charity Shield against Manchester United at Wembley. Ian Wright scored the first of his 35 League and Cup goals in the game, which finished as a 1-1 draw. Goalkeeper David Seaman missed the decisive penalty as United won 5-4. Then, in the opening League fixture, Coventry's Mick Quinn scored a hat-trick in a 3-0 win at Highbury – though Arsenal were to concede only another 12 at home all season. September brought a home demolition of Ipswich and a 5-0 thrashing at Huddersfield in the Coca-Cola Cup but, suddenly, the goals dried up. Wright, inevitably, ended a run of 463 minutes of League football without a goal when he fired home a winner against Aston Villa at the start of November. The goal drought was all the more surprising given Arsenal's excellent form in Europe during the run: Standard Liege were beaten 3-0 at Highbury and 7-0 in the return in Brussels – the Gunners' highest score under George Graham and their best ever in Europe.

The defence of the Coca-Cola Cup ended in the fourth round with a 1-0 home defeat by Aston Villa in November. January brought on more disappointment as Bolton went to Highbury for an FA Cup fourth round replay and won 3-1. League form was moderate and, while the club hovered around third place for much of the season, they were never able to mount a serious challenge to Manchester United – which meant that the Cup-Winners' Cup was now the prime target.

Torino were the quarter-final opposition and, after a 0-0 draw in Turin, a Tony Adams header sealed the game at Highbury and sent Arsenal through to a semi-final against Paris St Germain. The game in Turin came during the club's best patch of the season, along with league wins against Blackburn, Ipswich (5-0 away) and Southampton (4-0 away), and a 2-2 draw with Manchester United.

Another Wright goal earned a 1-1 draw in Paris in the semi-final, and a Kevin Campbell header secured a 1-0 win to send Arsenal through to the European final for the first time since 1980. But Arsenal's plans were hit by suspension and injury: Ian Wright, booked in the second leg of the semi-final, was suspended and John Jensen, injured playing for Denmark against Hungary, was ruled out. Despite their losses Arsenal battled to a 1-0 win over holders Parma in the final. A great defensive performance ensured the victory, and Graham's sixth major trophy in eight years in charge.

The season ended with an international call-up for defender Steve Bould, at 31 the oldest England debutant for over 40 years, and a first start at Wembley for Paul Merson in England's 5-0 win over Greece.

Aston Villa

Founded in 1874 by cricketers from the Aston Wesleyan Chapel, Lozells, who played on Aston Park, moving to a field in Wellington Road, Perry Barr in 1876. Prominent nationally, the club was a founder member of the Football League in 1888.

The landlord at Perry Barr made such demands that the club sought its own ground and eventually moved back to Aston occupying the Aston Lower Grounds, which had already been used for some big games. Not known as Villa Park until some time later, the ground first saw League football in 1897. Premier League founder members 1992.

Ground: Villa Park, Trinity Rd, Birmingham, B6 6HE
Phone: 021-327 2299   **Nickname:** The Villains
Colours: Claret/Blue, White, Blue/Claret
Change Colours: White, Black, White
Capacity: 40,530   **Pitch:** 115 yds x 75 yds
Directions: M6 J6, follow signs for Birmingham NE. 3rd exit at roundabout, then right into Ashton Hall Rd after 1/2 mile.
Rail: Witton

President: H.J. Musgrove   **Chairman:** H.D. Ellis
Secretary: Steven Stride
Manager: Ron Atkinson   **Assistant:** Jim Barron
First Team Coach: Dave Sexton   **Physio:** Jim Walker

Record FAPL Win: 5-0 v Swindon Town, 12/2/94
Record FAPL Defeat: 1-5 v Newcastle United, 27/4/94
Record FL Win: 12-2 v Accrington S, Division 1, 12/3/1892
Record FL Defeat: 1-8 v Blackburn R, FA Cup R3, 16/2/1889
Record Cup Win: 13-0 v Wednesbury Old Ath, FA Cup R1, 30/10/1886
Record Fee Received: £5.5m from Bari for David Platt, 8/1991
Record Fee Paid: £1.7m to Oldham Athletic for Earl Barrett, 2/1992
Most FAPL Appearances: Kevin Richardson, 82, 1992-94
Most FL Appearances: Charlie Aitken, 561, 1961-76
Record Attendance (all-time): 76,588 v Derby Co, FA Cup R6, 2/2/1946
Record Attendance (FAPL): 45,347 v Liverpool, 7/5/94
Highest Scorer in FAPL season: Dean Saunders, 17, 1992-93
Most FAPL Goals in season: 57, 1992-93
Most FAPL Points in season: 74, 1992-93
Most Capped Player: Peter McParland, N. Ireland: 33 out of 34

Season 1993-94

Biggest Home Win: 5-0 v Swindon Town, 2/4/94

Biggest Home Defeat: 0-2 Newcastle United, 2/10/93
0-2 Southampton, 24/11/93

Biggest Away Win: 1-2 Arsenal, Ipswich Town, Norwich City,
Sheffield United, Swindon Town

Biggest Away Defeat: 1-5 Newcastle United, 27/4/94

Biggest Home Attendance: 45,347 v Liverpool, 7/5/94

Smallest Home Attendance: 16,180 v Southampton, 24/11/93

Average Attendance: 28,967 (-2.3%)

Last Season: *PL:* 10th *FA Cup:* 5th round *Coca-Cola Cup:* Winners *UEFA Cup:* 2nd round

Leading Scorer: Dean Saunders (10)

League History: 1888 Founder Member of the League; 1936-38 Division 2; 1938-59 Division 1; 1959-60 Division 2; 1960-67 Division 1; 1967-70 Division 2; 1970-72 Division 3; 1972-75 Division 2; 1975-87 Division 1; 1987-88 Division 2; 1988-92 Division 1; 1992- FA Premier League

Honours: FA Premier League – Runners-up 1992-93; Football League: Division 1 – Champions 1893-94, 1895-96, 1896-97, 1898-99, 1899-1900, 1909-10, 1980-81; Runners-up 1888-89, 1902-03, 1907-08, 1910-11, 1912-13, 1913-14, 1930-31, 1932-33, 1989-90; Division 2 – Champions 1937-38, 1959-60; Runners-up 1974-75, 1987-88; Division 3 – Champions 1971-72. FA Cup: Winners 1887, 1895, 1897, 1905, 1913, 1920, 1957; Runners-up 1892, 1924. League-Cup Double Performed: 1896-97. Football League Cup: Winners 1961, 1975, 1977, 1994; Runners-up 1963, 1971

European Competitions: European Cup: 1981-82 (winners), 1982-83; UEFA Cup: 1975-76, 1977-78, 1983-84, 1990-91, 1993-94. World Cup Championship: 1982-83; European Super Cup: 1982-83 (winners)

Managers (and Secretary-managers): George Ramsay 1884-1926, W.J. Smith 1926-34, Jimmy McMullan 1934-35, Jimmy Hogan 1936-44, Alex Massie 1945-50, George Martin 1950-53, Eric Houghton 1953-58, Joe Mercer 1958-64, Dick Taylor 1965-67, Tommy Cummings 1967-68, Tommy Docherty 1968-70, Vic Crowe 1970-74, Ron Saunders 1974-82, Tony Barton 1982-84, Graham Turner 1984-86, Billy McNeill 1986-87, Graham Taylor 1987-90, Dr Jozef Venglos 1990-91, Ron Atkinson June 1991-.

5-Year League Record

	Div.	P	W	D	L	F	A	Pts	Pos	FAC	FLC
89-90	1	38	21	7	10	57	38	70	2	6	3
90-91	1	38	9	14	15	46	58	41	17	3	5
91-92	1	42	17	9	16	48	44	60	7	2	6
92-93	PL	42	21	11	10	57	40	74	2	4	4
93-94	PL	42	15	12	15	46	50	57	10	5	W

Summary of Appearances and Goals 1993-94

Player	A	G	B	Player	A	G	B
Atkinson	29	8	1	Kubicki	1(1)		
Barrett	39		2	McGrath	30		2
Beinlich	6(1)	1		Parker	17(2)	2	1
Bosnich	28		1	Richardson	40	5	1
Breitkreutz	1(1)			Saunders	37(1)	10	
Cowans	10(2)			Small	8(1)		
Cox	16(4)	2	2	Spink	14(1)		(1)
Daley	19(8)	1		Staunton	24	3	2
Ehiogu	14(3)		1	Teale	37(1)	1	5
Farrell	4			Townsend	31	3	2
Fenton	9(3)	1	1	Whittingham	13(5)	3	1
Froggatt	8(1)	1		Yorke	2(10)	2	
Houghton	25(5)	2					

A=Appearances (as Sub)   G=Goals   B=Bookings (Sent Off)

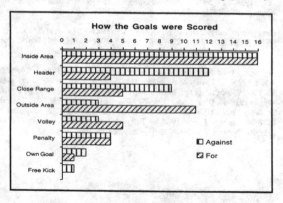

How the Goals were Scored

Villa Fizz in the Coca-Cola Cup

Ron Atkinson spent heavily in the pre-season to strengthen a squad which had chased Manchester United all the way to the title in 1993. Republic of Ireland midfielder Andy Townsend arrived from Chelsea for £2.1 million, prolific striker Guy Whittingham came from Portsmouth for £1.2 million and former Villa Park favourite Gordon Cowans returned on a free from Blackburn. But Whittingham and Cowans hardly established themselves, and both had left the club by the end of the season, moving to Wolves and Derby respectively.

The League campaign began encouragingly with a 4-1 home win over QPR, but away draws at Sheffield Wednesday and Wimbledon and a 2-1 defeat at home to Manchester United set the precedent for a mediocre League season – too many draws and as many defeats as wins.

The European campaign also resulted in disappointment. After a nervous, unconvincing first-round victory over modest Slovan Bratislava, Villa fell to Deportivo La Coruna in the next round having, it seemed, done the hard bit with a 1-1 draw in Spain thanks to a late goal by Dean Saunders. But Deportivo came back to win 1-0 in the return and Villa were out.

The Coca-Cola Cup, though, was another story. The second round paired Villa with city rivals Birmingham, and 1-0 wins in both legs was all that separated the two. At Sunderland, in the third round, goalkeeper Mark Bosnich performed heroics as Sunderland ran Villa ragged in the first half. But Villa's counter-attacking tactics worked wonders as they came away with a 4-1 win.

Holders Arsenal were waiting in the fourth round, but a Dalian Atkinson goal after just four minutes – and a stubborn defensive performance – earned a 1-0 win at Highbury and a trip to Tottenham for the quarter-final. Goals by Ray Houghton and Earl Barrett secured a 2-1 win there and Villa were through to the semi-finals against First Division Tranmere, and clear favourites to reach Wembley. But any thoughts of an easy passage to the final were smashed when Tranmere won the first leg 3-1 at home, with Villa's goal coming from Atkinson in the last minute. Villa took a 2-0 lead in the return, but a penalty from John Aldridge – having been brought down by Bosnich – put Tranmere back in front after 27 minutes. The Villa Park faithful had to wait until two minutes from time for the tie-saving goal, again provided by Atkinson. In the penalty shoot-out which followed, Bosnich saved three penalties as Villa won 5-4, though Tranmere will argue he should not have been on the pitch.

In the final, against favourites Manchester United, Villa completely out-played the manager's old club to win 3-1 with goals by Atkinson and Saunders (two). Boss Atkinson had won the League Cup for the second time in four years and Villa were back in Europe for the third time in four seasons.

Hopes of FA Cup glory had lasted until late February when Bolton won 1-0 at Burnden Park in the fifth round. But the season ended on a definite high: 45,347 turned out for the final game, a 2-1 win over Liverpool, the biggest attendance in the Premiership all season.

Blackburn Rovers

Founded in 1875 by local school-leavers. Used several pitches, including Alexander Meadows, the East Lancashire Cricket Club ground, and became known nationally for their FA Cup exploits, eclipsing the record of Blackburn Olympic, the first club to take the trophy away from London. Three consecutive wins in the 1880s, when in the finals Queen's Park (twice) and West Bromwich Albion were beaten, brought recognition by way of a special shield awarded by the FA to commemorate the achievement.

Founder member of the Football League in 1888, the club settled at Ewood Park in 1890, purchasing the ground outright in 1893-94. Premier League founder member 1992.

Ground: Ewood Park, Blackburn, BB2 4JF
Phone: (0254) 698888   **Nickname:** Blue and Whites
Colours: Blue/White, White, Blue   **Change:** Black/Red, Black, Black/Red
Capacity: 30,591   **Pitch:** 115yds x 76yds
Directions: *From North, South & West:* M6 J31 follow signs for Blackburn then Bolton Rd. Turn left after 1½ miles into Kidder St. *From East:* A677 or A679 following signs for Bolton Rd, then as above.
Rail: Blackburn Central

Chairman: R.D. Coar BSC   **Vice-Chairman:** R.D. Coar BSC
Secretary: John W. Howarth FAAI
Manager: Kenny Dalglish MBE   **Assistant:** Ray Harford
Physio: M. Pettigrew

Record FAPL Win: 7-1 v Norwich City, 3/10/92
Record FAPL Defeat: 2-5 v Coventry City, 26/1/93 *and*
                      2-5 v Leeds United, 10/4/93
Record FL Win: 9-0 v Middlesbrough, Division 2, 6/11/1954
Record FL Defeat: 0-8 v Arsenal, Division 1, 25/2/1933
Record Cup Win: 11-0 v Rossendale, FA Cup R1, 13/10/1884
Record Fee Received: £800,000 from Borusssia Moenchengladbach for Patrik Andersson
Record Fee Paid: £3.3m to Southampton for Alan Shearer, 7/1992
Most FAPL Appearances: Stuart Ripley, 78, 1992-94
Most FL Appearances: Derek Fazackerley, 596, 1970-86
Record Attendance (all-time): 61,783 v Bolton W, FA Cup R6, 2/3/1929
Record Attendance (FAPL): 21,462 v Everton, 29/12/93
Highest Scorer in FAPL Season: Alan Shearer, 31, 1993-94
Most FAPL Goals in season: 68, 1992-93

Most FAPL Points in season: 84, 1993-94
Most Capped Player: Bob Crompton, England: 41

Season 1993-94
Biggest Home Win: 3-0 v Wimbledon, 5/2/94
Biggest Home Defeat: 0-2 v West Ham, 18/9/93
Biggest Away Win: 3-0 v Everton, 4/4/94
Biggest Away Defeat: 1-4 v Wimbledon, 29/3/94
Biggest Home Attendance: 21,462 v Everton, 29/12/94
Smallest Home Attendance: 13,505 v Sheffield United, 18/10/94
Average Attendance: 17,303 (+6.5%)
Last Season: *PL:* 2nd *FA Cup:* 4th round *Coca-Cola Cup:* 4th round
Leading Scorer: Alan Shearer (31)

League History: 1888 Founder member of the League; 1936-39 Division 2; 1946-48 Division 1; 1948-58 Division 2; 1958-66 Division 1; 1966-71 Division 2; 1971-75 Division 3; 1975-79 Division 2; 1979-80 Division 3; 1980-92 Division 2; 1992 – FA Premier League.

Honours: FA Premier League: Runners up 1993-94; Football League: Division 1 – Champions 1911-12, 1913-14; Division 2 – Champions 1938-39; Runners-up 1957-58; Division 3 – Champions 1974-75; Runners-up 1979-1980. FA Cup : Winners 1884, 1885, 1886, 1890, 1891, 1928; Runners-up 1882, 1960. Football League Cup: Semi-final 1961-62. Full Members' Cup: Winners 1986-87.

Managers (and Secretary-managers): Thomas Mitchell 1884-96, J. Walmsley 1896-1903, R.B. Middleton 1903-25, Jack Carr 1922-26 (TM under Middleton to 1925), Bob Crompton 1926-31 (Hon. TM), Arthur Barritt 1931-36 (had been Secretary from 1927), Reg Taylor 1936-38, Bob Crompton 1938-41, Eddie Hapgood 1944-47, Will Scott 1947, Jack Burton 1947-49, Jackie Bestall 1949-53, Johnny Carey 1953-58, Dally Duncan 1958-60, Jack Marshall 1960-67, Eddie Quigley 1967-70, Johnny Carey 1970-71, Ken Furphy 1971-73, Gordon Lee 1974-75, Jim Smith 1975-78, Jim Iley 1978, John Pickering 1978-79, Howard Kendall 1979-81, Bobby Saxton 1981-86, Don Mackay 1987-91, Kenny Dalglish October 1991-.

5-Year League Record

	Div.	P	W	D	L	F	A	Pts	Pos	FAC	FLC
89-90	2	46	19	17	10	74	59	74	5	3	2
90-91	2	46	14	10	22	51	66	52	19	3	3
91-92	2	46	21	11	14	70	53	74	6	4	1
92-93	PL	42	20	11	11	68	46	71	4	6	SF
93-94	PL	42	25	9	8	63	36	84	2	4	4

Summary of Appearances and Goals 1993-94

Player	A	G	B	Player	A	G	B
Andersson	1		1	Mimms	13		
Atkins	8(7)	1	1	Morrison	1(4)		2
Batty	26		3	Newell	27(1)	6	2
Berg	38(3)	1	1	Pearce	1(4)	1	
Flowers	29			Ripley	40	4	2
Gallacher	27(3)	7	2	Shearer	34(6)	31	2
Hendry	22(1)			Sherwood	38	2	
Moran	19	1		Warhurst	4(5)		1
Le Saux	40(1)	2	6	Wilcox	31(2)	6	1
Makel	(2)			Wright	7(5)		
Marker	16(7)		1				
May	40	1	1				

A=Appearances (as Sub)   G=Goals   B=Bookings (Sent Off)

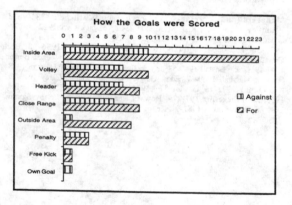

72

Shearer Returns as Rovers Reach Europe

Blackburn manager Kenny Dalglish resisted the temptation to spend more of Jack Walker's millions in the pre-season, despite facing the prospect beginning the campaign without injured Alan Shearer. The first four games brought nine points and, in the fifth, Shearer went on as a substitute and scored against Newcastle. It was the start of an incredible run for Shearer, now the best striker in the country bar none.

In September Dalglish did open the Walker wallet, to sign versatile Paul Warhurst from Sheffield Wednesday for £2.3 million. In October England midfielder David Batty moved from Leeds for £2.3 million, and a month later Dalglish splashed out £2.4 million for Southampton's Tim Flowers – now the most expensive goalkeeper in Britain. Dalglish did recoup £800,000 though, with the sale of mis-fit Swedish defender Patrik Andersson to Germany's Borussia Moenchengladbach.

In the League, Rovers were still picking up points regularly, and were unlucky to come away with only a point from Old Trafford after a last-minute equaliser by Paul Ince. The Coca-Cola Cup run ended in December with a 1-0 fourth-round defeat at Tottenham, but Rovers had moved into second place in the League and looked like the only club capable of challenging Manchester United.

A shock third-round exit from the FA Cup also looked likely as Portsmouth fought out a deserved 3-3 draw at Ewood Park. But, in the replay, Rovers made their superiority count to win 3-1. But they again fell in the fourth round, beaten by First Division Charlton in a replay. Attention now turned squarely towards the League and, when Shearer scored the opener in a 2-0 win at Tottenham, it was his 50th goal for the club.

Two goals from Shearer against Swindon in March closed the gap on United to just three points, and there seemed a real possibility that the champions could be caught – something thought unlikely back in December when United held a 16-point lead. But a disastrous 4-1 defeat at Wimbledon in their next game dented confidence and robbed Rovers of the chance to go clear at the top.

They responded, though, in dramatic fashion by beating Manchester United 2-0 at home at the start of April with two goals from the unstoppable Shearer. A 1-0 home win over Aston Villa nine days later put Rovers level on points, though United had a game in hand. Then, a 3-1 defeat at struggling Southampton meant the balance of power swung back to United. Rovers stuttered in the run-in, struggling to a 1-1 home draw with QPR and a 2-1 win at West Ham. But a 2-1 midweek defeat at Coventry ended all hopes – United had retained their title. Blackburn can look forward to a place in the UEFA Cup next term and reflect on a fine season which ended with an England call-up for converted left-back Graeme Le Saux and another England goal for that man Shearer – against Greece – his first for his country for 18 injury-wrecked months, and his 36th of a memorable season.

73

Chelsea

Founded in 1905. The Mears brothers developed Stamford Bridge Athletic Ground, which they owned, into a football stadium for use for prestigious matches and, prospectively, nearby Fulham FC. But Fulham did not take up the chance so the Mears brothers established their own club, rejecting possible names such as 'London' and 'Kensington' in favour, eventually, of Chelsea.

Judging that the club would not be accepted into the Southern League, it sought membership of the Football League. This was gained at the first attempt and it started the 1906-07 season in Division Two. Premier League founder members 1992.

Ground: Stamford Bridge, London SW6
Phone: 071-385 5545 **Nickname:** The Blues
Colours: Royal Blue, Royal Blue, White
Change: White/Red, Black, Black
Capacity: 41,050 **Pitch:** 110 yds x 72 yds
Directions: *From North & East:* A1 or M1 to central London and Hyde Park corner. Follow signs for Guildford (A3) and then Knightsbridge (A4). After a mile turn left into Fulham Rd. *From South:* A219 Putney Bridge then follow signs for West End joining A308 and then into Fulham Rd. *From West:* M4 then A4 to central London. Follow A3220 to Westminster, after ¾ miles right at crossroads into Fulham Rd.
Rail/Tube (District line): Fulham Broadway

President: G.M. Thomson **Chairman:** Ken W. Bates
Company Secretary/Director: Yvonne Todd
Manager: Glenn Hoddle **Assistant:** Peter Shreeves
First Team Coach: Don Howe **Physio:** Bob Ward

Record FAPL Win: 4-0 v Middlesbrough, 3/4/93
Record FAPL Defeat: 1-4 v Leeds United, 6/11/93
Record FL Win: 9-2 v Glossop N E, Division 2, 1/9/1906
Record FL Defeat: 1-8 v Wolverhampton W, Division 1, 26/9/1953
Record Cup Win: 13-0 v Jeunesse Hautcharage, ECWC, R1 L2, 29/9/1971
Record Fee Received: £2.2m from Tottenham H for Gordon Durie, 7/1991
Record Fee Paid: £1.6m to Wimbledon for Dennis Wise, 7/1990
　　　　　　　　　£1.6m to Stoke City for Mark Stein
Most FAPL Appearances: Frank Sinclair, 66, 1992-94
Most FL Appearances: Ron Harris, 655, 1962-80
Record Attendance (all-time): 82,905 v Arsenal, Div 1, 12/10/1935

Record Attendance (FAPL): 37,064 v Manchester United, 11/9/93
Highest Scorer in FAPL Season: Stein, 13, 1993-94
Most FAPL Goals in Season: 51, 1992-93
Most FAPL Points in Season: 56, 1992-93
Most Capped Player: Ray Wilkins, England: 24 out of 84

Season 1993-94
Biggest Home Win: 4-2 v Everton, 3/1/94
Biggest Home Defeat: 0-2 v Arsenal, 20/11/93
Biggest Away Win: 3-1 v Swindon Town, 2/10/93
Biggest Away Defeat: 1-4 v Leeds United, 6/11/93
Biggest Home Attendance: 37,064 v Manchester United, 11/9/93
Smallest Home Attendance: 8,923 v Coventry City, 4/5/94
Average Attendance: 19,211 (+1.0%)
Last Season: *PL:* 14th *FA Cup:* Runners-up *Coca-Cola Cup:* 3rd round
Leading Scorer: Mark Stein (13)

League History: 1905 Elected to Division 2; 1907-10 Division 1; 1910-12 Division 2; 1912-24 Division 1; 1924-30 Division 2; 1930-62 Division 1; 1962-63 Division 2; 1963-75 Division 1; 1975-77 Division 2; 1977-79 Division 1; 1979-84 Division 2; 1984-88 Division 1; 1988-89 Division 2; 1989-92 Division 1; 1992- FA Premier League.

Honours: Football League: Division 1 – Champions 1954-55; Division 2 – Champions 1983-84, 1988-89; runners-up 1906-7, 1911-12, 1929-30,1962-63, 1976-77. FA Cup: Winners 1970; Runners-up 1914-15, 1966-67, 1993-94. Football League Cup: Winners 1964-65; Runners-up 1971-72. Full Members' Cup: Winners 1985-86. Zenith Data Systems Cup: Winners 1989-90.

European Competitions: Cup-Winners' Cup: 1970-71 (winners), 1971-72. Fairs Cup: 1965-66, 1968-69.

Managers (and Secretary-managers): John Tait Robertson 1905-07, David Calderhead 1907-33, A. Leslie Knighton 1933-39, Billy Birrell 1939-52, Ted Drake 1952-61, Tommy Docherty 1962-67, Dave Sexton 1967-74, Ron Stuart 1974-75, Eddie McCreadie 1975-77, Ken Shellito 1977-78, Danny Blanchflower 1978-79, Geoff Hurst 1979-81, John Neal 1981-85 (Director to 1986), John Hollins 1985-88, Bobby Campbell 1988-91, Ian Porterfield June 1991-1993, Dave Webb 1993, Glenn Hoddle 1993-.

5-Year League Record

	Div.	P	W	D	L	F	A	Pts	Pos	FAC	FLC
89-90	1	38	16	12	10	58	50	60	5	4	2
90-91	1	38	13	10	15	58	69	49	11	3	SF
91-92	1	42	13	14	13	50	60	53	14	6	2
92-93	PL	42	14	14	14	51	54	56	11	3	4
93-94	PL	42	13	12	17	49	53	51	14	F	3

Summary of Appearances and Goals 1993-94

Player	A	G	B	Player	A	G	B
Barnard	9(3)	1		Johnsen	27(1)	1	4
Burley	20(3)	3	1	Kharin	40		1
Cascarino	16(4)	4		Kjeldberg	29	1	3
Clarke	39		2	Lee	3(4)	1	(1)
Donaghy	24(4)	1	1	Myers	7		
Dow	13(1)			Newton	33(3)		1
Duberry	1			Peacock	38	8	2
Fleck	7(2)	1	1	Shipperley	18(6)	4	
Hall	4(3)			Sinclair	34		6
Hitchcock	2			Spackman	5(4)		
Hoddle	16(3)	1		Stein	18	13	
Hopkin	12(9)	1	1	Wise	34	4	2(1)

A=Appearances (as Sub)   G=Goals   B=Bookings (Sent Off)

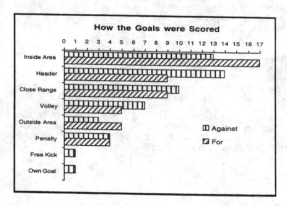

How the Goals were Scored

Inside Area, Header, Close Range, Volley, Outside Area, Penalty, Free Kick, Own Goal

⊞ Against   ▨ For

Hoddle's Kids on a Learning Curve

The season opened with an unfamiliar air of optimism around Stamford Bridge. Glenn Hoddle, the new manager, seemed set to introduce his own superb style of play and, after winning the Makita Trophy at White Hart Lane – beating Spurs 4-0 – all looked set for a promising season. Andy Townsend had been sold to Aston Villa, but Hoddle had strengthened his attacking line with a £1 million move for Newcastle's Gavin Peacock.

The optimism soon faded as Chelsea clocked up four 1-1 draws from their opening eight games. There was, however, a significant 1-0 home win over Manchester United thanks to a predatory strike from Peacock. Graham Stuart's transfer to Everton brought in £750,000 and Hoddle used the cash to sign tiny striker Mark Stein from Stoke for a whopping £1.6 million.

October ended with elimination from the Coca-Cola Cup, and a run of five consecutive defeats left Chelsea languishing in the bottom three. A 3-1 defeat at Southampton in late December left Chelsea just one place off the bottom, but after 12 games without a goal, Stein had finally scored. It was the start of a rich vein of scoring form which brought him eight from his next six games.

Stein's goals moved Chelsea away from danger and were instrumental in the club's FA Cup run, which began at rock-bottom Barnet. Sheffield Wednesday presented a sterner task in the fourth round, and the prospects looked grim after a 1-1 draw at the Bridge. But in the replay, Chelsea saved their season with two goals in extra time for a 3-1 win and a trip to Oxford.

A 2-1 win at the Manor Ground prompted greater effort in the League as the Blues beat Tottenham, Manchester United – Peacock again got the winner – Wimbledon and West Ham during March to ensure their Premiership status. The FA Cup quarter-final yielded a home tie against First Division Wolves, and a single goal from Peacock earned a victory without Stein, who was injured in the win at Old Trafford.

With League safety guaranteed, Chelsea now looked to the Cup for their first major trophy since the Cup-Winners' Cup in 1971. In the semi-final at Wembley, against Luton Town, Hoddle's side played it perfectly and were never in danger as two more goals from Peacock earned them a place in the final against Manchester United.

Though distinct underdogs, Chelsea were confident having been the only side to beat United twice in the League. They had the best of the first half in the final and almost took the lead when Peacock's shot thumped against the crossbar with Peter Schmeichel well beaten. But the match turned in 10 crazy second-half minutes. Two penalties – the first clear-cut, the second highly debatable – by Eric Cantona and a Mark Hughes goal after a slip by Frank Sinclair drained Chelsea's reserves and belief. A last-minute goal by Brian McClair made it 4-0 and a result wholly unfair to Chelsea, who were far better than the scoreline suggests.

But, as Hoddle was quick to point out, his young side had learned a great deal about winning and losing at Wembley; and could look forward to European football in 1994-95.

Coventry City

Founded as Singer's FC, cycle manufacturers, in 1883. Joined the
Birmingham and District League in 1894; in 1898 changed name to Coventry
City; and in 1905 moved to the Athletic Ground, Highfield Road. Elected to
Division One of the Southern League in 1908, but relegated to the Second in
1914.

Joined the Wartime Midland Section of the Football League in 1918 and
elected to an expanded Second Division of the Football League for 1919-20.
Founder members of the Fourth Division in 1958. Promoted to Division One
for the first time in 1967 and never relegated. Premier League founder
members 1992.

Ground: Highfield Road Stadium, King Richard Street, Coventry, CV2 4FW
Phone: (0203) 223535   **Nickname:** Sky Blues
Colours: All Sky Blue   **Change Colours:** Yellow, Blue, Yellow
Capacity: 24,021   **Pitch:** 110 yds x 75 yds
Directions: *From North & West:* M6 J3, after 3½ miles turn left into Eagle St
and straight on to Swan Lane. *From South & East:* M1 to M45 then A45 to
Ryton-on-Dunsmore where 3rd exit at roundabout is A423. After 1 mile turn
right into B4110. Left at T-junction then right into Swan Lane.
Rail: Coventry

Life President: Derrick H. Robbins   **Chairman:** P.D.H. Robins
Vice-chairman: B.A. Richardson   **Secretary:** Graham Hover
Manager: Phil Neal   **Assistant:**
Physio: George Dalton

Record FAPL Win: 5-1 v Liverpool, 19/12/92
Record FAPL Defeat: 0-5 v Manchester United, 28/12/92
Record FL Win: 9-0 v Bristol C, Division 3 (S), 28/4/1934
Record FL Defeat: 2-10 v Norwich C, Division 3 (S), 15/3/1930
Record Cup Win: 7-0 v Scunthorpe U, FA Cup R1, 24/11/1934
Record Fee Received: £1.25m from Nottingham F for Ian Wallace, 7/1980
Record Fee Paid: £900,000 to Dundee U for Kevin Gallacher, 1/1990
Most FAPL Appearances: Peter Atherton, 78 (+1), 1992-94
Most FL Appearances: George Curtis, 486, 1956-70
Record Attendance (all-time): 51,455 v Wolves, Division 2, 29/4/1967
Record Attendance (FAPL): 24,410 v Manchester United
Highest Scorer in FAPL Season: Mick Quinn, 17, 1992-93
Most FAPL Goals in Season: 62, 1992-93

Most FAPL Points in Season: 56, 1993-94
Most Capped Player: Dave Clements, N. Ireland: 21 out of 48 *and*
Ronnie Rees, Wales: 21 out of 39

Season 1993-94
Biggest Home Win: 4-0 v Manchester City, 19/2/94
Biggest Home Defeat: 0-2 Leeds United, 25/9/93
Biggest Away Win: 3-0 Arsenal, 14/8/93
Biggest Away Defeat: 0-4 Newcastle United, 23/2/94
Biggest Home Attendance: 17,020 v Manchester United, 27/11/94
Smallest Home Attendance: 9,984 v Southampton, 16/10/93
Average Attendance: 13,564 (-9.5%)
Last Season: *PL:* 11th *FA Cup:* 3rd round *Coca-Cola Cup:* 3rd round
Leading Scorer: Peter Ndlovu (11)

League History: 1919 Elected to Division 2; 1925-26 Division 3 (N); 1926-36 Division 3 (S); 1936-52 Division 2; 1952-58 Division 3 (S); 1958-59 Division 4; 1959-64 Division 3; 1964-67 Division 2; 1967-92 Division 1; 1992 – FA Premier League.

Honours: Football League: Division 1 best season: 6th, 1969-70; Division 2 Champions 1966-67: Division 3 Champions 1963-64; Division 3 (S) Champions 1935-36; Runners-up 1933-34; Division 4 Runners-up 1958-59. FA Cup: Winners 1986-87. Football League Cup: best season: Semi-final 1980-81, 1989-90

European Competitions: Fairs Cup: 1964-65

Managers (and Secretary-managers): H.R. Buckle 1909-10, Robert Wallace 1910-13, Frank Scott-Walford 1913-15, William Clayton 1917-19, H. Pollitt 1919-20, Albert Evans 1920-24, Jimmy Ker 1924-28, James McIntyre 1928-31, Harry Storer 1931-45, Dick Bayliss 1945-47, Billy Frith 1947-48, Harry Storer 1948-53, Jack Fairbrother 1953-54, Charlie Elliott 1954-55, Jesse Carver 1955-56, Harry Warren 1956-57, Billy Firth 1957-61, Jimmy Hill 1961-67, Noel Cantwell 1967-72, Bob Dennison 1972, Joe Mercer 1972-75, Gordon Milne 1972-81, Dave Sexton 1981-83, Bobby Gould 1983-84, Don Mackay 1985-86, George Curtis 1986-87 (became MD), John Sillett 1987-90, Terry Butcher 1990-92, Don Howe 1992, Bobby Gould July 1992-93, Phil Neal November 1993–.

5-Year League Record

	Div.	P	W	D	L	F	A	Pts	Pos	FAC	FLC
89-90	1	38	14	7	17	39	59	49	12	3	SF
90-91	1	38	11	11	16	42	49	44	16	4	5
91-92	1	42	11	11	20	35	44	44	19	3	4
92-93	PL	42	13	13	16	52	57	52	15	3	2
93-94	PL	42	14	14	14	43	45	56	11	3	3

Summary of Appearances and Goals 1993-94

Player	A	G	B	Player	A	G	B
Atherton	39(1)			McGrath	10(1)		
Babb	40	3	2	Morgan	39(1)	2	
Boland	24(3)		1	Ndlovu	40	11	2
Booty	2			Ogrizovic	33		
Borrows	29			Pickering	1(2)		
Busst	2(1)			Quinn	28(4)	8	1
Darby	25(1)	5	2	Rennie	34	1	
Flynn	33(3)	3	3	Robertson	(3)		
Gayle	3			Robson	1		
Gould	9			Sheridan	4(4)		
Harford	(1)	1		Wegerle	20(1)	6	1
Jenkinson	10(6)			Williams J	27(5)	3	1
Kruszynski	1(1)			Williams P	3(6)		
Marsden	5(2)		1				

A=Appearances (as Sub)   G=Goals   B=Bookings (Sent Off)

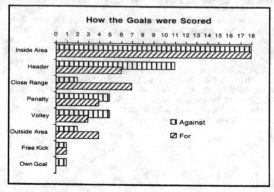

Straight Down the Middle

Coventry City's FA Premiership record could hardly have been more even. They finished 11th, exactly halfway, with 14 wins, 14 draws and 14 defeats – and scored two goals fewer than they conceded, 43 to 45. Such a solid, mid-table finish would not do for some, but for Coventry, relegation candidates with many in August, it was an acceptable return.

It all started in brilliant fashion with a storming 3-0 win at Arsenal on the opening day, terrace hero Micky Quinn scoring all three. Bobby Gould's team kept the momentum going through August and took the Premiership's longest unbeaten run from the start of the season going until their ninth game against Leeds in late September, when they lost 2-0.

In the Coca-Cola Cup Wycombe Wanderers proved stubborn opponents in the second round. The Third Division side recovered from a 3-0 beating in the first leg to take the tie to extra-time. But a 117th minute goal from full-back Phil Babb took the Sky Blues through.

October proved an unhappy month for the club though. After a 5-1 defeat at QPR Gould quit amid rumours that the club's board of directors were considering selling their prize asset, Zimbabwean Peter Ndlovu. A 2-0 defeat in the Coca-Cola Cup at Oldham three days later compounded the feeling of gloom around the club. In November, on the day England manager Graham Taylor quit, his coach, Phil Neal, was appointed as Coventry's new manager.

Neal's appointment helped steady the team as they beat Arsenal and Wimbledon and drew with Oldham in December. January brought two pieces of bad news, though, as top striker Roy Wegerle suffered a knee ligament injury in a 2-0 FA Cup defeat at Newcastle that kept him out for the rest of the season. With no money available for a replacement, the team were forced to carry on without him as best they could.

The results in the League were mixed from that point, although three consecutive 1-0 defeats to Liverpool, Aston Villa and Leeds in the spring threatened their postition. But eight points from 15 in April moved them back up to the security of mid-table, where they stayed.

Coventry did, however, have a say in the destination of the title. A 2-1 win over Blackburn at Highfield Road, with two goals by unsung Julian Darby, gave United their second consecutive title. Coventry went on to finish the season in good form, beating Cup-finalists Chelsea 2-1 and holding double-winners Manchester United to a 0-0 draw at Old Trafford in the last game of the season.

There was encouraging news, also, for Babb when he was capped by the Republic of Ireland in Holland. He did enough to book a place in Jack Charlton's squad for the finals and has attracted interest from big-spending Newcastle.

Crystal Palace

Founded in 1905 to play at the Crystal Palace Ground where, earlier, a Crystal Palace staff team had successfully played. Joined the Southern League for 1905/06 when they were Champions of Division Two. Soon moved to Herne Hill, then to The Nest, Selhurst. Founder members and first champions of the Football League Third Division 1920/21. Moved to Selhurst Park in 1924.

Founder members of the old Fourth Division in 1958, they reached the First Division for the first time as Second Division runners-up in 1969. Premier League founder members 1992. Relegated after one season, but promoted back at the first attempt.

Ground: Selhurst Park, South Norwood, London SE25 6PU
Phone: (081) 653 1000   **Club Nickname:** The Eagles
Colours: Red/Blue, Red, Red
Change: White/Red/Royal, White, Red/Royal
Capacity: 26,995   **Pitch:** 110 x 74 yd.
Directions: *From North:* M1 or A1 to A406 for Chiswick, then A205 to Wandsworth. A3 and then A214 for Streatham, And then A23 to B273 for Whitehorse Lane. *From South:* A23 and then B266. Turn right onto High Street and left into Whitehorse Lane. *From East:* A232 and then A215 to B266 for High Street, and then as above. *From West:* M4 To Chiswick, and then as for North.
Rail: Thornton Heath, Northwood Junction or Selhurst.

President: S. Stephenson
Chairman: Ron G. Noades
Club Secretary: Mike Hurst
Manager: Alan Smith
First Team Coach: Steve Harrison   **Physio:** David West

Record FAPL Win: 4-1 v. Middlesbrough 12/4/93
Record FAPL Defeat: 0-5 v. Liverpool 28/11/92
Record FL Win: 9-0 v. Barrow, Division 4, 10/10/1959
Record FL Defeat: 0-9 v. Burnley, FA Cup R2 replay, 10/2/1909,
                    0-9 v, Liverpool, Division 1, 12/9/90
Record Cup Win: 8-0 v. Southend U, Rumbelows League Cup, R2 L2 25/9/90
Record Fee Received: £2.5m from Arsenal for Ian Wright, 9/91
Record Fee Paid: £1.8m to Sunderland for Marco Gabbiadini, 9/91

Most FAPL Appearances: Nigel Martyn and Eddie McGoldrick, 42, 92-93
Most FL Appearances: Jim Cannon, 571, 1973-88
Record Attendance (all-time): 41,482 v. Burnley, Division 2, 11/5/1979
Record Attendance (FAPL): 36,380 Away v. Liverpool 28/11/92
Highest Scorer in FAPL season: Chris Armstrong,15, 1992-93
Most FAPL Goals in Season: 48, 1992-93
Most FAPL Points in Season: 49, 1992-93
Most Capped Player: Eric Young, Wales: 15 out of 16

Season 1993-94
Biggest Home Win: 5-1 v Portsmouth
Biggest Home Defeat: 0-2 v Watford
Biggest Away Win: 4-1 v West Bromwich Albion
Biggest Away Defeat: 0-3 v Millwall
Biggest Home Attendance: 28,749
Smallest Home Attendance: 10,925
Average Attendance: 15,314
Last Season: *Div 1:* 1st *FA Cup:* 3rd round *Coca-Cola Cup:* 4th Round
Leading Scorer: Chris Armstrong (23)

League History: 1920 Original Members of Division 3; 1921-25 Division 2; 1925-58 Division 3(S); 1958-61 Division 4; 1961-64 Division 3, 1964-69 Division 2; 1969-73 Division 1; 1973-74 Division 2; 1974-77 Division 3; 1977-79 Division 2; 1979-81 Division 1; 1981-89 Division 2; 1989-92 Division 1; 19992-93 FA Premier League; 1993-94 Division 1; 1994- FA Premier League

Honours: *Football League:* Division 1 best season: Champions 1993/94; Division 2 – Champions 1978-79; Runners-up 1968-69; Division 3 – Runners-up 1963-64; Division 3(s) – Champions 1920-21; Runners-up 1928-29, 1930-31, 198-39; Division 4 – Runners-up 1960-61. *FA Cup:* best season: Runners-up 1989-90. *Football League Cup:* best season: Semi-final 1992-93. *Zenith Data System Cup:* Winners: 1991

Managers (and Secretary-managers): John T. Robson 1905-07, Edmund Goodman 1907-25 (had been secretary since 1905 and afterwards continued in this position to 1933), Alec Maley 1925-27, Fred Maven 1927-30, Jack Tresadern 1930-35, Tom Bromilow 1935-36, R.S. Moyes 1936, tom Bromilow 1936-39, George Irwin 1939-47, Jack Butler 1947-49, ronnie Rooke 1949-50, Charlie Slade and Fred Dawes (joint managers) 1950-51, Laurie Scott 1951-54, Cyril Spiers 1954-58, George Smith 1958-60, Authur Rowe 1960-62, Dick Graham 1962-66, Bert Head 1966-72 (continued as GM until 1973), Malcolm Allison 1973-76, Terry Venables 1976-80, Ernie Walley 1980, Malcolm Allison 1980-81, Dario Gradi 1981, Steve Kember 1981-82, Alan Mullery 1982-84, Steve Coppell 1984-93, Alan Smith June 1993-.

5-Year League Record

	Div.	P	W	D	L	F	A	Pts	Pos	FAC	FLC
89/90	1	38	13	9	16	42	66	48	15	F	3
90/91	1	38	20	9	9	50	41	69	3	3	4
91/92	1	42	14	15	13	53	61	57	10	3	5
92/93	PL	42	11	16	15	48	61	49	20	3	SF
93/94	1	46	27	9	10	73	46	90	1	3	3

Summary of Appearances and Goals 1993-94

Player	A	G	B	Player	A	G	B
Armstrong	43	23	2	O'Connor	2		
Bowry	17(4)		(1)	Osborn	5(1)		
Coleman	46	3	5	Rodger	37(5)	3	2
Dyer	2(9)			Salako	34(4)	8	
Gordon	39(6)	5	2	Shaw	30(4)	2	2
Humphrey	32	1	1	Southgate	46	9	2
Martyn	46		1	Stewart	18	3	4
Massey	1			Thorn	10		2
Mathew	11(1)	1		Whyte	10(6)	3	
Mortimer				Williams	21(3)	7	1
Ndah	(1)			Young	46	5	5
Newman	10(1)		1				

A=Appearances (as Sub)   G=Goals   B=Bookings (Sent Off)

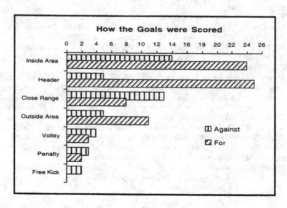

84

Consistency the Key for the Eagles

Crystal Palace, having been relegated the previous season, felt a change of management was required in their quest for an automatic return to the Premiership. Long-serving manager Steve Coppell was duly dismissed, with his assistant Alan Smith becoming number one at Selhurst Park.

Smith's first task was to try to persuade internationals Eddie McGoldrick and Geoff Thomas to stay at the club, but his efforts were in vain. Surprisingly, Smith did not sign immediate replacements, preferring instead to work with what he already had. After earning only one point from their opening two games Palace then won maximum points from their next three, which included a 5-1 win over much-fancied Portsmouth. Chris Armstrong emerged as the team's brigh star on with eight goals in the opening 10 games.

Although a 4-1 defeat to Everton ended their Coca-Cola Cup hopes for the season, Palace were soon setting the pace at the top of the First Division. Gareth Southgate was pulling the strings in midfield, while England winger John Salako was enjoying his first full season after overcoming a horrendous knee injury.

December brought the Eagles four wins from five games but they then suffered an unhappy New Year. Having lost at local-rivals Millwall, they then crashed out of the FA Cup at Wolves, and suffered another defeat on the same ground in the League a week later. This prompted Smith to move into the transfer marke. Paul Stewart was the new man as he moved down to London from Liverpool on loan, with a view to a permanent transfer. The former England player switched from midfield to his old forward role to partner Armstrong in the attack, as Smith sought new ideas.

Palace immediately went on a nine-game unbeaten run, which confirmed them as favourites to win promotion. Smith again moved into the transfer market to sign Chelsea midfielder Damien Matthew, and to extend Stewart's loan period.

During March the Eagles managed to keep four clean sheets from six games even without defender Andy Thorn, who had been ruled out since early November through injury. But in Chris Coleman and Eric Young they had a solid foundation to build around, a fact recognised by Wales manager Terry Yorath who called both of them up for international duty.

Just before transfer-deadline day Smith splashed out £1 million on Watford's exciting winger Bruce Dyer, But Palace made sure of promotion without him, with successive 2-1 wins against Oxford and Southend leaving them one win short of automatic promotion. Chris Coleman turned out to be the unlikely hero as he scored the only goal in a 1-0 win away to David Pleat's Luton Town which took Palace back up at the first attempt. The First Division title was clinched with a Young goal in a 1-0 win against Barnsley.

The key to Palace's success lay in consistency. Goalkeeper Nigel Martyn was an ever-present, John Humphrey, Dean Gordon, Coleman and Young played every game from February on, and influential midfielder Gareth Southgate also maintained a 100 per cent record.

Everton

The cricket team of St. Domingo's Church turned to football around 1878. Playing in Stanley Park, in late 1879 changed name to Everton FC, the name of the district to the west of the park.

Moved to a field at Priory Road in 1882 and then, in 1884, moved to a site in Anfield Road. As one of the country's leading teams, became founder members of the Football League in 1888. Moved to Goodison Park, a field on the north side of Stanley Park, in 1892 following a dispute with the ground's landlord. Premier League founder members 1992.

Ground: Goodison Park, Liverpool, L4 4EL
Phone: 051-521 2020   **Club Nickname:** The Toffees
Colours: Royal Blue, White, Blue
Change: Salmon/Dark Blue, Salmon, Salmon
Capacity: 40,160   **Pitch:** 112 yds x 78 yds
Directions: *From North:* M6 J8 take A58 to A580 and follow into Walton Hall Ave. *From South & East:* M6 J21A to M62, turn right into Queen's Drive then, after 4 miles, left into Walton Hall Ave. *From West:* M53 through Wallasey Tunnel, follow signs for Preston on A580. Walton Hall Ave is signposted.
Rail: Liverpool Lime Street

Chairman: Dr. D.M. Marsh
Chief Executive & Secretary: Jim Greenwood
Manager: Mike Walker
First Team Coach: Jimmy Gabriel   **Physio:** Les Helm

Record FAPL Win: 6-2 v Swindon Town, 15/1/94
Record FAPL Defeat: 1-5 v Norwich City 25/9/93 and
　　　　　　　　　　　　　　　1-5 v Sheffield Wednesday 2/4/94
Record FL Win: 9-1 v Manchester City, Division 1, 3/9/1906 *and*
　　　　　　　　　　　9-1 v Plymouth Argyle, Division 2, 27/12/1930
Record FL Defeat: 4-10 v Tottenham H, Division 1, 11/10/1958
Record Cup Win: 11-2 v Derby County, FA Cup R1, 18/1/1890
Record Fee Received: £2.75m from Barcelona for Gary Lineker, 7/1986
Record Fee Paid: £2m to West Ham United for Tony Cottee, 7/1988
Most FAPL Appearances: Neville Southall, 82,1992-94
Most FL Appearances: Ted Sagar, 465, 1929-53
Record Attendance (all-time): 78,299 v Liverpool, Division 1, 18/9/1948
Record Attendance (FAPL): 38,157 v Liverpool, 18/9/93

Highest Scorer in FAPL season: Tony Cottee, 16, 1993-94
Most FAPL Goals in Season: 53, 1992-93
Most FAPL Points in Season: 53, 1992-93
Most Capped Player: Neville Southall, Wales: 61

Season 1993-94
Biggest Home Win: 6-2 v Swindon Town, 15/1/94
Biggest Home Defeat: 1-5 v Norwich City, 25/9/93
Biggest Away Win: 2-0 v Ipswich Town, 12/2/94
                v Southampton, 27/12/93
Biggest Away Defeat: 1-5 v Sheffield Wednesday, 2/4/94
Biggest Home Attendance: 38,157 v Liverpool, 18/9/93
Smallest Home Attendance: 13,660 v Southampton, 4/12/93
Average Attendance: 22,900 (+11.9%)
Last Season: *PL:* 17th *FA Cup:* 3rd round *Coca-Cola Cup:* 4th round
Leading Scorer: Tony Cottee (16)

League History: 1888 Founder Member of the Football League; 1930-31 Division 2; 1931-51 Division 1; 1951-54 Division 2; 1954-92 Division 1; 1992-FA Premier League.

Honours: Football League: Division 1 – Champions 1890-91, 1914-15, 1927-28, 1931-32, 1938-39, 1962-63, 1969-70, 1984-85, 1986-87; Runners-up 1889-90, 1894-95, 1901-02, 1904-05, 1908-09, 1911-12, 1985-86; Division 2 Champions 1930-31; Runners-up 1953-54. FA Cup: Winners 1906, 1933, 1966, 1984; Runners-up 1893, 1897, 1907, 1968, 1985, 1986, 1989. Football League Cup: Runners-up 1976-77, 1983-84. League Super Cup: Runners-up 1986. Simod Cup: Runners-up 1989. Zenith Data Systems Cup: Runners-up 1991.

European Competitions: Champions' Cup: 1963-64, 1970-71. Cup-Winners' Cup: 1966-67, 1984-85 Winners). Fairs Cup: 1962-63, 1964-65, 1965-66. UEFA Cup: 1975-76, 1978-79, 1979-80.

Managers (and Secretary-managers): W.E. Barclay 1888-89, Dick Molyneux 1889-1901, William C. Cuff 1901-18, W.J. Sawyer 1918-19, Thomas H. McIntosh 1919-35, Theo Kelly 1936-48, Cliff Britton 1948-56, Ian Buchan 1956-58, Johnny Carey 1958-61, Harry Catterick 1961-73, Billy Bingham 1973-77, Gordon Lee 1977-81, Howard Kendall 1981-87, Colin Harvey 1987-90, Howard Kendall November 1990 -93, Mike Walker 1993-.

5-Year League Record

	Div.	P	W	D	L	F	A	Pts	Pos	FAC	FLC
89-90	1	38	17	8	13	57	46	59	6	5	4
90-91	1	38	13	12	13	50	46	51	9	6	3
91-92	1	42	13	14	15	52	51	53	12	4	4
92-93	PL	42	15	8	19	53	55	53	13	3	4
93-94	PL	42	12	8	22	42	63	44	17	3	4

Summary of Appearances and Goals 1993-94

Player	A	G	B	Player	A	G	B
Ablett	32	1	3	Radosavijevic	9(14)	1	
Angell	13(3)	1		Rideout	21(3)	6	
Barlow	6(16)	3		Rowett	(2)		
Beagrie	29	4	1	Snodin	28(1)		4
Cottee	36(3)	16	1	Southall	42		
Ebbrell	39	4	7	Stuart	26(4)	3	
Hinchcliffe	25(1)		1	Unsworth	7(1)		1
Holmes	15		1	Ward	26(1)	1	5
Horne	28(4)	1	3	Warzycha	3(4)		
Jackson	37(1)		4	Watson	27(1)	1	1
Limpar	9						
Moore	4						

A=Appearances (as Sub)   G=Goals   B=Bookings (Sent Off)

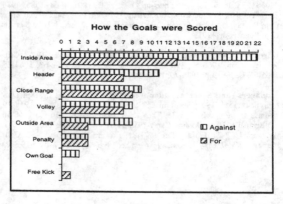

88

Narrow Escape for Walker

The season started brightly for Howard Kendall's Everton, but by the end of it, Mike Walker's Everton were nine only minutes away from relegation. It all started in fine fashion when a 2-0 away win at Southampton, and wins over Manchester City and Sheffield United, lifted Everton to the top of the table.

But three consecutive defeats set the tone for a season in which Everton slid steadily toward the bottom of the table. Scoring goals was a constant problem, and the sale of Peter Beardsley to Newcastle hardly helped.

Three back-to-back wins at the start of September – including a 2-0 win in the Merseyside derby – helped arrest the decline, but the end of the month brought a 5-1 thrashing by Norwich City... at Goodison Park!

Coca-Cola progress was made via Lincoln and Crystal Palace, but eight League matches in October and November brought just one win and a poor return of five points from a possible 24, while a 2-0 home defeat by Manchester United ended hopes in the Coca-Cola Cup.

December proved to be even worse. A 1-0 win over Southampton was followed by four defeats, with only a 0-0 draw at Sheffield United breaking the monotony. Manager Kendall, unable to bring the style or the trophies back to Goodison Park, decided enough was enough, and quit. Coach Jimmy Gabriel took over as caretaker manager but could do little to revitalise a dejected squad.

The new full-time manager, Mike Walker, arrived from Norwich in January in the middle of contract negotiations, and Everton were later penalised by the League for "poaching". Walker's first game produced a worrying 1-1 home draw with Bolton in the FA Cup, but his first League game in charge seemed to herald a new era as Swindon were crushed 6-2 at Goodison. The new mood of optimism was short-lived, though, as Everton crashed out of the FA Cup at Bolton four days later.

The position in the boardroom, with rivals Bill Kenwright and Peter Johnson bidding to take control of the club, meant that little money was available for new players, although striker Brett Angell was signed from Southend United at the end of January.

Everton had taken just one point from 21 before Walker's arrival, but early spring provided some breathing space as two wins and two draws moved them up to 15th, just out of the relegation dog-fight.

A 2-1 defeat at Anfield in mid-March signalled another decline, even though Anders Limpar had arrived from Arsenal but the Swedish international could not solve the problem. The next nine games brought just five points, leaving the club third from bottom with one game left.

In the final game Everton went two down at home to Wimbledon, before recovering to win 3-2 with an 81st-minute winner by Graham Stuart, who had joined the club in August from Chelsea. His goal maintained Everton's 40-year run in the top division of English football and, with Johnson successfully gaining control of the club, Walker should be able to strengthen his hand for the 1994-95 season.

Ipswich Town

Originally founded in the 1880s, a strictly amateur set up and founder member of the AFA's Southern Amateur League in 1907. Four times League champions and seven times County Cup winners. In 1936 under the leadership of the Cobbold family a professional Ipswich Town was formed.

The new club used Portman Road, only recently occupied by the amateur side and the site of several sporting activities. After two Southern League campaigns and one championship, elected to Football League Division Three (South) in 1938. Football League Champions in 1963, the club's debut season in the top section. Premier League founder member 1992.

Ground: Portman Road, Ipswich, Suffolk, IP1 2DA
Phone: (0473) 219211   **Nickname:** Blues or Town
Colours: Blue/White, White, Blue   **Change:** Red/Black, Black, Red/Black
Capacity: 22,823   **Pitch:** 112 yds x 70 yds
Directions: Follow A45 and signs for Ipswich West. Through Post House traffic lights and turn right at second roundabout into West End Rd. Ground on left.
Rail: Ipswich

President: P.M. Cobbold   **Vice-Presidents:** J.M. Sangster
Chairman: J. Kerr MBE   **Secretary:** David C. Rose
Manager: John Lyall   **Assistant:** Charlie Woods
Team Manager: Mick McGiven   **Physio:** D. Bingham

Record FAPL Win: 4-2 v Leeds United, 1992-93
Record FAPL Defeat: 0-5 v Sheffield Wednesday 23/4/94
Record FL Win: 7-0 v Portsmouth, Division 2, 7/11/64 *and*
           7-0 v West Bromwich Albion, Division 1, 11/64
Record FL Defeat: 1-10 v Fulham, Division 1, 26/12/63
Record Cup Win: 10-0 v Floriana, European Cup, PrRd 25/9/62
Record Fee Received: £1.75m to Tottenham H for Jason Dozzell
Record Fee Paid: £650,000 Geraint Williams to Derby County, 7/92
Most FAPL Appearances: Mick Stockwell, 80 (+1), 1992-94
Most FL Appearances: Mick Mills, 591, 1966-82
Record Attendance (all-time): 38,010 v Leeds Utd, FA Cup R6, 8/3/75
Record Attendance (FAPL): 22,559 v Manchester United, 1/5/94

Highest Scorer in FAPL Season: Chris Kiwomya, 10, 1992-93 *and*
Ian Marshall, 10, 1993-94
Most FAPL Goals in Season: 50, 1992-93
Most FAPL Points in Season: 52, 1992-93
Most Capped Player: Allan Hunter, N Ireland: 47 out of 53

Season 1993-94
Biggest Home Win: 3-2 v Sheffield United, 22/2/94
Biggest Home Defeat: 1-5 Arsenal, 5/2/94
Biggest Away Win: 3-0 v Oldham Athletic, 14/8/93
Biggest Away Defeat: 0-5 v Sheffield Wednesday, 23/4/94
Biggest Home Attendance: 22,559 v Manchester United, 1/5/94
Smallest Home Attendance: 10,747 v Sheffield United, 22/2/94
Average Attendance:
Last Season: *PL:* 19th. *FA Cup:* 5th round. *Coca-Cola Cup:* 3rd round
Leading Scorer: Ian Marshall (10)

League History: 1938 Elected to Division 3 (S); 1954-55 Division 2; 1955-57 Division 3 (S); 1957-61 Division 2; 1961-64 Division 1; 1964-68 Division 2; 1968-86 Division 1; 1986-92 Division 2; 1992- FA Premier League.

Honours: Football League: Division 1 – Champions 1961-62; Runners-up 1980-81, 1981-82; Division 2 – Champions 1960-61, 1967-68, 1991-92; Division 3 (S) – Champions 1953-54, 1956-57. FA Cup: Winners 1977-78. Football League Cup: best season: Semi-final 1981-82, 1984-85. Texaco Cup: 1972-73.

European Competitions: Champions' Cup: 1962-63. Cup-Winners' Cup: 1978-79. UEFA Cup: 1973-74, 1974-75, 1975-76, 1977-78, 1979-80, 1980-81 (winners), 1981-82, 1982-83.

Managers (and Secretary-managers): Mick O'Brien 1936-37, Scott Duncan 1937-55 (continued as secretary), Alf Ramsey 1955-63, Jackie Milburn 1963-64, Bill McGarry 1964-68, Bobby Robson 1969-82, Bobby Ferguson 1982-87, Johnny Duncan 1987-90, John Lyall, May 1990-July 1992, Mick McGiven July 1992-93, John Lyall 1993-.

5-Year League Record

	Div.	P	W	D	L	F	A	Pts	Pos	FAC	FLC
89-90	2	46	19	12	15	67	66	69	9	4	2
90-91	2	46	13	18	15	60	68	57	14	3	3
91-92	2	46	24	12	10	70	50	84	1	5	2
92-93	PL	42	12	16	14	50	55	52	16	6	5
93-94	PL	42	9	16	17	35	58	43	19	5	3

FA Premier League Appearances and Goals 1993-94

Player	A	G	B	Player	A	G	B
Baker	15			Palmer	31(5)	1	2
Durrant	3(3)			Slater	28	1	
Forrest	27			Stockwell	42	1	
Goddard	3(1)			Thompson	32		1
Guentchev	9(14)	2	1	Wark	38	3	3
Johnson	16	1		Whelan	28(1)		4
Kiwomya	34(3)	5	3	Whitton	8(4)	1	1
Linighan	38	3	2	Williams	34		1
Marshall	28(1)	10		Yallop	2(5)		
Mason	18(4)	3		Youds	18(5)	1	4
Milton	10(4)	1	2				

A=Appearances (as Sub)   G=Goals   B=Bookings (Sent Off)

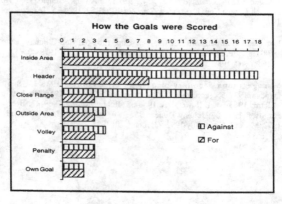

Lack of Punch Proves McGiven's Undoing

Ipswich narrowly avoided relegation in 1992-93 – their first season back in the top flight – and 1993-94 was to end with an even closer brush with the dreaded drop.

Manager Mick McGiven added midfielder Paul Mason, £400,000 from Aberdeen, and versatile Ian Marshall, £750,000 from Oldham, to his squad for the new season, but the loss of midfielder Jason Dozzell to Tottenham was a big blow.

Marshall proved his worth as a striker with three goals in the opening three matches, which left Ipswich joint-top of the first published table. Injury then forced Marshall out of the next four games, and his loss coincided with a loss of form as, without him and with Chris Kiwomya struggling, the team found goals hard to come by.

A 4-0 thumping at Highbury at the start of September highlighted two big problems – a lack of punch in attack, and a lack of pace at the back, where 37-year-old John Wark controlled things. In an attempt to remedy half the problem, winger Stuart Slater was signed from Celtic for £750,000 in October, but his unhappy time in Scotland had clearly affected his form and he failed to find top gear all season.

McGiven's answer to the second problem was less enterprising. A blanket defence system was introduced with Kiwomya or Marshall left as the lone attacker, with five at the back and four in midfield. The system worked well enough for a home win against Blackburn and draws at Manchester United and Leeds in the autumn, but was highly unpopular with the fans and the media, who soon dubbed Ipswich the most boring team in the Premiership.

A 2-1 win over Norwich in December promised better things in the New Year, and when Swindon and Spurs were beaten in the FA Cup, the promise seemed to have a ring of truth to it. But January and most of February passed without another League success, and when Wolves won an FA Cup fifth round replay at Portman Road, another collapse seemed highly possible.

Without money to spend, McGiven was forced to continue with his cautious approach, but such a style can, at best, bring only draws and, at worst, defeats. That was certainly Ipswich's story in the run-in, as their last 11 games produced just four points from four draws. And yet, ironically, Ipswich's defensive nature proved their salvation in their last game – away to Blackburn. A dogged 0-0 draw gave them the point they needed to ensure their survival, at Sheffield United's expense. A record of just nine wins from 42 games and only 35 goals, the lowest in the country, added to the defensive approach, rankled with Ipswich's supporters who have become accustomed to a stylish, attacking brand of football. The protests which went on throughout the final third of the campaign forced the board to act. In late May McGiven was moved sideways into a new job as football development officer, with John Lyall resuming control of the first team with Paul Goddard and Wark as his first-team coaches. It remains to be seen whether the switch will save Ipswich this term.

Leeds United

Leeds City, founded in 1904, took over the Elland Road ground of the defunct Holbeck Club and in 1905 gained a Football League Division Two place. The club was, however, expelled in 1919 for disciplinary reasons associated with payments to players during the War. The club closed down.

Leeds United FC, a new professional club, emerged the same year and competed in the Midland League. The club was elected to Football League Division Two for season 1920-21, both clubs up for re-election failing. The club has subsequently never been out of the top two divisions. Premier League founder member 1992.

Ground: Elland Road, Leeds, LS11 0ES
Phone: (0532) 716037   **Nickname:** United
Colours: All White   **Change Colours:** All Yellow
Capacity: 39,704   **Pitch:** 117 yds x 76 yds
Directions: *From North & East:* A58, A61, A63 or A64 into city centre and then onto M621. Leave Motorway after 1½ miles onto A643 and Elland Rd. *From West:* take M62 to M621 then as above. *From South:* M1 then M621 then as above
Rail: Leeds City

President: The Right Hon. The Earl of Harewood LLD
Chairman: L. Silver OBE   **Vice-Chairman:** P.J. Gilman
Secretary: Nigel Pleasants
Manager: Howard Wilkinson   **Assistant:** Mike Hennigan
First Team Coaches: Peter Gunby, Paul Hart
Physios: Alan Sutton, Geoff Ladley

Record FAPL Win: 5-0 v Tottenham Hotspur, 25/8/92 *and* v Swindon Town, 7/5/94
Record FAPL Defeat: 0-4 v Manchester City, 7/11/92 *and* 0-4 v Tottenham Hotspur, 20/2/93 *and* 0-4 v Norwich City, 21/8/93
Record FL Win: 8-0 v Leicester City, Division 1, 7/4/1934
Record FL Defeat: 1-8 v Stoke City, Division 1, 27/8/1934
Record Cup Win: 10-0 v Lyn (Oslo), European Cup, R1 1st leg, 17/9/1969
Record Fee Received: £2.75 from Blacburn R. for David Batty, 10/1993
Record Fee Paid: £2.9m to Sheffield Wednesday for Brain Deane, 7/93
Most FAPL Appearances: Gary Speed, 74(+1), 1992-94
Most FL Appearances: Jack Charlton, 629, 1953-73

Record Attendance (all-time): 57,892 v Sunderland, FA Cup 5R replay, 15/3/1967
Record Attendance (FAPL): 41,125 v Manchester United, 27/4/94
Highest Scorer in FAPL Season: Rod Wallace, 17, 1993-94
Most FAPL Goals in Season: 65, 1993-94
Most FAPL Points in Season: 70, 1993-94
Most Capped Player: Billy Bremner, Scotland: 54

Season 1993-94
Biggest Home Win: 4-0 v Wimbledon, 2/10/93
Biggest Home Defeat: 0-4 v Norwich City, 21/8/93
Biggest Away Win: 5-0 v Swindon Town, 7/5/94
Biggest Away Defeat: 0-2 v Liverpool, 28/8/93
Biggest Home Attendance: 41,125 v Manchester United, 27/4/94
Smallest Home Attendance: 28,717 v Oldham Athletic, 30/8/93
Average Attendance: 36,368 (+26.1%)
Last Season: *PL:* 5th *FA Cup:* 4th round *Coca-Cola Cup:* 2nd round
Leading Scorer: Ray Wallace (17)

League History: 1920 Elected to Division 2; 1924-27 Division 1; 1927-28 Division 2; 1928-31 Division 1; 1931-32 Division 2; 1932-47 Division 1; 1947-56 Division 2; 1956-60 Division 1; 1960-64 Division 2; 1964-82 Division 1; 1982-90 Division 2; 1990-92 Division 1; 1992- FA Premier League.

Honours: Football League: Division 1 – Champions 1968-69, 1973-74, 1991-92; Runners-up 1964-65, 1965-66, 1969-70, 1970-71, 1971-72; Division 2 – Champions 1923-24, 1963-64, 1989-90; Runners-up 1927-28, 1931-32, 1955-56. FA Cup: Winners 1972; Runners-up 1965, 1970, 1973. Football League Cup: Winners 1967-68.

European Competitions: Champions' Cup: 1969-70, 1974-75 (runners-up), 1992-93. Cup-Winners' Cup: 1972-73 (runners-up). Fairs Cup: 1965-66, 1966-67 (runners-up), 1967-68 (winners), 1968-69, 1970-71 (winners). UEFA Cup: 1971-72, 1973-74, 1979-80.

Managers (and Secretary-managers): Dick Ray 1919-20, Arthur Fairclough 1920-27, Dick Ray 1927-35, Bill Hampson 1935-47, Willis Edwards 1947-48, Major Frank Buckley 1948-53, Raich Carter 1953-58, Bill Lambton 1958-59, Jack Taylor 1959-61, Don Revie 1961-74, Brian Clough 1974, Jimmy Armfield 1974-78, Jock Stein 1978, Jimmy Adamson 1978-80, Allan Clarke 1980-82, Eddie Gray 1982-85, Billy Bremner 1985-88, Howard Wilkinson October 1988 -.

5-Year League Record

	Div.	P	W	D	L	F	A	Pts	Pos	FAC	FLC
89-90	2	46	24	13	9	79	52	85	1	3	2
90-91	1	38	19	7	12	65	47	64	4	4	SF
91-92	1	42	21	16	4	74	37	82	1	3	5
92-93	PL	42	12	15	15	57	62	51	17	4	3
93-94	PL	42	18	16	8	65	39	70	5	4	2

Summary of Appearances and Goals 1993-94

Player	A	G	B	Player	A	G	B
Batty	8(1)		1	Pemberton	7(3)		4
Beeney	22			Rocastle	6(1)	1	
Deane	41	11	2	Sharp	7(3)		1
Dorigo	37		2	Speed	35(1)	10	3
Fairclough	40	4	4	Strachan	32(1)	3	
Ford	(1)			Strandli	(4)		
Forrester	2(1)			Tinkler	(2)		
Hodge	7(1)	1	1	Wallace, Ray	(1)		
Kelly	42		2	Wallace, Rod	34(3)	17	3
Lukic	20			Wetherall	30(1)	1	1
McAllister	42	9	3	Whelan	6(10)		1
Newsome	25(4)	1	6	White	9(6)	5	
O'Leary	10		1				

A=Appearances (as Sub)   G=Goals   B=Bookings (Sent Off)

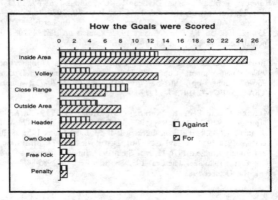

How the Goals were Scored

Better, but Still Room for Improvement

The new season at Leeds started with the opening of the refurbished, all-seater Elland Road, and a new centre-forward – Brian Deane, signed from Sheffield United for a club record £2.7 million. After the disasters of 1992-93, Leeds were clearly anxious to re-establish themselves among the leaders.

Deane scored on his debut in a 1-1 draw against Manchester City, but struggled to find the net regularly and ended the campaign with a disappointing total of 10. The problems in defence were overcome, though, thanks largely to the partnership of Chris Fairclough and David Weatherall in the middle, with emerging Republic of Ireland right-back Gary Kelly's form a real bonus.

The first game of September produced a 2-0 win at Southampton – United's first win on the road in a staggering 17 months! With that bogey broken, and with the defence far more solid, Howard Wilkinson's team started to look more like the champions they were in 1992.

There was, however, an early exit from the Coca-Cola Cup at the hands of Sunderland, and further upset when England midfielder David Batty was sold to Blackburn for £2.5 million, the money apparently needed to pay for the ground improvements. But a glorious run of 29 points from their 13 games up to the beginning of December took Leeds into second place in the table behind Manchester United.

A scoring slump in December prompted Wilkinson to sign striker David White from Manchester City, with unsettled midfielder David Rocastle moving in the opposite direction. But White, like Deane, also struggled for form and had to wait until April for his first goal.

A 0-0 draw at Old Trafford on New Year's Day was earned more by defence than attack, but served to boost the team's new-found confidence. But in January and February, it all fell apart. Defeats by Blackburn and Aston Villa in the League came just before a 3-2 defeat at home to Oxford United in an FA Cup fourth round replay. With Manchester United showing no signs of slipping, another trophy-less year was assured for the Elland Road faithful.

With White and Deane struggling, the responsibility fell on the midfield. Gary McAllister and Gary Speed responded in brilliant fashion with 20 goals between them, and Rod Wallace also came more into his own as the season went on, finishing with 16 to his credit.

In the spring Leeds re-gained their forward momentum and consolidated their position in the table with notable wins over Villa, QPR and Tottenham. But they also drew as many matches as they won and a 2-0 defeat at home to Manchester United in late April served to highlight the gap between the two sides.

If Leeds can convert even half their total of 16 draws into wins next season, and if White and Deane can find their old form, Leeds could well be challenging for honours again next year.

Leicester City

Founded in 1884 as Leicester Fosse by former pupils of the Wyggeston School from the western part of the city near the old Roman Fosse. Moved to their present ground in 1891 and, from the Midland League joined Division Two of the Football League in 1894. Promoted for the first time in 1908, they have been relegated seven times from the top flight.

FA Cup runners-up four times, they gained European Cup-Winners' Cup experience in 1961/62. Members of the new Division One in its first season, 1992/93, and promoted to the Premier League following play-off success in 1994.

Ground: City Stadium, Filbert Street, Leicester LE2 7FL
Phone: (0533) 555000   **Club Nickname:** Fiberts or Foxes
Colours: All Blue   **Change:** All White
Capacity: 24,000   **Pitch:** 112x75 yd.
Directions: *From North:* Leave M1 at junction 22, or take A46, A607 to town centre. Towards Rugby via Almond Road, Alyestone Road, and then left into Walnut Street and Filbert Street for the ground. *From South:* M1 or M69 and then A46 to Upperton Road and Filbert Street. *From East:* A47 into town centre, then right along Oxford Street to Alyestone Road and as North. *From West:* M69 and A50 to Alyestone Road, and then as North.
Rail: Leicester

President: K.R. Brigstock
Chairman: Martin George
General Secretary: Alan Bennett
Manager: Brian Little
First Team Coach: Allan Evans   **Physio:** Alan Smith

Record FAPL Win: –
Record FAPL Defeat: –
Record FL Win: 10-0 v Portsmouth, Division 1, 20/10/1928
Record FL Defeat: 0-12 v Nottingham Forest, Division 1, 21/4/1909
Record Cup Win: 8-1 v. Coventry City (away), League Cup R5, 1/12/64
Record Fee Received: £1.35m from Derby County for Paul Kitson, 3/92
Record Fee Paid: £500,000 to Everton for Wayne Clarke, 7/89
Most FAPL Appearances: –
Most FL Appearances: 528: Adam Black 1920-35
Record Attendance (all-time): 47,298 v. Tottenham H, FA Cup R5, 18/2/1928

Record Attendance (FAPL): –
Highest Scorer in FAPL season: –
Most FAPL Goals in Season: –
Most FAPL Points in Season: –
Most Capped Player: John O'Neill, N Ireland: 39

Season 1993-94
Biggest Home Win: v Millwall 4-0
Biggest Home Defeat: v Portsmouth 0-3
Biggest Away Win: v Birmingham 3-0
Biggest Away Defeat: v Nottingham Forest 0-4
Biggest Home Attendance: 21,744
Smallest Home Attendance: 10,366
Average Attendance: 16,007
Last Season: Division 1 – 4th
Leading Scorer: Iwan Roberts (13)

League History: 1894 Elected to Division 2; 1908-09 Division 1; 1009-25 Division 2; 1925-35 Division 1; 1935-37 Division 2; 1937-39 Division 1; 1946-54 Division 2; 19954-55 Division 1; 1955-57 Divsion 2; 1957-69 Division 1; 1969-71 Division 2; 1971-78 Division 1; 1978-80 Division 2; 1980-81 Division 1; 1981-83 Division 2; 1983-87 Division 1; 1987-92 Division 2; 1992-94 Division 1; 1994- FA Premier League.

Honours: *Football League:* Division 1 – Runners-up 1928-29; Division 2 – Champions 1924-25, 1936-37, 1953-54, 1956-57, 1970-71, 1979-80; Runners-up 1907-08. *FA Cup:* Runners-up 1949, 1961, 1963, 1969. *Football League Cup:* Winners 1964; Runners-up 1965.

European Competitions: Cup-Winners' Cup 1961-62

Managers (and Secretary-managers): William Clarke 1896-97, George Johnson 1898-1907*, James Blessington 1907-09, Andy Aitkin 1909-11, J.W. Bartlett 1912-14, Peter Hodge 1919-26, William Orr 1926-32, Peter Hodge 1932-34, Andy Lochead 1934-36, Frank Womack 1936-39, Tom Bromilow 1939-45, Tom Mather 1945-46, Johnnny Duncan 1946-49, Norman Bullock 1949-55, David Halliday 1955-58, Matt Gillies 1959-68, Frank O'Farrell 1968-71, Jimmy Bloomfield 1971-77, Frank McLintock 1977-78, Jock Wallace 1978-82 Gordon Milne 1982-86, Bryan Hamilton 1986-87, David Pleat 1987-91, Brian Little May 1991-.

5-Year League Record

	Div.	P	W	D	L	F	A	Pts	Pos	FAC	FLC
89/90	2	42	15	14	17	67	79	59	13	3	2
90/1	2	46	14	8	24	60	83	50	22	3	2
91/2	2	46	23	8	15	62	55	77	4	4	2
92/3	1	46	22	10	14	71	64	76	6	3	3
93/4	1	46	19	16	11	72	59	73	4	3	3

Summary of Appearances and Goals 1993-94

Player	A	G	B	Player	A	G	B
Agnew	36	3	4	Mills	21(2)		1
Blake	10(1)	1	2	Oldfield	24(3)	4	1(1)
Carey	24(3)		5	Ormondroyd	30(1)	4	
Coatsworth	15(4)	2	3(1)	Philpott	10(9)		
Gee	6(6)	1		Poole	14		
Gibson	11(4)		3	Roberts	26	13	3
Grayson	39(1)	1	6(1)	Smith	2(6)		2
Hill	30(1)		6(1)	Speedie	37	12	8
James	4(5)	1		Thompson	30	7	3
Joachim	27(9)	11		Walsh	9(1)	4	3
Kerr	4(3)	2		Ward	32		1
Lewis	24		1	Whitlow	31	2	5
Lowe	1(4)			Willis	9	1	2(1)
Eustace	(1)						

A=Appearances (as Sub)　　　　G=Goals　　　　B=Bookings (Sent Off)

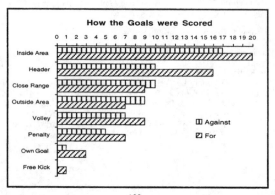

Third time lucky for Little

In successive seasons Brian Little's Leicester City side had been beaten by a single goal in Wembley Play-off Finals. He, and the club's tormented fans, must have hoped that promotion could be won at the third attempt without yet another nerve-jangling trip to North-West London. But, as the season unfolded, Little once again found himself facing the famous Twin Towers.

With little cash available Leicester started the new campaign with a relatively unchanged squad apart from the signing of David Speedie. The Filberts started the season remarkably well, winning four of their first six games with converted defender Steve Walsh again among the goals in his new role as a striker.

During October and November more impressive results were gained, but their Coca-Cola Cup campaign ended with a 5-1 thrashing at Manchester United. Little was then forced into the transfer market when striker Steve Walsh sustained a serious knee ligament injury. His replacement was Welsh international striker Iwan Roberts, from Huddersfield, who brought back themissing aerial threat with two goals on his debut at Wolves.

After four draws in five games, Leicester found themselves slipping off the pace at the top. The FA Cup came as a welcome diversion, but a 4-1 defeat at Manchester City was hardly the tonic Little was hoping for. Wins against West Brom and Charlton followed, but then two successive defeats against pace-setters Crystal Palace and Nottingham Forest highlighted Leicester's real problem – inconsistency.

They then went through the middle of February and early March unbeaten, but then suffered three successive defeats, two of them at home. Little made two more signings before the transfer deadline to give his side a boost. Paul Kerr came from Port Vale, in exchange for David Lowe, and a record £350,000 was spent on Mark Blake from Portsmouth.

But, despite nine unbeaten games at the end of the season, Leicester had to settle for fourth place and a place in the Play-offs against Tranmere Rovers. Young goalkeeper Gavin Ward was the hero in the first leg with a string of fine saves to earn a 0-0 draw. An injury crisis forced Little to recall Walsh, missing through injury since February, for the return. Goals by Ian Ormondroyd and Speedie edged Leicester through to the final once again, but a red card for Speedie in the last minute meant he would miss the final, against big-spending Derby County.

Despite going behind to an early Tommy Johnson goal, Leicester battled back and snatched an equaliser from Walsh just before the interval. With players tiring in the heat during the second half, chances were more plentiful and, after John Harkes had missed a glorious chance for the Rams, Walsh pounced to score his second after Derby keeper Martin Taylor had brilliantly saved Ormondroyd's initial header with only minutes remaining. Leicester had finally won the First Division Play-off Final – and promotion to the Premiership.

Liverpool

Following a dispute between Everton and its Anfield landlord a new club, Liverpool AFC, was formed in 1892 by the landlord, former Everton committee-man John Houlding, with its headquarters at Anfield. An application for Football League membership was rejected without being put to the vote. Instead the team joined the Lancashire League and immediately won the championship.

After that one campaign, when the Liverpool Cup was won but there was early FA Cup elimination, Liverpool was selected to fill one of two vacancies in an expanded Football League Second Division in 1893. Premier League founder members 1992.

Ground: Anfield Road, Liverpool L4 0TH
Phone: 051-263 2361   **Nickname:** Reds or Pool
Colours: All Red/White Trim   **Change:** Racing Green/White Trim
Capacity: 44,243   **Pitch:** 110 yds x 75 yds
Directions: *From North:* M6 J8, follow A58 to Walton Hall Ave and pass Stanley Park then turn left into Anfield Rd. *From South & East:* to end of M62 and right into Queens Drive (A5058). Left after 3 miles into Utting Ave and right after another mile into Anfield Rd. *From West:* M53 through Wallasey Tunnel, follow signs for Preston then turn into Walton Hall Ave and right into Anfield Rd before Stanley Park.
Rail: Liverpool Lime Street

Chairman: D.R. Moores   **Vice-Chairman:** S.T. Moss JP, DL
Chief Executive/General Secretary: Peter Robinson
Manager: Roy Evans   **Coach:** Ron Moran

Record FAPL Win: 5-0 v Crystal Palace, 28/11/92 *and*
                               v Swindon Town, 22/8/93
Record FAPL Defeat: 1-5 v Coventry City, away, 19/12/92
Record FL Win: 10-1 v Rotherham Town, Division 2, 18/2/1896 *and*
                      9-0 v Crystal Palace, Division 1, 12/9/89
Record FL Defeat: 1-9 v Birmingham C, Division 2, 11/12/1954
Record Cup Win: 11-0 v Stromsgodset Drammen, ECWC R1 1L, 17/9/1974
Record Fee Received: £3.2m from Juventus for Ian Rush, 6/1986
Record Fee Paid: £2.9m to Derby County for Dean Saunders, 7/1991
Most FAPL Appearances: Ian Rush, 72(+2), 1992-94
Most FL Appearances: Ian Callaghan, 640, 1960-78
Record Attendance (all-time): 61,905 v Wolves, FA Cup R4, 2/2/1952
Record Attendance (FAPL): 44,619 v Everton, 20/3/93

Highest Scorer in FAPL Season: Ian Rush, 14, 1992-93 *and* 1993-94
Most FAPL Goals in Season: 62, 1992-93
Most FAPL Points in Season: 60, 1993-94
Most Capped Player: Emlyn Hughes, England: 59 out of 62

Season 1993-94
Biggest Home Win: 4-2 v Southampton, 30/10/93
Biggest Home Defeat: 0-2 v Newcastle United, 16/4/94
Biggest Away Win: 5-0 v Swindon Town, 22/8/93
Biggest Away Defeat: 0-3 v Newcastle United, 21/11/93
Biggest Home Attendance: 44,601 v Newcastle United, 16/4/94
Smallest Home Attendance: 24,501 v Queens Park Rangers, 8/12/93
Average Attendance: 38,503 (+4.0%)
Last Season: *PL:* 8th *FA Cup:* 3rd round *Coca-Cola Cup:* 4th round
Leading Scorer: Ian Rush (14)

League History: 1893 Elected to Division 2; 1894-95 Division 1; 1895-96
Division 2; 1896-1904 Division 1; 1904-05 Division 2; 1905-54 Division 1;
1954-62 Division 2; 1962-92 Division 1; 1992- FA Premier League.

Honours: Football League: Division 1 – Champions 1900-01, 1905-06,
1921-22, 1922-23, 1946-47, 1963-64, 1965-66, 1972-73, 1975-76, 1976-77,
1978-79, 1979-80, 1981-82, 1982-83, 1983-84, 1985-86, 1987-88, 1989-90
(Liverpool have a record number of 18 League Championship wins);
Runners-up 1898-99, 1909-10, 1968-69, 1973-74, 1974-75, 1977-78, 1984-
85, 1986-87, 1988-89, 1990-91; Division 2 – Champions 1893-94, 1895-96,
1904-05, 1961-62. FA Cup: Winners 1965, 1974, 1986, 1989, 1992; Runners-
up 1914, 1950, 1971, 1977, 1988; Football League Cup: Winners 1981, 1982,
1983, 1984; Runners-up 1977-78, 1986-87 League Super Cup: Winners 1985-
86.
European Competitions: Champions' Cup: 1964-65, 1966-67, 1973-
74,1976-77 (winners), 1977-78 (winners), 1978-79, 1979-80, 1980-81
(winners), 1981-82, 1982-83, 1983-84 (winners), 1984-85 (runners-up); Cup-
Winners' Cup: 1965-66 (runners-up), 1971-72, 1974-75, 1992-93; Fairs Cup:
1967-68, 1968-69, 1969-70, 1970-71; UEFA Cup: 1972-73 (winners), 1975-
76 (winners), 1991-92; Super Cup: 1977 (winners), 1978, 1984; World Club
Championship: 1981 (runners-up).

Managers (and Secretary-managers):
W.E. Barclay 1892-96, Tom Watson 1896-1915, David Ashworth 1920-22,
Matt McQueen 1923-28, George Patterson 1928-36 (continued as secretary),
George Kay 1936-51, Don Welsh 1951-56, Phil Taylor 1956-59, Bill Shankly
1959-74, Bob Paisley 1974-83, Joe Fagan 1983-85, Kenny Dalglish 1985-91,
Graeme Souness 1991-94, Roy Evans January 1994-.

5-Year League Record

	Div.	P	W	D	L	F	A	Pts	Pos	FAC	FLC
89-90	1	38	23	10	5	78	37	79	1	SF	3
90-91	1	38	23	7	8	77	40	76	2	5	3
91-92	1	42	16	16	10	47	40	64	6	W	4
92-93	PL	42	16	11	15	62	55	59	6	3	4
93-94	PL	42	17	9	16	59	55	60	8	3	4

Summary of Appearances and Goals 1993-94

Player	A	G	B	Player	A	G	B
Barnes	24(2)	3		Molby	11	2	1
Bjornebye	6(3)		1	Nicol	27(4)	1	1
Burrows	3(1)		1	Piechnik	1		
Clough	25(2)	7	2	Redknapp	29(6)	4	4
Dicks	24	3	1	Rosenthal	(3)		
Fowler	27(1)	12		Ruddock	39	3	5
Grobbelaar	29			Rush	41(1)	14	2
Harkness	10		2	Stewart	7(1)		2
Hutchison	6(5)		1	Thomas	1(6)		
James	13(1)			Walters	7(10)		1
Jones	38		2(1)	Whelan	23	1	3
Marsh	(2)	1		Wright	31	1	2
Matteo	11	1					
McManaman	29(1)	2					

A=Appearances (as Sub) G=Goals B=Bookings (Sent Off)

How the Goals were Scored

□ Against
▨ For

104

Inglorious end for The Kop

For almost 90 years the Spion Kop at Anfield witnessed all the great triumphs of Liverpool Football Club, but in its final season, the club could not honour it with a trophy. Worse still, Liverpool were never really in the running for anything.

Manager Graeme Souness paid Nottingham Forest £2 million for Nigel Clough in the close season, and it started promisingly with three wins out of three and a place at the head of the table. Clough was even getting among the goals, with four in his first five games, as August ended with Liverpool in second spot with 12 points from five games.

Three consecutive defeats in September were accompanied by drama on and off the pitch. Defender Neil Ruddock was fined by the FA when video evidence revealed that he had thrown a punch during the defeat by Blackburn, and Souness stunned the city when he traded Mike Marsh and David Burrows to West Ham in exchange for Julian Dicks. Those who had witnessed the glory years of Shankly, Paisley and Fagan shook their heads in disbelief.

By October attention had switched to another new face. Teenage striker Robbie Fowler's form in the reserves earned him a call to the first team, and he responded with 10 goals in his first eight senior appearances, including all five against Fulham in a Coca-Cola Cup tie and a hat-trick at Southampton.

Indifferent League form, coupled with defeat on penalties by Wimbledon in the Coca-Cola Cup, put further pressure on Souness. A 3-3 draw at home to Manchester United – having been 3-0 down – in one of the best games of the season eased the situation, but when the FA Cup third round replay with Bristol City was lost at Anfield, Souness had no option but to resign, taking with him a £400,000 golden handshake.

On the last day of January assistant manager Roy Evans was appointed manager. Evans is a life-long Liverpool fan and is one of the legendary Anfield boot-room boys, having coached the reserves to seven Central League titles in eight years.

The decision to appoint Evans is clearly a move by the club to return to the former practice of promotion from within, a system which made Liverpool the most successful team in the country. His first task was to rubber-stamp Ronny Rosenthal's £300,000 move to Tottenham, which was followed by Mark Walters and Paul Stewart moving to Stoke and Crystal Palace on loan respectively.

Under Evans the team finished eighth in the Premiership, but the final match in front of The Kop ended in a muted 1-0 defeat by Norwich.

The challenge for Evans now is to return the club to their former dominant position. With talented youngsters such as Fowler, Jamie Redknapp, Steve McManaman, Dominic Matteo and Don Hutchison learning alongside experienced men such as Rush, Steve Nicol, Mark Wright and John Barnes, the future prospects are good... though they will have to do it without the aid of the 30,000-strong Kop choir at every home game.

Manchester City

Founded in 1880 as West Gorton AFC. Following ground difficulties, having lost the use of the Kirkmanshulme Cricket Ground, was relaunched as Gorton AFC in 1884. There were more ground problems before, in 1889, the Club moved to Hyde Road, adopted the title of Ardwick, and employed its first professional.

Joined the Football Alliance in 1891, finishing seventh, and was founder member of Football League Division Two in 1892. Ardwick too encountered difficulties and the club was restarted as Manchester City in 1894, retaining the Football League place. In 1923 the club moved to Maine Road. Premier League founder member 1992.

Ground: Maine Road, Moss Side, Manchester, M14 7WN
Phone: 061-226 1191/2   **Nickname:** Blues or The Citizens
Colours: Sky Blue, White, Sky Blue
Change: Purple/Candystripe, Purple, Purple
Capacity: 45,053   **Pitch:** 117 yds x 77 yds
Directions: *From North & West:* M61 to M63 J9. Follow signs into Manchester (A5103). Turn right after 3 miles into Claremont Rd. Turn right after 400 yards into Maine Rd. *From South:* M6 J19 to A556 joining M56. Leave at junction 3 following A5103 as above. *From East:* M62 J17 and follow signs for Manchester Airport (A56 and A57(M)). Then follow Birmingham signs to A5103. Left into Claremont Rd after 1 mile then right into Maine Rd.
Rail: Manchester Piccadilly

Chairman: Francis Lee   **Vice-Chairman:** F. Pye
Secretary: J.B.Halford   **General Manager:** Jimmy Frizzell
Manager: Brian Horton **Assistant:** Sam Ellis
First Team Coach: Tony Book   **Physio:** Eammon Salmon

Record FAPL Win: 4-0 v Leeds United, 7/11/92
Record FAPL Defeat: 0-4 v Coventry City, 19/2/94
Record FL Win: 10-1 v Huddersfield Town, Division 2, 7/11/1987
Record FL Defeat: 1-9 v Everton, Division 1, 3/9/1906
Record Cup Win: 10-1 v Swindon Town, FA Cup R4, 29/1/1930
Record Fee Received: £1.7m from Tottenham H for Paul Stewart, 6/1988
Record Fee Paid: £2.5m to Wimbledon for Keith Curle, 8/1991
Most FAPL Appearances: Tony Coton, 71, 1992-94
Most FL Appearances: Alan Oakes, 565, 1959-76

Record Attendance (all-time): 84,569 v Stoke C, FA Cup R6, 3/3/1934
British record for any game outside London or Glasgow
Record Attendance (FAPL): 37,136 v Manchester United
Highest Scorer in FAPL season: David White, 16, 1992-93
Most FAPL Goals in Season: 56, 1992-93
Most FAPL Points in Season: 57, 1992-93
Most Capped Player: Colin Bell, England: 48

Season 1993-94
Biggest Home Win: 3-0 v Aston Villa, 2/4/94 *and* 3-0 v QPR, 11/9/93
Biggest Home Defeat: 1-3 v Sheffield Wednesday, 27/11/93
Biggest Away Win: 3-1 v Swindon Town, 1/9/93
Biggest Away Defeat: 0-4 v Coventry City, 19/2/94
Biggest Home Attendance: 35,155 v Manchester United, 7/11/93
Smallest Home Attendance: 20,513 v Everton, 8/12/93
Average Attendance: 26,709 (+9.2%)
Last Season: *PL:* 16th *FA Cup:* 4th round *Coca-Cola Cup:* 4th round
Leading Scorer: Mike Sheron (6)

League History: 1892 Ardwick elected founder member of Division 2; 1894 Newly-formed Manchester C elected to Division 2; Division 1 1899-1902, 1903-09, 1910-26, 1928-38, 1947-50, 1951-63, 1966-83, 1985-87, 1989-92; Division 2 1902-03, 1909-10, 1926-28, 1938-47, 1950-51, 1963-66, 1983-85, 1987-89; 1992 – FA Premier League.

Honours: Football League: Division 1 – Champions 1936-37, 1967-68; Runners-up 1903-04, 1920-21, 1976-77; Division 2 – Champions 1898-99, 1902-03, 1909-10, 1927-28, 1946-47, 1965-66; Runners-up 1895-96, 1950-51, 1987-88. FA Cup: Winners1969-70, 1976; Runners-up 1973-74, 1980-81.

European Competitions: Champions' Cup: 1968-69. Cup-Winners' Cup: 1969-70 (winners), 1970-71. UEFA Cup: 1972-73, 1976-77, 1977-78, 1978-79.

Managers (and Secretary-managers): Joshua Parlby 1893-95, Sam Omerod 1895-1902, Tom Maley 1902-06, Harry Newbould 1906-12, Ernest Magnall 1912-24, David Ashworth 1924-25, Peter Hodge 1926-32, Wilf Wild 1932-46 (continued as secretary to 1950), Sam Cowan 1946-47, John 'Jock' Thomson 1947-50, Leslie McDowall 1950-63, George Poyser 1963-65, Joe Mercer 1965-71 (continued as GM to 1972), Malcolm Allison 1972-73, Johnny Hart 1973, Ron Saunders 1973-74, Tony Book 1974-79, Malcolm Allison 1979-80, John Bond 1980-83, John Benson 1983, Billy McNeill 1983-86, Jimmy Frizzell 1986-87 (continued as GM), Mel Machin 1987-89, Howard Kendall 1990, Peter Reid 1990-93, Brian Horton September 1993-.

5-Year League Record

	Div.	P	W	D	L	F	A	Pts	Pos	FAC	FLC
89-90	1	38	12	12	14	43	52	48	14	3	4
90-91	1	38	17	11	10	64	53	62	5	5	3
91-92	1	42	20	10	12	61	48	70	5	3	4
92-93	PL	42	15	12	15	56	51	57	9	6	3
93-94	PL	42	9	18	15	38	49	45	16	4	4

Summary of Appearances and Goals 1993-94

Player	A	G	B	Player	A	G	B
Beagrie	9	1	1	Kerr	3		
Brightwell	19(3)	1		Lomas	17(6)		1
Brightwell I	6(1)			McMahon	35		4
Coton	31		2	Mike	1(7)	1	
Curle	29	1	3	Phelan	30	1	1
Dibble	11			Quigley	2		1
Edgehill	21(1)		1	Quinn	14(1)	5	
Flitcroft	19(2)	3	2	Reid	1(3)		
Foster	1			Rocastle	21	2	3
Griffiths	11(5)	4		Rosler	12	5	1
Groenendijk	9		2	Sheron	29(4)	6	
Hill	15(2)			Shutt	5(1)		1
Holden	9			Simpson	12(3)		
Ingebrigtsen	2(6)		1	Vonk	34(1)	1	6
Karl	4(2)	1		Walsh	11	4	
Kernaghan	23(1)		2	White	16	1	2

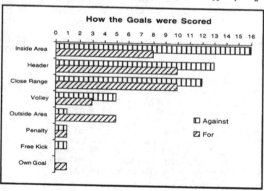

How the Goals were Scored

108

Lee Hailed as the Saviour

The 1993-94 season will long be remembered at Maine Road for the events which took place in the boardroom, rather than on the pitch. By the end of a traumatic season the club had a new manager and, crucially, a new chairman.

The discontent among City's fans, fuelled by the success of United across the City, erupted as early as August when the first four games produced a draw and three defeats. Chairman Peter Swales responded by bringing in journalist John Maddock as general manager of the club, above, and unknown to, manager Peter Reid. Within six days Reid had been fired, the 10th manager to be shown the Maine Road door in the 20 years of Swales's reign. The fans were furious and demanded that Swales should also leave.

A day later Oxford United manager Brian Horton was, surprisingly, named as the new boss at Manchester City, who finished the month third from bottom with only two points from their first five games. September brought a vast improvement in performances on the pitch, with three wins out of four, but the fans were still unsettled. So when it was revealed in the press that former Maine Road favourite Francis Lee was considering trying to take over the club, the fans had their new champion. The cry from the terraces now was "Swales out, Franny in!"

October brought narrow victories over Reading and Chelsea in the Coca-Cola Cup, plus three valuable League points. Then, in the derby against United in early November, City led 2-0 before going down 3-2 at home. The fans reacted in familiar fashion with a demonstration and Swales decided to step down as chairman. Lee and his consortium had long negotiations to conduct before they could take over, and the situation on the playing side took a turn for the worse when a serious injury to giant striker Niall Quinn ruled him out for the rest of the season and blew a gaping hole in the team's forward line. Striker Carl Griffiths was signed from Shrewsbury but his tally of four goals was not enough to compensate for Quinn's loss.

The Coca-Cola Cup run ended in a 2-1 defeat at home to Nottingham Forest in December, and the next five League games produced just two points. City could, however, feel that even the Gods were against them when, two-up at home to Ipswich, the game was abandoned because of torrential rain – the only Premiership clash abandoned all season long.

Lee finally took control – after Cardiff had knocked a ragged City side out of the FA Cup – by paying £3 million for 30 per cent of the shares. The team responded by beating Ipswich 2-1. New players had also arrived to help the fight against relegation: David Rocastle from Leeds, Peter Beagrie from Everton, Paul Walsh from Portsmouth, Uwe Rosler and Stefan Karl from Germany, while David White and Rick Holden had moved on.

The new players took time to settle, but three wins and seven draws from their last 12 games ensured safety. The challenge to Lee, Horton and Co now is to start making up ground on United. Until that happens, City's fans will continue to look enviously towards Old Trafford.

Manchester United

Came into being in 1902 upon the bankruptcy of Newton Heath. Predecessors appear to have been formed in 1878 as Newton Heath (LYR) when workers at the Carriage and Wagon Department at the Lancashire and Yorkshire Railway formed a club. This soon outgrew railway competition.

Turned professional in 1885 and founder member of Football Alliance in 1889. In 1892 Alliance runners-up Newton Heath was elected to an enlarged Division One of the Football League. In 1902 the club became Manchester United and, in February 1910, moved from Bank Street, Clayton, to Old Trafford. Premier League founder member 1992.

Ground: Old Trafford, Manchester, M16 0RA
Phone: 061-872 1661   **Nickname:** Red Devils
Colours: Red, White, Black   **Change:** All Black
Capacity: 44,622   **Pitch:** 116yds x 76yds
Directions: *From North:* M63 J4 follow signs for Manchester (A5081). Right after 2½ miles into Warwick Rd. *From South:* M6 J19 follow A556 then A56 (Altrincham). From Altrincham follow signs for Manchester turning left into Warwick Rd after 6 miles. *From East:* M62 J17 then A56 to Manchester. Follow signs for South and then Chester. Turn right into Warwick Rd after two miles.

Chairman/Chief Executive: C.M. Edwards
Vice-Presidents: J.A. Gibson, W.A. Young, J.G. Gulliver, R.L. Edwards
Secretary: Kenneth Merrett.   **Manager:** Alex Ferguson
Assistant: Brian Kidd   **Physio:** Jim McGregor

Record FAPL Win: 5-0 v Coventry City, 28/12/92 *and*
                     v Sheffield Wednesday, 16/3/94
Record FAPL Defeat: 0-3 v Everton, 19/8/92
Record FL Win: 10-1 v Wolverhampton W, Division 2, 15/10/1892
Record FL Defeat: 0-7 v Blackburn R, Division 1, 10/4/1926 *and*
                      0-7 v Aston Villa, Division 1, 27/12/1930 *and*
                      0-7 v Wolves, Division 2, 26/12/1931
Record Cup Win: 10-0 v RSC Anderlecht, European Cup, PR L2, 26/9/1956
Record Fee Received: £1.8m from Barcelona for Mark Hughes, 8/1986
Record Fee Paid: £3.75m to Nottingham F. for Roy Keane 6/93
Most FAPL Appearances: Steve Bruce and Peter Schmeichel, 83, 1992-94
Most FL Appearances: Bobby Charlton, 606, 1956-73
Record Attendance (all-time): 70,504 v Aston Villa, Division 1, 27/12/1920

Record Attendance (FAPL): 44,751 v Liverpool, 30/3/94
Highest Scorer in FAPL Season: Cantona, 18, 1993-94
Most FAPL Goals in Season: 80, 1993-94
Most FAPL Points in Season: 92, 1993-94
Most Capped Player: Bobby Charlton, England: 106

Season 1993-94
Biggest Home Win: 5-0 v Sheffield Wednesday, 16/3/94
Biggest Home Defeat: 0-1 v Chelsea, 5/2/94
Biggest Away Win: 5-2 v Oldham Athletic 29/12/93
Biggest Away Defeat: 0-2 v Blackburn Rovers, 2/4/94
Biggest Home Attendance: 44,751 v Liverpool 30/3/94
Smallest Home Attendance: 41,829* v Newcastle United 21/8/93
Average Attendance: 44,244 (+26.0%)
Last Season: *PL:* 1st *FA Cup:* winners *Coca-Cola Cup:* runners-up. *European Cup:* 2nd round
Leading Scorer: Eric Cantona (18)
* Higher than all except 11 Premiership gates in the 1993-94 season.

League History: 1892 Newton Heath elected to Division 1; 1894-1906 Division 2; 1906-22 Division 1; 1922-25 Division 2; 1925-31 Division 1; 1931-36 Division 2; 1936-37 Division 1; 1937-38 Division 2; 1938-74 Division 1; 1974-75 Division 2; 1975-92 Division 1; 1992 – FA Premier League.

Honours: FA Premier League – Champions 1992-93, 1993-94; Football League: Division 1 – Champions 1907-8, 1910-11, 1951-52, 1955-56, 1956-57, 1964-65, 1966-67; Runners-up 1946-47, 1947-48, 1948-49, 1950-51, 1958-59, 1963-64, 1967-68, 1979-80, 1987-88, 1991-92. Division 2 – Champions 1935-36, 1974-75; Runners-up 1896-97, 1905-06, 1924-25, 1937-38. FA Cup: Winners 1909, 1948, 1963, 1977, 1983, 1985, 1990, 1994; Runners-up 1957, 1958, 1976, 1979. Football League Cup: Winners 1991-92; Runners-up 1982-83, 1990-91, 1993-94.
European Competitions: Champions' Cup: 1956-57 (s-f), 1957-58 (s-f), 1965-66 (s-f), 1967-68 (winners), 1968-69 (s-f), 1993-94 (s-f). Cup-Winners' Cup: 1963-64, 1977-78, 1983-84, 1990-91 (winners), 1991-92. Fairs Cup: 1964-65. UEFA Cup: 1976-77, 1980-81, 1982-83, 1984-85, 1992-93.
Managers (and Secretary-managers): Ernest Magnall 1900-12, John Robson 1914-21, John Chapman 1921-26, Clarence Hildrith 1926-27, Herbert Bamlett 1927-31, Walter Crickmer 1931-32, Scott Duncan 1932-37, Jimmy Porter 1938-44, Walter Crickmer 1944-45*, Matt Busby 1945-69 (continued as GM then Director), Wilf McGuinness 1969-70, Frank O'Farrell 1971-72, Tommy Docherty 1972-77, Dave Sexton 1977-81, Ron Atkinson 1981-86, Alex Ferguson November 1986-.

5-Year League Record

	Div.	P	W	D	L	F	A	Pts	Pos	FAC	FLC
89-90	1	38	13	9	16	46	47	48	13	W	3
90-91	1	38	16	12	10	58	45	59	6	5	F
91-92	1	42	21	15	6	63	33	78	2	4	W
92-93	PL	42	24	12	6	67	31	84	1	5	3
93-94	PL	42	27	11	4	80	38	92	1	W	F

Summary of Appearances and Goals 1992-93

Player	A	G	B	Player	A	G	B
Bruce	41	3	2	McKee	1		
Butt	(1)			Neville	1		
Cantona	34	18	2(2)	Pallister	41	1	2
Dublin	1(4)	1		Parker	39(1)		3
Ferguson	1(2)			Phelan	1(1)		
Giggs	32(6)	13		Robson	10(5)	1	
Hughes	36	12	4	Schmeichel	40		
Ince	39	8	6	Sealey			
Irwin	42	2	3	Sharpe	26(4)	9	1
Kanchelskis	28(3)	6	1	Thornley	(1)		
Keane	34(3)	5	6	Walsh	2(1)		
Martin	1						
McClair	12(14)	1	1				

A=Appearances (as Sub)   G=Goals   B=Bookings (Sent Off)

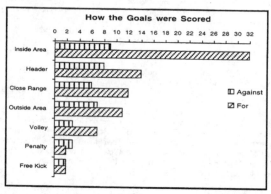

Busby Honoured with the Double

The 1993-94 season will long be remembered at Old Trafford for two momentous events: the death of the club's father figure, Sir Matt Busby, and the winning of the League and Cup double, the first in the club's illustrious history and only the fifth ever.

The season began at Wembley in August for the Charity Shield, with record buy Roy Keane on parade following his £3.75 million transfer from Nottingham Forest. After a 1-1 draw United won the penalty shoot-out, when Arsenal keeper David Seaman missed, and the first trophy in a memorable season. The defence of their title began with a 3-0 win at Norwich, and, by the end of the month, they were back on top and looking good.

Progress in both the Champions' and Coca-Cola Cups was steady if not spectacular, while in the League United went from strength to strength, leading by 11 points at the end of November. The European drive stalled when United were held 3-3 at home by Galatasaray, and then knocked out following a 0-0 draw in Istanbul. To make matters worse, Eric Cantona was dismissed after the final whistle for remarks made to the referee, and several players were involved in ugly scuffles with over-zealous riot police.

At home United continued to consolidate their grip on the title by moving 15 points clear by December. Everton was dispatched in the Coca-Cola Cup and when United overcame bogey-men Sheffield United in the third round of the FA Cup, an unprecedented treble suddenly looked possible.

But on January 20, all thoughts of titles and Cups was forgotten when Busby died. The football family united in mourning, and at the next home game against Everton, a lone Scots piper led the teams onto the pitch in utter silence, a true reflection of Busby's lasting influence. United beat Everton that day, and by the end of February had reached the final of the Coca-Cola Cup and the quarter-finals of the FA Cup.

But March proved a troublesome month for the club. Goalkeeper Peter Schmeichel was sent off in the FA Cup win over Charlton, ruling him out of the Coca-Cola Cup final, and Eric Cantona was dismissed against Swindon and Arsenal in consecutive matches. His subsequent five-match ban upset the balance of the side, and they were outplayed by Aston Villa in the Coca-Cola Cup Final, going down 3-1 with Andrei Kanchelskis becoming the fifth United dismissal of the season. League defeats at Blackburn and Wimbledon caused worries, but when Cantona, the PFA Player of the Year, returned with both goals in a 2-0 win over Manchester City, United regained the upper hand over persistent challengers Blackburn.

The team had reached the FA Cup Final without Cantona, after a replay victory against Oldham, and when Rovers lost at Coventry in the League, United retained their title with two games to spare. The icing on the cake came at Wembley with a run-away 4-0 win over Chelsea, though the match was much closer than the scoreline suggests.

Newcastle United

Formed 1882 as Newcastle East End on the amalgamation of Stanley and Rosewood. Founder members, as a professional club, of the Northern League in 1889. Moved from Chillington Road, Heaton in 1892 to take over the home of the defunct Newcastle West End, with several of those associated with the West End side joining the newcomers.

Applied for Football League Division One membership in 1892, failed and decided against a place in the new Second Division, staying in the Northern League. Later in 1892 changed name to Newcastle United. Elected to an expanded Football League Division Two in 1893.

Ground: St James' Park, Newcastle-upon-Tyne, NE1 4ST
Phone: 091-232 8361   **Nickname:** Magpies
Colours: Black/White, Black, Black   **Change:** All Blue
Capacity: 36,401   **Pitch:** 115 yds x 75 yds.
Directions: *From South:* Follow A1, A68 then A6127 to cross the Tyne. At roundabout, first exit into Moseley St. Left into Neville St, right at end for Clayton St. and then Newgate St. Left for Leaze Park Rd. *From West:* A69 towards city centre. Left into Clayton Street for Newgate St, left again for Leaze Park Rd. *From North:* A1 then follow signs for Hexham until Percy St. Right into Leaze Park Rd. *Rail:* Newcastle Central (¹/₂ mile).

President: T.L. Bennett
Chairman: Sir John Hall   **Vice-Chairman:** W.F. Shepherd
General Manager/Secretary: R. Cushing
Manager: Kevin Keegan   **Assistant:** Terry McDermott
Coaches: Derek Fazackerley and Colin Suggett   **Physio:** Derek Wright

Record FAPL Win: 7-1 v Swindon Town, 12/3/94
Record FAPL Defeat: 2-4 v Wimbledon, 12/2/94
Record FL Win: 13-0 v Newport County, Division 2, 5/10/1946
Record FL Defeat: 0-9 v Burton Wanderers, Division 2, 15/4/1895
Record Cup Win: 9-0 v Southport (at Hillsborough), FA Cup R4, 1/2/1932
Record Fee Received: £2m from Tottenham H for Paul Gascoigne, 7/1988
Record Fee Paid: £2.75 to QPR for Daren Peacock, 3/1994
Most FAPL Appearances: John Beresford, 84, 1992-94
Most FL Appearances: Jim Lawrence, 432, 1904-22
Record Attendance (all-time): 68,386 v Chelsea, Division 1, 3/9/1930
Record Attendance (FAPL): 36,388 v Manchester United, 11/12/93
Highest Scorer in FAPL Season: Andy Cole, 34, 1993-94

Most FAPL Goals in Season: 82, 1993-94
Most FAPL Points in Season: 77, 1993-94
Most Capped Player: Alf McMichael, N Ireland: 40

Season 1993-94
Biggest Home Win: 7-1 v Swindon Town, 12/3/94
Biggest Home Defeat: 1-2 v QPR, 16/10/93 *and* 1-2 v Southanpton, 22/1/94
Biggest Away Win: 4-2 v West Ham United, 19/3/94
Biggest Away Defeat: 2-4 v Wimbledon, 12/2/94
Biggest Home Attendance: 36,338 v Manchester United, 11/12/93
Smallest Home Attendance: 32,129 v Southampton, 22/1/94
Average Attendance: 33,792
Last Season: *Div 1:* 3rd *FA Cup:* 4th round *Coca-Cola Cup:* 3rd round
Leading Scorer: Andy Cole (34)

League History: 1893 Elected to Division 2; 1898-1934 Division 1; 1934-48 Division 2; 1948-61 Division 1; 1961-65 Division 2; 1965-78 Division 1; 1978-84 Division 2; 1984-89 Division 1; 1989-92 Division 2; 1992-1993 Division 1; 1993- FA Premier League.

Honours: Football League: Division 1 – Champions 1904-05, 1906-07, 1908-09, 1926-27, 1992-93; Division 2 – Champions 1964-65; Runners-up 1897-98, 1947-48. FA Cup: Winners 1910, 1924, 1932, 1951, 1952, 1955; Runners-up 1905, 1906, 1908, 1911, 1974. Football League Cup: Runners-up 1975-76. Texaco Cup: Winners 1973-74, 1974-75.

European Competitions: Fairs Cup: 1968-69 Winners, 1969-70, 1970-71.

Managers (and Secretary-managers): Frank Watt 1895-1932 (secretary until 1932), Andy Cunningham 1930-35, Tom Mather 1935-39, Stan Seymour 1939-47 (hon manager), George Martin 1947-50, Stan Seymour 1950-54 (hon manager), Duggie Livingstone, 1954-56, Stan Seymour (Non manager) 1956-58, Charlie Mitten 1958-61, Norman Smith 1961-62, Joe Harvey 1962-75, Gordon Lee 1975-77, Richard Dinnis 1977, Bill McGarry 1977-80, Arthur Cox 1980-84, Jack Charlton 1984, Willie McFaul 1985-88, Jim Smith 1988-91, Ossie Ardiles 1991-92, Kevin Keegan 1992-.

5-Year League Record

	Div.	P	W	D	L	F	A	Pts	Pos	FAC	FLC
89-90	2	46	22	14	10	78	55	80	3	5	3
90-91	2	46	14	17	15	49	56	59	11	4	2
91-92	2	46	13	13	20	66	84	52	20	3	3
92-93	1	46	29	4	8	85	37	93	1	5	3
93-94	PL	42	23	8	11	82	41	77	3	4	3

Summary of Appearances and Goals 1993-94

Player	A	G	B	Player	A	G	B
Allen	9	5		Lee	41	7	
Appleby	1			Mathie	(15)	3	
Beardsley	35	21	2	Neilson	10(4)		1
Beresford	32			O'Brien	4(2)		
Bracewell	32	1	3	Papavassilliou	7		
Clark	29	2	1	Peacock	9		
Cole	40	34	2	Robinson	11(4)		2
Elliott	13(2)		1	Scott	18		2
Fox	14	2		Sellars	29(1)	4	1
Holland	2(1)			Smicek	23		(1)
Hooper	19			Venison	38(1)		3
Howey	13(1)			Watson	30(3)	2	1
Jeffrey	2		1	Wright	(1)		
Kilcline	1						

A=Appearances (as Sub)   G=Goals   B=Bookings (Sent Off)

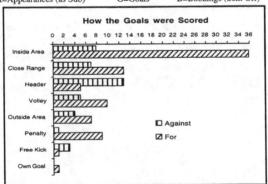

116

Just Like Old Times on Tyneside

Kevin Keegan's status as a hero on Tyneside was strengthened by his side's promotion to the FA Premiership, and moved up several notches further when he brought another Geordie hero, Peter Beardsley, back to St James' Park from Everton in the summer for £1 million. The old boys reunion took on a surreal note when the first visitors came to town on the opening day of the season – Tottenham, now led by former Newcastle manager Ossie Ardiles. Spurs won that day, but from then on Keegan's "Toon Army" simply got better and better.

A 1-1 draw at Manchester United earned their first point in the Premiership and, more significantly, marked the start of an astonishing run of goals from striker Andy Cole. Beardsley's return after injury in September ignited the team and he soon built up a potent understanding with Cole, which brought them an incredible tally of 65 goals between them.

Cole scored hat-tricks in both legs of the Coca-Cola Cup win over Notts County, another against Liverpool in November, and another against Coventry in February on the way to a new club record of 41. Beardsley added 24 to his team's account and his outstanding form earned him a recall to the England side, and his 50th cap against Denmark at Wembley. Just prior to that, he scored twice in a 7-1 thrashing of Swindon – the biggest win of the season in the Premiership, though, curiously, Cole failed to score!

All these goals kept United well up the table, and, while never really in contention for the title, they were always in the running for a UEFA Cup place. The cup competitions proved more difficult, with defeats in the Coca-Cola third round at Wimbledon, and in the FA fourth round in a replay at Luton. Despite this, capacity crowds at virtually every home game kept the cash rolling in to help fund the redevelopment of the ground.

Meanwhile, Keegan began strengthening his squad for a serious challenge for honours in the coming seasons. Gavin Peacock, David Kelly, Liam O'Brien, Mick Quinn, Franz Carr, Brian Kilcline and Kevin Scott were allowed to leave, while several big-money moves brought fresh talent. Scott Sellars arrived from Leeds for £750,000 in October, Ruel Fox moved from Norwich in February for a club record £2 million, and on transfer deadline-day in March, Keegan splashed out a further £2.7 million on QPR centre-back Darren Peacock.

With the redevelopment of St James' Park complete, Keegan has a further £5 million to spend and some of British football's biggest names have been linked with the club. Given that UEFA maintained their ban on Serbian clubs, UEFA Cup football is a just reward for a season of goals, sell-outs and stylish football under "King Kev".

Norwich City

Formed following a June 1902 public meeting organised by two local schoolteachers which agreed the desirability of a Norwich City Football Club. Started in the Norwich & Suffolk League. Turned professional and elected to the Southern League in 1905. Moved from Newmarket Road to The Nest, Rosary Road in 1908.

Founder members of Football League Divison Three with other Southern Leaguers in 1920, this becoming Divison Three (South) in 1921. Moved to Carrow Road, the home of Boulton & Paul Sports Club in 1935. Founder members of Division Three on the end of regionalisation in 1958. Premier League founder members 1992.

Ground: Carrow Road, Norwich, NR1 1JE
Phone: (0603) 612131   **Nickname:** The Canaries
Colours: Yellow, Green, Yellow   **Change:** All White
Capacity: 25,000   **Pitch:** 114yds x 74 yds
Directions: *From North:* A140 to ring road and follow signs for Yarmouth A47. Turn right at T junction after 3 1/2 miles then left after 1/2 mile into Carrow Rd. *From South & West:* A11/A140 onto ring road. Follow signs for Yarmouith A47 etc. *From East:* A47 into Norwich then left onto ring road.

President: G.C. Watling   **Chairman:** Robert T. Chase JP
Vice-Chairman: J.A. Jones   **Secretary:** A.R.W. Neville
Manager: John Deehan
Physio: Tim Sheppard MCSP, SRP

Record FAPL Win: 5-1 v Everton 25/9/93
Record FAPL Defeat: 1-7 v Blackburn Rovers, 3/10/92
Record FL Win: 10-2 v Coventry City, Division 3 (S), 15/3/1930
Record FL Defeat: 2-10 v Swindon Town, Southern League, 5/9/1908
Record Cup Win: 8-0 v Sutton United, FA Cup R4, 28/1/1989
Record Fee Received: £1.2m from Arsenal for Andy Linighan, 6/1990 *and* from Chelsea for Andy Townsend, 6/1990
Record Fee Paid: £925,000 to Port Vale for Darren Beckford, 6/1991
Most FAPL Appearances: Bryan Gunn, Ian Culverhouse and Mark Bowen, 83, 1992-94
Most FL Appearances: Ron Ashman, 592, 1947-64
Record Attendance (all-time): 43,984 v Leicester C, FA Cup R6, 30/3/1963
Record Attendance (FAPL): 21,181 v Tottenham Hotspur, 2/4/94
Highest Scorer in FAPL Season: Chris Sutton, 25, 1993-94

Most FAPL Goals in Season: 65, 1993-94
Most FAPL Points in Season: 72, 1992-93
Most Capped Player: Martin O'Neill, N. Ireland: 18 out of 64

Season 1993-94
Biggest Home Win: 3-0 v Everton, 20/3/94
Biggest Home Defeat: 0-2 v Manchester United, 15/8/93
Biggest Away Win: 5-1 v Everton, 25/9/93
Biggest Away Defeat: 0-3 v Newcastle United, 29/3/94
Biggest Home Attendance: 21,181 v Tottenham Hotspur, 2/4/94
Smallest Home Attendance: 14,851 v Wimbledon, 11/9/93
Average Attendance: 18,179 (+11.9%)
Last Season: *PL:* 12th *FA Cup:* 4th round *Coca-Cola Cup:* 3rd round *UEFA Cup:* 3rd round
Leading Scorer: Chris Sutton (25)

League History: 1920 Original Member of Division 3; 1921 Division 3 (S); 1934-39 Division 2; 1946-58 Division 3 (S); 1958-60 Division 3; 1960-72 Division 2; 1972-74 Division 1; 1974-75 Division 2; 1975-81 Division 1; 1981-82 Division 2; 1982-85 Division 1; 1985-86 Division 2; 1986-92 Division 1; 1992 – FA Premier League.

Honours: Football League: Division 1 best season: 4th, 1988-89; Division 2 – Champions 1971-72, 1985-86. Division 3 (S) – Champions 1933-34; Division 3 – Runners-up 1959-60. FA Cup: Semi-finals 1959, 1989, 1992. Football League Cup: Winners 1962, 1985; Runners-up 1973, 1975.

European Competitions: UEFA Cup: 1993-94

Managers (and Secretary-managers):
John Bowman 1905-07, James McEwen 1907-08, Arthur Turner 1909-10, Bert Stansfield 1910-15, Major Frank Buckley 1919-20, Charles O'Hagan 1920-21, Albert Gosnell 1921-26, Bert Stansfield 1926, Cecil Potter 1926-29, James Kerr 1929-33, Tom Parker 1933-37, Bob Young 1937-39, Jimmy Jewell 1939, Bob Young 1939-45, Cyril Spiers 1946-47, Duggie Lochhead 1945-50, Norman Low 1950-55, Tom Parker 1955-57, Archie Macaulay 1957-61, Willie Reid 1961-62, George Swindin 1962, Ron Ashman 1962-66, Lol Morgan 1966-69, Ron Saunders 1969-73, John Bond 1973-80, Ken Brown 1980-87, Dave Stringer December 1987-92, Mike Walker 1992-93, John Deehan January 1994- .

5-Year League Record

	Div.	P	W	D	L	F	A	Pts	Pos	FAC	FLC
89-90	1	38	13	14	11	44	42	53	10	4	3
90-91	1	38	13	6	19	41	64	45	15	6	3
91-92	1	42	11	12	19	47	63	45	18	SF	5
92-93	PL	42	21	9	12	61	65	72	3	4	3
93-94	PL	42	12	17	13	65	61	53	12	4	3

Summary of Appearances and Goals 1993-94

Player	A	G	B	Player	A	G	B
Adams	11(3)			Johnson	(2)		
Akinbiyi	(2)			Megson	21(1)		3
Bowen	41	5		Newman	32	2	4
Butterworth	23(2)		1	Polston	24		2(1)
Crook	38		1	Power	2(3)		1(1)
Culverhouse	42	1	3	Prior	13		1
Eadie	9(6)	3		Robins	9(4)	1	
Ekoku	20(7)	12	1	Smith	5(2)		
Fox	25	7		Sutch	1(2)		
Goss	34	6	2	Sutton	41	25	3
Gunn	41		1(1)	Ullathorne	11(5)	2	1
Howie	1(1)			Woodthorpe	18(2)		1

A=Appearances (as Sub)   G=Goals   B=Bookings (Sent Off)

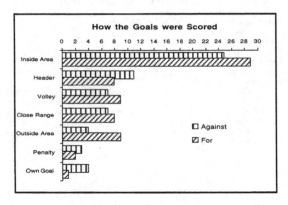

How the Goals were Scored

120

Goss Goals Not Enough

Following the unexpected success of 1992-93, much was expected of Norwich this time round, but little was delivered. The new season started well enough with a brilliant maiden voyage into uncharted waters in Europe, impressive League form and the emergence of Chris Sutton as a goalscorer of real quality. But it lasted only until the New Year.

After an opening-day defeat at home to Manchester United, the League campaign flourished with wins over Blackburn, Leeds and East Anglian rivals Ipswich. The Leeds game was notable for a goal by Jeremy Goss who, after just five goals in 10 seasons, suddenly found out how to find the net.

Norwich's first season in Europe brought Dutch side Vitesse to Carrow Road in the UEFA Cup, and Mike Walker's side showed great maturity with a 3-0 win, Goss again on the score-sheet. A disciplined 0-0 draw in the away leg ensured safe passage and a tie against mighty Bayern Munich in the second round. Between those two European ties, Norwich won 5-1 at Everton, where Efan Ekoku created a new Premiership record with four goals.

October brought progress in the Coca-Cola Cup, via Bradford City, and an amazing 2-1 victory in the Olympic Stadium in Munich in the first leg against Bayern, with Goss again among the scorers. The return produced another Goss goal, a 1-1 draw and a tie against another continental giant, Internazionale, in the next round. Things were going well in the League, too, and at the end of October Norwich lay second – 11 points behind the leaders.

November, though, marked the beginning of a decline. After a 0-0 home draw with Arsenal in the Coca-Cola Cup, the Canaries were battered 3-0 in the replay and League points were dropped against Manchester City and Oldham. The first leg of the UEFA Cup tie with Inter produced a 1-0 defeat at Carrow Road, and suddenly Norwich looked vulnerable. Another 1-0 defeat at the San Siro ended Norwich's European dreams, and a 2-1 defeat at struggling Ipswich 10 days later did little to lift the gloom.

But worse was just around the corner. On the eve of the FA Cup third round tie with Wycombe, manager Mike Walker announced he was quitting to take over at Everton. Walker claimed that the club's ambition did not match his, and that the offer of a one-year contract was a poor reward for his efforts.

Assistant manager John Deehan took over, and immediately had to deal with several players who were unsettled by Walker's move. Ruel Fox's disatisfaction was most evident, and he jumped at a move to Newcastle. The rest, however, decided to stay – at least until the end of the season. Fox's last game for Norwich was the 2-0 FA Cup defeat at home to Manchester United. From then on it was all downhill as their League form slumped. Five consecutive draws in February, four defeats in March, and three defeats in April – including an amazing 5-4 loss at home to Southampton – meant that Norwich finished a disappointing 12th.

Sutton, whose 28 goals took him to the fringes of the England squad, looked set to move in the summer, leaving Deehan the sizeable task of rebuilding the squad and the whole club's morale.

Nottingham Forest

Founded in 1865 by players of a hockey-like game, shinney, who played at the Forest Recreation Ground, and played their first game in 1866. Had several early homes, including a former Notts County ground, The Meadows, and Trent Bridge Cricket Ground.

Founder members of the Football Alliance in 1889 and champions in 1892 when elected to an extended Football League top division. In 1898 moved from the Town Ground to the City Ground at West Bridgford. Run by a Committee until 1982, the last League club to become a limited company. Premier League founder members 1992. Relegated after one season, but promoted back at the first attempt.

Ground: City Ground, Nottingham NG2 5FJ
Phone: (0602) 526000   **Club Nickname:** Reds
Colours: Red, White, Red
Change: Blue, Green, Blue
Capacity: 24,000   **Pitch:** 115x78 yd.
Directions: *From North:* Leave M1 at Junction 26 for A610 And A606, left into Radcliffe Road for the ground. *From South:* Leave M1 at Junction 24 to Trent Bridge right into Radcliffe Road. *From East:* A52 to West Bridgford and right to the ground. *From West:* A52 To A606 and then as for the North.
Rail: Nottingham

Chairman: Fred Reacher
Secretary: Paul White
Manager: Frank Clark   **Assistant Manager:** Ron Fenton
First Team Coach: Liam O'Kane   **Physio:** Graham Lyas

Record FAPL Win: 4-1 v Leeds United, 5/12/92, 3-0 v. Chelsea, 16/1/93
Record FAPL Defeat: 1-4 v Blackburn, 0-3 v Everton *and* Norwich
Record FL Win: 12-0 v Leicester Fosse, Division 1, 12/4/1909
Record FL Defeat: 1-9 v Blackburn R. Division 2, 10/4/1937
Record Cup Win: 14-0 v Clapton (away), FA Cup R1, 17/1/1891
Record Fee Received: £3.75m from Manchester Utd. for Roy Keane 6/94
Record Fee Paid: £2m to Millwall for Teddy Sheringham, 7/91 and £2m to Southend United for Stan Collymore, 6/93
Most FAPL Appearances: Nigel Clough, 42, 1992/93
Most FL Appearances: Bob McKinlay, 614, 1951-70
Record Attendance (all-time): 49,945 v Manchester Utd., Division 1 28/10/1967
Record Attendance (FAPL): 40,453 Away v. Liverpool 6/2/93

Highest Scorer in FAPL season: Nigel Clough, 10, 1992/93
Most FAPL Goals in Season: 41
Most FAPL Points in Season: 40
Most Capped Player: Stuart Pearce, England: 55

Season 1993-94
Biggest Home Win: 4-0 v Leister City 6/2/94
Biggest Home Defeat: 1-3 v Millwall 3/11/93
Biggest Away Win: 0-3 v Birmingham City 6/11/93 *and*
1-4 v Bristol City 28/12/93
Biggest Away Defeat: 0-2 v Crystal Palace 24/8/93
Biggest Home Attendance: 27,010 v Sunderland 8/5/94
Smallest Home Attendance: 17,584 v Millwall 3/11/93
Average Attendance: 23,051
Last Season: *Division 1:* 2nd, *FA Cup:* 3rd round, *Coca-Cola Cup:* 5th round
Leading Scorer: Stan Collymore (18)

League History: 1892 elected to Division 1; 1906-07 Divison 2; 1907-11 Division 1, 1911-22 Division 2, 1922-25 Division 1, 1925-49 Division 2; 1949-51 Division 3(S); 1951-57 Division 2; 1957-72 Division 1; 1972-77 Division 2, 1977-92 Division 1, 1992-93 FA Premier League, 1993-94 Division 1, 1994- FA Premier League.

Honours: *Football League:* Division 1 – Champions 1977-78; Runners-up 1966-67, 1978-79; Division 2 – Champions 1906-07, 1921-22; Runners-up 1956-57; Division 3(S) – Champions 1950-51. *FA Cup:* Winners 1898, 1959; Runners-up 1991. *Anglo-Scottish Cup:* Winners 1976-77. *Football League Cup:* Winners 1977-78, 1978-79, 1988-89, 1989-90, Runners-up 1979-80, 1991-92. *Simod Cup:* Winners 1989. *Zenith Data Systems Cup:* Winners 1991-92

European Competitions: *Fairs Cup:* 1961-62, 1967-68. *Champions' Cup:* 1978-79 (winners), 1979-80(winners), 1980-81. *Super Cup:* 1979-80 (winners), 1980-81 (runners-up). *World Club Championship:* 1980-81 (runners-up). *UEFA Cup:* 1983-84, 1984-85.

Managers (and Secretary-managers): Harry Radford 1889-97, Harry Haslam 1897-09, Fred Earp 1909-12, Bob Masters 1912-25, Jack Baynes 1925-29, Stan Hardy 1930-31, Noel Watson 1931-36, Harold Wightman 1936-39, Billy Walker 1939-60, Andy Beattie 1960-63, John Carey 1963-68, Matt Gillies 1969-72, Dave Mackay 1972-73, Allan Brown 1973-75, Brian Clough 1975-93, Frank Clark June 1993-.

5-Year League Record

	Div.	P	W	D	L	F	A	Pts	Pos	FAC	FLC
89/90	1	38	15	9	14	55	47	54	9	3	W
90/91	1	38	14	12	12	65	50	54	8	F	4
91/92	1	42	16	11	15	60	58	59	8	6	F
92/93	PL	42	10	10	22	41	62	40	22	5	5
93/94	1	46	23	14	9	74	49	83	2	3	5

Summary of Appearances and Goals 1993-94

Player	A	G	B	Player	A	G	B
Black	30(6)	3	1	Kilford	(1)		
Blatherwick	3			Laws	6(1)		2
Bohinen	22(1)	1	1	Lee	10(2)	2	1
Bull	3(8)			Lyttle	37	1	3(1)
Chettle	46	1	3	Pearce	42	6	5
Collymore	27(1)	19	4(1)	Phillips	39(3)	4	1
Cooper	36(1)	7	9	Rosario	15(1)	2	2
Crosby	4(2)			Stone	45	5	2
Crossley	36(1)			Tiler	3		
Gemmill	30(1)	8	3	Warner	1		
Glover	15(3)	5		Webb	17(4)	3	
Haaland	3			Woan	24(1)	5	1
Harvey	(2)			Wright	10		
Howe	2(2)						

A=Appearances (as Sub) G=Goals B=Bookings (Sent Off)

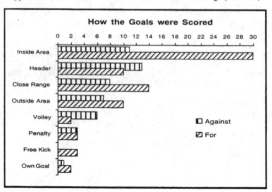

Fired-up Forest Manage without Clough

For a club of Nottingham Forest's size and tradition, an instant return to the FA Premiership was an absolute must. Under manager Frank Clark, who had the difficult task of leading the club into the post-Clough era, they always looked likely to achieve that aim.

Clark's first job was to rebuild a depleted squad, which had lost Nigel Clough to Liverpool and Roy Keane to Manchester United for a record £3.7 million. Crucially, though, England left-back Stuart Pearce was persuaded to stay at the City Ground.

Des Lyttle, a full-back from Swansea, and former England under-21 international Colin Cooper, from Millwall, both joined the club in the summer and made their debuts in a 1-1 draw at Southend. The most notable absentee, however, was Forest's new £2 million signing Stan Collymore, who missed the game against his former club through illness.

When Collymore did return he scored eight goals in seven games, but struggling Forest won only two of their first nine. Clark's answer to this alarming form was to sign Norwich's Welsh international midfielder David Phillips, and Newcastle goalkeeper Tommy Wright, an international with Northern Ireland and a direct replacement for the off-form Mark Crossley.

The performances improved dramatically as Forest suffered only one defeat during the whole of October – at promotion-rivals Leicester City. The run was maintained through November, December and into early January, with success in the Coca-Cola Cup against West Ham and Manchester City from the Premiership.

The central defensive partnership of Steve Chettle and Cooper gave Forest a solid look, and Cooper even gave Collymore a hand at the other end with goals in consecutive games against Watford and Sheffield Wednesday in the FA Cup, and against Tranmere. However, defeats to Wednesday and Tranmere, in the Coca-Cola Cup, meant that Forest had no other distractions in the final promotion run-in.

Bolstered by the signing of Norwegian internationals Lars Bohinen and Alf-Inge Håland, plus Southend striker Jason Lee, an impressive run of five victories was put together. And, with the City Ground now drawing Premiership-standard crowds of over 20,000, promotion seemed all the more vital.

After a 1-0 win at Charlton and a classic 2-2 draw at Millwall, Forest were in sight of the finishing post. Wins against West Brom and Midland neighbours Derby left them needing three points for an automatic ticket back to the top flight. The required points were gained at the expense of already-relegated Peterborough, Collymore again the hero with two goals to clinch the runners-up spot, and a place in the FA Premiership once again.

Queens Park Rangers

Founded in 1885 as St. Jude's Institute. Changed name to Queens Park Rangers in 1887; joined the London League in 1896; and turned professional in 1898. Moved to the Southern League, 1899, and were twice champions.

Lead a nomadic existence in West London but in 1917 took over the home of the amateurs Shepherds Bush, Loftus Road, where, apart from a couple of seasons at White City, it has stayed. Founder members of Football League Division Three in 1920 (this becoming Division Three (South) the following season); of Division Three at the end of regionalisation in 1958; and of the Premier League, 1992.

Ground: Loftus Road, South Africa Road, W12 7PA
Phone: 081-743 0262   **Nickname:** Rangers or Rs
Colours: Blue/White Hoops, White, White
Change: Red/Black Hoops, Black, Black
Capacity: 19,300   **Pitch:** 112 yds x 72 yds
Directions: *From North:* M1 to north circular A406 towards Neasden. Turn left onto A404 follow signs for Hammersmith past White City Stadium then right into South Africa Rd. *From South:* A3 across Putney Bridge and signs for Hammersmith. Follow A219 to Shepherds Bush and join A4020 towards Acton. Turn right after ¼ mile into Loftus Rd. *From East:* From A40(M) towards M41 roundabout. Take 3rd exit at roundabout to A4020 then as above. *From West:* M4 to Chiswick then A315 and A402 to Shepherd's Bush joining A4020 (then as above).
Rail: Shepherd's Bush   **Tube** (Central Line): White City

Chairman/Chief Executive: R.C. Thompson
Secretary: Miss S.F. Marson
Manager: Gerry Francis   **Assistant/Coach:** Frank Sibley
Physio: Brian Morris

Record FAPL Win: 5-1 v Coventry City 23/10/93
Record FAPL Defeat: 0-4 v Leeds United 4/4/94
Record FL Win: 9-2 v Tranmere R, Division 3, 3/12/1960
Record FL Defeat: 1-8 v Mansfield Town, Division 3, 15/3/1965 *and* 1-8 v Manchester United, Division 1, 19/3/1969
Record Cup Win: 8-1 v Bristol Rovers (away), FA Cup R1, 27/11/1937 *and* 8-1 v Crewe Alexandra, Milk Cup R1, 3/10/1983
Record Fee Received: £2.75m from Newcastle for Daren Peacock, 3/94
Record Fee Paid: £1m to Luton Town for Roy Wegerle, 12/1989

Most FAPL Appearances: Clive Wilson, 83, 1992-94
Most FL Appearances: Tony Ingham, 519, 1950-63
Record Attendance (all-time): 35,353 v Leeds U, Division 1, 27/4/1974
Record Attendance (FAPL): 21,267 v Manchester United, 5/2/94
Highest Scorer in FAPL Season: 20: Les Ferdinand, 1992-93
Most FAPL Goals in Season: 63, 1992-93
Most FAPL Points in Season: 63, 1992-93
Most Capped Player: Don Givens, Republic of Ireland: 26 out of 56

Season 1993-94
Biggest Home Win: 5-1 v Coventry City, 23/10/93
Biggest Home Defeat: 0-4 v Leeds United, 4/4/94
Biggest Away Win: 4-0 v West Ham United, 28/8/93
Biggest Away Defeat: 1-4 v Aston Villa, 14/8/93 *and*
v Oldham Athletic, 2/4/94
Biggest Home Attendance: 21,267 v Manchester United 5/2/94
Smallest Home Attendance: 9,875 v Southampton, 21/8/93
Average Attendance: 14,133 (-5.8%)
Last Season: *PL:* 9th *FA Cup:* 3rd round *Coca-Cola Cup:* 4th round
Leading Scorer: Les Ferdinand (17)

League History: 1920 Original Member of Divison 3; 1921 Division 3 (S); 1948-52 Division 2; 1952-58 Division 3 (S); 1958-67 Division 3; 1967-68 Division 2; 1968-69 Division 1; 1969-73 Division 2; 1973-79 Division 1; 1979-83 Division 2; 1983-92 Division 1; 1992 – FA Premier League.

Honours: Football League: Division 1 – Runners-up 1975-76; Division 2 – Champions 1982-83; Runners-up 1967-68, 1972-73; Division 3 (S) – Champions 1947-48; Runners-up 1946-47; Division 3 – Champions 1966-67. FA Cup: Runners-up 1982. Football League Cup: Winners 1966-67; Runners-up 1985-86. (In 1966-67 won Division 3 and Football League Cup.)

European Competitions: UEFA Cup: 1976-77, 1984-85.

Managers (and Secretary-managers): James Cowan 1906-13, James Howie 1913-20, Ted Liddell 1920-24, Will Wood 1924-25 (had been secretary since 1903), Bob Hewison 1925-30, John Bowman 1930-31, Archie Mitchell 1931-33, Mick O'Brien 1933-35, Billy Birrell 1935-39, Ted Vizard 1939-44, Dave Mangnall 1944-52, Jack Taylor 1952-59, Alec Stock 1959-65 (GM to 1968), Jimmy Andrews 1965, Bill Dodgin Jnr 1968, Tommy Docherty 1968, Les Allen 1969-70, Gordon Jago 1971-74, Dave Sexton 1974-77, Frank Sibley 1977-78, Steve Burtenshaw 1978-79, Tommy Docherty 1979-80, Terry Venables 1980-84, Gordon Jago 1984, Alan Mullery 1984, Frank Sibley 1984-85, Jim Smith 1985-88, Trevor Francis 1988-90, Don Howe 1990-91, Gerry Francis June 1991-.

5-Year League Record

	Div.	P	W	D	L	F	A	Pts	Pos	FAC	FLC
89-90	1	38	13	11	14	45	44	50	11	6	3
90-91	1	38	12	10	16	44	53	46	12	3	4
91-92	1	42	12	18	12	48	47	54	11	3	3
92-93	PL	42	17	12	13	63	55	63	5	4	4
93-94	PL	42	16	12	14	62	61	60	9	3	4

Summary of Appearances and Goals 1993-94

Player	A	G	B	Player	A	G	B
Allen	14(7)	7		Penrice	23(3)	8	1
Bardsley	32		4	Ready	19(3)	1	4(1)
Barker	35(2)	5	5(1)	Roberts	16		
Brevett	3(4)			Sinclair	30(2)	3	
Doyle	1			Stejskal	26		
Ferdinand	35(1)	17	2(1)	White	12(5)	8	2
Holloway	19(6)		1	Wilkins	39	1	1
Impey	31(2)	3	2	Wilson	42	3	
McCarthy	4			Witter	1		
McDonald	12	1	2	Yates	27(2)		
Meaker	11(2)	1					
Peacock	30	3	4				

A=Appearances (as Sub)   G=Goals   B=Bookings (Sent Off)

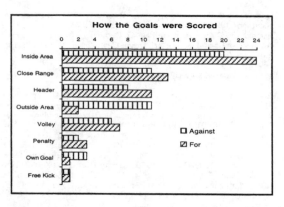

128

Uncertain Times at Loftus Road

Having finished as London's top club in 1992-93, QPR fans might have been expecting another season of progression in 1993-94. They were wrong. Uncertainty over the future of the club's manager and several key players undermined all that the team did on the pitch.

The first bad sign for QPR fans came in the pre-season when England winger Andy Sinton was sold to Sheffield Wednesday for £2.5 million. Just when it seemed that Rangers had put together a side capable of challenging for honours, the old problem of having to sell players to stay afloat resurfaced. Manager Gerry Francis used the cash to sign centre-back Steve Yates from his old club Bristol Rovers, and promising young Blackpool forward Trevor Sinclair. These modest, though shrewd investments, did little to appease the fans, who once again felt the board had sold out.

Rangers' FA Premiership campaign opened disastrously with 4-1 and 3-1 defeats against Aston Villa and Liverpool respectively. But by October they were back on the right track with impressive victories against Ipswich, Newcastle and Coventry. In the Coca-Cola Cup Barnet were swept aside in the first round, with Bradley Allen scoring a hat-trick in a 4-0 second-leg victory. Millwall were beaten 3-0 in the next round and, despite losing to Manchester United, the good run continued in the League with wins against Blackburn and Everton – where Allen scored another hat-trick – which took them up to eighth, three points behind Leeds in second place.

Sheffield Wednesday won 2-1 at Loftus Road in the Coca-Cola Cup in December, the prelude to a run of erratic performances which culminated in a humiliating third-round FA Cup exit at Second Division Stockport County in early January.

Les Ferdinand's recurring injury problems meant that he was in and out of the side during the winter, and without their top striker QPR became more and more inconsistent. But, when defender Darren Peacock was sold to Newcastle on transfer-deadline day in March, the side and the fans seemed to lose interest.

April produced three 1-1 draws and four defeats, including an embarrassing 3-1 loss at home to relegated Swindon! Some pride was restored in May with a draw against West Ham and a win at Spurs, but Rangers finished the season in ninth place – not the outcome they were hoping for.

QPR fans looked forward to a tense time as the uncertainty over Ferdinand's future increases. He was linked with a move to Newcastle and seemed certain to leave. Manager Francis is also thought to be considering his future and, when these factors are taken into account, it is easier to understand the fans' frustration, and their anger towards chairman Richard Thompson.

Sheffield Wednesday

Founded in 1867 by members of the Wednesday Cricket Club and played at Highfield before moving to Myrtle Road. Were first holders of the Sheffield FACup. The club played at Sheaf House then Endcliff and became professionals in 1886. In 1887 moved to Olive Grove.

Refused admission to the Football League, the club was founder member, and first champions, of the Football Alliance in 1889. In 1892 most Alliance clubs became founder members of Football League Division Two, but Wednesday were elected to an enlarged top division. The club moved to Hillsborough in 1899. Founder member of the Premier League 1992.

Ground: Hillsborough, Sheffield, S6 1SW
Phone: (0742) 343122   **Nickname:** The Owls
Colours: Blue/White, Blue, Blue   **Change:** All Black with Yellow/Grey trim
Capacity: 40,000   **Pitch:** 115 yds x 75 yds
Directions: *From North:* M1 J34 then A6109 to Sheffield. At roundabout after 1½ miles take 3rd exit then turn left after 3 miles into Herries Rd. *From South & East:* M1 junction 31 or 33 to A57. At roundabout take Prince of Wales Rd exit. A further 6 miles then turn left into Herries Rd South. *From West:* A57 to A6101 then turn left after 4 miles at T junction into Penistone Road.
Rail: Sheffield Midland

Chairman: D.G. Richards   **Vice-chairman:** K.T. Addy
Secretary: G.H. Mackrell FCCA
Manager: Trevor Francis   **Assistant:** Richie Barker
Physio: A. Smith

Record FAPL Win: 5-0 v Ipswich Town, 23/4/94 *and*
                          v West Ham, 18/12/93
Record FAPL Defeat: 0-5 v Manchester United, 16/3/94
Record FL Win: 9-1 v Birmingham, Division 1, 13/12/1930
Record FL Defeat: 0-10 v Aston Villa, Division 1, 5/10/1912
Record Cup Win: 12-0 v Halliwell, FA Cup R1, 17/1/1891
Record Fee Received: £2.7m from Blackburn R. for Paul Warhurst, 9/1993
Record Fee Paid: £2.7m to Sampdoria for Des Walker, 7/1993 *and*
                          £2.7m to QPR for Andy Sinton, 8/1993
Most FAPL Appearances: Carlton Palmer and Nigel Worthington, 70(+1) 1992-94
Most FL Appearances: Andy Wilson, 502, 1900-20

Record Attendance (all-time): 72,841 v Man City, FA Cup R5, 17/2/1934
Record Attendance (FAPL): 37,708 v Manchester United
Highest Scorer in FAPL Season: Bright, 19, 1993-94
Most FAPL Goals in Season: 76, 1993-94
Most FAPL Points in Season: 64, 1993-94
Most Capped Player: Nigel Worthington, N. Ireland: 37 out of 44

Season 1993-94
Biggest Home Win: 5-0 v Ipswich Town, 23/4/94 *and*
                        v West Ham, 18/12/93
Biggest Home Defeat: 2-3 v Manchester United, 2/10/93
Biggest Away Win: 4-1 v Ipswich Town, 6/11/93
Biggest Away Defeat: 0-5 v Manchester United, 16/3/94
Biggest Home Attendance: 34,959 v Sheffield United, 22/1/94
Smallest Home Attendance: 18,509 v Oldham Athletic, 24/11/94
Average Attendance: 27,187 (-0.25%)
Last Season: *PL:* 7th *FA Cup:* 4th *Coca-Cola Cup:* Semi-finals
Leading Scorer: Mark Bright (19)

League History: 1892 Elected to Division 1; 1899-1900 Division 2; 1900-20
Division 1; 1920-26 Division 2; 1926-37 Division 1; 1937-50 Division 2;
1950-51 Division 1; 1951-52 Division 2; 1952-55 Division 1; 1955-56
Division 2; 1956-58 Division 1; 1958-59 Division 2; 1959-70 Division 1;
1970-75 Division 2; 1975-80 Division 3; 1980-84 Division 2; 1984-90
Division 1; 1990-91 Division 2; 1991-92 Division 1; 1992- FA Premier
League.

Honours: Football League: Division 1 – Champions 1902-03, 1903-04,
1928-29, 1929-30; Runners-up 1960-61; Division 2 – Champions 1899-1900,
1925-26, 1951-52, 1955-56, 1958-59; Runners-up 1949-50, 1983-84. FA
Cup: Winners 1896, 1907, 1935; Runners-up 1890, 1966, 1993. Football
League Cup: Winners 1990-91, Runners-up 1993.

European Competitions: Fairs Cup: 1961-62, 1963-64. UEFA Cup: 1992-93

Managers (and Secretary-managers): Arthur Dickinson 1891-1920. Robert
Brown 1920-33, Billy Walker 1933-37, Jimmy McMullan 1937-42, Eric
Taylor 1942-58 (continued as GM to 1974), Harry Catterick 1958-61, Vic
Buckingham 1961-64, Alan Brown 1964-68, Jack Marshall 1968-69, Danny
Williams 1969-71, Derek Dooley 1971-73, Steve Burtenshaw 1974-75, Len
Ashurst 1975-77, Jackie Charlton 1977-83, Howard Wilkinson 1983-88, Peter
Eustace 1988-89, Ron Atkinson 1989-91, Trevor Francis June 1991-.

5-Year League Record

	Div.	P	W	D	L	F	A	Pts	Pos	FAC	FLC
89-90	1	38	11	10	17	35	51	43	18	4	3
90-91	2	46	22	16	8	80	51	82	3	5	W
91-92	1	42	21	12	9	62	49	75	3	4	3
92-93	PL	42	15	14	13	55	51	59	7	F	F
93-94	PL	42	16	16	10	76	54	64	7	4	SF

Summary of Appearances and Goals 1993-94

Player	A	G	B	Player	A	G	B
Bart-Williams	30(7)	9	1	Pearson	4(1)		
Bright	36(4)	19	3	Poric	2(4)		1
Briscoe	(1)			Pressman	32		
Coleman	10(5)	1		Sheridan	19(1)	3	4
Francis	(1)			Sinton	25	3	
Hirst	6(1)	1		Waddle	19	3	
Hyde	27(9)	1	1	Walker	42		1
Jemson	10(8)	5		Warhurst	4		
Jones	24(3)	5	1	Watson	15(8)	12	2
King	7(3)			Watts	1		
Linighan	1			Williams	4		
Nilsson	38		1	Woods	10		
Palmer	37	5	4(1)	Worthington	30(1)	1	
Pearce	29(3)	3	2(1)				

A=Appearances (as Sub)   G=Goals   B=Bookings (Sent Off)

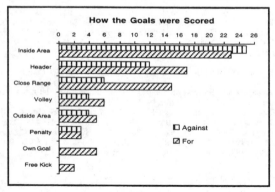

132

After the Lord Mayor's Show...

Disappointment is the only word to describe Sheffield Wednesday's season, especially after the multiple Wembley outings of the previous season. Expectations were high at Hillsborough after a seventh-place finish in the League, two Cup final appearances and the arrival of several new, expensive players at the club.

England defender Des Walker was the first to join, for £2 million from Trevor Francis's former Italian club Sampdoria. Walker had endured a torrid time in his single season in Italy, and took several months to settle back into the hectic pace of English football. The next arrival was England's new winger Andy Sinton. He arrived from QPR in a £2.5 million deal and, with the return of broken-leg victim Nigel Pearson and injured striker David Hirst, the situation looked promising.

How deceptive appearances can be! The first four games produced a 0-0 draw and three defeats, with no Wednesday player able to find the net. Mark Bright finally broke the spell in a 1-1 draw at Chelsea, which left them second from bottom at the end of August. Worse still, Hirst's injury problems kept recurring and effectively wrecked his season, restricting him to just 11 appearances.

The next home game, against Norwich, produced a 3-3 thriller, but after a 4-2 defeat at Newcastle – in a match best remembered for the horrendous clash of colours – and a 2-0 win over Southampton, Wednesday drew five of their next six League games, losing the other to Manchester United to finish the month third from bottom with 11 points from 12 games.

But a thumping 4-1 win at Ipswich at the start of November proved to be a turning point as Wednesday went on to win five and draw three of their next nine games, to move up to a far more respectable 10th at the turn of the year.

The good League form was matched in the Coca-Cola Cup, where Bolton, Middlesbrough and QPR were beaten in the first three rounds. January brought further League wins over QPR, Spurs and Sheffield United in the derby, another Coca-Cola victory, against Wimbledon at Selhurst Park, and success in the FA Cup third round, against Nottingham Forest in a replay. The Owls were looking more like their old selves again, with a double assault on Wembley, and steady progress up the League.

But an injury to Chris Waddle ruled him out for the second half of the season, and his loss proved a serious blow to the side. The FA Cup adventure ended in February with a home defeat in a fourth round replay against Chelsea, the challenge for the Coca-Cola Cup ended at the semi-final stage with defeat in both legs to Manchester United, 1-0 at Old Trafford and 4-1 at Hillsborough.

Despite these set-backs Wednesday maintained their League form to finish seventh, the same as the previous season. They even turned up the heat in the run-in, beating Everton 5-1 and Ipswich 5-0 to finish as the third-highest scorers in the division.

Southampton

Formed 1885 by members of the St Mary's Young Men's Association, St Mary's FC. The church link was dropped, though the name retained, in 1893. In 1895 applied for a Southern League place, but was refused only to be invited to fill a subsequent vacancy. 'St. Mary's' was dropped after two seasons. Moved from the County Cricket Ground to the Dell in 1898.

Six times Southern League champions, Southampton were founder members of Football League Division Three in 1920 (this becoming Division Three (South) the following season); of Division Three at the end of regionalisation in 1958; and of the Premier League, 1992.

Ground: The Dell, Milton Road, Southampton, SO9 4XX
Phone: (0703) 220505   **Nickname:** The Saints
Colours: Red/White, Black, Black
Change: Turquoise/Royal Blue, Turquoise, Royal Blue
Capacity: 15,288   **Pitch:** 110 yds x 72 yds
Directions: *From North:* A33 into The Avenue then right into Northlands Rd. Right at the end into Archer's Rd. *From East:* M27 then A334 and signs for Southampton along A3024. Follow signs for the West into Commercial Rd, right into Hill Lane then first right into Milton Rd. *From West:* Take A35 then A3024 towards city centre. Left into Hill Lane and first right into Milton Rd.
Rail: Southampton Central

President: J. Corbett   **Chairman:** F.G. Askham FCA/Lawrie McMenemy
Vice-chairman: K. St. J. Wiseman   **Secretary:** Brian Truscott
Manager: Alan Ball   **Assistant:** John Mortimore
First Team Coach: Lew Chatterley   **Physio:** Don Taylor

Record FAPL Win: 5-1 v Swindon Town, 25/8/93
Record FAPL Defeat: 2-5 v Sheffield Wednesday, 12/4/93
Record FL Win: 9-3 v Wolverhampton Wanderers, Division 2, 18/9/1965
Record FL Defeat: 0-8 v Tottenham Hotspur, Division 2, 28/3/1936 *and*
                  0-8 v Everton, Division 1, 20/11/1971
Record Cup Win: 7-1 v Ipswich Town, FA Cup R3, 7/1/1961
Record Fee Received: £2.4m from Blackburn R. for Tim Flowers, 7/1991
Record Fee Paid: £1m to Swindon Town for Alan McLoughlin, 11 /1993
Most FAPL Appearances: Matthew Le Tissier, 78, 1992-94
Most FL Appearances: Terry Payne, 713, 1956-74
Record Attendance (all-time): 31,044 v Man United, Division 1, 8/10/1969
Record Attendance (FAPL): 19,654 v Tottenham Hotspur, 15/8/92
Highest Scorer in FAPL Season: 25, Matthew Le Tissier, 1993-94

Most FAPL Goals in Season: 54, 1992-93
Most FAPL Points in Season: 50, 1992-93
Most Capped Player: Peter Shilton, England: 49 out of 125

Season 1993-94
Biggest Home Win: 5-1 v Swindon Town
Biggest Home Defeat: 0-4 v Arsenal
Biggest Away Win: 2-0 v Aston Villa
Biggest Away Defeat: 0-3 v Tottenham Hotspur
Biggest Home Attendance: 19,105 v Blackburn Rovers
Smallest Home Attendance: 9,028 v Ipswich Town
Average Attendance: 14,764 (-4.0%)
Last Season: *PL:* 18th *FA Cup:* 3rd round *Coca-Cola Cup:* 2nd round
Leading Scorer: Matthew Le Tissier (25)

League History: 1920 Original Member of Division 3; 1921 Division 3 (S); 1922-53 Division 2; 1953-58 Division 3 (S); 1958-60 Division 3; 1960-66 Division 2; 1966-74 Division 1; 1974-78 Division 2; 1978-92 Division 1; 1992 – FA Premier League.

Honours: Football League: Division 1 – Runners-up 1983-84; Division 2 – Runners-up 1965-66, 1977-78; Division 3 (S) – Champions 1921-22; Runners-up 1920-21; Division 3 – Champions 1959-60. FA Cup: Winners 1975-76; Runners-up 1900, 1902. Football League Cup: Runners-up 1978-79.

European Competitions: European Cup-Winners' Cup: 1976-77. Fairs Cup: 1969-70.-70. UEFA Cup: 1971-72, 1981-82, 1982-83, 1984-85. Zenith Data Systems Cup: Runners-up 1991-92.

Managers (and Secretary-managers): Cecil Knight 1894-95, Charles Robson 1895-97, E. Arnfield 1897-1911 (continued as secretary), George Swift 1911-12, E. Arnfield 1912-19, Jimmy McIntyre 1919-24, Arthur Chadwick 1925-31, George Kay 1931-36, George Cross 1936-37, Tom Parker 1937-43, J.R. Sarjantson stepped down from the board to act as secretary-manager 1943-47 with the next two listed being team managers during this period), Arthur Dominy 1943-46, Bill Dodgin Snr 1946-49, Sid Cann 1949-51, George Roughton 1952-55, Ted Bates 1955-73, Lawrie McMenemy 1973-85, Chris Nicholl 1985-91, Ian Branfoot 1991-94, Alan Ball January 1994-.

5-Year League Record

	Div.	P	W	D	L	F	A	Pts	Pos	FAC	FLC
89-90	1	38	15	10	13	71	63	55	7	5	5
90-91	1	38	12	9	17	58	69	45	14	5	5
91-92	1	42	14	10	18	39	55	52	16	6	4
92-93	PL	42	13	11	18	54	61	50	18	3	3
93-94	PL	42	12	7	23	49	66	43	18	3	2

Summary of Appearances and Goals 1993-94

Player	A	G	B	Player	A	G	B
Adams	17(2)		2	Heaney	2		
Allen	29(3)	1	6	Hughes	(2)		
Andrews	5			Hurlock	2		1
Banger	4(10)		1	Kenna	40(1)	2	4
Bartlett	4(3)			Le Tissier	38	25	5
Beasant	25		1	Maddison	41	7	1
Benali	34(3)		4(1)	Magilton	15		
Bennett	(8)	1		Maskell	6(4)	1	
Bound	1			Monkou	35	4	5
Charlton	29(4)	1	1	Moody	3(2)		
Cockerill	12(2)			Moore	14		
Cramb	(1)			Powell	1		
Dodd	5(5)		1	Reid	7		
Dowie	39	5	7	Widdrington	11	1	2
Flowers	12			Wood	27		2
Hall	4						

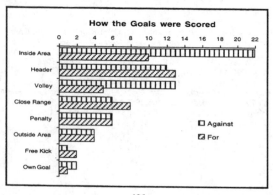

Figure: How the Goals were Scored — Inside Area, Header, Volley, Close Range, Penalty, Outside Area, Free Kick, Own Goal (Against / For)

Le Tissier Comes of Age

Matthew Le Tissier finally came of age in the 1993-94 season, taking on the mantle of responsibility for his team, scoring enough spectacular goals to warrant a one-man goal of the year contest, and finally winning his first England cap – becoming the first Channel Islander to do so in the process.

Not that it was all sweetness and light down at The Dell. The first nine League games produced one win – 5-1 against Swindon – and eight defeats, leaving them second from bottom, level on points with Swindon. The fans had had enough of Ian Branfoot and, when Le Tissier was dropped from the side for five games in September and October, they protested angrily and demanded his resignation.

Branfoot's position weakened further as the League results continued to go against him, and an early exit from the Coca-Cola Cup to Shrewsbury hardly helped his cause. Le Tissier returned for the home game with Newcastle in October and stole the show with a brilliant performance and two wonderful goals, but England goalkeeper Tim Flowers was sold to Blackburn for £2.4 million, with Dave Beasant moving from Chelsea as his replacement, in another development which displeased the fans.

With Le Tissier back at the helm, the Saints began to look livelier during November, but in December things went badly awry once more. Three consecutive 1-0 defeats to Everton, Ipswich and QPR, plus a 2-1 defeat at Swindon, increased the pressure on Branfoot, and he finally gave way in January after a disastrous FA Cup defeat by Port Vale. Former captain Alan Ball took over as manager, with Lawrie McMenemy working behind the scenes, in a new-look set-up which Saints fans had dreamed of for months.

Performances improved immediately. Ball's first game in charge brought a 2-1 win at Newcastle, and in his first home game Le Tissier smacked home a hat-trick in a 4-2 win over Liverpool. Le Tissier scored the winner in a 1-0 win against Wimbledon in late February, and two draws at the start of March moved them out of the relegation zone.

But another reversal of fortune struck in late March and early April as Southampton lost four and drew one of five games which produced only one goal, courtesy of Le Tissier. But, in an amazing game at Norwich, they hit back from 3-1 down to win 5-4 with a last-minute goal by Ken Monkou to keep their hopes of survival alive.

The final five games of the season were nerve-wracking for Saints fans as their side beat Blackburn, lost at Tottenham, thrashed Aston Villa, lost at Manchester United and then secured survival with a twice-halted 3-3 draw at West Ham on the final day, where Le Tissier's two goals took his season's total to 25. It would be churlish to suggest that Le Tissier kept Southampton up single-handedly, but without him and his goals, it is likely that the Saints would be looking forward to life in the Endsleigh League this term.

Tottenham Hotspur

Formed in 1882 by members of the schoolboys' Hotspur Cricket Club as Hotspur FC and had early Church connections. Added 'Tottenham' to distinguish club from others with similar names in 1885. Turned professional in 1895 and elected to the Southern League in 1896 having been rebuffed by the Football League.

Played at several places before moving to the site which became known as White Hart Lane in 1899. Joined the Football League Second Division 1908. Having failed to gain a place in the re-election voting, it secured a vacancy caused by a late resignation. Premier League founder members 1992.

Ground: 748 High Road, Tottenham, London, N17 0AP
Phone: 081-808 6666   **Nickname:** Spurs
Colours: White, Navy Blue, White   **Change:** All Yellow or all Sky Blue
Capacity: 30,246   **Pitch:** 110yds x 73 yds
Directions: A406 North Circular to Edmonton. At traffic lights follow signs for Tottenham along A1010 then Fore St for ground.
Rail: White Hart Lane (adjacent)
Tube: Seven Sisters (Victoria Line) or Manor House (Piccadilly Line).

Chairmen: Alan Sugar and A.G. Berry
Vice-presidents: F.P. Sinclair and N. Soloman
Secretary: Peter Barnes
Manager: Ossie Ardiles   **Assistant:** Steve Perryman MBE
First Team Coach: Doug Livermore
Physio: John Sheridan and Dave Butler

Record FAPL Win: 5-0 v Oldham Athletic, 18/9/93
Record FAPL Defeat: 0-6 v Sheffield United, 2/3/93
Record FL Win: 9-0 v Bristol Rovers, Division 2, 22/10/1977
Record FL Defeat: 0-7 v Liverpool, Division 1, 2/9/1978
Record Cup Win: 13-2 v Crewe Alex, FA Cup, R4 replay, 3/2/1960
Record Fee Received: £5.5m from Lazio for Paul Gascoigne, 5/1992
Record Fee Paid: £2.2m to Chelsea for Gordon Durie, 8/1991
Most FAPL Appearances: Vinny Samways, 73, 1992-94
Most FL Appearances: Steve Perryman, 655, 1969-86
Record Attendance (all-time): 75,038 v Sunderland, FA Cup R6, 5/3/1938
Record Attendance (FAPL): 33,709 v Arsenal, 12/12/92
Highest Scorer in FAPL Season: Teddy Sheringham, 21, 1992-93
Most FAPL Goals in Season: 60, 1992-93
Most FAPL Points in Season: 59, 1992-93

Most Capped Player: Pat Jennings, N. Ireland: 74 out of 119

Season 1993-94
Biggest Home Win: 5-0 v Oldham Athletic, 18/9/93
Biggest Home Defeat: 1-4 v West Ham United, 4/4/94
Biggest Away Win: 3-1 v West Ham United, 28/12/93
Biggest Away Defeat: 0-2 v Leeds United, 17/4/94
Biggest Home Attendance: 33,130 v Norwich City, 27/12/93
Smallest Home Attendance: 17,452 v Aston Villa, 2/3/94
Average Attendance: 27,255(-2.3%)
Last Season: *PL:* 15th *FA Cup:* 4th round *Coca-Cola Cup:* 5th round
Leading Scorer: Teddy Sheringham (13)

League History: 1908 Elected to Division 2; 1909-15 Division 1; 1919-20 Division 2; 1920-28 Division 1; 1928-33 Division 2; 1933-35 Division 1; 1935-50 Division 2; 1950-77 Division 1; 1977-78 Division 2; 1978-92 Division 1; 1992- FA Premier League.

Honours: Football League: Division 1 – Champions 1950-51, 1960-61; Runners-up 1921-22, 1951-52, 1956-57, 1962-63; Division 2 – Champions 1919-20, 1949-50; Runners-up 1908-09, 1932-33; Promoted 1977-78 (3rd). FA Cup: Winners 1901 (as non-League club), 1921, 1961, 1962, 1967, 1981, 1982, 1991 (8 wins stands as the record); Runners-up 1986-87. Football League Cup: Winners 1970-71, 1972-73; Runners-up 1981-82.

European Competitions: Champions' Cup: 1961-62 Cup-Winners' Cup: 1962-63 (winners), 1963-64, 1967-68, 1981-82 (runners-up), 1982-83, 1991-92. UEFA Cup: 1971-72 (winners), 1972-73, 1973-74 (runners-up), 1983-84 (winners), 1984-85.

Managers (and Secretary-managers): Frank Brettell 1898-99, John Cameron 1899-1906, Fred Kirkham 1907-08, Peter McWilliam 1912-27, Billy Minter 1927-29, Percy Smith 1930-35, Jack Tresadern 1935-38, Peter McWilliam 1938-42, Arthur Turner 1942-46, Joe Hulme 1946-49, Arthur Rowe 1949-55, Jimmy Anderson 1955-58, Bill Nicholson 1958-74, Terry Neill 1974-76, Keith Burkinshaw 1976-84, Peter Shreeves 1984-86, David Pleat 1986-87, Terry Venables 1987-91, Peter Shreeves 1991-92. Ossie Ardiles June 1993-.

5-Year League Record

	Div.	P	W	D	L	F	A	Pts	Pos	FAC	FLC
89-90	1	38	19	6	13	59	47	63	3	3	5
90-91	1	38	11	16	11	51	50	49	10	W	5
91-92	1	42	15	7	20	58	63	52	15	3	SF
92-93	PL	42	16	11	15	60	66	59	8	SF	4
93-94	PL	42	11	12	19	54	59	45	15	4	5

Summary of Appearances and Goals 1993-94

Player	A	G	B	Player	A	G	B
Allen	(1)			Howells	15(3)	1	
Anderton	35(2)	6		Kerslake	16(1)		
Austin	20(3)		2	Mabbutt	29		1
Barmby	27	5		Mahorn	1		
Calderwood	26		2(1)	Moran	(5)		
Campbell	27(7)		1	Nethercott	9		
Carr	1			Robinson	1(1)		
Caskey	16(8)	4	2	Rosenthal	11(4)	2	
Dozzell	28(4)	8	1	Samways	39	3	7
Durie	10	1		Scott	12	1	1
Edinburgh	24(1)		5	Sedgley	42	5	1
Gray	(2)	1		Sheringham	17(2)	14	2
Hazard	13(4)	2		Thorstvedt	32		
Hendry	(3)			Turner	(1)		
Hill	1(2)			Walker	10(1)		

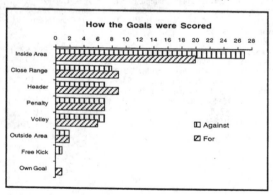

How the Goals were Scored

□ Against
☑ For

Trials and Tribulations

Not exactly a vintage season for Tottenham, but an interesting one none the less. At the end of it the club had narrowly avoided relegation, moulded a new England international in Darren Anderton, lost one of their most famous Spurs, had another badly injured, another maimed in an ugly incident, and were under investigation by the authorities, again, this time for alleged illegal payments to players which ultimately lead to record punishments.

During the summer new manager Ossie Ardiles used the £2.5 million he got from Liverpool, for Neil Ruddock, to sign Swindon centre-back Colin Calderwood and Ipswich midfielder Jason Dozzell, for £1.8 million, while midfield grafter Paul Hazard left for Southampton early in the season.

An opening-day win at Newcastle was an encouraging start and a 1-0 defeat in the North London derby at White Hart Lane two days later was soon forgotten about with a 1-0 win over Manchester City, and a 2-1 win at Anfield, where Sheringham scored both. Sheringham scored seven goals in eight games during September and October. But, in the last of those games, at Old Trafford, Sheringham suffered an injury which kept him out until April. Without him, Tottenham won only two out of their next 20 League games.

The maiming referred to earlier occured in November, when Wimbledon striker John Fashanu caught skipper Gary Mabbutt across the face with his elbow. Mabbutt suffered a fractured cheekbone, a dislocated eye-socket and damage to his face which kept him out until the end of February. In December, Danny Blanchflower – captain of the glorious double-winning side of 1961 – died aged 67.

On the playing side, Tottenham fared better in the Coca-Cola Cup, reaching the quarter-finals but in January they lost 2-1 to Aston Villa in the quarter-final, and then needed a penalty shoot-out to get past the First Division's bottom club, Peterborough, in the third round of the FA Cup. Late in the month they lost 3-0 at Ipswich in the fourth round to end all hopes of a trophy, leaving only an increasingly serious battle against relegation to concentrate on. A 2-0 defeat at Blackburn in early February meant the club had gone since October without a home win, and were sliding toward the relegation zone, a cause not helped by a 4-3 defeat at Chelsea, where misfit midfielder Andy Gray missed a penalty.

In desperation Ardiles paid Liverpool £300,000 for Israeli striker Ronny Rosenthal, and he responded with a vital equaliser in a 1-1 draw with Aston Villa. Tottenham then seemed to turn their season round with two draws and a win in late March, and when Sheringham returned with a goal in a 2-1 win at Norwich in early April, they seemed safe. But three consecutive defeats dropped them back in to danger, before wins over struggling Southampton and Oldham guaranteed Premiership football for next season. In theory at least. The FA investigation ended in the docking of 12 points and banishment from the FA Cup for 94-95 along with a £600,000 fine. On appeal the points deduction was reduced to six, but the fine increased to £1.5 million.

West Ham United

Thames Ironworks founded 1895, to give recreation for the shipyard workers. Several different grounds were used as the club entered the London League (1896) and won the championship (1898). In 1899, having become professional, won the Southern League Second Division (London) and moved into Division One.

On becoming a limited liability company the name was changed to West Ham United. Moved from the Memorial Ground to a pitch in the Upton Park area, known originally as 'The Castle', in 1904. Elected to an expanded Football League Division Two for the 1919-20 season and never subsequently out of the top two divisions.

Ground: Boleyn Ground, Green Street, Upton Park, London E13
Phone: 081-472 2740   **Nickname:** The Hammers
Colours: Claret, White, White   **Change:** All Blue
Capacity: 24,500   **Pitch:** 112 yds x 72 yds
Directions: *From North & West:* North Circular to East Ham then Barking Rd for 1½ miles until traffic lights. Turn right into Green St. *From South:* Blackwall Tunnel then A13 to Canning Town. Then A124 to East Ham, Green St on left after 2 miles. *From East:* A13 then A117 and A124. Green St on right after ¾ miles.
Rail/Tube: Upton Park (¼ mile)

Chairman: T.W. Brown FCIS, ATII, FCCA   **Vice-Chairman:** M.W. Cearns
Secretary: T.M. Finn
Manager: Billy Bonds MBE   **Assistant:** Harry Redknapp
First Team Coach: Paul Hilton, Tony Carr
Physio: John Green BSC (Hons) MCSP, SRP

Record FAPL Win: 4-1 v Tottenham Hotspur, 4/4/94
Record FAPL Defeat: 0-5 v Sheffield Wednesday, 18/12/93
Record FL Win: 8-0 v Rotherham United, Division 2, 8/3/1958 *and*
         8-0 v Sunderland, Division 1, 19/10/1968
Record FL Defeat: 2-8 v Blackburn Rovers, Division 1, 26/12/1963
Record Cup Win: 10-0 v Bury, League Cup, R2 2nd leg, 25/10/1983
Record Fee Received: £2m from Everton for Tony Cottee, 7/1988
Record Fee Paid: £1.25m to Celtic for Frank McAvennie, 3/1989
Most FAPL Appearances: Ludek Miklosko, 42, 1993-94
Most FL Appearances: Billy Bonds, 663, 1967-88
Record Attendance (all-time): 42,322 v Tottenham H, Div 1, 17/10/1970

Record Attendance (FAPL): 28,832 v Manchester United, 26/2/94
Highest Scorer in FAPL Season: Trevor Morley, 13, 1993-94
Most FAPL Goals in Season: 47, 1993-94
Most FAPL Points in Season: 52, 1993-94
Most Capped Player: Bobby Moore, England: 108

Season 1993-94
Biggest Home Win: 3-1 v Manchester City, 1/11/93
Biggest Home Defeat: 0-4 v Queens Park Rangers, 28/8/94
Biggest Away Win: 4-1 v Tottenham Hotspur, 4/4/94
Biggest Away Defeat: 0-5 v Sheffield Wednesday, 18/12/93
Biggest Home Attendance: 28,832 v Manchester United, 26/2/94
Smallest Home Attendance: 15,777 v Swindon Town, 11/9/93
Average Attendance: 20,595 (+28.7%)
Last Season: *PL:* 13 *FA Cup:* 6th round *Coca-Cola Cup:* 3rd round
Leading Scorer: Trevor Morley (13)

League History: 1919 Elected to Division 2; 1923-32 Division 1; 1932-58 Division 2; 1958-78 Division 1; 1978-81 Division 2; 1981-89 Divison 1; 1989-91 Division 2; 1991-1993 Division 1; 1993- FA Premier League.

Honours: Football League: Division 1 Runners-up 1992-93; Division 2 Champions 1957-58, 1980-81; Runners-up 1922-23, 1990-91. FA Cup: Winners 1964, 1975, 1980; Runners-up 1922-23. Football League Cup: Runners-up 1966, 1981.

European Competitions: Cup-Winners' Cup: 1964-65 (winners), 1965-66, 1975-76 (runners-up), 1980-81.

Managers (and Secretary-managers): Syd King 1902-32, Charlie Paynter 1932-50, Ted Fenton 1950-61, Ron Greenwood 1961-74 (continued as GM to 1977), John Lyall 1974-89, Lou Macari 1989-90, Billy Bonds February 1990-

5-Year League Record

	Div.	P	W	D	L	F	A	Pts	Pos	FAC	FLC
89-90	2	46	20	12	14	80	57	72	7	3	SF
90-91	2	46	24	15	7	60	34	87	2	SF	3
91-92	1	42	9	11	22	37	59	38	22	5	4
92-93	1	46	26	10	10	81	41	88	2	4	2
93-94	PL	42	13	13	16	47	58	52	13	6	3

Summary of Appearances and Goals 1993-94

Player	A	G	B	Player	A	G	B
Allen C	7	2		Holmes	33(1)	3	1
Allen M	20(6)	7	2	Jones	3(5)	2	
Bishop	36	1	1	Marquis	(1)		
Boere	(4)		(1)	Marsh	33	1	2
Breacker	40	3		Martin	6(1)	2	
Brown	6(3)			Miklosko	42		
Burrows	25	1	3	Mitchell	(1)		
Butler	26	1	3	Morley	39(3)	13	3
Chapman	26(4)	7	1	Potts	41		3
Dicks	7		1	Robson	1(2)		
Foster	5			Rowland	16(7)		2
Gale	31(1)		1	Rush	9(1)	1	1
Gordon	8	1		Williams	2(1)	1	

A=Appearances (as Sub) G=Goals B=Bookings (Sent Off)

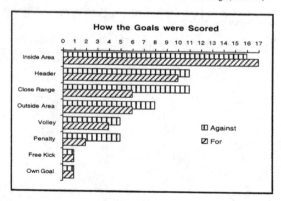

How the Goals were Scored

Inside Area / Header / Close Range / Outside Area / Volley / Penalty / Free Kick / Own Goal

□ Against ▨ For

144

Solid Start for the Hammers

Many had West Ham down as relegation candidates before the start of the season, and after a poor start, those doubters must have thought they were correct. But Billy Bonds proved what a shrewd customer he can be in the transfer market, and pulled the Hammers round in the end.

The only major moves of note during the summer were Kevin Keen's sale to Wolves, and the £750,000 purchase of winger Dale Gordon from Rangers, where he had become surplus to requirements.

The season got off to a bad start with two defeats, before a Gordon goal ensured a point at Coventry. Veteran Clive Allen, who finished the season at Millwall, scored both in a 2-0 win over Sheffield Wednesday, but the next two games resulted in 4-0 and 3-0 defeats. That was enough to convince Bonds that quick action was needed, and he moved swiftly to set up a swap deal with Liverpool – Julian Dicks moving to Anfield in return for defender David Burrows, midfielder Mike Marsh and enough cash to buy veteran striker Lee Chapman from Portsmouth. It turned out to be one of the best deals of the whole season as the trio brought new life to the team.

All three lined up for their debuts away to Blackburn, where West Ham outplayed the big-spending Lancashire side in a splendid 2-0 win, with Chapman opening the scoring. Chapman and Burrows both scored in a 5-1 romp over Chesterfield in the Coca-Cola Cup in the next game, and the Hammers suddenly looked a much tighter outfit.

With their form in the Premiership improving, it was something of a disappointment to lose 2-1 at Nottingham Forest in the next round of the Coca-Cola Cup, though they continued their progress in the League with a 3-1 home win over Manchester City.

November and December brought a mixed bag of results – five wins, two draws and four defeats – to leave them lying exactly half-way at the start of January.

The FA Cup now provided a welcome source of income with a run to the quarter-finals. Watford, Notts County and Kidderminster were all beaten en route to an epic battle with Luton Town. After a 0-0 draw at home, West Ham fell in the replay, to a hat-trick from Scott Oakes in a 3-2 defeat.

Prior to that, in late February, the club opened the new Bobby Moore stand and almost honoured it with a win against the champions, Manchester United, who were lucky to scrape a 2-2 draw thanks to a last-minute equaliser from Upton Park old boy Paul Ince, who was booed every time he touched the ball!

West Ham were not firing on all cylinders in the final months of the season, but had done enough to ensure safety. Forgotten man Martin Allen did, however, discover his scoring boots with five goals in the last six games as the Irons rose to an acceptable 13th in the table. One problem for Bonds to deal with in the summer, though. Marsh asked for a transfer because his family are unable to settle in the south. His loss will be a big blow to the club.

Wimbledon

Founded 1889 as Wimbledon Old Centrals, an old boys' side of the Central School playing on Wimbledon Common. Member of the Southern Suburban League, the name was changed to Wimbledon in 1905. Moved to Plough Lane in 1912. Athenian League member for two season before joining the Isthmian League in 1921.

FA Amateur Cup winners 1963 and seven times Isthmian League champions. Turned professional in 1965 joining the Southern League of which they were champions three times before being elected to Football League Division Four in 1977. Started ground sharing at Selhurst Park in 1991 and founder member of the Premier League 1992.

Ground: Selhurst Park, South Norwood, London SE25 6PU
Phone: 081-771 2233   **Nickname:** The Dons
Colours: All Blue with Yellow trim   **Change:** All Red
Capacity: 26,995   **Pitch:** 110 yds x 74 yds
Directions: *From North:* M1/A1 to North Circular A406 and Chiswick. Follow South Circular A205 to Wandsworth then A3 and A214 towards Streatham and A23. Then left onto B273 for 1 mile and turn left at end into High St and Whitehorse Lane. *From South:* On A23 follow signs for Crystal Palace along B266 going through Thornton Heath into Whitehorse Lane. *From East:* A232 Croydon Rd to Shirley joining A215, Norwood Rd. Turn left after 2½ miles into Whitehorse Lane. *From West:* M4 to Chiswick then as above.
Rail: Selhurst, Norwood Junction or Thornton Heath.

President: Rt. Hon. Lord Michael Havers of Bury St. Edmunds.
Chairman: Sam Hammam   **Vice-Chairman:** J. Lelliott
Secretary: Steve Rooke   **Manager:** Joe Kinnear
Assistant: Terry Burton   **Physio:** Steve Allen

Record FAPL Win: 4-0 v Crystal Palace, 9/4/1993
Record FAPL Defeat: 2-6 v Oldham Athletic, 3/4/1993
Record FL Win: 6-0 v Newport County, Division 3, 3/9/1983
Record FL Defeat: 0-8 v Everton, League Cup R2, 29/8/1978
Record Cup Win: 7-2 v Windsor & Eton, FA Cup R1, 22/11/1980
Record Fee Received: £2.5m from Manchester City for Keith Curle, 8/1991
Record Fee Paid: £775,000 to Port Vale for Robbie Earle, 7/1991
Most FAPL Appearances: Robbie Earle, 84, 1992-94
Most FL Appearances: Alan Cork, 430, 1977-92

Record Attendance (all-time): 18,000 v HMS Victory, FA Amateur Cup, R3, 1934-35
Record Attendance (FAPL): 30,115 v Manchester United, 8/5/93
Record Scorer in FAPL Season: Holdsworth, 19, 1992-93
Most FAPL Goals in Season: 56, 1992-93 *and* 56 , 1993-94
Most FAPL Points in Season: 65, 1993-94
Most Capped Player: Glyn Hodges, Wales: 5 out of 16

Season 1993-94
Biggest Home Win: 4-1 v Blackburn Rovers, 29/3/94
Biggest Home Defeat: 0-3 v Arsenal, 1/1/94
Biggest Away Win: 4-2 v Swindon Town, 23/4/94
Biggest Away Defeat: 0-4 v Leeds United, 2/10/93 *and*
v Newcastle United, 30/10/93
Biggest Home Attendance: 28,553 v Manchester United, 16/4/94
Smallest Home Attendance: 4,739 v Coventry City, 16/12/93
Average Attendance: 10,462(+ 24.7%)
Last Season: *PL:* 6th *FA Cup:* 5th round *Coca-Cola Cup:* 5th round
Leading Scorer: Dean Holdsworth (17)

League History: 1977 Elected to Division 4; 1979-80 Division 3; 1980-81 Division 4; 1981-82 Division 3; 1982-83 Division 4; 1983-84 Division 3; 1984-86 Division 2; 1986-92 Division 1; 1992- FA Premier League.

Honours: Football League: Division 1 best season: 6th, 1986-87; Division 3 – Runners-up 1983-84; Division 4 – Champions 1982-83. FA Cup: Winners 1987-88. Football League Cup: best season: 4th round, 1979-80, 1983-84, 1988-89. League Group Cup: Runners-up 1981-82.

European Competitions: None

Managers (and Secretary-managers): Les Henley 1955-71, Mike Everitt 1971-73, Dick Graham 1973-74, Allen Batsford 1974-78, Dario Gradi 1978-81, Dave Bassett 1981-87, Bobby Gould 1987-90, Ray Harford 1990-91, Peter Withe 1991, Joe Kinnear January 1992-.

5-Year League Record

	Div.	P	W	D	L	F	A	Pts	Pos	FAC	FLC
89-90	1	38	13	16	9	47	40	55	8	3	4
90-91	1	38	14	14	10	53	46	56	7	4	2
91-92	1	42	13	14	15	53	53	53	13	3	2
92-93	PL	42	14	12	16	56	55	54	12	5	3
93-94	PL	42	18	11	13	56	53	65	6	5	5

Summary of Appearances and Goals 1993-94

Player	A	G	B	Player	A	G	B
Ardley	14(2)	1		Gayle	10		1
Barton	37(2)	2	5	Holdsworth	42	17	4
Berry	4(1)	1		Jones	33	2	8
Blackwell	16(1)		1	Joseph	13		2
Blissett	6(11)	3	1	Kimble	14		
Castledine	3	1		McAllister	13		2
Clarke	9(14)	2	1	Perry	(1)		
Dobbs	3(7)			Sanchez	15	2	
Earle	42	9		Scales	37		3
Elkins	18	1	1	Segers	41		
Fashanu	35(1)	11	5	Sullivan	1(2)		
Fear	23	1	2	Talboys	6(1)		1
Fitzgerald	27(1)						

A=Appearances (as Sub)   G=Goals   B=Bookings (Sent Off)

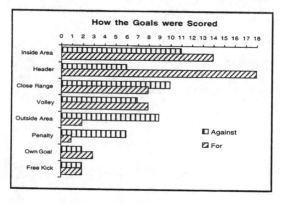

How the Goals were Scored

Dons Graduate... with Honours

Love them or loathe them, it is getting harder and harder to ignore Wimbledon. The club everybody loves to not bother going to see equalled their best-ever finishing position in 1993-94, sixth, and had three players called up for England duty. Not bad for a team run on a shoe-string, with no ground, precious few fans and a reputation for being long-ball merchants.

For once, the Dons were not forced to part with any players to balance the books in the summer, though this also meant that manager Joe Kinnear had no money to spend on new players. As it turned out, those under his control at the start of the season were more than capable anyway.

August began with a win, two draws, a defeat, and another draw before a run of four consecutive 1-0 wins – three in the Premiership and one in the Coca-Cola Cup against Hereford – which took them up to fourth and earned Kinnear the Manager of the Month award. Money was even found to buy striker Gary Blissett from Brentford.

Following a sound 4-0 beating at Leeds in October, the Dons finished off Hereford with a 4-1 win at their adopted Selhurst Park home, before going on to beat Newcastle 2-1 in the third round thanks to a winner from the fast-developing Dean Holdsworth.

Three consecutive 1-1 draws in November and December, two of them at Tottenham and Liverpool, showed that Wimbledon had lost none of their competitive spirit, and had merely added more finesse to their play. The draw at Tottenham will, however, be remembered for the clash between John Fashanu and Spurs skipper Gary Mabbutt, which left Mabbutt with facial injuries. This may have affected Fash's form, as he only scored another seven goals all season. Thankfully for the team, Holdsworth was about to enter a hot streak which brought him 24 goals in all, including two hat-tricks, against Scunthorpe, in the FA Cup, and Oldham, in the Premiership.

Meanwhile, in the Coca-Cola Cup, Wimbledon pulled off a major upset when they knocked Liverpool out on penalties in a replay after the 1-1 draw at Anfield. The quarter-finals was the end of the line, though, as they lost 2-1 at home to Sheffield Wednesday.

In the FA Cup, Sunderland were beaten 2-1 in the fourth round to set up a clash with Manchester United which attracted a crowd of over 27,000 to Selhurst Park. The game, however, belonged to United who ran out easy 3-0 winners.

For many teams, that would have been pretty much the end of the season. Not Wimbledon. In the final three months of the season, the Dons were at their best, chalking up notable victories over Leeds, Blackburn, Manchester United and Tottenham as they surged up to sixth place.

Such sterling effort deserved recognition, and that duly arrived when John Scales, Warren Barton and Holdsworth were all called up for England duty, albeit with the B team. Owner Sam Hammam maintains that he aims to get the club into Europein the 1994-95 season and, the way things are going, they could well do it.

FA PREMIER LEAGUE
CLUB TRANSFERS 1993-94

Top 10 Transfers 1993-94

No	Player	From	To	Fee
1	Roy Keane	Nottingham Forest	Man Utd	£3,750,000
2	Brian Deane	Sheff Utd	Leeds Utd	£2,900,000
3	David Batty	Leeds	Blackburn	£2,750,000
4	Darren Peacock	QPR	Newcastle	£2,750,000
5	Andy Sinton	QPR	Sheff Wed	£2,700,000
6	Des Walker	Sampdoria	Sheff Wed	£2,700,000
7	Paul Warhurst	Sheff Wed	Blackburn	£2,700,000
8	Neil Ruddock	Tottenham	Liverpool	£2,500,000
9	Tim Flowers	Southampton	Blackburn	£2,400,000
10	Nigel Clough	Nottingham Forest	Liverpool	£2,275,000

SUMMER 1993

Player	From	To	Fee
Roy Keane	Nottingham Forest	Manchester United	£3,750,000
Brian Deane	Sheffield United	Leeds United	£2,900,000
Des Walker	Sampdoria	Sheffield Wednesday	£2,700,000
Neil Ruddock	Tottenham Hotspur	Liverpool	£2,500,000
Nigel Clough	Nottingham Forest	Liverpool	£2,275,000
Andy Townsend	Chelsea	Aston Villa	£2,100,000
Peter Beardsley	Everton	Newcastle	£1,400,000
Gavin Peacock	Newcastle United	Chelsea	£1,250,000
Guy Whittingham	Portsmouth	Aston Villa	£1,200,000
Eddie McGoldrick	Crystal Palace	Arsenal	£1,000,000
Dale Gordon	Rangers	West Ham United	£750 000
Simon Webster	Charlton	West Ham United	£525,000
Jan-Aage Fjortoft	Rapid Vienna	Swindon Town	£500,000
Alphonse Groenendijk	Ajax	Manchester City	£500,000
Andy Pearce	Coventry City	Sheffield Wednesday	£500,000
Paul Mason	Aberdeen	Ipswich Town	£400,000
Gary Blissett	Brentford	Wimbledon	£350,000
David Tuttle	Tottenham Hotspur	Sheffield United	£350,000
Alex Mathie	Morton	Newcastle United	£285,000
Simon Charlton	Huddersfield Town	Southampton	£250,000
Mick Harford	Sunderland	Coventry City	£200,000
Spencer Prior	Southend United	Norwich City	£200,000
Alan Kimble	Cambridge United	Wimbledon	£175,000
Luc Nijholt	Motherwell	Swindon Town	£175,000

Andy Morrison	Plymouth Argyle	Blackburn Rovers	£150,000
Steve Morgan	Plymouth Argyle	Coventry City	£110,000
Keith Rowland	Bournemouth	West Ham United	£110,000
Jason Dozzell	Ipswich Town	Tottenham Hotspur	undecided
Andy Dow	Dundee	Chelsea	tribunal

AUGUST 1993

Player	From	To	Fee
Andy Sinton	QPR	Sheff Wed	£2,700,000
Jason Dozzell	Ipswich	Tottenham	£1,750,000
Colin Calderwood	Swindon	Tottenham	£1,250,000
Graham Stuart	Chelsea	Everton	£850,000
Ian Marshall	Oldham	Ipswich	£750,000
Trevor Sinclair	Blackpool	QPR	£750,000
Steve Yates	Bristol Rovers	QPR	£750,000
David Phillips	Norwich	Nottingham Forest	£600,000
Jakob Kjeldberg	Silkeborg	Chelsea	£400,000
Willie Falconer	Middlesbrough	Sheff Utd	£400,000
Jostein Flo	Sojndal	Sheff Utd	£400,000
Scott Howie	Clyde	Norwich	£350,000
Malcolm Allen	Millwall	Newcastle	£300,000
Lee Chapman	Leeds	Portsmouth	£250,000
Andy Dow	Dundee	Chelsea	£250,000
Danny Wilson	Sheff Wed	Barnsley	£250,000
Alan Thompson	Newcastle	Bolton	£250,000
Peter Shirtliff	Sheff Wed	Wolves	£250,000
Andy Mutch	Wolverhampton	Swindon	£250,000
Chris Whyte	Leeds	Birmingham	£250,000
Paul Williams	Stockport	Coventry	£150,000
Martin Carruthers	Aston Villa	Stoke	£100,000
Steve Cotterill	Wimbledon	Bournemouth	£80,000
Jonas Wirmola	Sparvagens	Sheff Utd	£50,000
Ian Hendon	Tottenham	L Orient	£50,000
Mark Foran	Millwall	Sheff Utd	£25,000
Ian Bryson	Sheff Utd	Barnsley	£20,000
Rob Scott	Sutton	Sheff Utd	£20,000
Ashley Fickling	Sheff Utd	Darlington	£10,000
John Harkes	Sheff Wed	Derby	
David Johnson	Sheff Wed	Lincoln	
Mark Blake	Aston Villa	Portsmouth	swap
Wayne Burnett	Blackburn	Plymouth	swap
Lee Bradford	Dorchester	Everton	trial
Terry Fenwick	Tottenham	Swindon	trial
Alan Harper	Everton	Stoke	trial
Dragan Lukic	Belgrade	Newcastle	trial
Peter Shearer	Bournemouth	Coventry	trial

Viv Anderson	Sheff Wed	Barnsley	free
John Burridge	Hibernian	Newcastle	free
Perry Digweed	Brighton	Wimbledon	free
Darren Donelly	Blackburn	Chester	free
Micky Gynn	Coventry	Stoke	free
Terry Fleming	Coventry	Northampton	free
Damian Henderson	Leeds	Scarborough	free
Scott Houghton	Tottenham	Luton	free
Iain Jenkins	Everton	Chester	free
Istvan Kozma	Liverpool	Ujpesti Te	free
David MacDonald	Tottenham	Peterborough	free
Ray Ranson	Man City	Reading	free
Glyn Roberts	Norwich	Rotherham	free
Paul Robertson	Sheff Wed	Scarborough	free
Cyrille Regis	Aston Villa	Wolves	free
George Switzer	Man Utd	Darlington	free
Garry Thompson	QPR	Cardiff	free

SEPTEMBER 1993

Player	From	To	Fee
Paul Warhurst	Sheff Wed	Blackburn	£2,700,000
Julian Dicks	West Ham	Liverpool	*£1,600,000
Alan Kernaghan	Middlesbrough	Man City	£1,600,000
Stuart Slater	Celtic	Ipswich	£750,000
Paul Allen	Tottenham	Southampton	£550,000
Mike Hooper	Liverpool	Newcastle	£550,000
David Kerslake	Leeds	Tottenham	£450,000
Tommy Wright	Newcastle	Nottingham Forest	£450,000
Jeroen Boere	Go Ahead Eagles	West Ham	£250,000
Lee Chapman	Portsmouth	West Ham	£250,000
Mike Marsh	Liverpool	West Ham	*swap
David Burrows	Liverpool	West Ham	*swap
Detzi Kruszynski	Brentford	Coventry	trial
Zsolt Petry	Ghent	Southampton	trial
Agent Sawu	Zimbabwe	Liverpool	trial
Terry Fenwick	Tottenham	Swindon	free
Alan Harper	Everton	Luton	free
Pat van den Hauwe	Tottenham	Millwall	free
John Gayle	Birmingham	Coventry	unknown
Peter Duffield	Sheff Utd	Hamilton	unknown

Mike Marsh + David Burrows = Julian Dicks

OCTOBER 1993

Player	From	To	Fee
David Batty	Leeds	Blackburn	£2,750,000
Mark Stein	Stoke	Chelsea	£1,600,000
Carl Griffiths	Shrewsbury	Man City	£500,000
Tore Pedersen	FK Brann	Oldham	£500,000
Rick Holden	Man City	Oldham	£450,000
Roger Nilsson	Stavanger	Sheff Utd	£400,000
Ian Pearce	Chelsea	Blackburn	£300,000
Danny Wallace	Man Utd	Birmingham	£250,000
Julian Darby	Bolton	Coventry	£150,000
Ally Pickering	Rotherham	Coventry	£80,000
Mike Jeffrey	Doncaster	Newcastle	*£60,000
Nathan Peel	Sheff Utd	Burnley	£60,000
Adam Poric	St George, Australia	Sheff Wed	£60,000
Carl Shutt	Leeds	Birmingham	£50,000
David Roche	Newcastle	Doncaster	swap
Mo Johnston	Everton	Hearts	free
Peter Reid	N/c	Southampton	free
Emeko Izeugo	Nigeria	Oldham	trial
Carl Veart	Australia	Everton	trial

plus swap involving David Roche
N/c = non-contract player

NOVEMBER 1993

Player	From	To	Fee
Tim Flowers	Southampton	Blackburn	£2,400,000
Gordon Durie	Tottenham	Rangers	£1,200,000
Sean McCarthy	Bradford	Oldham	£500,000
Patrik Andersson	Blackburn	B.Monchengladbach	£400,000
Dave Beasant	Chelsea	Southampton	£300,000
Keith Scott	Wycombe	Swindon	£300,000
John Pemberton	Sheff Utd	Leeds	£250,000
Mark Robson	West Ham	Charlton	£125,000
Mickey Hazard	Swindon	Tottenham	£50,000
Neil Tolson	Oldham	Bradford	£50,000
Bobby Davison	Leicester	Sheff Utd	free
Johnny Hansen	Ajax	Newcastle	trial
Martin McIntosh	Clydebank	Oldham	trial
Guiseppe Morisco	Messina	Sheff Wed	trial
Soren Frederiksen	Viborg	Southampton	trial

DECEMBER 1993

Player	From	To	Fee
David White	Man City	Leeds	swap*
David Rocastle	Leeds	Man City	swap*
Tony Dobson	Blackburn	Portsmouth	£150,000
Alex Bunbury	West Ham	S Maritimo	£50,000
Glenn Cockerill	Southampton	Leyton Orient	free
Simon Oliver	Leeds	Halifax	free
Ben Price	Havant	Sheff Utd	trial

* valued at £2,000,000

JANUARY 1994

Player	From	To	Fee
Brett Angell	Southend	Everton	£500,000
Liam O'Brien	Newcastle	Tranmere	£300,000
Simon Coleman	Derby	Sheffield Wed	£250,000
Darren Ferguson	Man Utd	Wolves	£250,000
Ronny Rosenthal	Liverpool	Tottenham	£250,000
Sandy Robertson	Rangers	Coventry	£250,000
Steve Livingstone	Chelsea	Grimsby	£140,000
Chris Holland	Preston	Newcastle	£100,000
David Barnes	Sheffield Utd	Watford	£50,000
Lee Martin	Man Utd	Celtic	tribunal
Gerry Creaney	Celtic	Everton	trial
Ralf Hassenhuttl	Rapid Vienna	Chelsea	trial

FEBRUARY 1994

Player	From	To	Fee
Ruel Fox	Norwich	Newcastle	£2,250,000
Kevin Scott	Newcastle	Tottenham	£850,000
Jim Magilton	Oxford	Southampton	£650,000
Willie Falconer	Sheff Utd	Celtic	£350,000
Nathan Blake	Cardiff	Sheff Utd	£300,000
Neil Adams	Oldham	Norwich	£250,000
Craig Maskell	Swindon	Southampton	£250,000
Gary Rowett	Cambridge	Everton	*£200,000
Damian Matthew	Chelsea	Crystal Palace	£150,000
Gordon Cowans	Aston Villa	Derby	£80,000
Paul Moody	Southampton	Oxford	**£60,000
Ryan Anderson	Portsmouth	Tottenham	trial
Terry Hurlock	Southampton	Millwall	trial
Niels Jorgensen	Aalborg	QPR	trial
Dragan Lukovic	Red Star Belgrade	West Ham	trial
Michael Stensgard	Denmark	Everton	trial
Joel Swain	Arsenal	Brighton	trial
Mark Walton	Norwich	Dundee	trial

Terry Gibson	Wimbledon	Barnet	free
Gerry Peyton	West Ham	Japan	free
* rising to £300,000	** rising to £100,000		

MARCH 1994

Player	From	To	Fee
Darren Peacock	QPR	Newcastle	£2,750,000
Anders Limpar	Arsenal	Everton	£1,600,000
Peter Beagrie	Everton	Man City	£1,100,000
Joe Parkinson	Bournemouth	Everton	£800,000
Neil Heaney	Arsenal	Southampton	£300,000
Marcus Gayle	Brentford	Wimbledon	£250,000
Greg Berry	Wimbledon	Millwall	£200,000
Colin Foster	West Ham	Watford	£100,000
Clive Allen	West Ham	Millwall	£75,000
Steve Whitton	Ipswich	Colchester	£10,000
Michael Basham	West Ham	Swansea	undisclosed
Mickey Adams	Southampton	Stoke	free
Mitchell Thomas	West Ham	Luton	free

FA PREMIER LEAGUE CLUBS
PLAYER LOANS 1993-94

AUGUST 1993

Player	From	To
Tony Barness	Chelsea	Middlesbrough
Matthew Bound	Southampton	Hull
Kerry Dixon	Southampton	Luton
Chris Lambert	Reading	Blackburn
Lee Power	Norwich	Sunderland
Carl Shutt	Leeds	Birmingham
Mark Walton	Norwich	Wrexham

SEPTEMBER 1993

Player	From	To
Brian Borrows	Coventry	Bristol City
Nick Colgan	Chelsea	Crewe
Tony Dobson	Blackburn	Portsmouth
Keith Gillespie	Man Utd	Wigan
Steve Harkness	Liverpool	Huddersfield
Nigel Jemson	Sheff Wed	Grimsby
Phil Jones	Liverpool	Crewe
Steve Livingstone	Chelsea	Port Vale
Paul Mahorn	Tottenham	Fulham
Chris Makin	Oldham	Preston
John Reed	Sheffield Utd	Mansfield
Mike Small	West Ham	Wolves

OCTOBER 1993

Player	From	To
Dennis Bailey	QPR	Charlton
Chris Boden	Aston Villa	Barnsley
Tom Cowan	Sheff Utd	Stoke
Paul Dickov	Arsenal	Luton
Mark Flatts	Arsenal	Cambridge
Robert Herrera	QPR	Fulham
Lance Key	Sheff Wed	Oldham
Phil King	Sheff Wed	Notts Co
Steve Livingstone	Chelsea	Grimsby
Lee Power	Norwich	Portsmouth
Neil Whitworth	Man Utd	Rotherham
Daniel Williamson	West Ham	Doncaster

NOVEMBER 1993

Player	From	To
Matt Appleby	Oldham	Bradford
Andy Barlow	Oldham	Bradford
Mike Basham	West Ham	Colchester
Simon Coleman	Derby	Sheff Wed
Martin Davies	Coventry	Stafford
Matt Dickens	Blackburn	Lincoln
John Gannon	Sheff Utd	Middlesbrough
Leigh Jenkinson	Coventry	Birmingham
Chris Marsden	Huddersfield	Coventry
Alan McCarthy	QPR	Watford
Martin McIntosh	Clydebank	Sheff Wed
Carl Muggleton	Leicester	Sheff Utd
Michael Oakes	Aston Villa	Scarborough
Zeke Rowe	Chelsea	Barnet
Mitchell Thomas	West Ham	Luton
Gary Walsh	Man Utd	Oldham
Dave Walton	Sheff Utd	Shrewsbury
Paul Williams	Coventry	West Bromwich

DECEMBER 1993

Player	From	To
Brian Croft	QPR	Shrewsbury
Simon Davies	Man Utd	Exeter
Mark Flatts	Arsenal	Brighton
Robert Fleck	Chelsea	Bolton
Martyn Margetson	Man City	Bristol Rovers
Aiden Newhouse	Wimbledon	Tranmere
Carl Shutt	Birmingham	Man City
Neil Whitworth	Man Utd	Blackpool

JANUARY 1994

Player	From	To
Ade Akinbiyi	Norwich	Hereford
Steve Anthrobus	Wimbledon	Port Vale
Graham Fenton	Aston Villa	WBA
Colin Foster	West Ham	Notts County
Stuart Kerr	Celtic	Swindon
Aidan Newhouse	Wimbledon	Port Vale
Matthew Rush	West Ham	Swansea
Jon Sheffield	Cambridge	Swindon
Paul Stewart	Liverpool	Crystal Palace
Mark Warren	Leyton Orient	West Ham

FEBRUARY 1994

Player	From	To
Kevin Brock	Newcastle	Cardiff
Mark Gayle	Crewe	Liverpool
Neil Gregory	Ipswich	Colchester
Gary Kelly	Bury	West Ham
Pal Lydersen	Arsenal	Start
Martyn Margetson	Man City	Bolton
Frank McAvennie	Celtic	Swindon
Alan McCarthy	QPR	Plymouth
Lee Williams	Aston Villa	Peterborough
Tony Witter	QPR	Reading

MARCH 1994

Player	From	To
Kevin Ashley	Wolves	Norwich
Dennis Bailey	QPR	Watford
Joeren Boere	West Ham	Portsmouth
David Carmichael	Coventry	Nuneaton
Jimmy Carter	Arsenal	Oxford
Tom Cowan	Sheffield Utd	Huddersfield
Danny Dichio	QPR	Barnet
Paul Dickov	Arsenal	Brighton
Terry Jones	Everton	Northwich
Scott Marshall	Arsenal	Oxford
Paul McGee	Wimbledon	Peterborough
Michael Oakes	Aston Villa	Tranmere
Brian Reid	Rangers	Newcastle
Mark Walters	Liverpool	Stoke
Mark Ward	Everton	Birmingham
Kevin Watson	Tottenham	Brentford

A-Z
FA Premier League Players
1994-95

1994-95 FA Premier League Players

ABLETT Gary — Everton

Full Name: ABLETT, Gary Ian   DOB: 19/11/65, Liverpool
FAPL Debut: Home v Sheffield Wednesday 15/8/92
Debut Goal: Away v Southampton 14/8/93

Previous Club Details

Club	Signed	Fee	Apps Lge	FLC	FAC	Goals Lge	FLC	FAC
Liverpool	11/83	–	103+6	10+1	16+2	1		
Derby County	1/85	Loan	3+3					
Hull City	9/86	Loan	5					
Everton	1/92	£750,000	88	11	4	2		

FA Premier Lge Record

Everton	92/93-93/94		71			1		

ADAMS Tony — Arsenal

Full Name: ADAMS, Anthony   DOB: 10/10/66, Romford
FAPL Debut: Home v Norwich City 15/8/92   Debut Goal:
England International Debut: Away v Spain 18/2/87

Previous Club Details

Club	Signed	Fee	Apps Lge	FLC	FAC	Goals Lge	FLC	FAC
Arsenal	1/84	–	248+1	33+1	18	20	2	1

FA Premier Lge Record

Arsenal	92/94		74			0		

ADAMS Micky — Southampton

Full Name: ADAMS, Michael Richard   DOB: 8/11/61, Sheffield
FAPL Debut: Home v Tottenham Hotspur 15/8/92
Debut Goal: Home v Aston Villa 22/8/92

Previous Club Details

Club	Signed	Fee	Apps Lge	FLC	FAC	Goals Lge	FLC	FAC
Gillingham	11/79	–	85+7	5	6	5		
Coventry City	7/83	£75,000	85+5	9	7	9	1	
Leeds United	1/87	£110,000	72+1	4	6	2		1
Southampton	3/89	£250,000	141+3	16	7	7		
Stoke City	3/94	Loan	10			3		

FA Premier Lge Record

Southampton	92/93-93/94		55+2			4		

† denotes as substitute

ADAMS Neil   Norwich City
Full Name: ADAMS, Neil James   DOB: 23/11/65, Stoke
FAPL Debut: Home v Nottingham Forest 22/8/92
Debut Goal: Home v Nottingham Forest 22/8/92

Previous Club Details			*Apps*			*Goals*		
Club	Signed	Fee	Lge	FLC	FAC	Lge	FLC	FAC
Stoke City	6/85	–	31+1	3	1	4		
Everton	6/86	£150,000	17+3	4+1				1
Oldham Ath	1/89	Loan	9					
Oldham Ath	6/89	£100,000	93+36	13+2	10+2	23	1	2
Norwich City	2/94	£250,000	11+2					
FA Premier Lge Record								
Oldham Ath	92/93-93/94		33+12			9		
Norwich City	93/94		11+2			0		

AGNEW Steve   Leicester City
Full Name: AGNEW, Steve   DOB: 9/11/65, Shipley

Previous Club Details			*App*			*Goals*		
Club	Signed	Fee	Lge	FLC	FAC	Lge	FLC	FAC
Barnsley	11/83	–	186+8	13	20	30	3	4
Blackburn Rov	6/91	£700,000	2	2				
Portsmouth	11/92	Loan	3+2					
Leicester City	2/93	£250,000	45	3	1	4		

AKINBIYI Ade   Norwich City
Full Name: AKINBIYI, Adeola Peter   DOB: 10/10/74, Hackney
FAPL Debut: Home v QPR † 12/3/94   Debut Goal:

Previous Club Details			*App*			*Goals*		
Club	Signed	Fee	Lge	FLC	FAC	Lge	FLC	FAC
Norwich City	2/93	–	0+2					
FA Premier Lge Record								
Norwich City	93/94		0+2			0		

ALLEN Bradley   Queens Park Rangers
Full Name: ALLEN, Bradley James   DOB: 13/9/71, Romford
FAPL Debut: Away v Norwich City † 17/10/92
Debut Goal: Away v Norwich City 17/10/92

Previous Club Details			*Apps*			*Goals*		
Club	Signed	Fee	Lge	FLC	FAC	Lge	FLC	FAC
QPR	9/88	–	49+19	4+2	1	24	4	
FA Premier Lge Record								
QPR	92/93-93/94		34+11			17		

ALLEN Malcolm   Newcastle United
Full Name: ALLEN, Malcolm   DOB: 21/3/67, Carnarvon
FAPL Debut: Home v Tottenham Hotspur 14/8/93
Debut Goal: Home v Everton 25/8/93

Previous Club Details

Club	Signed	Fee	Apps Lge	FLC	FAC	Goals Lge	FLC	FAC
Watford	3/85	–	27+12	4+1	6+8	5	2	6
Aston Villa	9/87	Loan	4					
Norwich City	8/88	£175,000	24+11	0+3	5	8		7
Millwall	3/90	£400,000	64+17	7	0+1	24	2	
Newcastle Utd	8/93	£300,000	9	3		5	2	

FA Premier Lge Record

Newcastle Utd	93/94		9			5		

ALLEN Martin   West Ham United

Full Name: ALLEN, Martin   DOB: 18/8/65, Reading
FAPL Debut: Home v Wimbledon 14/8/93
Debut Goal: Away v Aston Villa 15/1/94

Previous Club Details

Club	Signed	Fee	Apps Lge	FLC	FAC	Goals Lge	FLC	FAC
QPR	6/83	–	128+8	15+3	9	16	1	1
West Ham Utd	8/89	£660,000	133+24	12+2	13	22	5	3

FA Premier Lge Record

West Ham Utd	93/94		19+6			6		

ALLEN Paul   Southampton

Full Name: ALLEN, Paul Kevin   DOB: 28/8/62, Aveley
FAPL Debut: Away v Southampton 15/8/92
Debut Goal: Home v Everton 5/9/92

Previous Club Details

Club	Signed	Fee	Apps Lge	FLC	FAC	Goals Lge	FLC	FAC
West Ham Utd	8/79	–	149+3	20+4	15+3	6	2	3
Tottenham H	6/85	£400,000	276+17	42+8	22+1	23	4	1
Southampton	9/93	£550,000	28+3	2	2	1		

FA Premier Lge Record

Tottenham H	92/93-93/94		38+1			3		
Southampton	93/94		29+3			1		

ALLEN Peter   Southampton

Full Name: ALLEN, Peter   DOB:
FAPL Debut: Home v Manchester City † 1/5/93 Debut Goal:

Previous Club Details

Club	Signed	Fee	Apps Lge	FLC	FAC	Goals Lge	FLC	FAC
Southampton		–	0+1					

FA Premier Lge Record

Southampton	92/93		0+1			0		

ANDERTON Darren   Tottenham Hotspur

Full Name: ANDERTON, Darren Robert   DOB: 3/3/72, Southampton
FAPL Debut: Away v Southampton 15/8/92

Debut Goal: Home v Southampton 7/2/93
England International Debut: Home v Denmark 9/3/94

Previous Club Details

Club	Signed	Fee	Lge	FLC	FAC	Lge	FLC	FAC
			Apps			Goals		
Portsmouth	2/90	–	53+9	3+2	7	7	1	5
Tottenham H	5/92	£1.75m	66+4	7	7+1	12	1	1

FA Premier Lge Record

Tottenham H	92/93-93/94		66+4			12		

ANDREWS Ian   Southampton
Full Name: ANDREWS, Ian   DOB: 1/12/64, Nottingham
FAPL Debut: Home v Everton 14/9/93   Debut Goal:

Previous Club Details

Club	Signed	Fee	Lge	FLC	FAC	Lge	FLC	FAC
			Apps			Goals		
Leicester City	12/82		126	6	7			
Swindon Town	1/84	Loan	1					
Celtic	7/88	£300,000						
Leeds United	12/88	Loan	1					
Southampton	12/89	£200,000	10					

FA Premier Lge Record

Southampton	93/94		5			0		

ANGELL Brett   Everton
Full Name: ANGELL, Brett   DOB: 20/8/68, Marlborough
FAPL Debut: Home v Norwich City † 25/9/93
Debut Goal: Home v Chelsea 5/2/94

Previous Club Details

Club	Signed	Fee	Lge	FLC	FAC	Lge	FLC	FAC
			Apps			Goals		
Derby County	2/88	£40,000						
Stockport Co	10/88	£33,000	60+10	3	3	28		1
Southend Utd	8/90	£100,000	109+6	7	3+	47	4	2
Everton	9/93	Loan						
Everton	1/94	£500,000	13+3			1		

FA Premier Lge Record

Everton	93/94		13+3			1		

ANTHROBUS Steve   Wimbledon
Full Name: ANTHROBUS, Steven   DOB: 10/11/68, Lewisham
FAPL Debut: Home v Coventry City 22/8/92   Debut Goal:

Previous Club Details

Club	Signed	Fee	Lge	FLC	FAC	Lge	FLC	FAC
			Apps			Goals		
Millwall	8/86		19+2	3		4		
Wimbledon	2/90	£150,000	27+1	1	2			

FA Premier Lge Record

Wimbledon	92/93		4+1			0		

APPLEBY Matthew   Newcastle United

Full Name: APPLEBY, Matthew   DOB: 16/4/72, Middlesbrough
FAPL Debut: Home v Coventry City   Debut Goal:

Previous Club Details		*Apps*			*Goals*		
Club	Signed Fee	Lge	FLC	FAC	Lge	FLC	FAC
Newcastle Utd	5/90 –	15+1	1				

FA Premier Lge Record

Newcastle Utd	92/93	1			0		

ARDLEY Neal   Wimbledon

Full Name: ARDLEY, Neal Christopher   DOB: 1/9/72, Epsom
FAPL Debut: Home v Arsenal † 5/9/92
Debut Goal: Home v Blackburn Rovers 19/9/92

Previous Club Details		*Apps*			*Goals*		
Club	Signed Fee	Lge	FLC	FAC	Lge	FLC	FAC
Wimbledon	7/91 –	46+5	6+1	6	5	2	

FA Premier Lge Record

Wimbledon	92/93-93/94	38+4			5		

ARMSTRONG Chris   Crystal Palace

Full Name: ARMSTRONG, Christopher P   DOB: 19/6/71, Newcastle
FAPL Debut: Away v Manchester United 2/9/92
Debut Goal: Home v Oldham Athletic 12/9/92

Previous Club Details		*Apps*			Goals		
Club	Signed Fee	Lge	FLC	FAC	Lge	FLC	FA
Wrexham	3/89 –	40+20	2+1	0+1	13		
Millwall	8/91 £50,000	11+17	3+1	0+1	5	2	
Crystal Palace	9/92 £1m	78	3	1	38		

FA Premier Lge Record

Crystal Palace	92/93	35			15		

ATHERTON Peter   Sheffield Wednesday

Full Name: ATHERTON, Peter   DOB: 6/4/70, Orrell
FAPL Debut: Home v Middlesbrough 15/8/92   Debut Goal:

Previous Club Details		*Apps*			*Goals*		
Club	Signed Fee	Lge	FLC	FAC	Lge	FLC	FAC
Wigan Athletic	2/88 –	145+4	8	7	1		
Coventry City	8/91 £300,000	112+1	4	2			
Sheffield Wed	6/94 Trib						

FA Premier Lge Record

Sheffield Wed	92/93-93/94	77+1			0		

ATKINS Mark · Blackburn Rovers

Full Name: ATKINS, Mark Nigel   DOB: 14/9/68, Doncaster
FAPL Debut: Away v Crystal Palace 15/8/92
Debut Goal: Away v Coventry City 29/8/92

Previous Club Details			*Apps*			*Goals*		
Club	Signed	Fee	Lge	FLC	FAC	Lge	FLC	FAC
Scunthorpe Utd	7/86	–	45+5	3+1	5	2		
Blackburn Rov	6/88	£45,000	192+24	17+4	9+3	28	4	

FA Premier Lge Record

Blackburn Rov	92/93-93/94		30+13			5		

ATKINSON Dalian · Aston Villa

Full Name: ATKINSON, Dalian Robert   DOB: 21/3/68, Shrewsbury
FAPL Debut: Away v Ipswich Town 15/8/92
Debut Goal: Away v Ipswich Town 15/8/92

Previous Club Details			*Apps*			*Goals*		
Club	Signed	Fee	Lge	FLC	FAC	Lge	FLC	FAC
Ipswich Town	6/85	–	49+11	5+1	–	18	3	
Sheff Wed	7/87	£450,000	38	3	2	10	3	1
Real Sociedad	8/90	£1.7m						
Aston Villa	7/91	£1.6m	68+3	13	8	20	8	

FA Premier Lge Record

Aston Villa	92/93-93/94		57			19		

AUSTIN Dean · Tottenham Hotspur

Full Name: AUSTIN, Dean Barry   DOB: 26/4/70, Hemel Hempstead
FAPL Debut: Home v Crystal Palace † 22/8/92   Debut Goal:

Previous Club Details			*Apps*			*Goals*		
Club	Signed	Fee	Lge	FLC	FAC	Lge	FLC	FAC
Southend Utd	3/90	£12,000	96	4	2	2		
Tottenham H	5/92	£375,000	52+4	2+2	7			

FA Premier Lge Record

Tottenham H	92/93-93/94		52+4			0		

BABB Phil · Coventry City

Full Name: BABB, Phillip   DOB: 30/11/70, London
FAPL Debut: Home v Middlesbrough † 15/8/92
Debut Goal: Away v Arsenal 14/8/93
Eire International Debut: Home v Russia 23/3/94

Previous Club Details			*Apps*			*Goals*		
Club	Signed	Fee	Lge	FLC	FAC	Lge	FLC	FAC
Bradford City	8/90		73+7	5+1	3	14		
Coventry City	7/92	£500,000	66+7	5	2	3	1	

FA Premier Lge Record

Coventry City	92/93-93/94		66+7			3		

BAILEY Dennis — Queens Park Rangers

Full Name: BAILEY, Dennis Lincoln   DOB: 13/12/65, Lambeth
FAPL Debut: Away v Manchester City 17/8/92
Debut Goal: Home v Sheffield United 22/8/92

Previous Club Details

Club	Signed	Fee	Lge	FLC	FAC	Lge	FLC	FAC
			Apps			Goals		
Crystal Palace	12/87	310,000	0+5			1		
Bristol Rovers	2/89	Loan	17			9		
Birmingham C	8/89	£80,000	65+10	6	6	23	2	
Bristol Rovers	3/91	Loan	6			1		
QPR	6/91	£175,000	22+7	5	1+1	10	3	
Charlton Ath	10/93	Loan	0+4					
Watford	3/94	Loan	2+6					

FA Premier Lge Record

QPR	92/93		13+2			1		

BAKER Clive — Ipswich Town

Full Name: BAKER, Clive   DOB: 14/3/59, N Walsham
FAPL Debut: Home v Sheffield United † 26/9/92 Debut Goal:

Previous Club Details

Club	Signed	Fee	Lge	FLC	FAC	Lge	FLC	FAC
			Apps			Goals		
Norwich City	7/77		14		2			
Barnsley	8/84	Free	291	15	23			
Coventry City	8/91	Free			0+1			
Ipswich Town	8/92	Free	45+1	5	4			

FA Premier Lge Record

Ipswich Town	92/93-93/94		45+1			0		

BANGER Nicky — Southampton

Full Name: BANGER, Nicholas Lee   DOB: 25/4/71, Southampton
FAPL Debut: Home v Middlesbrough † 29/8/92
Debut Goal: Home v Middlesbrough 29/8/92

Previous Club Details

Club	Signed	Fee	Lge	FLC	FAC	Lge	FLC	FAC
			Apps			Goals		
Southampton	4/89	–	14+36	1+2	0+1	6	3	

FA Premier Lge Record

Southampton	92/93-93/94		14+26			6		

BARDSLEY David — Queens Park Rangers

Full Name: BARDSLEY, David John   DOB: 11/9/64, Manchester
FAPL Debut: Away v Manchester City 17/8/92
Debut Goal: Home v Southampton 19/8/92
Eire International Debut: Home v Russia 23/3/94

Previous Club Details

Club	Signed	Fee	Lge	FLC	FAC	Lge	FLC	FAC
			Apps			Goals		
Blackpool	11/82	–	45	2	2	1		

Watford	11/83	£150,000	97+3	6		13+1	7	1	1
Oxford United	9/87	£265,000	74	12		5	7		
QPR	9/89	£500,000	182	15		13	3		
FA Premier Lge Record									
QPR	92/93-93/94		72				3		

BARKER Simon   Queens Park Rangers
Full Name: BARKER, Simon   DOB: 4/11/64, Farnworth
FAPL Debut: Home v Sheffield United 22/8/92
Debut Goal: Home v Sheffield United 22/8/92

Previous Club Details			*Apps*			*Goals*		
Club	Signed	Fee	Lge	FLC	FAC	Lge	FLC	FAC
Blackburn Rov	11/82	–	180+2	11	12	35	4	
QPR	7/88	£400,000	107+15	13+2	13+1	11	3	2
FA Premier Lge Record								
QPR	92/93		21+4			1		

BARLOW Stuart   Everton
Full Name: BARLOW, Stuart   DOB: 16/7/68, Liverpool
FAPL Debut: Away v Tottenham Hotspur † 5/9/92
Debut Goal: Away v QPR 28/12/92

Previous Club Details			*Apps*			*Goals*		
Club	Signed	Fee	Lge	FLC	FAC	Lge	FLC	FAC
Everton	6/90	–	17+39	2+5	2+2	8	1	2
Rotherham Utd	1/92	Loan						
FA Premier Lge Record· .								
Everton	92/93-93/94		14+33			8		

BARMBY Nicky   Tottenham Hotspur
Full Name: BARMBY, Nicholas Jonathan   DOB: 11/2/74, Hull
FAPL Debut: Away v Sheffield Wednesday 27/9/92
Debut Goal: Home v Middlesbrough 17/10/92

Previous Club Details			*Apps*			*Goals*		
Club	Signed	Fee	Lge	FLC	FAC	Lge	FLC	FAC
Tottenham H	2/91	–	36+8	5+1	6+1	11	4	1
FA Premier Lge Record								
Tottenham H	92/93-93/94		36+8			11		

BARNARD Darren   Chelsea
Full Name: BARNARD, Darren Sean   DOB: 30/11/71, Germany
FAPL Debut: Away v Coventry City 24/10/92
Debut Goal: Home v Middlesbrough 3/4/93

Previous Club Details			*Apps*			*Goals*		
Club	Signed	Fee	Lge	FLC	FAC	Lge	FLC	FAC
Chelsea	7/90	£50,000	18+11	1+1	1+1	2		

BARNES John   Liverpool
Full Name: BARNES, John   DOB: 7/11/63, Jamaica, West Indies
FAPL Debut: Away v QPR † 23/11/92
Debut Goal: Home v Aston Villa 9/1/92
England International Debut: Away v Ireland † 28/5/83

Previous Club Details			*Apps*			*Goals*		
Club	Signed	Fee	Lge	FLC	FAC	Lge	FLC	FAC
Watford	7/81	–	232+1	21	31	65	7	11
Liverpool	6/87	£900,000	201+3	14	36	70	2	14

FA Premier Lge Record
Liverpool   92/93-93/94   48+1   8

BARNESS Tony   Chelsea
Full Name: BARNESS, Tony   DOB: 25/2/73, Lewisham, London
FAPL Debut: Home v Norwich City 12/9/92   Debut Goal:

Previous Club Details			*Apps*			*Goals*		
Club	Signed	Fee	Lge	FLC	FAC	Lge	FLC	FAC
Charlton Ath	3/91	–	21+6	2	3	1		
Chelsea	9/92	£350,000	2					

FA Premier Lge Record
Chelsea   92/93   2   0

BARRETT Earl   Aston Villa
Full Name: BARRETT, Earl Delisser   DOB: 28/4/67, Rochdale
FAPL Debut: Away v Ipswich Town 15/8/92
Debut Goal: Home v Everton 20/2/93
England International Debut: Away v New Zealand 3/6/91

Previous Club Details			*Apps*			*Goals*		
Club	Signed	Fee	Lge	FLC	FAC	Lge	FLC	FAC
Manchester C	4/85	–	2+1	1				
Chester City	3/86	Loan	12					
Oldham Ath	11/87	£35,000	181+2	20	14	7	1	1
Aston Villa	2/92	£1.7m	103+2	12	3	1	1	

FA Premier Lge Record
Aston Villa   92/93-93/94   80   1

BARTLETT Neal   Southampton
Full Name: BARTLETT, Neil   DOB: 7/4/75, Southampton
FAPL Debut: Home v Manchester City † 1/5/93 ‾‾ ‾‾‾ ‾

Previous Club Details   *Apps*   *Goals*
Club   Signed Fee   Lge   FLC FAC   Lge FLC FAC
Southampton   7/93   –   4+4   0+4
FA Premier Lge Record
Southampton   92/93   4+4   0

BARTON Warren   **Wimbledon**
Full Name: BARTON, Warren Dean   DOB: 19/3/69, Stoke Newington
FAPL Debut: Away v Leeds United 15/8/92
Debut Goal: Away v Leeds United 15/8/92

Previous Club Details   *Apps*   *Goals*
Club   Signed Fee   Lge   FLC FAC   Lge FLC FAC
Maidstone Utd   7/87   £10,000 41+1   0+2 3   1
Wimbledon   6/90   £300,000 138+2 13   8   48   1
FA Premier Lge Record
Wimbledon   92/93-93/94   59+2   4

BART–WILLIAMS Chris   **Sheffield Wednesday**
Full Name: BART–WILLIAMS, Christopher Gerald
DOB: 16/6/74, Sierra Leone
FAPL Debut: Away v Everton † 15/8/92
Debut Goal: Home v Coventry City 2/9/92

Previous Club Details   *Apps*   *Goals*
Club   Signed Fee   Lge   FLC FAC   Lge FLC FAC
Leyton Orient   7/91   –   34+2   4   2
Sheffield Wed   11/91   £275,000 63+23 6+6 5+3   15   2   1
FA Premier Lge Record
Sheffield Wed   92/93-93/94   50+20   15

BATTY David   **Blackburn Rovers**
Full Name: BATTY, David   DOB: 12/12/68, Leeds
FAPL Debut: Home v Wimbledon 15/8/92
Debut Goal: Home v Middlesbrough 30/1/93
England International Debut: Away v Spain † 9/9/93

Previous Club Details   *Apps*   *Goals*
Club   Signed Fee   Lge   FLC FAC   Lge FLC FAC
Leeds United   7/87   –   201+10 17 12   4
Blackburn Rov   10/93   £2.5m   26   2   4
FA Premier Lge Record
Leeds United   92/93- 93/94   38+1   0
Blackburn Rov   93/94   26   0

BEAGRIE Peter   **Manchester City**
Full Name: BEAGRIE, Peter Sydney DOB: 29/11/65, Middlesbrough
FAPL Debut: Home v Sheffield Wednesday 15/8/92
Debut Goal: Home v Coventry City 17/10/92

Previous Club Details			Apps			Goals		
Club	Signed	Fee	Lge	FLC	FAC	Lge	FLC	FAC
Middlesbrough	9/83	–	24+8	1		2		
Sheffield Wed	8/86	£35,000	81+3	5	5	11		
Stoke City	6/88	£210,000	54	4	3	7		1
Everton	11/89	£750,000	88+61	7+2	2	11	3	1
Sunderland	9/91	Loan	5					
Manchester C	3/94	£1.1m	8		1			
FA Premier Lge Record								
Everton	92/93- 93/94		40+11			6		
Manchester C	93/94		9			1		

BEARDSLEY Peter   Newcastle United
Full Name: BEARDSLEY, Peter Andrew   DOB: 18/1/61, Newcastle
FAPL Debut: Home v Sheffield Wednesday 15/8/92
Debut Goal: Away v Manchester United 19/8/92
England International Debut: Away v Egypt † 29/1/86

Previous Club Details			Apps			Goals		
Club	Signed	Fee	Lge	FLC	FAC	Lge	FLC	FAC
Carlisle Utd	8/79	–	93+11	6+1	15	2		7
Vancouver (US)	4/81	£275,000						
Manchester Utd	9/82	£300,000	1					
Vancouver (US)	9/83	–						
Newcastle Utd	9/83	£150,000	146+1	10	6	61		
Liverpool	7/87	£1.9m	120+11	13+1	22+3	46	1	11
Everton	8/91	£1m	42	4	2	15	3	1
Newcastle Utd	6/93	£1.4m	34	3	3	20	1	1
FA Premier Lge Record								
Everton	92/93		39			10		
Newcastle Utd	93/94		35			21		

BEASANT Dave   Southampton
Full Name: BEASANT, David John   DOB: 20/3/59, Willesden
FAPL Debut: Home v Oldham Athletic 15/8/92   Debut Goal:
England International Debut: Home v Italy † 15/11/89

Previous Club Details			Apps			Goals		
Club	Signed	Fee	Lge	FLC	FAC	Lge	FLC	FAC
Wimbledon	8/79	£1,000	340	21	27			
Newcastle Utd	6/88	£800,000	20	2	2			
Chelsea	1/89	£725,000	133	11	5			
Grimsby Town	10/92	Loan	6					
Wolves	1/93	Loan	4	1				
Southampton	11/93	£300,000	24		2			
FA Premier Lge Record								
Chelsea	92/93		17			0		
Southampton	93/94		25			0		

BEAUCHAMP Joe   West Ham United

Full Name: BEAUCHAMP, Joseph   DOB: 13/3/71, Oxford

Previous Club Details

Club	Signed	Fee	Lge	FLC	FAC	Lge	FLC	FAC
			Apps			*Goals*		
Oxford United	5/89	–	117+7	6+1	8	17	2	3
Swansea City	10/91	Loan	5			2		
West Ham Utd	6/94							

BEENEY Mark   Leeds United

Full Name: BEENEY, Mark   DOB: 30/12/67, Tunbridge Wells

FAPL Debut: Away v Coventry City 8/5/93   Debut Goal:

Previous Club Details

Club	Signed	Fee	Lge	FLC	FAC	Lge	FLC	FAC
			Apps			*Goals*		
Gillingham	8/86	–	2	1				
Maidstone Utd	2/87	–	50	3	11			
Aldershot	3/90	Loan	7					
Brighton	391	£30,000	68+1	6	7			
Leeds United	4/93	£350,000	23	2	3			

FA Premier Lge Record

Leeds United	92/93-93/94		23			0		

BEINLICH Stefan   Aston Villa

Full Name: BEINLICH, Stefan   DOB: 13/1/72, Berlin, Germany

FAPL Debut: Away v Coventry † 26/12/92

Debut Goal: Home v Sheffield Wednesday 8/12/93

Previous Club Details

Club	Signed	Fee	Lge	FLC	FAC	Lge	FLC	FAC
			Apps			*Goals*		
Bergmann B		–						
Aston Villa	10/91	£100,000	6+9			1		

FA Premier Lge Record

Aston Villa	92/93-93/94		6+7			1		

BENALI Francis   Southampton

Full Name: BENALI, Francis Vincent   DOB: 10/12/68, Southampton

FAPL Debut: Home v Tottenham Hotspur 15/8/92   Debut Goal:

Previous Club Details

Club	Signed	Fee	Lge	FLC	FAC	Lge	FLC	FAC
			Apps			*Goals*		
Southampton	12/86	–	118+19	10+6	2			

FA Premier Lge Record

Southampton	92/93-93/94		64+5			0		

BENNETT Frank   Southampton

Full Name: BENNETT, Frank   DOB: 3/1/69, Birmingham

FAPL Debut: Home v Everton †14/8/93

Debut Goal: Home v Chelsea 27/12/93

BERESFORD John   Newcastle United

Full Name: BERESFORD, John   DOB: 4/9/66, Sheffield
FAPL Debut: Home v Tottenham Hotspur 14/8/93

Previous Club Details

Club	Signed	Fee	Lge	FLC	FAC	Lge	FLC	FAC
			Apps			*Goals*		
Manchester C	9/83	–						
Barnsley	8/86	Free	79+9	5+2	5	5	2	1
Portsmouth	3/89	£300,000	102+5	12	11	8	2	
Newcastle Utd	6/92	£650,000	73	7	7			

FA Premier Lge Record

| Newcastle Utd | 93/94 | | 32 | | | 0 | | |

BERG Henning   Blackburn Rovers

Name: BERG, Henning   DOB: 1/9/69, Eidsvell
FAPL Debut: Home v Crystal Palace † 2/2/93
Debut Goal: Home v Chelsea 14/8/93
Norway International Debut: v Faeroe Islands 13/5/92

Previous Club Details

Club	Signed	Fee	Lge	FLC	FAC	Lge	FLC	FAC
			Apps			*Goals*		
KFMU Oslo, Valerengen, Lillestrom (all Norwegian)								
Blackburn Rov	12/92	£400,000	39+5	5	4	1		

FA Premier Lge Record

| Blackburn Rov | 92/93-93/94 | | 39+5 | | | 1 | | |

BISHOP Ian   West Ham United

Full Name: BISHOP, Ian   DOB: 29/5/65, Liverpool
FAPL Debut: Home v Swindon Town 11/9/93
Debut Goal: Away v Sheffield United 28/3/94

Previous Club Details

Club	Signed	Fee	Lge	FLC	FAC	Lge	FLC	FAC
			Apps			*Goals*		
Everton	6/83	–	0+1					
Crewe Alex	3/84	Loan	4					
Carlisle United	10/84	£15,000	131+1	8	5	14	1	1
Bournemouth	7/88	£35,000	44	4	5	2		
Manchester C	8/88	£465,000	18+1	4		2	1	
West Ham Utd	12/89	Exchange	144+11	10	14+1	9		2

FA Premier Lge Record

| West Ham Utd | 93/94 | | 36 | | | 1 | | |

BJORNEBYE Stig Inge

Liverpool

Full Name: BJORNEBYE, Stig Inge   DOB:
FAPL Debut: Away v Coventry City 19/12/92
Debut Goal:

Previous Club Details			Apps			Goals		
Club	Signed	Fee	Lge	FLC	FAC	Lge	FLC	FAC
Rosenborg (Nor)								
Liverpool	12/.92		17+3		2			
FA Premier Lge Record								
Liverpool	92-93/93-94		17+3		2			

BLACK Kingsley

Nottingham Forest

Full Name: BLACK, Kingsley   DOB: 22/6/68, Luton
FAPL Debut: Home v Liverpool 16/8/92
Debut Goal: Home v Middlesbrough 21/10/93
N Ireland International Debut Home v France † 27/4/88

Previous Club Details			App			Goals		
Club	Signed	Fee	Lge	FLC	FAC	Lge	FLC	FAC
Luton Town	7/86	–	123+4	16+2	5+1	25	1	2
Nottingham F	9/91	£1.5m	74+11	17+1	4	10	5	
FA Premier Lge Record								
Nottingham F	92/93		19+5			5		

BLACKWELL Dean

Wimbledon

Full Name: BLACKWELL, Dean Robert   DOB: 15/12/69, Camden
FAPL Debut: Away v Leeds United † 15/8/92 Debut Goal:

Previous Club Details			Apps			Goals		
Club	Signed	Fee	Lge	FLC	FAC	Lge	FLC	FAC
Wimbledon	7/88	–	66+16	3	7+1	1		
Plymouth Arg	3/90	Loan	5+2					
FA Premier Lge Record								
Wimbledon	92/93-93/94		34+6			0		

BLAKE Mark

Leicester City

Full Name: BLAKE, Mark   DOB: 16/12/70, Nottingham
FAPL Debut: Away v Middlesbrough † 26/9/92 Debut Goal:

Previous Club Details			App			Goals		
Club	Signed	Fee	Lge	FLC	FAC	Lge	FLC	FAC
Aston Villa	7/89	–	26+5	1+1	2	2		
Wolves	1/91	Loan	2					
Portsmouth		£600,000	15					
Leicester City	3/93	£360,000	10+1			1		
FA Premier Lge Record								
Aston Villa	92/93		0+1			0		

BLATHERWICK Steve   Nottingham Forest
Full Name: BLATHERWICK, Steven   DOB: 20/9/73, Nottingham

Previous Club details			*App*			*Goals*		
Club	Signed	Fee	Lge	FLC	FAC	Lge	FLC	FAC
Nottingham F		–	3					
Wycombe W	2/94	Loan	2					

BLISSETT Gary   Wimbledon
Name: BLISSETT, Gary   DOB: 26/6/64, Manchester

Previous Club Details			*Apps*			*Goals*		
Club	Signed	Fee	Lge	FLC	FAC	Lge	FLC	FAC
Crewe Alex	8/83	–	112+10	9	4	39	3	
Brentford	3/87	£60,000	220+13	16+3	14	79	9	7
Wimbledon	8/93	£350,000	6+11	0+2	1+1	3		
FA Premier Lge Record								
Wimbledon	92/93- 93/94		6+11			3		

BOERE Jeroem   West Ham United
Full Name: BOERE, Jeroem   DOB:
FAPL Debut: Away v Newcastle United † 25/9/93

Previous Club Details			*Apps*			*Goals*		
Club	Signed	Fee	Lge	FLC	FAC	Lge	FLC	FAC
Go Ahead Eag								
West Ham	9/93		0+4	0+1				
Fulham	3/94	Loan	4+1					
FA Premier Lge Record ·								
West Ham Utd	93/94		0+4			0		

BOHINEN Lars   Nottingham Forest
Full Name: BOHINEN, Lars   DOB: 8/9/69, Norway
Norway International Debut:v Kuwait 25/10/89

Previous Club Details			*App*			*Goals*		
Club	Signed	Fee	Lge	FLC	FAC	Lge	FLC	FAC
Langes, Baerum, Lyn, Valerengen, Lillestrom (all Norwegian)								
Nottingham F	10/93	£450,000	22+1	2+1	1	1		

BOLAND Willie   Coventry City
Full Name: BOLAND, Willie   DOB: 6/8/75, Eire
FAPL Debut: Away v Chelsea † 1/5/93   Debut Goal:

Previous Club Details			*Apps*			*Goals*		
Club	Signed	Fee	Lge	FLC	FAC	Lge	FLC	FAC
Coventry City	11/92	–	23+4	3				
FA Premier Lge Record								
Coventry City	92/93- 93/94		23+4			0		

BOOTY Martyn   Coventry City
Full Name: BOOTY, Martyn   DOB: 30/5/71, Kirby Muxloe
FAPL Debut: Away v Manchester City 27/8/93 Debut Goal:

Previous Club Details   *Apps*   *Goals*
Club	Signed	Fee	Lge	FLC	FAC	Lge	FLC	FAC
Coventry City	5/89	–	4+1	2	2			

FA Premier Lge Record
| Coventry City | 93/94 | | 2 | | | 0 | | |

BORROWS Brian   Coventry City
Full Name: BORROWS, Brian   DOB: 20/12/60, Liverpool
FAPL Debut: Away v Sheffield Wednesday † 2/9/92
Debut Goal: Home v Liverpool 19/12/92

Previous Club Details   *Apps*   *Goals*
Club	Signed	Fee	Lge	FLC	FAC	Lge	FLC	FAC
Everton	4/80	–	27	2				
Bolton W	3/83	£10,000	95	7	4			
Coventry City	6/85	£80,000	325+4	34	18	11	1	
Bristol City	9/93	Load	6					

FA Premier Lge Record
| Coventry City | 92/93- 93/94 | | 64+2 | | | 2 | | |

BOSNICH Mark   Aston Villa
Full Name: BOSNICH, Mark John   DOB: 13/1/72, Sydney, Aus
FAPL Debut: Away v Sheffield Wednesday 5/12/92 Debut Goal:
Australia International

Previous Club Details   *Apps*   *Goals*
Club	Signed	Fee	Lge	FLC	FAC	Lge	FLC	FAC
Manchester U	6/89	–	3					
Sydney	8/91	–						
Croatia (Aus)								
Aston Villa	2/92	–	45	7+1	4			

FA Premier Lge Record
| Aston Villa | 92/93- 93/94 | | 44 | | | 0 | | |

BOULD Steve   Arsenal
Full Name: BOULD, Stephen Andrew   DOB: 16/11/62, Stoke
FAPL Debut: Home v Norwich City 15/8/92
Debut Goal: Home v Norwich City 15/8/92
England International Debut: Home v Greece 17/5/94

Previous Club Details   *Apps*   *Goals*
Club	Signed	Fee	Lge	FLC	FAC	Lge	FLC	FAC
Stoke City	11/80	–	179+4	13	10	6	1	
Torquay Utd	10/82	Loan	9		2			
Arsenal	6/89	£390,000	153+7	17	16	5		

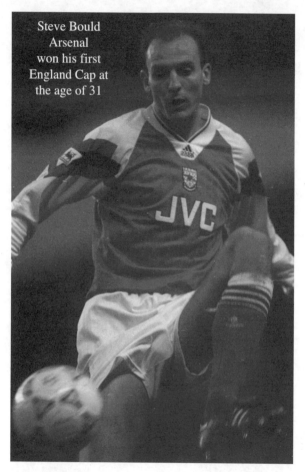

Steve Bould
Arsenal
won his first
England Cap at
the age of 31

FA Premier Lge Record
Arsenal   92/93- 93/94   46+2   1

BOUND Matthew   Southampton
Full Name: BOUND, Matthew Terence   DOB: 9/11/72, Melksham
FAPL Debut: Home v Blackburn Rovers † 9/3/93   Debut Goal:
Previous Club Details   *Apps*   *Goals*
Club   Signed Fee   Lge   FLC FAC   Lge FLC FAC
Southampton 5/91   –   2+3
FA Premier Lge Record
Southampton 92/93- 93/94   2+2   0

BOWEN Mark   Norwich City
Full Name: BOWEN, Mark Rosslyn   DOB: 7/12/63, Neath
FAPL Debut: Away v Arsenal †15/8/92
Debut Goal: Home v QPR 17/10/92
Wales International Debut: Away v Canada 10/5/86
Previous Club Details   *Apps*   *Goals*
Club   Signed Fee   Lge   FLC FAC   Lge FLC FAC
Tottenham H 12/81   –   14+3   3   2
Norwich City 7/87   £90,000 250+2 23 21   20   1   1
FA Premier Lge Record
Norwich City 92/93- 93/94   84   6

BOWMAN Robert   Leeds United
Full Name: BOWMAN, Robert   DOB: 6/8/75, Durham
FAPL Debut: Away v Wimbledon † 6/2/93   Debut Goal:
Previous Club Details   *Apps*   *Goals*
Club   Signed Fee   Lge   FLC FAC   Lge FLC FAC
Leeds United 11/92   3+1
FA Premier Lge Record
Leeds United 92/93   3+1   0

BOWRY Robert   Crystal Palace
Full Name: BOWRY, Robert   DOB: 19/5/71, Hampstead
FAPL Debut: Home v Sheffield United 5/12/93
Debut Goal: Home v Aston Villa 10/2/93
Previous Club Details   *Apps*   *Goals*
Club   Signed Fee   Lge   FLC FAC   Lge FLC FAC
QPR   8/90   –
Crystal Palace 4/92 Free   23+9   7   1   1
FA Premier Lge Record
Crystal Palace 92/93   6+5   0

BRACEWELL Paul   Newcastle United
Full Name: BRACEWELL, Paul   DOB: 19/7/62, Heswall,Cheshire

FAPL Debut: Home v TottenhamHotspur 14/8/93
Debut Goal: Home v Aston Villa 23/2/94
England International Debut: Away v West Germany †12/6/85

Previous Club Details

Club	Signed	Fee	Apps Lge	FLC	FAC	Goals Lge	FLC	FAC
Stoke City	2/80	–	123+6	6	6	5	1	
Sunderland	7/83	£250,000	38	4	2	4		
Everton	5/84	£425,000	95	11	19+2	7	2	
Sunderland	9/89	£250,000	112+1	9	10	2		
Newcastle Utd	6/92	£250,000	51+12	3	3+2	3		

FA Premier Lge Record

Newcastle Utd	93/94		32			1		

BREACKER Tim   West Ham United
Full Name: BREACKER, Tim   DOB: 2/7/65, Bicester
FAPL Debut: Home v Wimbledon 14/8/93   Debut Goal:

Previous Club Details

Club	Signed	Fee	Apps Lge	FLC	FAC	Goals Lge	FLC	FAC
Luton Town	5/83	–	204+6	22+2	21	3		
West Ham Utd	10/90	£600,000	134	8	19	8		

FA Premier Lge Record

West Ham Utd	93/94		40			3		

BREITKREUTZ Matthias   Aston Villa
Full Name: BREITKREUTZ, Matthias   DOB: 12/5/71, Berlin, Germany
FAPL Debut: Away v Manchester City † 19/12/92 Debut Goal:

Previous Club Details

Club	Signed	Fee	Apps Lge	FLC	FAC	Goals Lge	FLC	FAC
Bergmann B								
Aston Villa	10/91	£100,000	10+3	0+1				

FA Premier Lge Record

Aston Villa	92/93-93/94		3+2			0		

BREVETT Rufus   Queens Park Rangers
Full Name: BREVETT, Rufus Emanuel   DOB: 24/9/69, Derby
FAPL Debut: Away v Manchester United 26/9/92   Debut Goal:

Previous Club Details

Club	Signed	Fee	Apps Lge	FLC	FAC	Goals Lge	FLC	FAC
Doncaster Rov	6/88	–	106+3	5	4	3		
QPR	2/91	£250,000	32+6	2+1	1			

FA Premier Lge Record

QPR	92/93-93/94		16+5			0		

BRIGHT Mark   Sheffield Wednesday
Full Name: BRIGHT, Mark Abraham   DOB: 6/6/62, Stoke

FAPL Debut: Home v Blackburn Rovers 15/8/92
Debut Goal: Home v Blackburn Rovers 15/8/92

Previous Club Details			Apps			Goals		
Club	Signed	Fee	Lge	FLC	FAC	Lge	FLC	FAC
Port Vale	10/81	–	18+11	1+1	0+1	10		1
Leicester City	7/84	£33,000	26+16	3+1	1	6		
Crystal Palace	11/86	£75,000	219+3	22	13+1	88	11	2
Sheffield Wed	9/92	£375,000	63+6	14	9	30	8	5
FA Premier Lge Record								
Crystal Palace	92/93		5			0		
Sheffield Wed	92/93-93/94		63+6			30		

BRIGHTWELL David   Manchester City
Full Name: BRIGHTWELL, David John   DOB: 7/1/71, Lutterworth
FAPL Debut: Away v Coventry City † 21/11/92
Debut Goal: Home v Newcastle United 9/4/94

Previous Club Details			Apps			Goals		
Club	Signed	Fee	Lge	FLC	FAC	Lge	FLC	FAC
Manchester C	4/88	–	26+8	2+1	1	1		
Chester City	3/91	Loan	6					
FA Premier Lge Record								
Manchester C	92/93-93/94		23+7			1		

BRIGHTWELL Ian   Manchester City
Full Name: BRIGHTWELL, Ian Robert   DOB: 9/4/68, Lutterworth
FAPL Debut: Home v QPR 17/8/92
Debut Goal: Home v Leeds United 7/11/92

Previous Club Details			Apps			Goals		
Club	Signed	Fee	Lge	FLC	FAC	Lge	FLC	FAC
Manchester C	5/85	–	174+29	13+2	9+5	16		1
FA Premier Lge Record								
Manchester C	92/93-93/94		26+1			1		

BRISCOE Lee   Sheffield Wednesday
Full Name: BRISOE, Lee   DOB: 3/11/71, Tobago, West Indies
FAPL Debut: Away v Tottenham Hotspur † 5/2/94

Previous Club Details			Apps			Goals		
Club	Signed	Fee	Lge	FLC	FAC	Lge	FLC	FAC
Sheffield Wed			0+1					
FA Premier Lge Record								
Sheffield Wed	93/94		0+1			0		

BROWN Kenny — West Ham United

Full Name: BROWN, Kenny
DOB: 11/7/67, Barking
FAPL Debut: Away v Newcastle United 25/9/93

Previous Club Details

Club	Signed	Fee	Apps Lge	FLC	FAC	Goals Lge	FLC	FAC
Norwich City	7/85	–	24+1					
Plymouth Arg	8/88	–	126	9	6	4		
West Ham Utd	8/91	£175,000	44+7	1	7+1	5		

FA Premier Lge Record

West Ham Utd	93/94		6+3			0		

BROWN Richard — Blackburn Rovers

Full Name: BROWN, Richard Anthony
DOB: 13/1/67, Nottingham
FAPL Debut: Home v Norwich City 3/10/92
Debut Goal:

Previous Club Details

Club	Signed	Fee	Apps Lge	FLC	FAC	Goals Lge	FLC	FAC
Sheffield Wed	12/84	£10,000						
Blackburn Rov	9/90	£15,000	26+2	1+1	2			
Maidstone Utd	2/91	Loan	3					

FA Premier Lge Record

Blackburn Rov	92/93		2			0		

BRUCE Steve — Manchester United

Full Name: BRUCE, Stephen Roger
DOB: 31/12/60, Corbridge
FAPL Debut: Away v Sheffield United 15/8/93
Debut Goal: Home v Leeds United 6/9/93

Previous Club Details

Club	Signed	Fee	Apps Lge	FLC	FAC	Goals Lge	FLC	FAC
Gillingham	10/78	–	203+2	15	14	29	6	1
Norwich City	8/84	£125,000	141	20	9	14	5	1
Manchester U	12/87	£800,000	243	30+1	1	34	6	1

FA Premier Lge Record

Manchester U	92/93-93/94		82			8		

BULL Gary — Nottingham Forest

Full Name: BULL, Gary
DOB: 12/6/66, Tipton

Previous Club Details

Club	Signed	Fee	App Lge	FLC	FAC	Goals Lge	FLC	FAC
Cambridge Utd	3/88	–	13+6	0+1		4		
Barnet	3/89	£2,000	83	4	11	37	4	3
Nottingham F	7/93	Free	3+8	2	0+2			

BURLEY Craig — Chelsea

Full Name: BURLEY, Craig William
DOB: 24/9/71, Irvine
FAPL Debut: Away v Tottenham Hotspur 5/12/92

Debut Goal: Home v Everton 3/1/94

Previous Club Details			Apps			Goals		
Club	Signed	Fee	Lge	FLC	FAC	Lge	FLC	FAC
Chelsea	9/89	–	26+8	1	8	3		3

FA Premier Lge Record

Chelsea	92/93- 93/94		20+5			3		

BURROWS David   West Ham United
Full Name: BURROWS, David   DOB: 25/10/68, Dudley
FAPL Debut: Away v Nottingham Forest 16/8/92
Debut Goal: Home v Coventry City 11/12/93

Previous Club Details			Apps			Goals		
Club	Signed	Fee	Lge	FLC	FAC	Lge	FLC	FAC
West Brom Alb	10/86	–	37+9	3+1	2	1		
Liverpool	10/88	£550,000	135+11	16	16+1	3		
West Ham Utd	9/93	Swap	24	3	2	1	1	

FA Premier Lge Record

Liverpool	92/93		29+1			2		
West Ham Utd	93/94		25			1		

BUSST David   Coventry City
Full Name: BUSST, David John   DOB: 30/6/67, Birmingham
FAPL Debut: Away v Norwich City 16/1/93   Debut Goal: –

Previous Club Details			Apps			Goals		
Club	Signed	Fee	Lge	FLC	FAC	Lge	FLC	FAC
Coventry City	1/92	–	12+1	0+1	0+1			

FA Premier Lge Record

Coventry City	92/93-93/94		12+1			0		

BUTLER Peter   West Ham United
Full Name: BUTLER, Peter   DOB: 26/8/66, Halifax
FAPL Debut: Home v Wimbledon 14/8/93
Debut Goal: Home v Norwich City 25/10/92

Previous Club Details			Apps			Goals		
Club	Signed	Fee	Lge	FLC	FAC	Lge	FLC	FAC
Huddersfield T	8/84	–	0+5					
Cambridge Utd	1/86	Loan	14		1			
Bury	7/86	–	9+2	2	1	1		
Cambridge Utd	12/86	–	55	4	2	9		
Southend Utd	2/88	–	135+7	12	2	9	1	
Huddersfield T	3/92	Loan	7					
West Ham Utd	8/92	£170,000	64	4	2	3		

FA Premier Lge Record

West Ham Utd	93/94		26			1		

BUTT Nicky   Manchester United

Full Name: BUTT, Nicky   DOB: 21/1/75, Manchester
FAPL Debut: Home v Oldham Athletic† 21/11/92 Debut Goal:

Previous Club Details			Apps			Goals		
Club	Signed	Fee	Lge	FLC	FAC	Lge	FLC	FAC
Manchester U	1/93	–	0+2		0+1			
FA Premier Lge Record								
Manchester U	92/93-93/94		0+2			0		

BUTTERWORTH Ian   Norwich City

Full Name: BUTTERWORTH, Ian Stuart   DOB: 25/1/64, Crewe
FAPL Debut: Away v Arsenal 15/8/92
Debut Goal: Away v Liverpool 25/10/92

Previous Club Details			Apps			Goals		
Club	Signed	Fee	Lge	FLC	FAC	Lge	FLC	FAC
Coventry City	8/81	–	80+10	5	5+1	10		
Nottingham F	6/85	£250,000	26+1	6	1			
Norwich City	9/86	Loan	4					
Norwich City	12/86	£160,000	226+5	17+1	25		4	
FA Premier Lge Record								
Norwich City	92/93-93/94		49+2			0		

CALDERWOOD Colin   Tottenham Hotspur

Full Name: Calderwood, Colin   DOB: 20/1/65, Stranraer
FAPL Debut: Away v Newcastle United 14/8/93

Previous Club Details			Apps			Goals		
Club	Signed	Fee	Lge	FLC	FAC	Lge	FLC	FAC
Mansfield T	3/82	–	97+3	4	6	1		1
Swindon Town	7/85	£30.000	328+2	35	17	20		1
Tottenham H	7/93	£1.25m	26	5	3			
FA Premier Lge Record								
Tottenham H	93/94		26			0		

CAMPBELL Kevin   Arsenal

Full Name: CAMPBELL, Kevin Joseph   DOB: 4/2/70, Lambeth
FAPL Debut: Home v Norwich City 15/8/92
Debut Goal: Home v Norwich City 15/8/92

Previous Club Details			Apps			Goals		
Club	Signed	Fee	Lge	FLC	FAC	Lge	FLC	FAC
Arsenal	2/88	–	105+28	9+10	12+7	42	5	1
Leyton Orient	1/89	Loan	16			9		
Leicester City	11/89	Loan	11			5		
FA Premier Lge Record								
Arsenal	92/93-93/94		61+5			18		

CAMPBELL Sol — Tottenham Hotspur

Full Name: CAMPBELL, Sulzeer
DOB: 18/9/74, Newham, London
FAPL Debut: Home v Chelsea † 5/12/92
Debut Goal:

Previous Club Details

Club	Signed	Fee	Apps Lge	FLC	FAC	Goals Lge	FLC	FAC
Tottenham H	9/92	–	27+8	5	1+2		1	

FA Premier Lge Record

Tottenham H	92/93-93/94		27+8			0		

CANTONA Eric — Manchester United

Full Name: CANTONA, Eric
DOB: 24/5/66, Paris, France
FAPL Debut: Home v Wimbledon 15/8/92
Debut Goal: Away v Middlesbrough 22/8/92
French International

Previous Club Details

Club	Signed	Fee	Apps Lge	FLC	FAC	Goals Lge	FLC	FAC
Nimes (Fra)								
Leeds United	2/92	£900,000	12+1	1		6		
Manchester United	11/92	£1.2m	54+1	5	6	27	1	4

FA Premier Lge Record

Leeds United	92/93		12+1			6		
Manchester U	92/93-93/94		54+1			27		

CAREY Brian — Leicester City

Full Name: CAREY, Brian
DOB: 31/5/68, Cork

Previous Club Details

Club	Signed	Fee	App Lge	FLC	FAC	Goals Lge	FLC	FAC
Manchester U	9/89	£100,000						
Wrexham	1/91	Loan	3					
Wrexham	12/91	Loan	13		3	1		
Leicester City	7/93	£250,000	1	0+1				

CARR Stephen — Tottenham Hotspur

Full Name: CARR, Stephen
DOB:
FAPL Debut: Away v Ipswich Town 26/9/93
Debut Goal:

Previous Club Details

Club	Signed	Fee	Apps Lge	FLC	FAC	Goals Lge	FLC	FAC
Tottenham H	–		1	1				

FA Premier Lge Record

Tottenham H	93/94		1			0		

CARTER Jimmy — Arsenal

Full Name: CARTER, James William Charles
DOB: 9/11/65, Hammersmith

FAPL Debut: Away v Blackburn Rovers 18/8/92
Debut Goal: Home v Southampton 20/3/93

Previous Club Details

Club	Signed	Fee	Apps Lge	FLC	FAC	Goals Lge	FLC	FAC
QPR	12/85	–						
Millwall	3/87	£15,000	99+11	3+1	6+1	11		2
Liverpool	1/91	£800,000	2+3			2		
Arsenal	10/91	£500,000	16+6	1	2	2		1
Oxford United	3/94	Loan	5					

FA Premier Lge Record

Arsenal	92/93		11+5			2		

CASCARINO Tony   Chelsea
Full Name: CASCARINO, Anthony Guy   DOB: 1/9/62, Orpington
FAPL Debut: Away v Blackburn Rovers 21/2/93
Debut Goal: Home v Tottenham Hotspur 20/3/93
Eire International Debut: Away v Switzerland 11/9/85

Previous Club Details

Club	Signed	Fee	Apps Lge	FLC	FAC	Goals Lge	FLC	FAC
Gillingham	1/82	–	209+10	18	15+2	78	11	9
Millwall	6/87	£200,000	105	10	8	42	1	2
Aston Villa	3/90	£1.5m	43+3	2+1	2	11	1	
Celtic	7/91	£1.1m						
Chelsea	2/92	£750,000	35+5	1	3+1	8		

FA Premier Lge Record

Chelsea	92/93-93/94		24+5			6		

CASKEY Darren   Tottenham Hotspur
Full Name: CASKEY, Darren   DOB: 21/8/74, Basildon
FAPL Debut: Home v Arsenal †16/8/93
Debut Goal: Home v Everton 3/10/93

Previous Club Details

Club	Signed	Fee	Apps Lge	FLC	FAC	Goals Lge	FLC	FAC
Tottenham H	3/92	–	16+8	3+1	3	4	1	

FA Premier Lge Record

Tottenham Hotspur	93/94		16+8			4		

CASTLEDINE Stewart   Wimbledon
Full Name: CASTLEDINE, Stewart   DOB: 22/1/73, Wandsworth
FAPL Debut: Home v QPR † 27/9/93
Debut Goal: Away v Sheffield Wednesday 16/10/93

Previous Club Details

Club	Signed	Fee	Apps Lge	FLC	FAC	Goals Lge	FLC	FAC
Wimbledon	7/91	–	3+2	1				

CHARLTON Simon   Southampton

Name: CHARLTON, Simon   DOB: 25/10/71, Huddersfield
FAPL Debut: Home v Everton 14/8/93
Debut Goal: Home v Chelsea 27/12/93

Previous Club Details   *Apps*   *Goals*

Club	Signed	Fee	Lge	FLC	FAC	Lge	FLC	FAC
Huddersfield T	7/89		121+3	9	10	1	1	
Southampton	8/93	£250,000	28+4	1	1	1		

FA Premier Lge Record

Southampton	93/94	29+4		1

CHETTLE Steve   Nottingham Forest

Full Name: CHETTE, Steven   DOB: 27/9/68, Nottingham
FAPL Debut: Home v Liverpool 16/8/92   Debut Goal:

Previous Club Details   *App*   *Goals*

Club	Signed	Fee	Lge	FLC	FAC	Lge	FLC	FAC
Nottingham F	8/86	–	202+6	32+3	22+1	7	1	

FA Premier Lge Record

Nottingham F	92/93	30		0

CLARK Lee   Newcastle United

Full Name: CLARK, Lee   DOB: 27/10/72, Wallsend
FAPL Debut: Home v Tottenham Hotspur 14/8/93
Debut Goal: Away v Swindon Town 18/9/93

Previous Club Details   *Apps*   *Goals*

Club	Signed	Fee	Lge	FLC	FAC	Lge	FLC	FAC
Newcastle Utd	11/89		103+10	10	9	19		

FA Premier Lge Record

Newcastle Utd	93/94	29		2

CLARKE Andy   Wimbledon

Full Name: CLARKE, Andrew Weston   DOB: 22/7/67, Islington
FAPL Debut: Away v Leeds United 15/8/92
Debut Goal: Home v Aston Villa 3/10/92

Previous Club Details   *Apps*   *Goals*

Club	Signed	Fee	Lge	FLC	FAC	Lge	FLC	FAC
Non-League								
Wimbledon	2/91	£250,000	51+50	7+4	4+1	13	2	

FA Premier Lge Record

Wimbledon	92/93-93/94	31+24		7

CLARKE Steve   Chelsea

Full Name: CLARKE, Stephen   DOB: 29/8/63, Saltcoats
FAPL Debut: Home v Oldham Athletic 15/8/92   Debut Goal:
Scotland International

Previous Club Details			*Apps*			*Goals*		
Club	Signed	Fee	Lge	FLC	FAC	Lge	FLC	FAC
Chelsea	1/87	£422,000	217+4	14	17	6	1	1

FA Premier Lge Record
| Chelsea | 92/93-93/94 | | 56+2 | | | 0 | | |

CLOUGH Nigel   Liverpool

Full Name: CLOUGH, Nigel Howard   DOB: 19/3/66, Sunderland
FAPL Debut: Home v Liverpool 16/8/92
Debut Goal: Away v Norwich City 31/8/92
England International Debut: Home v Chile 23/5/89

Previous Club Details			Apps			Goals		
Club	Signed	Fee	Lge	FLC	FAC	Lge	FLC	FAC
Nottingham F	9/84	–	265+4	41	24	91	21	5
Liverpool	8/93	£2.275m	25+2	2	2	7	1	

FA Premier Lge Record
| Nottingham F | 92/93 | | 42 | | | 10 | | |
| Liverpool | 93/94 | | 25+2 | | | 7 | | |

COATSWORTH Gary   Leicester City

Full Name: COATSWORTH, Gary   DOB: 7/10/68, Sunderland

Previous Club Details			*App*			*Goals*		
Club	Signed	Fee	Lge	FLC	FAC	Lge	FLC	FAC
Barnsley	2/87	–	3+3					
Darlington	7/89	Free	15+7	1+1		2		
Leicester	10/91	£15,000	27+5		1	4		

COLE Andy   Newcastle United

Full Name: COLE, Andrew   DOB: 19/10/71, Nottingham
FAPL Debut: Home v Tottenham Hotspur 14/8/93
Debut Goal: Away v Manchester United 21/8/93

Previous Club Details			*Apps*			*Goals*		
Club	Signed	Fee	Lge	FLC	FAC	Lge	FLC	FAC
Arsenal	10/89		0+1					
Fulham	5/91	Loan						
Bristol City	3/92	£500,000	41			20		
Newcastle Utd	3/93	£1.75m	50+1	2	3	45	6	1

FA Premier Lge Record
| Newcastle Utd | 93/94 | | 40 | | | 34 | | |

COLEMAN Chris   Crystal Palace

Full Name: COLEMAN, Christopher   DOB: 10/6/70, Swansea
FAPL Debut: Home v Blackburn Rovers 15/8/92
Debut Goal: Away v Coventry City 3/12/92

Previous Club Details			*Apps*			*Goals*		
Club	Signed	Fee	Lge	FLC	FAC	Lge	FLC	FAC
Swansea City	9/87	–	159+1	8	13	2		
Crystal Palace	7/91	£275,000	91+11	13+2	2	12	2	
FA Premier Lge Record								
Crystal Palace	92/93		31+7			5		

COLEMAN Simon   Sheffield Wednesday

Full Name: COLEMAN, Simon   DOB: 13/3/68, Worksop
FAPL Debut: Home v Liverpool † 4/12/93
Debut Goal: Away v Tottenham Hotspur 5/2/94

Previous Club Details			*Apps*			*Goals*		
Club	Signed	Fee	Lge	FLC	FAC	Lge	FLC	FAC
Mansfield T	7/85	–	96	9	7	7		
Middlesbrough	9/89	£400,000	51+4		5	2		
Derby County	8/91	£300,000	62+8	5+1	5	2		
Sheffield Wed	1/94	£250,000	10+5	3	2	1		
FA Premier Lge Record								
Sheffield Wed	93/94		10+5			1		

COLLYMORE Stan   Nottingham Forest

Full Name: COLLYMORE, Stanley   DOB: 22/1/71, Stone
FAPL Debut: Home v Southampton † 26/9/92   Debut Goal:

Previous Club Details			*App*			*Goals*		
Club	Signed	Fee	Lge	FLC	FAC	Lge	FLC	FAC
Crystal Palace	1/91	£100,000	4+16	2+3		1		
Southend Utd	11/92	£100,000	30		3	15		3
Nottingham F	7/93	£2.1m	27+1	5		19	5	
FA Premier Lge Record								
Crystal Palace	92/93		0+2			0		

COOPER Colin   Nottingham Forest

Full Name: COOPER, Colin   DOB: 28/2/67, Durham

Previous Club Details			*App*			*Goals*		
Club	Signed	Fee	Lge	FLC	FAC	Lge	FLC	FAC
Middlesbrough	7/84	–	183+6	18	13	6		
Millwall	7/91	£300,000	77	6	2	6		
Nottingham F	6/93	£1.5m	36+1	4	2	7	1	1

COTON Tony — Manchester City
Full Name: COTON, Anthony Philip   DOB: 19/5/61, Tamworth
FAPL Debut: Home v QPR 17/8/92   Debut Goal:

Previous Club Details

Club	Signed	Fee	Lge	FLC	FAC	Lge	FLC	FAC
			Apps			*Goals*		
Birmingham C	10,78	–	94	10	10			
Watford	9/84	£300,000	233	18	32			
Manchester C	7/90	£1m	141	15	10			

FA Premier Lge Record

Manchester C	92/93-93/94	71				0		

COTTEE Tony — Everton
Full Name: COTTEE, Anthony   DOB: 11/7/65, West Ham
FAPL Debut: Away v Blackburn Rovers 15/9/92
Debut Goal: Away v Blackburn Rovers 15/9/92
England International Debut: Away v Sweden † 10/9/86

Previous Club Details

Club	Signed	Fee	Lge	FLC	FAC	Lge	FLC	FAC
			Apps			*Goals*		
West Ham Utd	9/82	–	203+9	19	24	92	14	11
Everton	8/88	£2.3m	157+23	19+4	15+6	72	10	4

FA Premier Lge Record

Everton	92/93-93/94	60+4				28		

CRAMB Colin — Southampton
Name: CRAMB, Colin   DOB: 23/6/74, Lanark
FAPL Debut: Away v Everton † 14/8/93

Previous Club Details

Club	Signed	Fee	Lge	FLC	FAC	Lge	FLC	FAC
			Apps			*Goals*		
Hamilton Acc								
Southampton	8/93	£150,000	0+1					

FA Premier Lge Record

Southampton	93/94	0+1				0		

CROOK Ian — Norwich City
Full Name: CROOK, Ian Stuart   DOB: 18/1/63, Romford
FAPL Debut: Home v Everton † 22/8/92
Debut Goal: Home v Nottingham Forest 31/8/92

Previous Club Details

Club	Signed	Fee	Lge	FLC	FAC	Lge	FLC	FAC
			Apps			*Goals*		
Tottenham H	8/80	–	10+10	1	0+1	1		
Norwich City	6/86	£80,000	221+21	21+4	13+4	14	3	

FA Premier Lge Record

Norwich City	92/93-93/94	70+2				3		

CROSBY Gary
Nottingham Forest

Full Name: CROSBY, Gary
DOB: 8/5/64, Sleaford
FAPL Debut: Home v Liverpool 16/8/92
Debut Goal: Home v QPR 24/2/93

Previous Club Details			App			Goals		
Club	Signed	Fee	Lge	FLC	FAC	Lge	FLC	FAC
Lincoln City	8/86		6+1	2				
Glentoran								
Nottingham F	12/87	£20,000	139+13	29+1	18+4	11	6	3
FA Premier Leg Record								
Nottingham F	92/93		20+3			1		

CROSSLEY Mark
Nottingham Forest

Full Name: CROSSLEY, Mark
DOB: 16/6/69, Barnsley
FAPL Debut: Home v Liverpool 16/8/92
Debut Goal:

Previous Club Details			App			Goals		
Club	Signed	Fee	Lge	FLC	FAC	Lge	FLC	FAC
Nottingham F	7/87	–	157+1	25	20			
FA Premier Lge Record								
Nottingham F	92/93		37			0		

CULVERHOUSE Ian
Norwich City

Full Name: CULVERHOUSE, Ian Brett
DOB: 22/9/64, Bishops Stortford
FAPL Debut: Away v Arsenal 15/8/92
Debut Goal: Home v Everton 21/3/94

Previous Club Details			Apps			Goals		
Club	Signed	Fee	Lge	FLC	FAC	Lge	FLC	FAC
Tottenham H	9/82	–	1+1					
Norwich City	10/85	£50,000	94+1			1		
FA Premier Lge Record								
Norwich City	92/93-93/94		83			1		

CUNDY Jason
Tottenham Hotspur

Full Name: CUNDY, Jason Victor
DOB: 12/11/69, Wandsworth
FAPL Debut: Away v Southampton 15/8/92
Debut Goal: Away v Ipswich Town 30/8/92

Previous Club Details			Apps			Goals		
Club	Signed	Fee	Lge	FLC	FAC	Lge	FLC	FAC
Chelsea	8/88	–	40+1	6	6	2		
Tottenham H	3/92	£750,000	23+2	2		1		
FA Premier Lge Record								
Tottenham H	92/93		23+2			1		

CURLE Keith
Manchester City

Full Name: CURLE, Keith
DOB: 14/11/63, Bristol
FAPL Debut: Home v QPR 17/8/92

Debut Goal: Away v Coventry City 21/11/92
England International Debut: Away v CIS † 29/4/92

Previous Club Details			*Apps*			*Goals*		
Club	Signed	Fee	Lge	FLC	FAC	Lge	FLC	FAC
Bristol Rovers	11/81	–	21+11	3	1	4		
Torquay Utd	11/83	£5,000	16		1	5		1
Bristol City	3/84	£10,000	113+8	7+1	5	1		
Reading	10/87	£150,000	40	8				
Wimbledon	10/88	£500,000	91+2	7	5	3		
Manchester C	8/91	£2.5m	108	12	6	9		
FA Premier Lge Record								
Manchester C	92/93-93/94		68			4		

DARBY Julian   Coventry City
Full Name: DARBY, Julian   DOB: 3/10/67, Bolton
FAPL Debut: Home v Everton 6/11/93
Debut Goal: Away v West Ham United 11/12/93

Previous Club Details			Apps			Goals		
Club	Signed	Fee	Lge	FLC	FAC	Lge	FLC	FAC
Bolton W	7/86	–	258+12	25+	19	36	8	3
Coventry City	10/93	£150,000	24+1		1	5		
FA Premier Lge Record								
Coventry City	93/94		25+1			5		

DAVIS Paul   Arsenal
Full Name: DAVIS, Paul Vincent   DOB: 9/12/61, Dulwich
FAPL Debut: Away v Norwich 3/3/93   Debut Goal:

Previous Club Details			*App*			*Goals*		
Club	Signed	Fee	Lge	FLC	FAC	Lge	FLC	FAC
Arsenal	7/79	–	301+18	42+3	19+5	29	4	3
FA Premier Lge Record								
Arsenal	92/93-93/94		27+1			0		

DEANE Brian   Leeds United
Full Name: DEANE, Brian Christopher   DOB: 7/2/68, Leeds
FAPL Debut: Home v Manchester United 15/8/93
Debut Goal: Home v Manchester United 15/8/93
England International Debut: Away v New Zealand † 10/5/86

Previous Club Details			*App*			*Goals*		
Club	Signed	Fee	Lge	FLC	FAC	Lge	FLC	FAC
Doncaster Rov	12/85		59+7	3	2+1	12		1
Sheffield Utd	7/88	£30,000	156	12	18	68	9	8
Leeds Utd	7/93	£2.7m	40	2	3	9		1
FA Premier Lge Record								
Sheffield Utd	92/93		41			15		
Leeds United	93/94		41			11		

DIBBLE Andy   Manchester City

Full Name: DIBBLE, Andrew Gerald   DOB: 8/5/65, Cwmbran
FAPL Debut: Away v QPR 6/2/93   Debut Goal:
Wales International Debut: Away v Canada †10/5/86

Previous Club Details			Apps			Goals		
Club	Signed	Fee	Lge	FLC	FAC	Lge	FLC	FAC
Cardiff City	8/82	–	62	4	4			
Luton Town	7/84	£125,000	30	4	1			
Sunderland	2/86	Loan	12					
Huddersfield T	2/87	Loan	5					
Manchester C	7/88	£240,000	85+1	7	5+1			
Middlesbrough	2/91	Loan	19					
Bolton W	9/91	Loan	13					
West Brom Alb	2/92	Loan	9					
Oldham Ath	2/93	Loan						

FA Premier Lge Record

Manchester C	92/93-93/94		11+1			0		

DICKOV Paul   Arsenal

Full Name: DICKOV, Paul   DOB: 1/11/72, Livingston
FAPL Debut: Home v Southampton † 20/3/93
Debut Goal: Home v Crystal Palace 8/5/93

Previous Club Details			Apps			Goals		
Club	Signed	Fee	Lge	FLC	FAC	Lge	FLC	FAC
Arsenal	12/90	–	1+3			2		
Luton Town	10/93	Loan	8+7			1		
Brighton	3/10	Loan	8					

FA Premier Lge Record

Arsenal	92/93-93/94		1+3			0		

DICKS Julian   Liverpool

Full Name: DICKS, Julian   DOB: 8/8/68, Bristol
FAPL Debut: Home v Wimbledon 14/8/93
Debut Goal: Away v Everton 18/9/93

Previous Club Details			Apps			Goals		
Club	Signed	Fee	Lge	FLC	FAC	Lge	FLC	FAC
Birmingham C	4/86		83+6	5+1	5	1		
West Ham Utd	3/88	£300,000	159	19	14	29	5	
Liverpool	9/93	£1.6m	23	3	1	3		

FA Premier Lge Record

West Ham Utd	93/94		7			0		
Liverpool	93/94		24			3		

DIXON Lee   Arsenal

Full Name: DIXON, Lee Michael   DOB: 17/3/64, Manchester
FAPL Debut: Home v Norwich City 15/8/92   Debut Goal:
England International Debut: Home v Czechoslovakia 25/4/90

Previous Club Details			Apps			Goals		
Club	Signed	Fee	Lge	FLC	FAC	Lge	FLC	FAC
Burnley	7/82	–	4	1				
Chester City	2/84	–	56+1	2	1	1		
Bury	7/85	–	45	4	8	6		1
Stoke City	7/86	£40,000	71	6	7	5		
Arsenal	1/88	£400,000	211+3	11	11			

FA Premier Lge Record

Arsenal	92/93-93/94		60+1			0		

DOBBS Gerald   Wimbledon

Full Name: DOBBS, Gerald Francis   DOB: 24/1/71, Lambeth
FAPL Debut: Away v Leeds United † 15/8/92
Debut Goal: Home v Sheffield United 20/2/93

Previous Club Details			Apps			Goals		
Club	Signed	Fee	Lge	FLC	FAC	Lge	FLC	FAC
Wimbledon	7/89	–	31+12	2	1+1	1		1

FA Premier Lge Record

Wimbledon	92/93-93/94		19+10			1		

DODD Jason   Southampton

Full Name: DODD, Jason Robert   DOB: 2/11/70, Bath
FAPL Debut: Home v Tottenham Hotspur 15/8/92
Debut Goal: Away v Sheffield Wednesday 13/4/93

Previous Club Details			Apps			Goals		
Club	Signed	Fee	Lge	FLC	FAC	Lge	FLC	FAC
Southampton	3/89	£50,000	95+14	17+1	13	13	1	

FA Premier Lge Record

Southampton	92/93-93/94		32+8			1		

DONAGHY Mal   Chelsea

Full Name: DONAGHY, Malachy   DOB: 13/9/57, Belfast
FAPL Debut: Home v Oldham Athletic 15/8/92
Debut Goal: Away v Leeds United 24/3/93
N Ireland International Debut: Home v Scotland 16/5/80

Previous Club Details			Apps			Goals		
Club	Signed	Fee	Lge	FLC	FAC	Lge	FLC	FAC
Luton Town	6/87	£20,000	410	34	36	2	3	
Manchester U	10/88	£650,000	76+12	9+5	10			
Luton Town	12/89	Loan	5					
Chelsea	8/92	£150,000	63+5	8	1+1	3		

DORIGO Tony   Leeds United
Full Name: DORIGO, Anthony Robert
DOB: 31/1/65, Melbourne, Australia
FAPL Debut: Home v Wimbledon 15/8/92
Debut Goal: Home v Ipswich Town 27/2/93
England International Debut: Home v Yugoslavia †13/12/89

Previous Club Details			*Apps*			*Goals*		
Club	Signed	Fee	Lge	FLC	FAC	Lge	FLC	FAC
Aston Villa	7/83	–	106+5	14+1	7	1		
Chelsea	5/87	£475,000	146	14	4	11		
Leeds United	5/91	£1.3m	108	8	8	4		

FA Premier Lge Record
Leeds United   92/93-93/94   70+1   1

DOW Andy   Chelsea
Full Name: Dow, Andy   DOB: 07/02/73, Dundee
FAPL Debut: Home v Blackburn Rovers 14/8/93

Previous Club Details			*Apps*			*Goals*		
Club	Signed	Fee	Lge	FLC	FAC	Lge	FLC	FAC
Dundee	11/90							
Chelsea	8/93		13+1	2	1			

FA Premier Lge Record
Chelsea   93/94   13+1   0

DOWIE Iain   Southampton
Full Name: DOWIE, Iain   DOB: 9/1/65, Hatfield
FAPL Debut: Away v QPR † 19/8/92
Debut Goal: Away v Crystal Palace 26/9/92
N Ireland International Debut: Home v Norway † 27/3/90

Previous Club Details			*Apps*			*Goals*		
Club	Signed	Fee	Lge	FLC	FAC	Lge	FLC	FAC
Luton Town	12/88	£30,000	53+13	3+1	1+2	15		
Fulham	9/89	Loan	5			1		
West Ham Utd	3/91	£480,000	12			4		
Southampton	9/91	£500,000	97+7	4	2	25		

FA Premier Lge Record
Southampton   92/93-93/94   72+2   16

DOYLE Maurice   Queens Park Rangers
Full Name: DOYLE, Maurice   DOB: 17/10/69, Ellesmere Port
FAPL Debut: Away v Ipswich Town 9/2/93   Debut Goal:

Previous Club Details			Apps			Goals		
Club	Signed	Fee	Lge	FLC	FAC	Lge	FLC	FAC
Crewe Alex	7/88	–	6+2			2		
QPR	4/89	£120,000	6					
Crewe Alex	1/91	Loan	6+1		2	2		
FA Premier Lge Record								
QPR	92/93-93/94		6			0		

DOZZELL Jason   Tottenham Hotspur

Full Name: DOZZELL, Jason Alvin Winans   DOB: 9/12/67, Ipswich
FAPL Debut: Home v Aston Villa 15/8/92
Debut Goal: Home v Liverpool 25/8/92

Previous Club Details			Apps			Goals		
Club	Signed	Fee	Lge	FLC	FAC	Lge	FLC	FAC
Ipswich Town	12/84	–	271+20	22+1	18	45	3	10
Tottenham H	8/93	Tribunal	28+4	4	2	8		1
FA Premier Lge Record								
Ipswich Town	92/93		41			7		
Tottenham H	92/93-93/94		28+4			0		

DUBERRY Michael   Chelsea

Full Name: DUBERRY, Michael Wayne   DOB: 14/10/75, London
FAPL Debut: Home v Coventry City 4/5/94
Debut Goal:

Previous Club Details			Goals			Apps		
Club	Signed	Fee	Lge	FLC	FAC	Lge	FLC	FAC
Chelsea	6/93		1					
FA Premier Lge Record								
Chelsea	93/94		1			0		

DUBLIN Dion   Manchester United

Full Name: DUBLIN, Dion   DOB: 22/4/69, Leicester
FAPL Debut: Away v Sheffield United † 15/8/92
Debut Goal: Away v Southampton 24/8/92

Previous Club Details			App			Goals		
Club	Signed	Fee	Lge	FLC	FAC	Lge	FLC	FAC
Norwich City	3/88	–						
Cambridge Utd	8/88	–	133+23	8+2	21	53	5	11
Manchester U	7/92	£1m	3+8	1+1	1+1	2	1	
FA Premier Lge Record								
Manchester U	92/93-93/94		3+8			2		

DURRANT Lee   Ipswich Town

Full Name: DURRANT, Lee   DOB: 18/12/73, Great Yarmouth
FAPL Debut: Away v Aston Villa 12/3/94   Debut Goal:

Previous Club Details			Apps			Goals		
Club	Signed	Fee	Lge	FLC	FAC	Lge	FLC	FAC
Ipswich Town	7/92	–	3+3					

FA Premier Lge Record

| Ipswich Town | 93/94 | | 3+3 | | | 0 | | |

DYER Bruce   Crystal Palace
Full Name: DYER, Bruce   DOB: 13/4/75, Ilford
FAPL Debut: Debut Goal:

Previous Club Details			Apps			Goals		
Club	Signed	Fee	Lge	FLC	FAC	Lge	FLC	FAC
Watford	4/93	–	29+2	4	1	6	1	
Crystal Palace	3/94	£1.1m	2+9					

EADIE Darren   Norwich City
Full Name: EADIE, Darren   DOB: 10/6/75, Chippenham
FAPL Debut: Away v QPR 18/9/93
Debut Goal: Away v QPR 18/9/93

Previous Club Details			Apps			Goals		
Club	Signed	Fee	Lge	FLC	FAC	Lge	FLC	FAC
Norwich City	2/93	–	9+6	3		3		

FA Premier Lge Record

| Norwich City | 93/94 | | 9+6 | | | 3 | | |

EARLE Robbie   Wimbledon
Full Name: EARLE, Robert Gerald   DOB: 27/1/65, Newcastle-U-Lyme
FAPL Debut: Away v Leeds United 15/8/92
Debut Goal: Home v Arsenal 5/9/92

Previous Club Details			Apps			Goals		
Club	Signed	Fee	Lge	FLC	FAC	Lge	FLC	FAC
Port Vale	7/82	–	284+10	21+2	20+1	77	4	4
Wimbledon	7/91	£775,000	123	12	8	60	3	1

FA Premier Lge Record

| Wimbledon | 92/93-93/94 | | 83 | | | 16 | | |

EBBRELL John   Everton
Full Name: EBBRELL, John Deith   DOB: 1/10/69, Bromborough
FAPL Debut: Home v Sheffield Wednesday 15/8/92
Debut Goal: Away v Blackburn Rovers 15/9/92

Previous Club Details			Apps			Goals		
Club	Signed	Fee	Lge	FLC	FAC	Lge	FLC	FAC
Everton	11/86	–	149+19	16+3+3	3	9	1	2

FA Premier Lge Record

| Everton | 92/93-93/94 | | 62 | | | 5 | | |

EDGEHILL Richard   Manchester City

Full Name: EDGEHILL, Richard   DOB: 23/9/74, Oldham
FAPL Debut: Away v Wimbledon 20/9/93   Debut Goal:

Previous Club Details			*Apps*			*Goals*		
Club	Signed	Fee	Lge	FLC	FAC	Lge	FLC	FAC
Manchester C	7/92	–	20+1	4	1			

FA Premier Lge Record
| Manchester C | 92/93-93/94 | 20+1 | | | 0 | | | |

EDINBURGH Justin   Tottenham Hotspur

Full Name: EDINBURGH, Justin Charles   DOB: 18/12/69, Brentwood
FAPL Debut: Away v Southampton 15/8/92   Debut Goal:

Previous Club Details			*Apps*			*Goals*		
Club	Signed	Fee	Lge	FLC	FAC	Lge	FLC	FAC
Southend Utd	7/88	–	36+1	2+1	2			
Tottenham H	7/90	£150,000	90+5	12+3	8	1		

FA Premier Lge Record
| Tottenham H | 92/93-93/94 | 54+2 | | | 0 | | | |

EHIOGU Ugo   Aston Villa

Full Name: EHIOGU, Ugochuku   DOB: 3/12/72, Hackney
FAPL Debut: Home v Southampton † 22/8/92   Debut Goal:

Previous Club Details			*Apps*			*Goals*		
Club	Signed	Fee	Lge	FLC	FAC	Lge	FLC	FAC
West Brom Alb	7/89	–	0+2					
Aston Villa	7/91	£40,000	18+10	1+1	0+2			

FA Premier Lge Record
| Aston Villa | 92/93-93/94 | 14+7 | | | 0 | | | |

EKOKU Efan   Norwich City

Full Name: EKOKU, Efan   DOB: 8/6/67, Manchester
FAPL Debut: Home v Manchester United † 5/4/93
Debut Goal: Away v Tottenham Hotspur 9/4/93

Previous Club Details			*Apps*			*Goals*		
Club	Signed	Fee	Lge	FLC	FAC	Lge	FLC	FAC
Bournemouth	5/90		53+19	0+2	5+2	20		1
Norwich City	3/93	£500,000	20+10	1	1+1	15	1	

FA Premier Lge Record
| Norwich City | 92/93-93/94 | 20+10 | | | 15 | | | |

ELKINS Gary   Wimbledon

Full Name: ELKINS, Gary   DOB: 4/5/66, Wallingford
FAPL Debut: Away v Leeds United 15/8/92
Debut Goal: Home v Liverpool 4/4/94

Previous Club Details			Apps			Goals		
Club	Signed	Fee	Lge	FLC	FAC	Lge	FLC	FAC
Fulham	12/83	–	100+4	6	2+2	2		
Exeter City	12/89	Loan	5					
Wimbledon	8/90	£20,000	59+4	4	6	2		
FA Premier Lge Record								
Wimbledon	92/93-93/94		34+1			1		

ELLIOT Robert   Newcastle United
Full Name: ELLIOT, Robert   DOB: 25/12/73, Newcastle
FAPL Debut: Away v Oldham Athletic 23/2/94 Debut Goal:

Previous Club Details			Apps			Goals		
Club	Signed	Fee	Lge	FLC	FAC	Lge	FLC	FAC
Newcastle Utd	4/91	–	27+3	1	2			
FA Premier Lge Record								
Newcastle Utd	92/93-93/94		13+2			0		

EUSTACE Scott   Leicester City
Full Name: EUSTACE, Scott   DOB: 3/6/75, Leicester

Previous Club Details			App			Goals		
Club	Signed	Fee	Lge	FLC	FAC	Lge	FLC	FAC
Leicester City	7/93		0+1					

FAIRCLOUGH Chris   Leeds United
Full Name: FAIRCLOUGH, Courtney Huw   DOB: 12/4/64, Nottingham
FAPL Debut: Home v Wimbledon 15/8/92
Debut Goal: Home v Coventry City 31/10/92

Previous Club Details			Apps			Goals		
Club	Signed	Fee	Lge	FLC	FAC	Lge	FLC	FAC
Nottingham F	10/81	–	102+5	9+1	6	1	1	
Tottenham H	6/87	£387,000	60	7	3	5		
Leeds United	3/89	£500,000	185+2	15+2	14+1	21	2	
FA Premier Lge Record								
Leeds United	92/93-93/94		68+1			6		

FARRELL Dave   Aston Villa
Full Name: FARRELL, David William   DOB: 11/11/71, Birmingham
FAPL Debut: Away v Oldham Athletic † 24/10/92 Debut Goal:

Previous Club Details			Apps			Goals		
Club	Signed	Fee	Lge	FLC	FAC	Lge	FLC	FAC
Aston Villa	1/92	£45,000	5+1					
Scunthorpe Utd	1/93	Loan	4+1					
FA Premier Lge Record								
Aston Villa	92/93-93/94		5+1			0		

FASHANU John   Wimbledon

Full Name: FASHANU, John   DOB: 18/9/62, Kensington
FAPL Debut: Home v Manchester City 1/9/92
Debut Goal: Home v Arsenal 5/9/93
England International Debut: Home v Chile 23/5/89

Previous Club Details			*Apps*			*Goals*		
Club	Signed	Fee	Lge	FFC	FAC	Lge	FLC	FAC
Norwich City	10/79	–	6+1			1		
Crystal Palace	8/83	Loan	1	1				
Lincoln City	9/83	–	31+5	2	2+1			
Millwall	11/84	£55,000	50	4	9	12	2	4
Wimbledon	3/86	£125,000	263+5	21+2	27	105	9	11
FA Premier Lge Record								
Wimbledon	92/93-93/94		62+3			17		

FEAR Peter   Wimbledon

Full Name: FEAR, Peter   DOB: 10/9/73, Sutton
F.●PL Debut: Away v Arsenal † 10/2/93
Debut Goal: Home v Leeds United 26/3/94

Previous Club Details			*Apps*			*Goals*		
Club	Signed	Fee	Lge	FLC	FAC	Lge	FLC	FAC
Wimbledon	6/92	–	24+2	2	1	1		
FA Premier Lge Record								
Wimbledon	92/93-93/4		24+2			1		

FENTON Graham   Aston Villa

Full Name: FENTON, Graham   DOB: 22/5/74, Wallsend
FAPL Debut: Home v Manchester City 22/2/94
Debut Goal: Away v Sheffield United 16/4/94

Previous Club Details			Apps			Goals		
Club	Signed	Fee	Lge	FLC	FAC	Lge	FLC	FAC
Aston Villa	3/92	–	9+3	1+1		1		
West BromAlb	1/94	Loan	7			3		
FA Premier Lge Record								
Aston Villa	93/94		9+3			1		

FERDINAND Les   Queens Park Rangers

Full Name: FERDINAND, Leslie   DOB: 18/12/66, Acton
FAPL Debut: Away v Manchester City 17/8/92
Debut Goal: Home v Southampton 19/8/92
England International Debut: Home v San Marino 17/2/93

Previous Club Details			*Apps*			*Goals*		
Club	Signed	Fee	Lge	FLC	FAC	Lge	FLC	FAC
QPR	4/87	£15,000	114+11	8+3	3+1	56	4	2
Brentford	3/88	Loan	3					

Besiktas (Tur)   6/88   Loan
FA Premier Lge Record
QPR   92/93-93/94   71+7   36

FITZGERALD Scott   Wimbledon
Full Name: FITZGERALD, Scott Brian   DOB: 13/8/69, Westminister
FAPL Debut: Away v Leeds United 15/8/92   Debut Goal:

Previous Club Details			*Apps*			*Goals*		
Club	Signed	Fee	Lge	FLC	FAC	Lge	FLC	FAC
Wimbledon	7/87	–	79+6	10	5	1		

FA Premier Lge Record
| Wimbledon | 92/93-93/94 | | 45+3 | | | 0 | | |

FLATTS Mark   Arsenal
Full Name: FLATTS, Mark Michael   DOB: 14/10/72, Islington
FAPL Debut: Away v Sheffield United † 19/9/92 Debut Goal:

Previous Club Details			*Apps*			*Goals*		
Club	Signed	Fee	Lge	FLC	FAC	Lge	FLC	FAC
Arsenal	12/90	–	8+5	1				
Cambridge Utd	10/93	Loan	5+1			1		
Brighton	12/93	Loan	9+1			1		

FA Premier Lge Record
| Arsenal | 92/93-93/94 | | 8+5 | | | 0 | | |

FLECK Robert   Chelsea
Full Name: FLECK, Robert   DOB: 11/8/65, Glasgow
FAPL Debut: Home v Oldham Athletic 15/8/92
Debut Goal: Away v Aston Villa 2/9/92
Scotland International Debut: Home v Argentina 28/3/90

Previous Club Details			*Apps*			*Goals*		
Club	Signed	Fee	Lge	FLC	FAC	Lge	FLC	FAC
Rangers								
Norwich City	12/87	£580,000	130+13	13	13+2	39	11	11
Chelsea	8/92	£2.1m	35+6	7	1	3	1	
Bolton	12/93	Loan	6+1					

FA Premier Lge Record
| Chelsea | 92/93-93/94 | | 35+6 | | | 3 | | |

FLITCROFT Gary   Manchester City
Full Name: FLITCROFT, Gary William   DOB: 6/12/72, Bolton
FAPL Debut: Home v Oldham Athletic † 29/8/92
Debut Goal: Away v Ipswich Town 12/12/92

Previous Club Details			*Apps*			*Goals*		
Club	Signed	Fee	Lge	FLC	FAC	Lge	FLC	FAC
Manchester C	7/91	–	47+5	5+1	6	8		1

Bury	3/92	Loan	12					

FA Premier Lge Record

Manchester C	92/93-93/94	47+5				8		

FLOWERS Tim Blackburn Rovers

Full Name: FLOWERS, Timothy David   DOB: 3/2/67, Kenilworth
FAPL Debut: Home v Tottenham H 15/8/92   Debut Goal:
England International Debut: Away v Brazil 13/6/93

Previous Club Details			*Apps*			*Goals*		
Club	Signed	Fee	Lge	FLC	FAC	Lge	FLC	FAC
Wolves	8/84	–	63	5	2			
Southampton	6/86	£70,000	190	26	16			
Swindon Town	3/87	Loan	2					
Swindon Town	11/87	Loan	5					
Blackburn Rov	11/93	£2.4m	28		4			

FA Premier Lge Record

Southampton	92/93-93/94	54			0			
Blackburn Rov	93/94	29			0			

FLYNN Sean Coventry City

Full Name: FLYNN, Sean Michael   DOB: 13/3/68, Birmingham
FAPL Debut: Home v Middlesbrough † 15/8/92
Debut Goal: Away v Arsenal 14/8/93

Previous Club Details			*Apps*			*Goals*		
Club	Signed	Fee	Lge	FLC	FAC	Lge	FLC	FAC
Halesowen (non-League).								
Coventry City	12/91	£30,000	57+7	2	1	5		

FA Premier Lge Record

Coventry City	92/93-93/94	36+6			3			

FORREST Craig Ipswich Town

Full Name: FORREST, Craig Lorne   DOB: 20/9/67, Vancouver, Canada
FAPL Debut: Home v Aston Villa 15/8/92   Debut Goal:
Canadian International

Previous Club Details			*Apps*			*Goals*		
Club	Signed	Fee	Lge	FLC	FAC	Lge	FLC	FAC
Ipswich Town	8/85	–	199	5	5			
Colchester Utd	3/88	Loan	11					

FA Premier Lge Record

Ipswich Town	92/93-93/94	37			0			

FORRESTER Jamie Leeds United

Full Name: FORRESTER, Jamie   DOB: 1/11/74, Bradford
FAPL Debut: Away v Nottingham Forest † 21/3/93   Debut Goal:

Previous Club Details			Apps			Goals		
Club	Signed	Fee	Lge	FLC	FAC	Lge	FLC	FAC
Auxerre (Fra)								
Leeds United	10/92	£120,000(jt)	7+6		1+1			2

FA Premier Lge Record

| Leeds United | 92/93-93/94 | | 7+6 | | | 0 | | |

FOSTER Colin
Nottingham Forest

Full Name: FOSTER, Colin
DOB: 16/7/64, Chislehurst
FAPL Debut: Away v Leeds United 17/8/93
Debut Goal:

Previous Club Details			App			Goals		
Club	Signed	Fee	Lge	FLC	FAC	Lge	FLC	FAC
Leyton Orient	2/82	–	173+1	12	19	10		5
Nottingham F	3/87	£70,000	68+4	8	5	5	1	
West Ham Utd	9/89	£750,000	88+5	5	9	4		1
Notts County	1/94	Loan	9					
Nottingham F	3/94	£100,000						

FA Premier Lge Record

| West Ham Utd | 93/94 | | 5 | | | 0 | | |

FOSTER John
Manchester City

Full Name: FOSTER, John
DOB: 19/9/73, Manchester
FAPL Debut: Away v Newcastle United 1/1/94
Debut Goal:

Previous Club Details			Apps			Goals		
Club	Signed	Fee	Lge	FLC	FAC	Lge	FLC	FAC
Manchester C	7/92	–	1		1			

FA Premier Lge Record

| Manchester C | 93/94 | | 1 | | | 0 | | |

FOWLER Robbie
Liverpool

Full Name: FOWLER, Robert
DOB: 9/4/74, Liverpool
FAPL Debut: Away v Chelsea 25/9/93
Debut Goal: Home v Oldham Athletic 16/10/93

Previous Club Details			Apps			Goals		
Club	Signed	Fee	Lge	FLC	FAC	Lge	FLC	FAC
Liverpool		–	27+1			12		

FA Premier Lge Record

| Liverpool | 93/94 | | 27+1 | | | 12 | | |

FOX Ruel
Newcastle United

Full Name: FOX, Ruel Adrian
DOB: 14/1/68, Ipswich
FAPL Debut: Away v Arsenal 15/8/92
Debut Goal: Away v Arsenal 15/8/92

Club	Signed	Fee	Lge	FLC	FAC	Lge	FLC	FAC
Norwich City	1/86	–	148+24	13+3	11+2	22	3	
Newcastle Utd	2/94	£2.25m	13			2		

FA Premier Lge Record

Norwich City	92/93-93/94		57+2			11		
Newcastle Utd	93/94		14			2		

FRANCIS Trevor   Sheffield Wednesday

Full Name: FRANCIS, Trevor John   DOB: 19/4/54, Plymouth
FAPL Debut: Home v Chelsea † 22/8/92   Debut Goal:
England International

Previous Club Details

Club	Signed	Fee	Lge	FLC	FAC	Lge	FLC	FAC
Birmingham C	5/71	–	278+2	18	19	118	3	6
Nottingham F	2/79	£1m	69+1	5	8	28		5
Manchester C	9/81	£1.2m	26	1	2	12		2
Sampdoria (Ita)	9/82	£800,000						
Atalanta (Ita)	7/86							
Rangers	9/87	£75,000						
QPR	3/88	–	30+2	8	1	12	3	
Sheffield Wed	2/90	–	29+47	5+2	2+1	5	3	1

FA Premier Lge Record

Sheffield Wed	92/93-93/94		1+5			0		

FURLONG Paul ·   Chelsea

Full Name: FURLONG, Paul   DOB: 1/10/68, Wood Green

Previous Club Details

Club	Signed	Fee	Lge	FLC	FAC	Lge	FLC	FAC
Coventry City	7/91	–	27+10	4	1+1	4	1	
Watford	7/92	£250,000	79	7	2	39	1	
Chelsea	6/94	£2.3m						

GALE Tony   West Ham United

Full Name: GALE, Tony   DOB:19/11/59 Westminster
FAPL Debut: Home v Wimbledon 14/8/93

Previous Club Details

Club	Signed	Fee	Lge	FLC	FAC	Lge	FLC	FAC
Fulham	8/77	–	277	22	16	19	2	
West Ham Utd	7/84	£150,000	292+7	28+2	29	5	1	1

FA Premier Lge Record

West Ham Utd	93/94		31+1			0		

GALLACHER Kevin   Blackburn Rovers

Full Name: GALLACHER, Kevin William   DOB: 23/11/66, Clydebank
FAPL Debut: Home v Blackburn Rovers 29/8/92
Debut Goal: Away v Oldham Athletic 5/9/92
Scotland International Debut: Home v Columbia 17/5/88

Previous Club Details			*Apps*			*Goals*		
Club	Signed	Fee	Lge	FLC	FAC	Lge	FLC	FAC
Coventry City	1/90	–	99+1	11	4	28	7	
Blackburn Rov	3/93	£1.6m	36+3	4	4	12		1
FA Premier Lge Record								
Coventry City	92/93		19+1			6		
Blackburn Rov	93/94		36+3			12		

GAYLE John   Coventry City

Full Name: GAYLE, John   DOB: 30/7/64, Bromsgrove
FAPL Debut: Home v Leeds United 25/9/93
Debut Goal:

Previous Club Details			Lge	FLC	FAC	Lge	FLC	FAC
Club	Signed	Fee	Lge	FLC	FAC	Lge	FLC	FAC
Wimbledon	3/89	£30,000	17+3	3		2		
Birmingham C	11/90	£175,000	39+5		2	10		
Coventry City			3					
FA Premier Lge Record								
Coventry City	93/94		3			0		

GAYLE Marcus   Wimbledon

Full Name: GAYLE, Marcus   DOB: 27/9/70, Hammersmith
FAPL Debut: Home v Leeds United 26/3/94
Debut Goal:

Previous Club Details			*Apps*			*Goals*		
Club	Signed	Fee	Lge	FLC	FAC	Lge	FLC	FAC
Brentford	7/89	–	83+38	5+3	4+2	16		
Wimbledon	3/94	£250,000	9					
FA Premier Lge Record								
Wimbledon	93/94		10			0		

GEE Phil   Leicester City

Full Name: GEE, Philip   DOB: 19/12/64, Pelsall

Previous Club Details			*App*			*Goals*		
Club	Signed	Fee	Lge	FLC	FAC	Lge	FLC	FAC
Derby County	9/85	£5,000	107+17	11+2	6+1	26	3	2
Leicester City	3/92	Swap	31+13	2+3		7		

GEMMILL Scot   Nottingham Forest

Full Name: GEMMILL, Scot   DOB: 2/1/71, Paisley

FAPL Debut: Home v Liverpool 16/8/92
Debut Goal: Away v Tottenham Hotspur 28/10/92

Previous Club Details

Club	Signed	Fee	App			Goals		
			Lge	FLC	FAC	Lge	FLC	FAC
Nottingham F	1/90	–	104+3	20+1	8	17	3	

FA Premier Lge Record

| Nottingham F | 92/93 | 33 | | | | 1 | | |

GIBSON Colin   Leicester City
Full Name: GIBSON, Colin   DOB: 6/4/60, Bridport

Previous Club Details

Club	Signed	Fee	App			Goals		
			Lge	FLC	FAC	Lge	FLC	FAC
Aston Villa	4/78	–	181+4	26	12	10	4	1
Manchester U	11/85	£275,000	74+5	7	8+1	9		
Port Vale	9/90	Loan	5+1			2		
Leicester City	12/90	£100,000	45+5	4	1	4		

GIGGS Ryan   Manchester United
Full Name: GIGGS, Ryan Joseph   DOB: 29/11/73, Cardiff
FAPL Debut: Away v Sheffield United 15/8/92
Debut Goal: Away v Nottingham Forest 29/8/92
Wales International Debut: Away v West Germany † 16/10/93

Previous Club Details

Club	Signed	Fee	Apps			Goals		
			Lge	FLC	FAC	Lge	FLC	FAC
Manchester U	12/90	–	95+14	14+4	10	26	6	9

FA Premier Lge Record

| Manchester U | 92/93-93/94 | 72+7 | | | | 22 | | |

GLOVER Lee   Nottingham Forest
Full Name: GLOVER, Edward Lee   DOB: 24/4/70, Kettering
FAPL Debut: Home v Middlesbrough † 21/10/92   Debut Goal:

Previous Club Details

Club	Signed	Fee	App			Goals		
			Lge	FLC	FAC	Lge	FLC	FAC
Nottingham F	7/86	–	61+15	6+5	8+2	9	2	1
Leicester City	Loan		3+2			1		
Barnsley	Loan		8					

FA Premier Lge Record

| Nottingham F | 92/93 | 9+5 | | | | 0 | | |

GODDARD Paul   Ipswich Town
Full Name: GODDARD, Paul   DOB: 12/10/59, Harlington
FAPL Debut: Home v Aston Villa 15/8/92

Debut Goal: Away v Middlesbrough 1/9/92
England International Debut: Away v Ireland † 2/6/82

Previous Club Details		Apps			Goals		
Club	Signed Fee	Lge	FLC	FAC	Lge	FLC	FAC
QPR	7/77 –	63+7	4+1		23		
West Ham Utd	8/80 £800,000	159+11	26	10+1	54	12	3
Newcastle Utd	11/86 £415,000	61	3	6	19	1	3
Derby County	8/88 £425,000	49	7	1+1	15	2	
Millwall	12/89 £800,000	17+3		4+1	1		1
Ipswich Town	1/91 –	59+13	5+1	2+2	12		

FA Premier Lge Record

Ipswich Town	92/93-93/94	22+7			3		

GORDON Dale   West Ham United
Name: GORDON, Dale   DOB: 1/1/67, Gt Yarmouth
FAPL Debut: Home v Wimbledon 14/8/93
Debut Goal: Away v Coventry City 21/8/93

Previous Club Details		Apps			Goals		
Club	Signed Fee	Lge	FLC	FAC	Lge	FLC	FAC
Norwich City	1/84 –	194+12	21	19	31	3	6
Rangers	11/91 £1.2m						
West Ham Utd	8/93 £750,000	202+12	22	19	32	3	6

FA Premier Lge Record

West Ham Utd	93/94	8			0		

GORDON Dean   Crystal Palace
Full Name: GORDON, Dean   DOB: 10/2/72, Croydon
FAPL Debut: Away v Oldham Athletic † 19/8/92
Debut Goal:

Previous Club Details		Apps			Goals		
Club	Signed Fee	Lge	FLC	FAC	Lge	FLC	FAC
Crystal Palace	7/91 –	47+12	3+3	1	5		

FA Premier Lge Record

Crystal Palace	92/93	6+4			0		

GOSS Jeremy   Norwich City
Full Name: GOSS, Jeremy   DOB: 11/5/65, Cyprus
FAPL Debut: Away v Arsenal 15/8/92
Debut Goal: Home v Crystal Palace 27/1/93
Welsh International Debut: Home v Iceland 1/5/91

Previous Club Details		Apps			Goals		
Club	Signed Fee	Lge	FLC	FAC	Lge	FLC	FAC
Norwich City	3/83 –	126+20	11	2+1	11	1	

FA Premier Lge Record

Norwich City	92/93-93/94	58			7		

GOULD Jonathon
Coventry City
Full Name: GOULD, Jonathon
DOB: 18/7/68, London
FAPL Debut: Home v Liverpool 19/12/92
Debut Goal:

Previous Club Details

Club	Signed	Fee	Lge	FLC	FAC	Lge	FLC	FAC
			Apps			*Goals*		
Coventry City	7/92	–	18					

FA Premier Lge Record

Coventry City	92/93-93/94	18			0			

GRAY Andy
Tottenham Hotspur
Full Name: GRAY, Andrew Arthur
DOB: 22/2/64, Lambeth
FAPL Debut: Away v Southampton † 15/8/92
Debut Goal: Away v Crystal Palace 30/1/93
England International Debut: Away v Poland 13/11/91

Previous Club Details

Club	Signed	Fee	Lge	FLC	FAC	Lge	FLC	FAC
			Apps			*Goals*		
Crystal Palace	11/84	£2,000	91+7	91	3	27	2	
Aston Villa	11/87	£150,000	34+3	3	3+1	4	1	1
QPR	2/89	£425,000	11			2		
Crystal Palace	8/89	£500,000	87+3	15	11	12	4	2
Tottenham H	2/92	£900,000	23+10			3		

FA Premier Lge Record

Tottenham H	92/93-93/94	9+10			2			

GRAYSON Simon
Leicester City
Full Name: Grayson N Simon
DOB: 16/12/69, Ripon

Previous Club Details

Club	Signed	Fee	Lge	FLC	FAC	Lge	FLC	FAC
			App			*Goals*		
Leeds Utd	6/88	–	2					
Leicester City	3/92	£50,000	66+11					

GREGORY David
Ipswich Town
Full Name: GREGORY, David Spencer
DOB: 23/1/70, Colchester
FAPL Debut: Home v Crystal Palace † 24/10/92
Debut Goal: Away v Crystal Palace 1/5/93

Previous Club Details

Club	Signed	Fee	Lge	FLC	FAC	Lge	FLC	FAC
			Apps			*Goals*		
Ipswich Town	3/87	–	16-15	3+2	1	2		

FA Premier Lge Record

Ipswich Town	92/93	1+2			1			

GRIFFITHS Carl   Manchester City

Full Name: GRIFFITHS, Carl   DOB: 16/7/71, Welshpool
FAPL Debut: Away v West Ham United 1/11/93
Debut Goal: Away v Leeds United 4/12/93

Previous Club Details			Apps			Goals		
Club	Signed	Fee	Lge	FLC	FAC	Lge	FLC	FAC
Shrewsbury	9/88	–	110+33	7+4	6	53	6	2
Manchester City	10/93	£500,000	11+5		2	4		

FA Premier Lge Record

Manchester City			11+5			4		

GROBBELAAR Bruce   Liverpool

Full Name: GROBBELAAR, Bruce David
DOB: 16/10/57, Durban, South Africa
FAPL Debut: Home v Wimbledon 26/9/92   Debut Goal:
Zimbabwe International

Previous Club Details			Apps			Goals		
Club	Signed	Fee	Lge	FLC	FAC	Lge	FLC	FAC
Crewe Alex	21/79	–	24					
Vancouver (US)	5/80	–						
Liverpool	3/81	£250,000	440	70	62			
Stoke City	3/93	Loan	4					

FA Premier Lge Record

Liverpool	92/93-93/94		34			0		

GROENENDIJK Alphonse   Manchester City

Name: GROENENDIJK, Alphonse   DOB:

Previous Club Details			Apps			Goals		
Club	Signed	Fee	Lge	FLC	FAC	Lge	FLC	FAC
Ajax (Hol)								
Manchester C	8/93	£500,000	9	1	2			

FA Premier Lge Record

Manchester C	93/94		9			0		

GROVES Perry   Southampton

Full Name: GROVES, Perry   DOB: 19/4/65, Bow
FAPL Debut: Away v Blackburn Rovers † 18/8/92
Debut Goal: Home v Leeds United 19/9/92

Previous Club Details			Apps			Goals		
Club	Signed	Fee	Lge	FLC	FAC	Lge	FLC	FAC
Colchester Utd	6/82	–	142+14	9+1	6	26	1	1
Arsenal	9/86	£50,000	91+65	18+8	11+6	21	5	1
Southampton	8/92	£750,000	13+2	2	0+1	2		

209

FA Premier Lge Record
Arsenal	92/93	0+1	
Southampton	92/93	13+2	2

GUENTCHEV Bontcho   Ipswich Town

Full Name: GUENTCHEV, Bontcho   DOB: 7/7/64, Bulgaria
FAPL Debut: Home v Manchester City 12/12/92
Debut Goal: Home v Blackburn Rovers 28/12/92
Bulgarian International

Previous Club Details			*Apps*			*Goals*		
Club	Signed	Fee	Lge	FLC	FAC	Lge	FLC	FAC
Sporting Lisbon								
Ipswich Town	12/92	£250,000	28+15	4	6+2	5		3

FA Premier Lge Record
Ipswich Town	92/93-93/94	28+15	5

GUNN Bryan   Norwich City

Full Name: GUNN, Bryan James   DOB: 22/12/63, Thurso
FAPL Debut: Away v Arsenal 15/8/92   Debut Goal:
Scotland International Debut: Home v Egypt 16/5/90

Previous Club Details			*Apps*			*Goals*		
Club	Signed	Fee	Lge	FLC	FAC	Lge	FLC	FAC
Norwich City	10/86	£150,000	282	6	4			

FA Premier Lge Record
Norwich City	92/93-93/94	82	0

HAALAND Alf Inge   Nottingham Forest

Full Name: HAALAND, Alf Inge   DOB:
Norway International

Previous Club Details			*App*			*Goals*		
Club	Signed	Fee	Lge	FLC	FAC	Lge	FLC	FAC
Nottingham F	–		3					

HALL Gareth   Chelsea

Full Name: HALL, Gareth David   DOB: 20/3/69, Croydon
FAPL Debut: Home v Oldham Athletic 15/8/92
Debut Goal: Home v Ipswich Town 17/10/92
Wales International Debut: Home v Yugoslavia † 23/3/88

Previous Club Details			*Apps*			*Goals*		
Club	Signed	Fee	Lge	FLC	FAC	Lge	FLC	FAC
Chelsea	5/86	–	111+16	11+1	6	3		

FA Premier Lge Record
Chelsea	92/93-93/94	40+4	2

HALL Richard   Southampton

Full Name: HALL, Richard Anthony   DOB: 14/3/72, Ipswich

210

FAPL Debut: Home v Tottenham Hotspur 15/8/92
Debut Goal: Away v Oldham Athletic 31/10/92

Previous Club Details			*Apps*			*Goals*		
Club	Signed	Fee	Lge	FLC	FAC	Lge	FLC	FAC
Scunthorpe Utd	3/90	–	22	2	3	3		
Southampton	2/91	£200,000	53+6	6+1	6	6		2
FA Premier Lge Record								
Southampton	92/93-93/94		32			4		

HARFORD Mick   Coventry City
Full Name: HARFORD, Mick   DOB: 12/5/59, Sunderland
FAPL Debut: Home v Oldham Athletic 15/8/92
Debut Goal: Home v Oldham Athletic 15/8/92
England International Debut: Away v Ireland † 17/2/88

Previous Club Details			*Apps*			*Goals*		
Club	Signed	Fee	Lge	FLC	FAC	Lge	FLC	FAC
Lincoln City	7/77	–	109+6	8	3	41	5	
Newcastle Utd	12/80	£180,000	18+1			4		
Bristol City	8/81	£160,000	30	5	5	11	1	2
Birmingham C	3/82	£100,000	92	10	7	25	6	2
Luton Town	12/84	£250,000	135+4	16	27	57	10	11
Derby County	1/90	£450,000	58	7	1	15	3	
Luton Town	9/91	£325,000	29	1		12		
Chelsea	8/92	£300,000	27+1	5	1	9	2	
Sunderland	3/93	£250,000	10+1			2		
Coventry City	7/93	£200,000	0+1			1		
FA Premier Lge Record								
Chelsea	92/93		27+1			9		
Coventry City	93/94		0+1			1		

HARKNESS Steve   Liverpool
Full Name: HARKNESS, Steven   DOB: 27/8/71, Carlisle
FAPL Debut: Away v Ipswich Town 25/8/92
Debut Goal: Home v Tottenham Hotspur 8/5/93

Previous Club Details			*Apps*			*Goals*		
Club	Signed	Fee	Lge	FLC	FAC	Lge	FLC	FAC
Carlisle Utd	3/89	–	12+1					
Liverpool	7/89	£75,000	26+5	4+2	2			
Huddersfield T	3/93	Loan	5					
FA Premier Lge Record								
Liverpool	92/93-93/94		19+1			1		

HAZARD Micky   Tottenham Hotspur
Full Name: Hazard, Micky   DOB: 5/2/60, Sunderland
Debut Goal: Home v Liverpool 18/12/93

211

Previous Club Details			*Apps*			*Goals*		
Club	Signed	Fee	Lge	FLC	FAC	Lge	FLC	FAC
Tottenham H	2/78	–	73+18	11+3	7+3	13	5	2
Chelsea	9/85	£310,000	78+3	7+3	4+2	9	1	1
Portsmouth	1/90	£100,000	8			1		
Swindon Town	9/90	£130,000	112+7	12	7	17	1	
Tottenham H	11/93	£50,000	13+3		2	2		
FA Premier Lge Record								
Swindon Town	93/94		7+2					
Tottenham H	93/94		13+4			2		

HEANEY Neil   Southampton

Full Name: HEANEY, Neil Andrew   DOB: 3/11/71, Middlesbrough
FAPL Debut: Home v Liverpool † 31/1/193   Debut Goal:

Previous Club Details			*Apps*			*Goals*		
Club	Signed	Fee	Lge	FLC	FAC	Lge	FLC	FAC
Arsenal	11/89		4+3	0+1				
Hartlepool Utd	1/91	Loan	2+1					
Cambridge Utd	1/92	Loan	9+4		1	2		
Southampton	3/94	£300,000	2					
FA Premier Lge Record								
Arsenal	92/93-93/94		4+2			0		
Southampton	93/94		2			0		

HENDRY Colin   Blackburn Rovers

Full Name: HENDRY, Edward Colin James DOB: 7/12/65, Keith
FAPL Debut: Away v Crystal Palace 15/8/92
Debut Goal: Home v Coventry City 26/1/93
Scotland International Debut: Away v Estonia 19/5/93

Previous Club Details			*Apps*			*Goals*		
Club	Signed	Fee	Lge	FLC	FAC	Lge	FLC	FAC
Blackburn Rov	3/87	£30,000	99+3	4	3	22		
Manchester C	11/89	£700,000	57+6	4+1	5	5	1	2
Blackburn Rov	11/91	£700,000	86+5	12	6+1	5		
FA Premier Lge Record								
Blackburn Rov	92/93-93/94		62+1			1		

HENDRY John   Tottenham Hotspur

Full Name: HENDRY, John   DOB: 6/1/70, Glasgow
FAPL Debut: Home v Manchester Utd † 19/9/92   Debut Goal:

Previous Club Details			*Apps*			*Goals*		
Club	Signed	Fee	Lge	FLC	FAC	Lge	FLC	FAC
Tottenham H	7/90	£50,000	5+12	0+2	0+1	3		
Charlton Ath	2/92	Loan	1+4			1		
FA Premier Lge Record								
Tottenham H	92/93-93/94		2+6			1		

HILL Andy — Manchester City

Full Name: HILL, Andrew Rowland DOB: 20/1/65, Maltby
FAPL Debut: Home v QPR 17/8/92
Debut Goal: Home v Leeds United 7/11/92

Previous Club Details			*Apps*			*Goals*		
Club	Signed	Fee	Lge	FLC	FAC	Lge	FLC	FAC
Manchester U	1/83	–						
Bury	7/84	–	264	22	12	10	1	
Manchester U	12/90	£200,000	81+4	8	2+1	6		
FA Premier Lge Record								
Manchester C	92/93-93/94		38+3			1		

HILL Colin — Leicester City

Full Name: HILL Colin DOB: 12/11/63 Uxbridge
N Ireland International Debut: Home v Norway 27/3/90

Previous Club Details			*App*			*Goals*		
Club	Signed	Fee	Lge	FLC	FAC	Lge	FLC	FAC
Arsenal	8/81	–	46	4	1	1		
Maritime(Port)		Free						
Colchester Utd	10/87	Free	64+5	2	7			2
Sheffield Utd	8/89	£85,000	77+5	5	10+2	1		
Leicester City	3/92	Loan	10					
Leicester City	7/92	£200,000	76+1			0		

HILL Danny — Tottenham Hotspur

Full Name: HILL, Danny DOB: 1/10/74, Edmonton, London
FAPL Debut: Away v Chelsea † 23/3/92 Debut Goal:

Previous Club Details			*Apps*			*Goals*		
Club	Signed	Fee	Lge	FLC	FAC	Lge	FLC	FAC
Tottenham H		–	2+4					
FA Premier Lge Record								
Tottenham H	92/93-93/94		2+4			0		

HILLIER David — Arsenal

Full Name: HILLIER, David DOB: 18/12/69, Blackheath
FAPL Debut: Home v Norwich 15/8/92
Debut Goal: Home v Sheffield United 9/1/93

Previous Club Details			*Apps*			*Goals*		
Club	Signed	Fee	Lge	FLC	FAC	Lge	FLC	FAC
Arsenal	2/88	–	86+4	12+2	6	2		
FA Premier Lge Record								
Arsenal	92/93-93/94		50+1			1		

HINCHCLIFFE Andy — Everton

Full Name: HINCHCLIFFE, Andrew DOB: 5/2/69, Manchester

FAPL Debut: Home v Sheffield Wednesday 15/8/92
Debut Goal: Home v Nottingham Forest 13/3/93

Previous Club Details			Apps			Goals		
Club	Signed	Fee	Lge	FLC	FAC	Lge	FLC	FAC
Manchester C	6/86	–	107+5	11	12	8	1	1
Everton	7/90	£800,000	196+22	12+7	7+5	84	10	6
FA Premier Lge Record								
Everton	92/93-93/94		28+1			12		

HIRST David   Sheffield Wednesday
Full Name: HIRST, David Eric   DOB: 7/12/67, Cudworth
FAPL Debut: Away v Everton 15/8/92
Debut Goal: Home v Nottingham Forest 19/8/92
England International Debut: Away v Australia 1/6/91

Previous Club Details			Apps			Goals		
Club	Signed	Fee	Lge	FLC	FAC	Lge	FLC	FAC
Barnsley	11/85	–	26+2	1		9		
Sheffield Wed	8/86	£200,000	168+21	8+5	4+2	72	7	5
FA Premier Lge Record								
Sheffield Wed	92/93-93/94		29			12		

HITCHCOCK Kevin   Chelsea
Full Name: HITCHCOCK, Kevin Joseph   DOB: 5/10/62, Canning Town
FAPL Debut: Away v Manchester City 20/9/92 Debut Goal:

Previous Club Details			Apps			Goals		
Club	Signed	Fee	Lge	FLC	FAC	Lge	FLC	FAC
Nottingham F	8/83	£15,000						
Mansfield T	2/84	Loan	14					
Mansfield T	6/84	£140,000	168	12	10			
Chelsea	3/88	£250,000	37	2	4			
Northampton T	12/90	Loan	17					
West Ham Utd	3/93	Loan						
FA Premier Lge Record								
Chelsea	92/93-93/94		22			0		

HODDLE Glenn   Chelsea
Full Name: HODDLE, Glenn   DOB: 27/10/57, Hayes
FAPL Debut: Home v Blackburn Rovers 14/8/93
Debut Goal: Away v West Ham United 26/3/93
England International Debut: Home v Bulgaria 22/11/79

Previous Club Details			Apps			Goals		
Club	Signed	Fee	Lge	FLC	FAC	Lge	FLC	FAC
Tottenham H	4/75	–	370+7	44	47+1	89	10	11
Monaco (Fra)	7/87	£800,000						
Swindon Town	8/91	–	63+1	6	1	1	1	
Chelsea	6/93	£75,000	16+2	2	0+2	1		

FA Premier Lge Record
Chelsea   93/94   16+3   1

HODGE Steve   **Leeds United**
Full Name: HODGE, Stephen Brian   DOB: 25/10/62, Nottingham
FAPL Debut: Home v Wimbledon † 15/8/92
Debut Goal: Home v Aston Villa 13/9/93
England International Debut: Away v Russia † 23/3/86

| *Previous Club Details* | | | *Apps* | | | *Goals* | | |
Club	Signed	Fee	Lge	FLC	FAC	Lge	FLC	FAC
Nottingham F	10/80	–	122+1	10	6	30	2	
Aston Villa	8/85	£450,000	53	12	4	12	3	1
Tottenham H	12/86	£650,000	44+1	2	7	7		2
Nottingham F	8/88	£550,000	79+3	20+1	11+1	20	6	2
Leeds United	7/91	£900,000	8+26	4+3	2+1	10		

FA Premier Lge Record
Leeds United   92/93-93/94   16+15   3

HODGES Lee   **Tottenham Hotspur**
Full Name: HODGES, Lee Leslie   DOB: 4/9/73, Epping
FAPL Debut: Home v Wimbledon 5/5/93   Debut Goal:

| *Previous Club Details* | | | *Apps* | | | *Goals* | | |
Club	Signed	Fee	Lge	FLC	FAC	Lge	FLC	FAC
Tottenham H	2/92	–	0+4					
Plymouth Arg	2/93	Loan	6+1			2		

FA Premier Lge Record
Tottenham H   92/93-93/94   0+4   0

HOLDSWORTH Dean   **Wimbledon**
Full Name: HOLDSWORTH, Dean   DOB: 8/11/68, London
FAPL Debut: Away v Leeds United 15/8/92
Debut Goal: Home v Coventry City 22/8/92

| *Previous Club Details* | | | *Apps* | | | *Goals* | | |
Club	Signed	Fee	Lge	FLC	FAC	Lge	FLC	FAC
Watford	11/86		2+14			3		
Carlisle Utd	2/88	Loan	4			1		
Port Vale	3/88	Loan	6			2		
Swansea City	8/88	Loan	4+1			1		
Brentford	10/88	Loan	2+5			1		
Brentford	9/89	£125,000	75+2	8+1	5+1	35	4	3
Wimbledon	7/92	£720,000						

FA Premier Lge Record
Wimbledon   92/93-93/94   75+2   35

HOLLAND Chris   **Newcastle United**
Full Name: HOLLAND, Christopher J   DOB:

215

FAPL Debut: Home v Ipswich Town 23/3/94   Debut Goal:

Previous Club Details			Apps			Goals		
Club	Signed	Fee	Lge	FLC	FAC	Lge	FLC	FAC
Preston	–		0+2					
Newcastle Utd	1/94	£100,000	2+1					
FA Premier Lge Record								
Newcastle Utd	93/94		2+1			0		

HOLLOWAY Ian   Queens Park Rangers
Full Name: HOLLOWAY, Ian Scott   DOB: 12/3/63, Kingswood
FAPL Debut: Away v Manchester City 17/8/92
Debut Goal: Home v Tottenham Hotspur 3/10/92

Previous Club Details			Apps			Goals		
Club	Signed	Fee	Lge	FLC	FAC	Lge	FLC	FAC
Bristol Rovers	3/81	–	104+7	10	8	14	1	2
Wimbledon	7/85	£35,000	19	3	1	2		
Brentford	3/86	£25,000	27+3	2	3	2		
Torquay Utd	1/87	Loan	5					
Bristol Rovers	8/87	£10,000	179	5		26		1
QPR	8/91	£230,000	73+13	7+1	3	2		
FA Premier Lge Record								
QPR	92/93-93/94		41+7			2		

HOLMES Matt   West Ham United
Full Name: HOLMES, Matthew J   DOB: 1/8/69, Luton
FAPL Debut: Home v Wimbledon 14/8/93
Debut Goal: Home v Manchester City 1/11/93

Previous Club Details			Apps			Goals		
Club	Signed	Fee	Lge	FLC	FAC	Lge	FLC	FAC
Bournemouth	9/88	–	105+9	7	8+2	8		
Cardiff City	3/89	Loan	0+1					
West Ham Utd	8/92	£40,000	39+12	3	5	4		
FA Premier Lge Record								
West Ham Utd	93/94		33+1			3		

HOLMES Paul   Everton
Full Name: HOLMES, Paul   DOB: 18/2/68, Wortley
FAPL Debut: Home v Ipswich Town 24/3/92   Debut Goal:

Previous Club Details			Apps			Goals		
Club	Signed	Fee	Lge	FLC	FAC	Lge	FLC	FAC
Doncaster Rov	2/86	–	45+2		3+1	1		1
Torquay Utd	8/88	£6,000	127+11	9	9+2	4		1
Birmingham C	6/92		12		1			
Everton	3/93	£100,000	19	4	1			
FA Premier Lge Record								
Everton	92/93-93/94		19+1			0		

HOOPER Mike   Newcastle United

Full Name: HOOPER, Michael Dudley   DOB: 10/2/64, Bristol
FAPL Debut: Home v Middlesbrough 7/11/92   Debut Goal:

Previous Club Details			*Apps*			*Goals*		
Club	Signed	Fee	Lge	FLC	FAC	Lge	FLC	FAC
Bristol City	1/84	–	1		1			
Wrexham	2/85	–	34	4				
Liverpool	10/85	£40,000	50+1	10	5			
Leicester City	9/90	Loan	14					
Newcastle Utd	9/93	£550,000	19	2	3			
FA Premier Lge Record								
Liverpool	92/93		8+1			0		
Newcastle Utd	93/94		19			0		

HOPKIN David   Chelsea

Full Name: HOPKIN, David   DOB: 21/8/70, Greenock
FAPL Debut: Away v Liverpool 10/2/92
Debut Goal: Away v Aston Villa 23/10/93

Previous Club Details			*Apps*			*Goals*		
Club	Signed	Fee	Lge	FLC	FAC	Lge	FLC	FAC
Morton								
Chelsea	9/92	£300,000	14+11	1	3+2	1		
FA Premier Lge Record								
Chelsea	92/93-93/94		14+11			1		

HORNE Barry   Everton

Full Name: HORNE, Barry   DOB: 18/5/62, St Asaph
FAPL Debut: Home v Sheffield Wednesday 15/8/92
Debut Goal: Home v Sheffield Wednesday 15/8/92
Wales International Debut: Home v Denmark † 9/9/87

Previous Club Details			*Apps*			*Goals*		
Club	Signed	Fee	Lge	FLC	FAC	Lge	FLC	FAC
Wrexham	6/84	–	136	10	7	17	1	2
Portsmouth	7/87	£60,000	66+4	3	6	7		
Southampton	3/89	£700,000	111+1	15+2	15	6	3	3
Everton	8/92	£695,000	63+4	10+1	2+1	1		
FA Premier Lge Record								
Everton	92/93-93/94		63+4			1		

HOUGHTON Ray   Aston Villa

Full Name: HOUGHTON, Raymond James   DOB: 9/1/62, Glasgow
FAPL Debut: Away v Ipswich Town 15/8/92
Debut Goal: Home v Norwich City 28/11/92
Eire International Debut: Home v Wales 23/3/86

Previous Club Details			Apps			Goals		
Club	Signed	Fee	Lge	FLC	FAC	Lge	FLC	FAC
West Ham Utd	7/89	–	0+1					
Fulham	7/82	–	129	12	4	16	2	3
Oxford United	9/85	£147,000	83	13	3	10	3	
Liverpool	10/87	£825,000	147+6	13	26+1	28	3	4
Aston Villa	7/92	£900,000	63+5	8+2	7	5	2	2
FA Premier Lge Record								
Aston Villa	92/93-93/94		63+5			5		

HOWE Stephen
Nottingham Forest

Full Name: HOWE, Stephen
DOB: 6/1/73, Annitsford

Previous Club Details			App			Goals		
Club	Signed	Fee	Lge	FLC	FAC	Lge	FLC	FAC
Nottingham F	–		2+2	1				

HOWELLS David
Tottenham Hotspur

Full Name: HOWELLS, David
DOB: 15/12/67, Guildford
FAPL Debut: Away v Southampton 15/8/92
Debut Goal: Away v Blackburn Rovers 7/11/92

Previous Club Details			Apps			Goals		
Club	Signed	Fee	Lge	FLC	FAC	Lge	FLC	FAC
Tottenham H	1/85	–	137+33	12+4	7+3	16	2	1
FA Premier Lge Record								
Tottenham H	92/93-93/94		31+5			2		

HOWEY Steve
Newcastle United

Full Name: HOWEY, Stephen
DOB: 26/10/71, Sunderland
FAPL Debut: Home v Tottenham 14/8/93

Previous Club Details			Apps			Goals		
Club	Signed	Fee	Lge	FLC	FAC	Lge	FLC	FAC
Newcastle	12/89	–	70+18	6+2	6	3	1	
FA Premier Lge Record								
Newcastle Utd	93/94		13+1			0		

HOWIE Scott
Norwich City

Full Name: HOWIE, Scott
DOB: 4/1/72, Glasgow
FAPL Debut: Home v Liverpool 5/2/94
Debut Goal:

Previous Club Details			Apps			Goals		
Club	Signed	Fee	Lge	FLC	FAC	Lge	FLC	FAC
Norwich City	8/93	£300,00	1+1					
FA Premier Lge Record								
Norwich City	93/94		1+1			0		

HUGHES David   Southampton
Full Name: HUGHES, David R   DOB: 30/12/72, St Albans
FAPL Debut: Away v Oldham † 5/12/94   Debut Goal:
Previous Club Details   *Apps*   *Goals*
Club   Signed Fee   Lge   FLC FAC   Lge FLC FAC
Southampton   7/91   –   0+2
FA Premier Lge Record
Southampton   93/94   0+2   0

HUGHES Mark   Manchester United
Full Name: HUGHES, Leslie Mark   DOB: 1/11/63, Wrexham
FAPL Debut: Away v Sheffield United 15/8/92
Debut Goal: Away v Sheffield United 15/8/92
Wales International Debut: Home v England 2/5/84
Previous Club Details   *Apps*   *Goals*
Club   Signed Fee   Lge   FLC FAC   Lge FLC FAC
Manchester U   11/80 –   85+4   5+1 10   37   4   4
Barcelona (Spa) 7/86   £2.5m
Bayern Munich   10/87 Loan
Manchester U   7/88   £1.5m   218+4 32   29+1   74   12   11
FA Premier Lge Record
Manchester U   92/93-93/94   77   27

HUMPHREY John   Crystal Palace
Full Name: HUMPHREY, John   DOB: 31/1/61, Paddington
FAPL Debut: Home v Blackburn Rovers 15/8/92 Debut Goal:
Previous Club Details   *Apps*   *Goals*
Club   Signed Fee   Lge   FLC   FAC   Lge FLC FAC
Wolves   2/79   –   149   8   7   3
Charlton Ath   7/85   £60,000 194   13   9   3
Reading   12/93   Loan   8
Crystal Palace 6/90   £400,000 134+5 19+2 5   2
FA Premier Lge Record
Crystal Palace 92/93   28+4   0

HURST Lee   Coventry City
Full Name: HURST, Lee Jason   DOB: 21/9/70, Nuneaton
FAPL Debut: Home v Middlesbrough 15/8/92
Debut Goal: Away v Sheffield United 2/9/92
Previous Club Details   *Apps*   *Goals*
Club   Signed Fee   Lge   FLC   FAC   Lge FLC FAC
Coventry City 5/89   –   46+3   3+1   1+1   2
FA Premier Lge Record
Coventry City 92/93-93/94   35   2

219

HUTCHISON Don   Liverpool
Full Name: HUTCHISON, Donald   DOB: 9/5/71, Gateshead
FAPL Debut: Away v Aston Villa 19/9/92
Debut Goal: Home v Sheffield Wednesday 3/10/92

Previous Club Details			Apps			Goals		
Club	Signed	Fee	Lge	FLC	FAC	Lge	FLC	FAC
Hartlepool Utd	3/90	–	19+5	1+1	2	3		
Liverpool	11/90	£175,000	32+12	7+1	1+2	7	2	
FA Premier Lge Record								
Liverpool	92/93-93/94		32+9			7		

HYDE Graham   Sheffield Wednesday
Full Name: HYDE, Graham   DOB: 10/11/70, Doncaster
FAPL Debut: Away v Everton 15/8/92
Debut Goal: Away v Nottingham Forest 12/9/92

Previous Club Details			Apps			Goals		
Club	Signed	Fee	Lge	FLC	FAC	Lge	FLC	FAC
Sheffield Wed	5/88	–	50+18	10+2	5+5	2	1	1
FA Premier Lge Record								
Sheffield Wed	92/93-93/94		41+14			2		

IMPEY Andy   Queens Park Rangers
Full Name: IMPEY, Andrew Rodney   DOB: 30/9/71, Hammersmith
FAPL Debut: Away v Manchester City 17/8/92
Debut Goal: Away v Coventry City 26/8/92

Previous Club Details			Apps			Goals		
Club	Signed	Fee	Lge	FLC	FAC	Lge	FLC	FAC
QPR	6/90	£35,000	83+2	7+1	0+2	5	1	
FA Premier Lge Record								
QPR	92/93-93/94		70+2			5		

INCE Paul   Manchester United
Full Name: INCE, Paul Emerson Carlyle   DOB: 21/10/67, Ilford
FAPL Debut: Away v Sheffield United 15/8/92
Debut Goal: Home v Manchester City 6/12/92
England International Debut: Away v Spain 9/9/92

Previous Club Details			Apps			Goals		
Club	Signed	Fee	Lge	FLC	FAC	Lge	FLC	FAC
West Ham Utd	7/85	–	66+6	9	8+2	7	3	1
Manchester U	8/89	£125,000	167+3	18+1	15+1	20	2	1
FA Premier Lge Record								
Manchester U	92/93-93/94		80			14		

INGEBRIGTSEN Kare   Manchester City
Full Name: Ingebrigtsen, Kare   DOB:11/11/65
FAPL Debut: Home v Blackburn Rovers † 30/1/93 Debut Goal:

Norway International Debut: Away v Tunisia 7/11/90

Previous Club Details

Club	Signed	Fee	Apps Lge	FLC	FAC	Goals Lge	FLC	FAC
Utleira, Malvik, Frigg, Rosenborg (all Norwegian)								
Manchester C		–	4+11		2			

FA Premier Lge Record

| Manchester C | 92/93-93/94 | 4+11 | | | 0 | | | |

IRELAND Simon — Blackburn Rovers

Full Name: IRELAND, Simon DOB: 23/11/71, Barnstaple
FAPL Debut: Away v Manchester City † 30/1/93 Debut Goal:

Previous Club Details

Club	Signed	Fee	Apps Lge	FLC	FAC	Goals Lge	FLC	FAC
Huddersfield	7/90	–	10+9	1	0+1	1		
Wrexham	2/92	Loan	2+3					
Blackburn Rov	10/92	£200,000	0+1					

FA Premier Lge Record

| Blackburn Rov | 92/93 | 0+1 | | | 0 | | | |

IRWIN Dennis — Manchester United

Full Name: IRWIN, Dennis Joseph DOB: 31/10/65, Cork
FAPL Debut: Away v Sheffield United 15/8/92
Debut Goal: Home v Ipswich Town 22/8/92
Eire International Debut: Home v Morocco 12/9/90

Previous Club Details

Club	Signed	Fee	Apps Lge	FLC	FAC	Goals Lge	FLC	FAC
Leeds United	10/83	–	72	5	3	1		
Oldham Ath	5/86	–	166+1	19	13	4	3	
Manchester U	6/90	£625,000	151+2	25+2	16	11		2

FA Premier Lge Record

| Manchester U | 92/93-93/94 | 82 | | | 7 | | | |

JACKSON Matthew — Everton

Full Name: JACKSON, Matthew Alan DOB: 19/10/71, Leeds
FAPL Debut: Home v Sheffield Wednesday 15/8/92
Debut Goal: Away v Crystal Palace 9/1/93

Previous Club Details

Club	Signed	Fee	Apps Lge	FLC	FAC	Goals Lge	FLC	FAC
Luton Town	7/90	–	7+2	2				
Preston	3/91	Loan	3+1					
Everton	10/91	£600,000	92+3	7	6	4		

FA Premier Lge Record

| Everton | 92/93-93/94 | 62+3 | | | 3 | | | |

JAMES Anthony   Leicester City
Full Name: JAMES, Anthony   DOB: 27/6/67, Sheffield

Previous Club Details			App			Goals		
Club	Signed	Fee	Lge	FLC	FAC	Lge	FLC	FAC
Lincoln City	8/88	–	24+5	2				
Leicester City	8/89	£150,000	79+28	6	2	11		1

JAMES David   Liverpool
Full Name: JAMES, David   DOB: 1/8/70, Welwyn Garden City
FAPL Debut: Away v Nottingham Forest 16/8/92   Debut Goal:

Previous Club Details			Apps			Goals		
Club	Signed	Fee	Lge	FLC	FAC	Lge	FLC	FAC
Watford	7/88	–	89	6	2			
Liverpool	6/92	£1m	41+1	1				
FA Premier Lge Record								
Liverpool	92/93-93/94		41+1			0		

JEFFREY Mike   Newcastle United
Full Name: JEFFREY, Michael   DOB: 11/8/71, Liverpool
FAPL Debut: Away v Tottenham Hotspur 4/12/93 Debut Goal:

Previous Club Details			Apps			Goals		
Club	Signed	Fee	Lge	FLC	FAC	Lge	FLC	FAC
Bolton W	2/89	–	9+6	1+2	1			
Doncaster Rov	3/92	£20,000	48+1	4		19		
Newcastle Utd	10/93	£60,000	2					
FA Premier Lge Record								
Newcastle Utd	93/94		2			0		

JEMSON Nigel   Sheffield Wednesday
Full Name: JEMSON, Nigel Bradley   DOB: 10/8/69, Preston
FAPL Debut: Away v Arsenal † 29/8/92
Debut Goal: Away v Ipswich Town 6/11/93

Previous Club Details			Apps			Goals		
Club	Signed	Fee	Lge	FLC	FAC	Lge	FLC	FAC
Preston	6/87	–	28+4		2	8		1
Nottingham F	3/88	£150,000	45+2	9	3	13	4	3
Bolton W	12/88	Loan	4+1					
Preston	3/89	Loan	6+3			2		
Sheffield Wed	9/91	£800,000	26+25	3+4	3+3	9	1	
Grimsby Town	9/93	Loan	6			2		
FA Premier Lge Record								
Sheffield Wed	92/93-93/94		15+16			5		

JENKINSON Leigh   Coventry City
Full Name: JENKINSON, Leigh   DOB: 9/7/69, Thorne
FAPL Debut: Home v Arsenal 13/3/93   Debut Goal:

Previous Club Details			Apps			Goals		
Club	Signed	Fee	Lge	FLC	FAC	Lge	FLC	FAC
Hull City	6/87	–	95+35	7+2	6	13	1	
Rotherham Utd	9/90	Loan	5+2					
Coventry City	3/93	£300,000	11+9	0+1				
Birmingham C	11/93	Loan	2+1					

FA Premier Lge Record

Coventry City	92/93-93/94		11+9			0		

JENSEN John — Arsenal

Full Name: JENSEN, John   DOB: 3/5/65 Copenhagen
FAPL Debut: Home v Norwich City 15/8/92   Debut Goal:
Danish International

Previous Club Details			Apps			Goals		
Club	Signed	Fee	Lge	FLC	FAC	Lge	FLC	FAC
Brondby (Den), Hamburg (Ger), Brondby								
Arsenal	8/92	£1.1m	56+3	8	4+1			

FA Premier Lge Record

Arsenal	92/93-93/94		56+3			0		

JOACHIM Julian — Leicester City

Full Name: JOACHIM, Julian   DOB: 12/9/74, Peterborough

Previous Club Details			App			Goals		
Club	Signed	Fee	Lge	FLC	FAC	Lge	FLC	FAC
Leicester City	9/92		52+10	3+1	3	21	2	1

JOHNSEN Erland — Chelsea

Full Name: JOHNSEN, Erland   DOB: 5/4/67, Fredrikstad, Norway
FAPL Debut: Away v Nottingham Forest 16/1/93
Debut Goal: Home v Blackburn Rovers 14/8/93

Previous Club Details			Apps			Goals		
Club	Signed	Fee	Lge	FLC	FAC	Lge	FLC	FAC
Chelsea	11/89	£306,000	69+2	2	9	1		

FA Premier Lge Record

Chelsea	92/93-93/94		39+1			1		

JOHNSON Andrew — Norwich City

Full Name: JOHNSON, Andrew James   DOB: 2/5/74, Bath
FAPL Debut: Home v Manchester City † 20/2/93
Debut Goal: Away v Middlesbrough 8/5/93

Previous Club Details			Apps			Goals		
Club	Signed	Fee	Lge	FLC	FAC	Lge	FLC	FAC
Norwich City	3/92	–	3+3	1		1		

FA Premier Lge Record

Norwich City	92/93-93/94		1+3			1		

JOHNSON Gavin — Ipswich Town

Full Name: JOHNSON, Gavin DOB: 10/10/70, Eye
FAPL Debut: Home v Aston Villa 15/9/92
Debut Goal: Home v Aston Villa 15/9/92

Previous Club Details			*Apps*			*Goals*		
Club	Signed	Fee	Lge	FLC	FAC	Lge	FLC	FAC
Ipswich Town	2/89	–	100+15	8+1	12	11	2	2

FA Premier Lge Record
Ipswich Town 92/93-93/94 55+1 6

JONES Rob — Liverpool

Full Name: JONES, Robert Marc DOB: 5/11/71, Wrexham
FAPL Debut: Home v Sheffield Utd 19/8/92 Debut Goal:
England International Debut: Home v France 9/2/92

Previous Club Details			*Apps*			*Goals*		
Club	Signed	Fee	Lge	FLC	FAC	Lge	FLC	FAC
Crewe Alex	12/88	–	60+16	9	0+3	2		
Liverpool	10/91	£300,000	95	7+1	13	2		

FA Premier Lge Record
Liverpool 92/93-93/94 67 0

JONES Ryan — Sheffield Wednesday

Full Name: JONES, Ryan DOB: 23/7/73, Sheffield
FAPL Debut: Away v Coventry City 3/3/93
Debut Goal: Home v Wimbledon 16/10/93

Previous Club Details			*Apps*			*Goals*		
Club	Signed	Fee	Lge	FLC	FAC	Lge	FLC	FAC
Sheffield Wed	6/91		32+3	4	3	5	1	

FA Premier Lge Record
Sheffield Wed 92/93-93/94 32+3 5

JONES Steve — West Ham United

Full Name: JONES, Stephen Gary DOB: 17/3/70, Cambridge
FAPL Debut: Home v Swindon Town 11/9/93
Debut Goal: Home v Norwich City 24/1/94

Previous Club Details			*Apps*			*Goals*		
Club	Signed	Fee	Lge	FLC	FAC	Lge	FLC	FAC
West Ham Utd	11/92	£22,500	7+7		2+1	5		1

FA Premier Lge Record
West Ham Utd 93/94 3+5 2

JONES Vinny — Wimbledon

Name: JONES, Vincent Peter DOB: 5/1/65, Watford
Debut Goal:
Away v Sheffield Wednesday 22/8/92

Previous Club Details			Apps			Goals		
Club	Signed	Fee	Lge	FLC	FAC	Lge	FLC	FAC
Wimbledon	11/86	£10,000	77	6+2	2+2	9		1
Leeds United	6/89	£650,000	44+2	2	1	5		
Sheffield Utd	9/90	£700,000	35	4	1	2		
Chelsea	8/91	£575,000	42	1	4	3		1
Wimbledon	9/92	£700,000	58	9	6	3	2	
FA Premier Lge Record								
Chelsea	92/93		7			1		
Wimbledon	92/93-93/94		58+2			3		

JOSEPH Roger   Wimbledon
Name: JOSEPH, Roger Anthony   DOB: 24/12/65, Paddington
FAPL Debut: Away v Leeds United 15/8/92   Debut Goal:

Previous Club Details			Apps			Goals		
Club	Signed	Fee	Lge	FLC	FAC	Lge	FLC	FAC
Brentford	10/84		103+1	7	1	2		
Wimbledon	8/88	£150,000	152+7	16+1	11+1			
FA Premier Lge Record								
Wimbledon	92/93-93/94		44+1			0		

KANCHELSKIS Andrei   Manchester United
Full Name: KANCHELSKIS, Andrei   DOB: 23/1/69, Kirovograd, USSR
FAPL Debut: Away v Sheffield United 15/8/93
Debut Goal: Home v Leeds United 6/9/93
Russian International

Previous Club Details			Apps			Goals		
Club	Signed	Fee	Lge	FLC	FAC	Lge	FLC	FAC
Shakhtyor D								
Manchester U	3/91		71+22	15+1	9	13	3	4
FA Premier Lge Record								
Manchester U	92/93-93/94		42+15			9		

KEANE Roy   Manchester United
Name: KEANE, Roy Maurice   DOB:10/8/71, Cork
FAPL Debut: Home v Liverpool 16/8/92
Debut Goal: Away v Leeds United 5/12/92
Eire International Debut: Home v Chile 22/5/92

Previous Club Details			Apps			Goals		
Club	Signed	Fee	Lge	FLC	FAC	Lge	FLC	FAC
Cobh Ramblers								
Nottingham F	5/90	£10,000	116	17	18	22	6	3
Man Utd	7/93	£3.75m	34+2	6+1	6	5		1
FA Premier Lge Record								
Nottingham F	92/93		42			6		
Manchester U	93/94		34+3			5		

KEARTON Jason   Everton
Full Name: KEARTON, Jason   DOB: 9/7/69, Australia
FAPL Debut: Away v QPR † 28/12/92   Debut Goal:

Previous Club Details   *Apps*   *Goals*
Club	Signed	Fee	Lge	FLC	FAC	Lge	FLC	FAC
Everton	10/88		2+3	1				
Stoke City	8/91	Loan	16					
Blackpool	1/92	Loan	14					

FA Premier Lge Record
Everton	92/93		2+3			0		

KELLY Gary   Leeds United
Full Name: KELLY, Gary   DOB: 9/7/74, Drogheda
FAPL Debut: Away v Manchester City 14/8/93   Debut Goal:
Eire International Debut: Home v Russia 23/3/94

Previous Club Details   Apps   Goals
Club	Signed	Fee	Lge	FLC	FAC	Lge	FLC	FAC
Leeds United	9/91	–	41+2	2	3			

FA Premier Lge Record
Leeds United	93/94		42			0		

KENNA Jeff   Southampton
Full Name: KENNA, Jeffrey Jude   DOB: 27/8/70, Dublin
FAPL Debut: Away v QPR † 19/8/92
Debut Goal: Home v Sheffield United 27/2/92

Previous Club Details   *Apps*   *Goals*
Club	Signed	Fee	Lge	FLC	FAC	Lge	FLC	FAC
Southampton	4/89	–	81+4	2	5+1	4		

FA Premier Lge Record
Southampton	92/93-93/94		66+3			4		

KENNY Billy   Everton
Full Name: KENNY, William Aiden   DOB: 19/9/73, Liverpool
FAPL Debut: Home v Manchester City 31/10/92
Debut Goal: Away v Chelsea 11/3/93

Previous Club Details   *Apps*   *Goals*
Club	Signed	Fee	Lge	FLC	FAC	Lge	FLC	FAC
Everton	6/92	–	16+1			1		

FA Premier Lge Record
Everton	92/93		16+1			1		

KEOWN Martin   Arsenal
Full Name: KEOWN, Martin Raymond   DOB: 24/7/66, Oxford
FAPL Debut: Home v Coventry City 17/10/92   Debut Goal:
England International Debut: Home v France 19/2/92

Previous Club Details			Apps			Goals		
Club	Signed	Fee	Lge	FLC	FAC	Lge	FLC	FAC
Arsenal	1/84	–	22		5			
Brighton	2/85	Loan	21+2	2		1	1	
Aston Villa	6/86	£200,000	109+3	12+1	6	3		
Everton	6/89	£750,000	92+4	11	12			
Arsenal	2/93	£2m	38+10	3	2+1			
FA Premier Lge Record								
Everton	92/93		13			0		
Arsenal	92/93-93/94		38+10			0		

KERNAGHAN Alan   Manchester City

Full Name: KERNAGHAN, Alan   DOB: 25/4/67, Otley
FAPL Debut: Away v Coventry City 15/8/93
Debut Goal: Home v Ipswich Town 1/9/93

Previous Club Details			Apps			Goals		
Club	Signed	Fee	Lge	FLC	FAC	Lge	FLC	FAC
Middlesbrough	3/85	–	172+40	22+7	7+4	16	1	3
Charlton Ath	1/91	Loan	13					
Manchester C	9/93	£1.6m	22+1	5	2			1
FA Premier Lge Record								
Middlesbrough	92/93		22			2		
Manchester C	93/94		22+1			0		

KERR David   Manchester City

Full Name: KERR, David William   DOB: 6/9/74, Dumfries
FAPL Debut: Home v Crystal Palace † 5/5/93   Debut Goal:

Previous Club Details			Apps			Goals		
Club	Signed	Fee	Lge	FLC	FAC	Lge	FLC	FAC
Manchester C	9/91	–	3+1					
FA Premier Lge Record								
Manchester C	92/93-93/94		3+1			0		

KERR Paul   Leicester City

Full Name: KERR, Paul   DOB: 9/6/64, Portsmouth

Previous Club Details			App			Goals		
Club	Signed	Fee	Lge	FLC	FAC	Lge	FLC	FAC
Aston Villa	5/82	–	16+8	5+1	2	3	2	1
Middlesbrough	1/87	£50,000	114+11	10	9+2	13	1	3
Millwall	3/91	£100,000	42+2	2	2	12		1
Port Vale	7/92	£200,000	58+5	4	4	15		1
Leicester City	3/94	Swap	4+3			2		

227

KERSLAKE David   Tottenham Hotspur

Full Name: KERSLAKE, David   DOB: 19/6/66, Stepney
FAPL Debut: Home v Manchester City 13/3/93   Debut Goal:

Previous Club Details

Club	Signed	Fee	Lge	FLC	FAC	Lge	FLC	FAC
			Apps			Goals		
QPR	6/83	–	38+20	6+2	2+2	6	4	
Swindon Town	11/89	£110,000	163+2	12	8	2		
Leeds United	3/93	£500,000	8					
Tottenham H	9/93	£450,000	16+1	3	1+1			

FA Premier Lge Record

Leeds United	92/93		8			0		
Tottenham H	93/94		16+1			0		

KHARIN Dimitri   Chelsea

Full Name: KHARIN, Dimitri   DOB: 16/8/68, Moscow
FAPL Debut: Away v QPR 27/1/93   Debut Goal:
Russian International

Previous Club Details

Club	Signed	Fee	Lge	FLC	FAC	Lge	FLC	FAC
			Apps			Goals		
CSKA Moscow		–						
Chelsea	11/92	£200,000	44	3	8			

FA Premier Lge Record

Chelsea	92/93-93/94		44			0		

KIMBLE Alan   Wimbledon

Full Name: KIMBLE, Alan   DOB: 6/8/66, Dagenham
FAPL Debut: Away v West Ham United 14/8/93   Debut Goal:

Previous Club Details

Club	Signed	Fee	Lge	FLC	FAC	Lge	FLC	FAC
			Apps			Goals		
Charlton Ath	8/84	–	6					
Exeter City	8/85	Loan	1	1				
Cambridge Utd	8/86	Free	295+4	23+1	29	24		1
Wimbledon	7/93	£175,000	14	3				

FA Premier Lge Record

Wimbledon	93/94		14			0		

KING Phil   Sheffield Wednesday

Full Name: KING, Philip Geoffrey   DOB: 28/12/67, Bristol
FAPL Debut: Away v Everton 15/8/92
Debut Goal: Home v Southampton 12/4/93

Previous Club Details

Club	Signed	Fee	Lge	FLC	FAC	Lge	FLC	FAC
			Apps			Goals		
Exeter City	1/85	–	24+3	1				
Torquay Utd	7/86	£3,00	24	2	1	3		
Swindon Town	2/87	£15,000	112+4	11	5	4		

Sheffield Wed	11/89	£400,000	124+15 17	9	2
Notts County	10/93	Loan	6		

FA Premier Lge Record

Sheffield Wed	92/93-93/94	18+4		1

KIWOMYA Chris   Ipswich Town

Full Name: KIWOMYA, Christopher Mark   DOB: 2/12/69, Huddersfield
FAPL Debut: Home v Aston Villa 15/8/92
Debut Goal: Away v Manchester United 22/8/92

Previous Club Details			*Apps*			*Goals*		
Club	Signed	Fee	Lge	FLC	FAC	Lge	FLC	FAC
Ipswich Town	3/87	–	183+26	14	13	47	8	2

FA Premier Lge Record

Ipswich Town	92/93-93/94	71+3		15

KJELDBERG Jakob   Chelsea

Name: KJELDBERG, Jakob   DOB:

Previous Club Details			*Apps*			*Goals*		
Club	Signed	Fee	Lge	FLC	FAC	Lge	FLC	FAC
Silkeborg (Den)								
Chelsea	8/93	£400,000	28	3	4+1			

FA Premier Lge Record

Chelsea	93/94	29		0

KUBICKI Dariusz   Aston Villa

Full Name: Kubicki, Dariusz   DOB: 6/6/63, Warsaw
FAPL Debut: Away v Swindon 30/10/93   Debut Goal:

Previous Club Details			*Apps*			*Goals*		
Club	Signed	Fee	Lge	FLC	FAC	Lge	FLC	FAC
Legia Warsaw		–						
Aston Villa	8/91	£200,000	24+1	3	4+1			
Sunderland	3/94	Loan	15					

FA Premier Lge Record

Aston Villa	93/94	1+1		0

LAWS Brian   Nottingham Forest

Full Name: LAWS, Brian   DOB: 14/10/61, Wallsend
FAPL Debut: Home v Liverpool 16/8/92   Debut Goal:

Previous Club Details			*App*			*Goals*		
Club	Signed	Fee	Lge	FLC	FAC	Lge	FLC	FAC
Burnley	10/79	–	125	14	15	12	2	1
Huddersfield T	8/83	£10,000	56	7	3	1		
Middlesbrough	3/85	£30,000	103+5	6+1	8+1	12	2	
Nottingham F	7/88	£120,000	136+11	28+4	16+2	4		1

FA Premier Lge Record

Nottingham F	92/93	32+1		0

LEE David   Chelsea

Full Name: LEE, David John   DOB: 26/11/69, Kingswood
FAPL Debut: Away v Aston Villa † 2/9/92
Debut Goal: Home v Manchester United 19/12/92

Previous Club Details			*Apps*			*Goals*		
Club	Signed	Fee	Lge	FLC	FAC	Lge	FLC	FAC
Chelsea	6/88	–	79+25	12+2	2+4	9	1	
Reading	1/92	Loan	5			5		
Plymouth Arg	3/92	Loan	9			1		
FA Premier Lge Record								
Chelsea	92/93-93/94		26+6			3		

LEE Jason   Nottingham Forest

Full Name: LEE, Jason   DOB: 9/5/71, Newham

Previous Club Details			*App*			*Goals*		
Club	Signed	Fee	Lge	FLC	FAC	Lge	FLC	FAC
Charlton Ath	6/89	–	0+1					
Stockport Co	2/91	Loan	2					
Lincoln City	3/91	£35,000	50+2	2	0+1	9		1
Southend Utd	7/93	–	96			21		
Nottingham F	3/94	£200,000	10+2			2		

LEE Robert   Newcastle United

Full Name: LEE, Robert   DOB: 1/2/66, West Ham
FAPL Debut: Home v Home v Tottenham Hotspur 14/8/93
Debut Goal: Home v Swindon Town 12/3/94

Previous Club Details			*Apps*			*Goals*		
Club	Signed	Fee	Lge	FLC	FAC	Lge	FLC	FAC
Charlton Ath	7/83	–	274+24	16+3	14	58	1	2
Newcastle Utd	9/92	£700,000	76	6	7	17	2	2
FA Premier Lge Record								
Newcastle Utd	93/94		41			7		

LE SAUX Graeme   Blackburn Rovers

Full Name: LE SAUX, Graeme Pierre   DOB: 17/10/68, Jersey
FAPL Debut: Home v Ipswich Town † 17/10/92
Debut Goal: Away v Chelsea 14/8/93
England International Debut: Home v Denmark 9/3/94

Previous Club Details			*Apps*			*Goals*		
Club	Signed	Fee	Lge	FLC	FAC	Lge	FLC	FAC
Chelsea	12/87	–	77+13	7+6	7+1	8	1	
Blackburn Rov	3/93	Swap	48+1	4	4	2		
FA Premier Lge Record								
Chelsea	92/93		10+4			0		
Blackburn Rov	92/93-93/94		48+1			2		

LE TISSIER Matthew
Southampton

Full Name: LE TISSIER, Matthew Paul   DOB: 14/10/68, Guernsey
FAPL Debut: Home v Tottenham Hotspur 15/8/92
Debut Goal: Away v QPR 19/8/92
England International Debut: Home v Denmark 9/3/94

Previous Club Details			Apps			Goals		
Club	Signed Fee		Lge	FLC	FAC	Lge	FLC	FAC
Southampton	10/86	–	240+30	23+6	18+1	98	13	6
FA Premier Lge Record								
Southampton	92/93-93/94		77			38		

LEWIS Neil
Leicester City

Full Name: LEWIS A Neil   DOB: 28/6/74, Wolverhampton

Previous Club Details			App			Goals		
Club	Signed Fee		Lge	FLC	FAC	Lge	FLC	FAC
Leicester City	7/92	–	26+5	2	1			

LIMPAR Anders
Everton

Full Name: LIMPAR, Anders   DOB: 24/9/65, Sweden
FAPL Debut: Home v Norwich City 15/8/92
Debut Goal: Away v Liverpool 23/8/92
Sweden International Debut: Away v USSR 8/4/87

Previous Club Details			Apps			Goals		
Club	Signed Fee		Lge	FLC	FAC	Lge	FLC	FAC
Arsenal	7/90	£1m	76+20	9	7	18		2
Everton	3/94	£1.6m	8					
FA Premier Lge Record								
Arsenal	92/93-93/94		21+12			2		
Everton	93/94		9			0		

LINIGHAN Andy
Arsenal

Full Name: LINIGHAN, Andrew   DOB: 18/6/62, Hartlepool
FAPL Debut: Away v Sheffield United † 19/9/92
Debut Goal: Away v Oldham Athletic 20/2/93

Previous Club Details			Apps			Goals		
Club	Signed Fee		Lge	FLC	FAC	Lge	FLC	FAC
Hartlepool Utd	9/80	–	110	7+1	8	4	1	
Leeds Utd	5/84	£200,000	66	6	2	3	1	
Oldham Ath	1/86	£65,000	87	8	3	6	2	
Norwich Cty	3/88	£350,000	86	6	10	8		
Arsenal	6/90	£1.25m	61+7	9+1	10+1	2	1	1
FA Premier Lge Record								
Arsenal	92/93-93/94		39+2			2		

Matthew
Le Tissier
Southampton

Scorer of brilliant
goals

LINIGHAN David   Ipswich Town
Full Name: LINIGHAN, David   DOB: 9/1/65, Hartlepool
FAPL Debut: Home v Aston Villa 15/8/92
Debut Goal: Away v Southampton 13/4/93

Previous Club Details			*Apps*			*Goals*		
Club	Signed	Fee	Lge	FLC	FAC	Lge	FLC	FAC
Hartlepool Utd	3/82	–	84+7	3+1	4	5	1	
Derby County	8/86	£25,000						
Shrewsbury T	12/86	£30,000	65	5	3	2		
Ipswich Town	6/88	£300,000	241+1	19	17	12		
FA Premier Lge Record								
Ipswich Town	92/93-93/94		79			4		

LOMAS Stephen   Manchester City
Full Name: LOMAS, Stephen   DOB: 18/1/74, Hanover
FAPL Debut: Away v Sheffield United 25/9/93 Debut Goal:

Previous Club Details			Apps			Goals		
Club	Signed	Fee	Lge	FLC	FAC	Lge	FLC	FAC
Manchester C	1/91	–	17+5	4	1+1		1	
FA Premier Lge Record								
Manchester C			17+6			0		

LUKIC John   Leeds United
Full Name: LUKIC, Jovan   DOB: 11/12/60, Chesterfield
FAPL Debut: Home v Wimbledon 15/8/92   Debut Goal:

Previous Club Details			*Apps*			*Goals*		
Club	Signed	Fee	Lge	FLC	FAC	Lge	FLC	FAC
Leeds United	12/78	–	146	7	9			
Arsenal	7/83	£75,000	223	32	21			
Leeds United	6/90	£1m	128	14	10			
FA Premier Lge Record								
Leeds United	92/93-93/94		59			0		

LYDERSON Pål   Arsenal
Full Name: LYDERSON, Pål   DOB: 10/9/65, Norway
FAPL Debut: Away v Tottenham Hotspur 12/11/92   Debut Goal:
Norwegian International

Previous Club Details			*Apps*			*Goals*		
Club	Signed	Fee	Lge	FLC	FAC	Lge	FLC	FAC
Arsenal	9/91	£500,000	12+4	1				
FA Premier Lge Record								
Arsenal	92/93		7+1			0		

LYTTLE Des   Nottingham Forest
Full Name: LYTTLE, Desmond   DOB: 24/9/71, Wolverhampton

Previous Club Details			*App*			*Goals*		
Club	Signed	Fee	Lge	FLC	FAC	Lge	FLC	FAC
Swansea City	7/92	£12,500	46	2	5	1		
Nottingham F	7/93	£375,000	37	6	2	1		

McALLISTER Brian   Wimbledon
Full Name: McALLISTER, Brian   DOB: 30/11/70, Glasgow
FAPL Debut: Away v Sheffield Utd 25/8/92   Debut Goal:

Previous Club Details			*Apps*			*Goals*		
Club	Signed	Fee	Lge	FLC	FAC	Lge	FLC	FAC
Wimbledon	2/89	–	39+1	5	3			
Plymouth Arg	12/90	Loan	7+1					

FA Premier Lge Record
Wimbledon	92/93-93/94	39+1		0	

McALLISTER Gary   Leeds United
Full Name: McALLISTER, Gary   DOB: 25/12/64, Motherwell
FAPL Debut: Home v Wimbledon 15/8/92
Debut Goal: Home v Liverpool 29/8/92
Scotland International Debut: Home v East Germany 25/4/90

Previous Club Details			*Apps*			*Goals*		
Club	Signed	Fee	Lge	FLC	FAC	Lge	FLC	FAC
Leicester City	8/85	£125,000	199+2	14+1	5	46	3	2
Leeds United	6/90	£1m	152+1	16	14	21	3	3

FA Premier Lge Record
Leeds United	92/93-93/94	73		14	

McCARTHY Alan   Queens Park Rangers
Full Name: McCARTHY, Alan   DOB: 11/1/72, Wandsworth
FAPL Debut: Away v Ipswich Town 26/3/94   Debut Goal:

Previous Club Details			Apps			Goals		
Club	Signed	Fee	Lge	FLC	FAC	Lge	FLC	FAC
QPR	12/89	–	8+1		0+1			
Watford	11/93	Loan	8+1					
Plymouth Arg	2/94	Loan	1+1					

FA Premier Lge Record
QPR	93/94	4		0	

McCLAIR Brian   Manchester United
Full Name: McCLAIR, Brian John   DOB: 8/12/63, Bellshill
FAPL Debut: Away v Sheffield United 15/8/92
Debut Goal: Away v Everton 12/9/92
Scotland International Debut: Home v Luxembourg 12/11/86

Previous Club Details			*Apps*			*Goals*		
Club	Signed	Fee	Lge	FLC	FAC	Lge	FLC	FAC
Celtic	7/83	–						

| Manchester U | 7/87 | £850,000 | 242+18 | 33+1 | 28+4 | 80 | 17 | 12 |

FA Premier Lge Record

| Manchester U | 92/93-93/94 | 52+15 | | | 10 | | |

McDONALD Alan   Queens Park Rangers
Full Name: McDONALD, Alan   DOB: 12/10/63, Belfast
FAPL Debut: Away v Manchester City 17/8/92
Debut Goal: Away v Wimbledon 27/9/93
Northern Ireland International Debut: Away v Romania 16/10/85

Previous Club Details

			Apps			Goals		
Club	Signed	Fee	Lge	FLC	FAC	Lge	FLC	FAC
QPR	8/81	–	293+5	35	24	9	2	1
Charlton Ath	3/83	Loan	9					

FA Premier Lge Record

| QPR | 92/93-93/94 | 51 | | | 1 | | |

McGEE Paul   Wimbledon
Full Name: McGEE, Paul   DOB: 17/5/68, Dublin
FAPL Debut: Away v Middlesbrough 21/11/92   Debut Goal:

Previous Club Details

			Apps			Goals		
Club	Signed	Fee	Lge	FLC	FAC	Lge	FLC	FAC
Colchester Utd	2/89	£35,000	3					
Wimbledon	3/89	£120,000	54+6	1+1	5	9	1	

FA Premier Lge Record

| Wimbledon | 92/93-93/94 | 1+2 | | | 0 | | |

McGOLDRICK Eddie   Arsenal
Full Name: McGOLDRICK, Edward John Paul DOB: 30/4/65, Islington
FAPL Debut: Home v Blackburn Rovers 15/8/92
Debut Goal: Away v Oldham Athletic 19/8/92
Eire International Debut: Home v Switzerland 25/3/92

Previous Club Details

			Apps			Goals		
Club	Signed	Fee	Lge	FLC	FAC	Lge	FLC	FAC
Northampton T	8/86	£10,000	97+10	9	6+1	9		1
Crystal Palace	1/89	£200,000	97+8	13+1	4	3		
Arsenal	7/93	£1m	22+3	4	1+1			

FA Premier Lge Record

| Crystal Palace | 92/93 | 42 | | | 8 | | |
| Arsenal | 93/94 | 23+3 | | | 0 | | |

McGOWAN Gavin   Arsenal
Full Name: McGOWAN, Gavin   DOB: 16/1/76, Blackheath
FAPL Debut: Away v Sheffield Wednesday 6/5/93

Previous Club Details

			Apps			Goals		
Club	Signed	Fee	Lge	FLC	FAC	Lge	FLC	FAC
Arsenal	–		0+2					

FA Premier Lge Record
Arsenal   92/93-93/94   0+2   0

McGRATH Lloyd   Coventry City
Full Name: McGRATH, Lloyd Anthony   DOB: 24/2/65, Birmingham
FAPL Debut: Away v Wimbledon † 22/8/92   Debut Goal:

Previous Club Details			*Apps*			*Goals*		
Club	Signed	Fee	Lge	FLC	FAC	Lge	FLC	FAC
Coventry City	12/82	–	200+14	22	16	4	1	

FA Premier Lge Record
Coventry City 92/93-93/94   30+6   0

McGRATH Paul   Aston Villa
Full Name: McGRATH, Paul   DOB: 4/12/69, Ealing
FAPL Debut: Home v Ipswich Town 15/8/92
Debut Goal: Home v Nottingham Forest 12/12/92
Eire International Debut: Home v Italy †

Previous Club Details			*Apps*			*Goals*		
Club	Signed	Fee	Lge	FLC	FAC	Lge	FLC	FAC
Manchester U	4/82	£30,000	159+4	13	15+2	12	2	2
Aston Villa	7/89	£400,000	182	21	18	6		1

FA Premier Lge Record
Aston Villa   92/93-93/94   71   4

McMAHON Steve   Manchester City
Full Name: McMAHON, Stephen   DOB: 20/8/61, Liverpool
FAPL Debut: Home v QPR 17/8/92
Debut Goal: Home v Norwich City 26/8/92
England International Debut: Away v Israel 17/2/88

Previous Club Details			*Apps*			*Goals*		
Club	Signed	Fee	Lge	FLC	FAC	Lge	FLC	FAC
Everton	8/79	–	99+1	11	9	11	3	
Aston Villa	5/83	£175,000	74+1	9	3	7		
Liverpool	9/85	£375,000	202+2	27	30	28	13	7
Manchester C	12/91	£900,000	76+3	7	3	1		

FA Premier Lge Record
Manchester C   92/93-93/94   58+3   1

McMANAMAN Steve   Liverpool
Full Name: McMANAMAN, Steven   DOB: 11/2/72, Bootle
FAPL Debut: Away v Nottingham Forest †16/8/92
Debut Goal: Home v Wimbledon 26/9/92

Previous Club Details			*Apps*			*Goals*		
Club	Signed	Fee	Lge	FLC	FAC	Lge	FLC	FAC
Liverpool	2/90	–	82+11	11+1	11+1	11	5	3

MABBUTT Gary   Tottenham Hotspur

Full Name: MABBUTT, Gary Vincent   DOB: 23/9/61, Bristol
FAPL Debut: Away v Wimbledon 25/10/92
Debut Goal: Home v Nottingham Forest 28/12/92
England International Debut: Home v West Germany 13/10/82

Previous Club Details			*Apps*			*Goals*		
Club	Signed	Fee	Lge	FLC	FAC	Lge	FLC	FAC
Bristol Rov	1/79	–	122+9	10	5+1	10	1	1
Tottenham H	8/82	£105,000	383+13	54+2	33+2	27	2	3

FA Premier Lge Record
Tottenham H   92/93-93/94   57   2

MADDISON Neil   Southampton

Full Name: MADDISON, Neil Stanley   DOB: 2/10/69, Darlington
FAPL Debut: Home v Middlesbrough 29/8/92
Debut Goal: Home v Arsenal 5/12/92

Previous Club Details			*Apps*			*Goals*		
Club	Signed	Fee	Lge	FLC	FAC	Lge	FLC	FAC
Southampton	4/88	–	81+12	3+2	3+3	12		

FA Premier Lge Record
Southampton   92/93-93/94   73+4   10

MADDIX Danny   Queens Park Rangers

Full Name: MADDIX, Daniel Shawn   DOB: 11/10/67, Ashford, Kent
FAPL Debut: Away v Southampton † 12/9/92   Debut Goal:

Previous Club Details			*Apps*			*Goals*		
Club	Signed	Fee	Lge	FLC	FAC	Lge	FLC	FAC
Tottenham H	7/85							
Southend Utd	10/86	Loan	2					
QPR	7/87	–	122+17	15	14	6	2	1

FA Premier Lge Record
QPR   92/93   9+5   0

MAGILTON Jim   Southampton

Full Name: MAGILTON, James   DOB: 6/5/69, Belfast
FAPL Debut: Home v Liverpool 14/2/94   Debut Goal:

Previous Club Details			*Apps*			*Goals*		
Club	Signed	Fee	Lge	FLC	FAC	Lge	FLC	FAC
Liverpool	5/86	–						
Oxford United	10/90	£100,000	154	10	8	34	1	4
Southampton	2/94	£600,000	14					

FA Premier Lge Record
Southampton 93/94   15   0

MAHORN Paul   Tottenham Hotspur

Full Name: MAHORN, Paul   DOB: 13/8/73, Whipp Cross, Essex
FAPL Debut: Away v Swindon Town 22/1/94   Debut Goal:

Previous Club Details			*Apps*			*Goal*		
Club	Signed	Fee	Lge	FLC	FAC	Lge	FLC	FAC
Tottenham H	1/92	–	1					
Fulham	9/93	Loan	1+2					

FA Premier Lge Record
Tottenham H 93/94   1   0

MAKEL Lee   Blackburn Rovers

Full Name: MAKEL, Lee   DOB: 11/1/73, Sunderland
FAPL Debut: Home v Middlesbrough 20/3/93   Debut Goal:

Previous Club Details			*Apps*			*Goals*		
Club	Signed	Fee	Lge	FLC	FAC	Lge	FLC	FAC
Newcastle Utd	2/91	–	6+6	1		1		
Blackburn Rov	6/92	£160,000	1+2	0+3		1		

FA Premier Lge Record
Blackburn Rov 92/93-93/94   1+2   0

MARGETSON Martyn   Manchester City

Full Name: MARGETSON, Martyn Walter   DOB: 8/9/71, Neath
FAPL Debut: Home v Everton 8/5/93   Debut Goal:

Previous Club Details			*Apps*			*Goals*		
Club	Signed	Fee	Lge	FLC	FAC	Lge	FLC	FAC
Manchester C	7/90	–	1+5	0+1				

FA Premier Lge Record
Manchester C 92/93   1   0

MARKER Nicky   Blackburn Rovers

Name: MARKER, Nicky   DOB: 03/06/65, Budleigh Salterton
FAPL Debut: Home v Oldham Athletic † 26/09/92   Debut Goal:

Previous Club Details			*Apps*			*Goals*		
Club	Signed	Fee	Lge	FLC	FAC	Lge	FLC	FAC
Exeter City	5/83		196+6	11	8	3	1	
Plymouth Arg	11/87		201+1	15	9	13	3	1
Blackburn R	9/92	£250,000 (+ exch)						
			28+10	3	5			

FA Premier Lge Record
Blackburn Rov 92/93-93/94   28+10   0

MARSH Mike   **West Ham United**
Full Name: MARSH, Michael Andrew   DOB: 21/7/69, Liverpool
FAPL Debut: Home v Arsenal † 23/8/92
Debut Goal: Home v Crystal Palace 28/11/92

Previous Club Details			Apps			Goals		
Club	Signed	Fee	Lge	FLC	FAC	Lge	FLC	FAC
Liverpool	8/87	–	42+27	10+1	6+2	2	3	
West Ham Utd	9/93	Swap	32	3	5	1		1
FA Premier Lge Record								
Liverpool	92/93-93/94		22+8			2		
West Ham Utd	93/94		33			1		

MARSHALL Ian   **Ipswich Town**
Full Name: MARSHALL, Ian Paul   DOB: 20/3/66, Liverpool
FAPL Debut: Away v Chelsea 15/8/92
Debut Goal: Home v Ipswich Town 19/9/92

Previous Club Details			App			Goals		
Club	Signed	Fee	Lge	FLC	FAC	Lge	FLC	FAC
Everton	3/84	–	9+6	1+1		1		
Oldham Ath	3/88	£100,000	165+5	17	14	36		3
Ipswich Town	8/93	£750,000	27+1	3	5	10	2	3
FA Premier Lge Record								
Oldham Ath	92/93		26+1			2		
Ipswich Town	93/94		28+1			10		

MARSHALL Scott   **Arsenal**
Full Name: MARSHALL, Scott Roderick   DOB: 1/5/73, Edinburgh
FAPL Debut: Away v Sheffield Wednesday 6/5/93   Debut Goal:

Previous Club Details			App			Goals		
Club	Signed	Fee	Lge	FLC	FAC	Lge	FLC	FAC
Arsenal	3/91	–	2					
FA Premier Lge Record								
Arsenal	92/93		2			0		

MARTIN Alvin   **West Ham United**
Full Name: MARTIN, Alvin   DOB: 29/7/58, Liverpool
FAPL Debut: Home v Manchester City 1/11/93
Debut Goal: Home v Oldham Athletic 20/11/93
England International Debut: Home v Brazil 2/5/81

Previous Club Details			App			Goals		
Club	Signed	Fee	Lge	FLC	FAC	Lge	FLC	FAC
West Ham Utd	8/74	–	428+3	67	36	27	6	
FA Premier Lge Record								
West Ham Utd	93/94		6+1			2		

MARTYN Nigel   Crystal Palace
Full Name: MARTYN, Nigel   DOB: 11/8/66, St Austell
FAPL Debut: Home v Blackburn Rovers 15/8/92   Debut Goal:
England International Debut: Away v CIS † 29/4/92

Previous Club Details			*Apps*			*Goals*		
Club	Signed	Fee	Lge	FLC	FAC	Lge	FLC	FAC
Bristol Rovers	8/87		101	6	6			
Crystal Palace	11/89	£1m	189	25	13			
FA Premier Lge Record								
Crystal Palace	92/93		42			0		

MASKELL Craig   Southampton
Name: MASKELL, Craig   DOB: 10/4/68, Aldershot
FAPL Debut: Away v Sheffield United 14/8/93
Debut Goal: Away v Southampton 25/8/93

Previous Club Details			*Apps*			*Goals*		
Club	Signed	Fee	Lge	FLC	FAC	Lge	FLC	FAC
Southampton	4/86	–	2+4			1		
Huddersfield T	5/88	£20,000	86+1	6	8	43	4	3
Reading	8/90	£250,000	60+12	2	5+1	27		
Swindon Town	7/92	Exchange	40+7	3+1	2+1	22	1	
Southampton	2/94	£250,000	6+4			1		
FA Premier Lge Record								
Swindon Town	93/94		8+6			3		
Southampton	93/94		6+4			1		

MASON Paul   Ipswich Town
Full Name: MASON, Paul   DOB: 03/9/63, Liverpool
FAPL Debut: Debut Goal:

Previous Club Details			*Apps*			*Goals*		
Club	Signed	Fee	Lge	FLC	FAC	Lge	FLC	FAC
Aberdeen								
Ipswich Town	8/93	£400,000	18+4	3	1+2	3	1	
FA Premier Lge Record								
Ipswich Town	93/94		18+4			3		

MASSEY Stuart   Crystal Palace
Full Name: MASSEY, Stuart   DOB: 17/11/64, Crawley
FAPL Debut: Away v Aston Villa 5/9/92   Debut Goal:

Previous Club Details			*Apps*			*Goals*		
Club	Signed	Fee	Lge	FLC	FAC	Lge	FLC	FAC
Crystal Palace	7/92	£20,000	1+1					
FA Premier Lge Record								
Crystal Palace	92/93		0+1			0		

240

MATHIE Alex   **Newcastle United**
Full Name: MATHIE, Alexander   DOB: 20/12/68, Bathgate
FAPL Debut: Home v Sheffield Wednesday 13/9/93
Debut Goal: Home v Sheffield Wednesday 13/9/93

Previous Club Details			App			*Goals*		
Morton								
Port Vale	3/93	Loan	0+3					
Newcastle Utd	7/93	£285,000	0+15	1		3		
FA Premier Lge Record								
Newcastle Utd	93/94		0+15			3		

MATTEO Dominic   **Liverpool**
Full Name: MATTEO, Dominic   DOB: 28/4/74, Dumfries
FAPL Debut: Away v Manchester City 23/10/93
Debut Goal:

Previous Club Details		Apps			*Goals*		
Club	Signed Fee	Lge	FLC	FAC	Lge	FLC	FAC
Liverpool	5/92 –	11	2				
FA Premier Lge Record							
Liverpool	93/94	11			1		

MATTHEW Damian   **Crystal Palace**
Full Name: MATTHEW, Damian   DOB: Islington, 23/9/70
Debut: Home v Oldham Athletic 15/8/92   Debut Goal:

Previous Club Details		App			*Goals*		
Club	Signed Fee	Lge	FLC	FAC	Lge	FLC	FAC
Chelsea	6/89 –	13+8					
Luton Town	9/92 Loan	3+2					
Crystal Palace	2/94 £150,000	11+1			1		
FA Premier Lge Record							
Chelsea	92/93	3+1			0		

MAY David   **Blackburn Rovers**
Full Name: MAY, David   DOB: 24/6/70, Oldham
FAPL Debut: Away v Crystal Palace 15/8/92
Debut Goal: Away v Everton 3/3/93

Previous Club Details		App			*Goals*		
Club	Signed Fee	Lge	FLC	FAC	Lge	FLC	FAC
Blackburn Rov	6/88 –	122	12+1	10	3	2	1
FA Premier Lge Record							
Blackburn Rov	92/93-93/94	73			2		

MEAKER Michael   **Queens Park Rangers**
Full Name: MEAKER, Michael John   DOB: 18/8/71, Greenford
FAPL Debut: Home v Norwich City 6/3/93   Debut Goal:

Previous Club Details			*App*			*Goals*		
Club	Signed	Fee	Lge	FLC	FAC	Lge	FLC	FAC
QPR	12/89	–	14+11	1	1	1	1	
Plymouth Arg	11/91	Loan	4					
FA Premier Lge Record								
QPR	92/93-93/94		14+2			1		

MEGSON Gary　　　　　　　　　　　Norwich City

Full Name:　MEGSON, Gary John　　　　　DOB: 2/5/59, Manchester
FAPL Debut:　Away v Arsenal 15/8/92
Debut Goal:　Away v Manchester City 26/8/92

Previous Club Details			*App*			*Goals*		
Club	Signed	Fee	Lge	FLC	FAC	Lge	FLC	FAC
Plymouth Arg	5/77	–	78	9	5	10		
Everton	12/79	£250,000	20+2		3	2		1
Sheffield Wed	8/81	£130,000	123	13	12	13	2	5
Nottingham F	8/84	£175,000						
Newcastle Utd	11/84	£130,000	21+3	1+1	2	1		1
Sheffield Wed	12/85	£60,000	107+3	10	15	12		1
Manchester C	1/89	£250,000	78+4	5	7+1	2		
Norwich City	7/92	Free	40+4	1	4	1		
FA Premier Lge Record								
Norwich City	92/93-93/94		40+4			1		

MERSON Paul　　　　　　　　　　　　　Arsenal

Full Name:　MERSON, Paul Charles　　　　　DOB: 20/3/68, Harlesden
FAPL Debut:　Home v Norwich City 15/8/92
Debut Goal:　Home v Sheffield Wednesday 29/8/92
England International Debut: Home v West Germany † 11/9/91

Previous Club Details			*App*			*Goals*		
Club	Signed	Fee	Lge	FLC	FAC	Lge	FLC	FAC
Arsenal	11/85	–	195+38	24+2	23+3	62	8	4
Brentford	1/87	Loan	6+1					
FA Premier Lge Record								
Arsenal	92/93-93/94		56+10			14		

MIKLOSKO Ludek　　　　　　　West Ham United

Full Name:　MIKLOSKO, Ludek　　　　　DOB:9/12/61 Protesov,Czech
FAPL Debut:　Home v Wimbledon 14/8/93
Czechoslovakian International

Previous Club Details			*Apps*			*Goals*		
Club	Signed	Fee	Lge	FLC	FAC	Lge	FLC	FAC
Banik Ostrava		–						
West Ham Utd	2/90	£300,000	187	13	15			
FA Premier Lge Record								
West Ham Utd	93/94		42			0		

MIKE Adrian   Manchester City
Full Name: MIKE, Adrian Roosevelt   DOB: 16/11/73, Manchester
FAPL Debut: Home v Middlesbrough † 12/9/92
Debut Goal: Away v Swindon Town 1/9/93

Previous Club Details			*App*			*Goals*		
Club	Signed	Fee	Lge	FLC	FAC	Lge	FLC	FAC
Manchester C	6/92	–	4+9	1+1		2		
Bury	3/93	Loan	5+2			1		
FA Premier Lge Record								
Manchester C	92/93-93/94		2+9			1		

MILLER Alan   Arsenal
Full Name: MILLER, Alan John   DOB: 29/3/70, Epping
FAPL Debut: Away v Leeds United † 21/11/92 Debut Goal:

Previous Club Details			*App*			*Goals*		
Club	Signed	Fee	Lge	FLC	FAC	Lge	FLC	FAC
Arsenal	5/88	–	5+2					
Plymouth Arg	11/88	Loan	13		2			
West Brom Alb	8/91	Loan	3					
Birmingham C	12/91	Loan	15					
FA Premier Lge Record								
Arsenal	92/93-93/94		5+2			0		

MILLER Paul   Wimbledon
Full Name: MILLER, Paul Anthony   DOB: 31/1/68, Woking
FAPL Debut: Away v Leeds United 15/8/92
Debut Goal: Home v Aston Villa 3/10/92

Previous Club Details			*App*			*Goals*		
Club	Signed	Fee	Lge	FLC	FAC	Lge	FLC	FAC
Wimbledon	8/87	–	65+15	3+3	3+1	10		
Newport Co	10/87	Loan	6			2		
Bristol City	1/90	Loan	0+3					
FA Premier Lge Record								
Wimbledon	92/93		11+8			1		

MILLS Gary   Leicester City
Full Name: MILLS, Gary   DOB: 11/11/61, Northampton

Previous Club Details			*App*			*Goals*		
Club	Signed	Fee	Lge	FLC	FAC	Lge	FLC	FAC
Nottingham F	11/78	–	50+8	7+3	3	8	2	
Seattle (US)								
Derby County	10/82		18	2	3	2		
Seattle (US)								
Nottingham F	12/83		63+15	9+2	2	4	1	
Notts County	8/87		75	6	5	8	1	
Leicester City	3/89	£150,000	194+5	9+1	7	15	1	

MILTON Simon   Ipswich Town

Full Name: MILTON, Simon Charles   DOB: 23/8/63, Fulham
FAPL Debut: Home v Aston Villa †15/8/92
Debut Goal: Away v Blackburn Rovers 13/4/93

Previous Club Details			App			Goals		
Club	Signed	Fee	Lge	FLC	FAC	Lge	FLC	FAC
Ipswich Town	7/87	£5,500	147+27	10+3	8	36	2	1
Exeter City	11/87	Loan	2			3		
Torquay Utd	3/88	Loan	4			1		
FA Premier Lge Record								
Ipswich Town	92/93-93/94		16+9			3		

MIMMS Bobby   Blackburn Rovers

Full Name: MIMMS, Robert Andrew   DOB: 12/10/63, York
FAPL Debut: Away v Crystal Palace 15/8/93   Debut Goal:

Previous Club Details			App			Goals		
Club	Signed	Fee	Lge	FLC	FAC	Lge	FLC	FAC
Halifax Town	8/81	–						
Rotherham Utd	11/81	£15,000	83	7	3			
Everton	6/85	£150,000	29	2	2			
Notts County	3/86	Loan	2					
Sunderland	12/86	Loan	4					
Blackburn Rov	1/87	Loan	6					
Manchester C	9/87	Loan	3					
Tottenham H	2/88	£325,000	37	5	2			
Aberdeen	2/90	Loan						
Blackburn Rov	12/90	£250,000	122	14	9			
FA Premier Lge Record								
Blackburn Rov	92/93-93/94		55			0		

MINTO Scott   Chelsea

Full Name: Minto, Scott   DOB: 6/8/71, Heswall

Previous Club Details			App			Goals		
Club	Signed	Fee	Lge	FLC	FAC	Lge	FLC	FAC
Charlton Ath	2/89	–	171/9	8	8+2	6	2	
Chelsea	6/94							

MITCHELL Paul   West Ham United

Full Name: MITCHELL, Paul   DOB: 20/10/71, Bournemouth
FAPL Debut: Home v Blackburn R † 27/4/94   Debut Goal:

Previous Club Details			Apps			Goals		
Club	Signed	Fee	Lge	FLC	FAC	Lge	FLC	FAC
Bournemouth	8/89	–	6+6					
West Ham Utd	8/93	£40,000	0+1					

244

FA Premier Lge Record
West Ham Utd 93/94   0+1   0

MOLBY Jan   **Liverpool**
Full Name: MOLBY, Jan   DOB: 4/7/63, Jutland, Denmark
FAPL Debut: Home v Arsenal 23/8/92
Debut Goal: Away v Ipswich Town 25/8/92
Danish International

Previous Club Details			*App*			*Goals*		
Club	Signed	Fee	Lge	FLC	FAC	Lge	FLC	FAC
Liverpool	8/84	£575,000	183+21	23+3	24+4	42	9	4

FA Premier Lge Record
Liverpool   92/93-93/94   19+2   5

MONCUR John   **West Ham United**
Full Name: MONCUR, John   DOB: 22/9/66, Stepney
FAPL Debut: Away v Sheffield United 14/8/93
Debut Goal: Away v Sheffield United 14/8/93

Previous Club Details			*App*			*Goals*		
Club	Signed	Fee	Lge	FLC	FAC	Lge	FLC	FAC
Tottenham H	8/84	–	10+11	1+2				
Doncaster Rov	9/86	Loan	4					
Cambridge Utd	3/87	Loan	3+1					
Portsmouth	3/89	Loan	7					
Brentford	10/89	Loan	5			1		
Ipswich Town	10/91	Loan	5+1					
Nottingham F	2/92	Loan						
Swindon Town	3/92	£80,000	51+5	6	2	5		
West Ham Utd	7/94							

FA Premier Lge Record
Swindon Town 93/94   40   4

MONKOU Ken   **Southampton**
Full Name: MONKOU, Kenneth John   DOB: 29/11/64, Necare, Surinam
FAPL Debut: Home v Manchester United 24/8/92
Debut Goal: Home v Sheffield Wednesday 28/12/92

Previous Club Details			*App*			*Goals*		
Club	Signed	Fee	Lge	FLC	FAC	Lge	FLC	FAC
Chelsea	3/89	£100,000	92+2	12	3	2		
Southampton	8/92	£750,000	67	4	3	5		

FA Premier Lge Record
Southampton 92/93-93/94   67   5

MOORE Kevin   **Southampton**
Full Name: MOORE, Thomas Kevin   DOB: 29/4/58, Grimsby
FAPL Debut: Home v QPR 19/8/92

Debut Goal: Home v Sheffield United 27/2/93

Previous Club Details			App			Goals		
Club	Signed	Fee	Lge	FLC	FAC	Lge	FLC	FAC
Grimsby Town	7/76	–	397+3	41	25	28	3	3
Oldham Ath	2/87	£100,000	13			1		
Southampton	7/87	£125,000	144+4	17	13	10	2	
Bristol Rovers	1/92	Loan	7			1		
Bristol Rovers	10/92	Loan						
FA Premier Lge Record								
Southampton	92/93-93/94		32			2		

MOORE Neil   Everton
Full Name: MOORE, Neil   DOB: 21/9/72, Liverpoool
FAPL Debut: Away v Manchester City † 8/5/93   Debut Goal:

Previous Club Details			App			Goals		
Club	Signed	Fee	Lge	FLC	FAC	Lge	FLC	FAC
Everton	6/91	–	4+1					
FA Premier Lge Record								
Everton	92/93-93/94		4+1			0		

MORAN Kevin   Blackburn Rovers
Full Name: MORAN, Kevin Bernard   DOB: 29/4/56, Dublin
FAPL Debut: Away v Crystal Palace 15/8/92   Debut Goal:

Previous Club Details			App			Goals		
Club	Signed	Fee	Lge	FLC	FAC	Lge	FLC	FAC
Manchester U	2/78	–	228+3	24+1	18	21	2	1
Gijon (Fra)	8/88	–						
Blackburn Rov	1/90	–	142+4	8+1	10+1	10		1
FA Premier Lge Record								
Blackburn Rov	92/93-93/94		54			5		

MORAN Paul   Tottenham Hotspur
Full Name: MORAN, Paul   DOB: 22/5/68, Enfield
FAPL Debut: Away v Norwich City † 26/12/92   Debut Goal:

Previous Club Details			App			Goals		
Club	Signed	Fee	Lge	FLC	FAC	Lge	FLC	FAC
Tottenham H	7/85		14+11	1+6	3+1	2		
Portsmouth	1/89	Loan	3					
Leicester City	11/89	Loan	10			2		
Newcastle Utd	2/91	Loan	1					
Southend Utd	3/91	Loan	1					
Cambridge Utd	9/92	Loan						
FA Premier Lge Record								
Tottenham H	92/93-93/94		0+8			0		

MORGAN Steve   Coventry City
Full Name: MORGAN, Stephen   DOB: 19/9/68, Oldham
FAPL Debut: Away v Arsenal 14/8/93
Debut Goal: Home v Chelsea 18/9/93

Previous Club Details			*App*			*Goals*		
Club	Signed	Fee	Lge	FLC	FAC	Lge	FLC	FAC
Blackpool	8/86	–	135+9	13	16	10	2	1
Plymouth Arg	7/90	£115,000	85	5	3	5		
Coventry City	7/93	£110,000	38+1	3	1	2	3	
FA Premier Lge Record								
Coventry City	93/94		39+1			2		

MORLEY Trevor   West Ham United
Full Name: MORLEY, Trevor   DOB: 20/3/62, Nottingham
FAPL Debut: Home v Wimbledon 14/8/93
Debut Goal: Away v Blackburn Rovers 18/9/93

Previous Club Details			*Apps*			*Goals*		
Club	Signed	Fee	Lge	FLC	FAC	Lge	FLC	FAC
Northampton T	6/85	£20,000	107	10	6	39	4	2
Manchester C	1/88	£175,000	69+3	7	1	18	3	
West Ham Utd	12/89	Exchange	168+15	10	13+4	57	5	7
FA Premier Lge Record								
West Ham Utd	93/94		39+3			13		

MORRISON Andy   Blackburn Rovers
Full Name: MORRISON, Andy   DOB: 30/7/70, Inverness

Previous Club Details			*Apps*			*Goals*		
Club	Signed	Fee	Lge	FLC	FAC	Lge	FLC	FAC
Plymouth Arg	7/88	–	105+8	9+1	6	6	1	
Blackburn Rov	8/93	£150,000	1+4		1			
FA Premier Lge Record								
Blackburn Rov	93/94		1+4			0		

MORROW Steve   Arsenal
Full Name: MORROW, Stephen Joseph   DOB: 2/7/70, Bangor, NI
FAPL Debut: Home v Oldham Athletic 26/8/92   Debut Goal:
N Ireland International Debut: Home v Hungary † 18/5/90

Previous Club Details			*App*			*Goals*		
Club	Signed	Fee	Lge	FLC	FAC	Lge	FLC	FAC
Arsenal	5/88	–	19+9	5+1	2+2	1		
Reading	1/91	Loan	10					
Watford	8/91	Loan	7+1					
Reading	10/91	Loan	3					
Barnet	3/92	Loan	1					

MORTIMER Paul   Crystal Palace
Full Name: MORTIMER, Paul   DOB: 8/5/68, Kensington
FAPL Debut: Home v Nottingham Forest 21/11/92 Debut Goal:

Previous Club Details			*Apps*			*Goals*		
Club	Signed	Fee	Lge	FLC	FAC	Lge	FLC	FAC
Charlton Ath	9/87	–	108+5	4	8	17		
Aston Villa	7/91	£350,000	10+2	2		1		
Crystal Palace	10/91	£500,000	18+4	1	1	2		
Brentford	1/93	Loan	6					

FA Premier Lge Record
Crystal Palace   92/93   1   0

MYERS Andy   Chelsea
Full Name: MYERS, Andrew John   DOB: 3/11/73, Hounslow
FAPL Debut: Away v Wimbledon 28/12/92   Debut Goal:

Previous Club Details			*App*			*Goals*		
Club	Signed	Fee	Lge	FLC	FAC	Lge	FLC	FAC
Chelsea	6/91	–	19+5	1+1	6	1		

FA Premier Lge Record
Chelsea   92/93-93/94   10   0

NDAH George   Crystal Palace
Full Name: NDAH, George   DOB: 23/12/74, Dulwich
FAPL Debut: Away v Liverpool † 28/11/92   Debut Goal:

Previous Club Details			*Apps*			*Goals*		
Club	Signed	Fee	Lge	FLC	FAC	Lge	FLC	FAC
Crystal Palace	8/92	–	4+10	2+3		1		

FA Premier Lge Record
Crystal Palace   92/93   4+9   0

NDLOVU Peter   Coventry City
Full Name: NDLOVU, Peter   DOB: 25/2/73, Bulawayo
FAPL Debut: Away v Tottenham Hotspur † 19/8/92
Debut Goal: Away v Sheffield Wednesday 2/9/92
Zimbabwean International

Previous Club Details			*App*			*Goals*		
Club	Signed	Fee	Lge	FLC	FAC	Lge	FLC	FAC
Coventry City	7/91	£10,000	75+19	3	2	20	1	

FA Premier Lge Record
Coventry City   92/93-93/94   66+5   18

NEILSON Alan — Newcastle United

Full Name: NIELSON, Alan   DOB: 26/9/72, Wegburg, Germany
Wales International Debut: Home v Eire † 19/2/92

Previous Club Details			*Apps*			*Goals*		
Club	Signed	Fee	Lge	FLC	FAC	Lge	FLC	FAC
Newcastle Utd	2/91		29+9	3		1		

FA Premier Lge Record

| Newcastle Utd | 93/94 | | 10+4 | | | 0 | | |

NETHERCOTT Stuart — Tottenham Hotspur

Full Name: NETHERCOTT, Stuart   DOB: 21/3/73, Ilford
FAPL Debut: Home v Norwich City † 9/4/93   Debut Goal:

Previous Club Details			*App*			*Goals*		
Club	Signed	Fee	Lge	FLC	FAC	Lge	FLC	FAC
Tottenham H	7/91	–	11+2		1			
Maidstone Utd	9/91	Loan	13			1		
Barnet	2/92	Loan	3					

FA Premier Lge Record

| Tottenham H | 92/93-93/94 | | 11+2 | | | 0 | | |

NEWELL Mike — Blackburn Rovers

Full Name: NEWELL, Michael Colin   DOB: 27/1/65, Liverpool
FAPL Debut: Away v Crystal Palace 15/8/92
Debut Goal: Home v Manchester City 22/8/92

Previous Club Details			*App*			*Goals*		
Club	Signed	Fee	Lge	FLC	FAC	Lge	FLC	FAC
Crewe Alex	9/83	–	3					
Wigan Ath	10/83	–	64+8	6	8	25	1	6
Luton Town	1/86	–	62+1		5	18		1
Leicester City	9/87	£350,000	81	9	2	21	5	
Everton	6/89	£1.1m	48+20	7+3	6+2	15	4	
Blackburn Rov	11/91	£1.1m	67+1	10	5	19	7	3

FA Premier Lge Record

| Blackburn Rov | 92/93-93/94 | | 67+1 | | | 19 | | |

NEWHOUSE Aiden — Wimbledon

Full Name: NEWHOUSE, Aiden Robert   DOB: 23/5/72, Wallasey
FAPL Debut: Home v Aston Villa † 3/10/92   Debut Goal:

Previous Club Details			*App*			*Goals*		
Club	Signed	Fee	Lge	FLC	FAC	Lge	FLC	FAC
Chester City	7/89		29+15	5+1	0+2	6		
Wimbledon	2/90	£100,000	7+16	1+1	2	2		
Port Vale	1/94	Loan	0+2					

FA Premier Lge Record

| Wimbledon | 92/93 | | 0+1 | | | 1 | | |

NEWMAN Richard   Crystal Palace
Full Name: NEWMAN, Richard   DOB: 5/8/70, Guildford
FAPL Debut: Home v Everton † 9/1/93   Debut Goal:

Previous Club Details			*Apps*			*Goals*		
Club	Signed	Fee	Lge	FLC	FAC	Lge	FLC	FAC
Crystal Palace	1/88	–	11+2		1			
Maidstone Utd	2/92	Loan	10+2			1		
FA Premier Lge Record								
Crystal Palace	92/93		1+1			0		

NEWMAN Rob   Norwich City
Full Name: NEWMAN, Robert Nigel   DOB: 13/12/63, Bradford on Avon
FAPL Debut: Away v Arsenal 15/8/92
Debut Goal: Home v Sheffield Wednesday 19/9/92

Previous Club Details			*App*			*Goals*		
Club	Signed	Fee	Lge	FLC	FAC	Lge	FLC	FAC
Bristol City	10/81	–	382+12	29+1	27	52	2	2
Norwich City	7/91	£600,000	89+2	10	8	11	1	1
FA Premier Lge Record								
Norwich City	92/93-93/94		48+2			4		

NEWSOME Jon   Leeds United
Full Name: NEWSOME, Jonathan   DOB: 6/9/70, Sheffield
FAPL Debut: Home v Wimbledon 15/8/92
Debut Goal: Home v Blackburn R 23/10/93

Previous Club Details			*App*			*Goals*		
Club	Signed	Fee	Lge	FLC	FAC	Lge	FLC	FAC
Sheffield Wed	7/81	–	6+1	3				
Leeds United	6/91	£150,000	62+14	3	3+1	3		
FA Premier Lge Record								
Leeds United	92/93-93/94		55+11			1		

NEWTON Eddie   Chelsea
Full Name: NEWTON, Edward John Ikem   DOB:13/12/71,Hammersmith
FAPL Debut: Away v Norwich City † 19/8/92
Debut Goal: Home v Sheffield Wednesday 22/8/92

Previous Club Details			*App*			*Goals*		
Club	Signed	Fee	Lge	FLC	FAC	Lge	FLC	FAC
Chelsea	5/90	–	64+6	9	7	6	1	
Cardiff City	1/92	Loan	16			4		
FA Premier Lge Record								
Chelsea	92/93-93/94		64+5			5		

NICOL Steve   Liverpool
Full Name: NICOL, Stephen   DOB: 1/12/61, Irvine
FAPL Debut: Away v Nottingham Forest 16/8/92
Debut Goal: Away v QPR 18/8/93
Scotland International Debut: Home v Yugoslavia 2/9/84

Previous Club Details			App			Goals		
Club	Signed	Fee	Lge	FLC	FAC	Lge	FLC	FAC
Liverpool	10/81	£300,000	323+15	28	48	36	4	3

FA Premier Lge Record

Liverpool	92/93-93/94		58+4			1		

NILSSON Roland   Sheffield Wednesday
Full Name: NILSSON, Nils Lennart Roland
DOB: 27/11/63, Helsingborg, Sweden
FAPL Debut: Away v Everton 15/8/92
Debut Goal: Away v Leeds United 12/12/92
Swedish International Debut: Home v Greece 1/5/86

Previous Club Details			App			Goals		
Club	Signed	Fee	Lge	FLC	FAC	Lge	FLC	FAC
Sheffield Wed	11/89	£375,000	150	16	15	2	1	

FA Premier Lge Record

Sheffield Wed	92/93-93/94		67			1		

O'CONNOR Martyn   Crystal Palace
Full Name: O'CONNOR, Martyn   DOB: 10/12/67, Walsall

Previous Club Details			Apps			Goals		
Club	Signed	Fee	Lge	FLC	FAC	Lge	FLC	FAC
Crystal Palace	7/92	–	2					
Walsall	3/93	Loan	10					

OGRIZOVIC Steve   Coventry City
Full Name: OGRIZOVIC, Steven   DOB: 12/9/57, Mansfield
FAPL Debut: Home v Middlesbrough 15/8/93 Debut Goal:

Previous Club Details			App			Goals		
Club	Signed	Fee	Lge	FLC	FAC	Lge	FLC	FAC
Chesterfield	7/77	–	16	2				
Liverpool	11/77	£70,000	4					
Shrewsbury T	8/82	£70,000	84	7	5			
Coventry City	6/84	£72,000	381	37	21	1		

FA Premier Lge Record

Coventry City	92/93-93/94		65			0		

OLDFIELD David   Leicester City
Full Name: OLDFIELD, David   DOB: 30/5/68, Perth, Australia

251

Previous Club Details			App			Goals		
Club	Signed	Fee	Lge	FLC	FAC	Lge	FLC	FAC
Luton Town	5/86	–	21+8	4+2	0+1	4	2	
Manchester C	3/89	£600,000	18+8	2+1		6	2	
Leicester City	1/90	£150,000	154+19	10+1	6	25	1	2

O'LEARY David   Leeds United
Full Name: O'LEARY, David Anthony   DOB: 2/5/58, Stoke Newington
FAPL Debut: Away v Wimbledon † 5/9/92   Debut Goal:
Eire International Debut: Away v England 8/9/76

Previous Club Details			App			Goals		
Club	Signed	Fee	Lge	FLC	FAC	Lge	FLC	FAC
Arsenal	7/75	–	523+35	68+2	66+3	11	2	3
Leeds United	6/93		9					
FA Premier Lge Record								
Arsenal	92/93		6+5			0		
Leeds United	93/94		10			0		

ORMONDROYD Ian   Leicester City
Full Name: ORMONDROYD , Ian   DOB: 22/9/64, Bradford

Previous Club Details			App			Goals		
Club	Signed	Fee	Lge	FLC	FAC	Lge	FLC	FAC
Bradford City	9/85	–	75+15	12+2	7	20	4	2
Oldham Ath	3/87	Loan	8+2			1		
Aston Villa	2/89	£600,000	41+15	4+2	5	6	2	2
Derby County	9/91	£350,000	25	3	3	8		1
Leicester City	3/92	Swap	61+10	6	1+1	7	2	

OSBORN Simon   Crystal Palace
Full Name: OSBORN, Simon   DOB: 19/1/72, Croydon
FAPL Debut: Home v Blackburn Rovers † 15/8/92
Debut Goal: Home v Blackburn Rovers † 15/8/92

Previous Club Details			Apps			Goals		
Club	Signed	Fee	Lge	FLC	FAC	Lge	FLC	FAC
Crystal Palace	1/90	47+8	11	2	4	1		
FA Premier Lge Record								
Crystal Palace	92/93		27+4			2		

PALLISTER Gary   Manchester United
Full Name: PALLISTER, Gary Andrew   DOB: 30/6/65, Ramsgate
FAPL Debut: Away v Sheffield Utd 15/8/92
Debut Goal: Home v Blackburn Rovers 3/5/93
England International Debut: Away v Hungary 27/4/88

Previous Club Details			App			Goals		
Club	Signed	Fee	Lge	FLC	FAC	Lge	FLC	FAC
Middlesbrough	11/84	–	156	10	10	5		1

Darlington	10/85	Loan	7					
Manchester U	8/89	£2.3m	190+3	32	24	6		

FA Premier Lge Record

Manchester U	92/93-93/94	82			2	

PALMER Carlton   Sheffield Wednesday
Full Name: PALMER, Carlton Lloyd   DOB: 5/12/65, Rowley Regis
FAPL Debut: Away v Everton 15/8/92
Debut Goal: Home v Oldham Athletic 17/10/92
England International Debut: Home v CIS 29/4/92

Previous Club Details			*App*			*Goals*		
Club	Signed	Fee	Lge	FLC	FAC	Lge	FLC	FAC
West Brom Alb	12/84	–	114+7	7+1	4	4	1	
Sheffield Wed	2/89	£750,000	203+1	31	18+1	14	3	

FA Premier Lge Record

Sheffield Wed	92/93-93/94	69+1			6	

PALMER Steve   Ipswich Town
Full Name: PALMER, Stephen Leonard   DOB: 31/3/68, Brighton
FAPL Debut: Away v Nottingham Forest 31/10/92
Debut Goal: Away v Oldham 14/8/93

Previous Club Details			*App*			*Goals*		
Club	Signed	Fee	Lge	FLC	FAC	Lge	FLC	FAC
Ipswich Town	8/89	–	66+22	2	8+3	2		1

FA Premier Lge Record

Ipswich Town	92/93-93/94	34+8			1	

PAPAVASSILLIOU Nicodenos   Newcastle United
Full Name: PAPAVASSILLIOU, Nicodenos DOB: 30/8/70, Limassol, Cyprus
FAPL Debut: Home v Tottenham Hotspur 14/8/93 Debut Goal:

Previous Club Details			*Apps*			*Goals*		
Club	Signed	Fee	Lge	FLC	FAC	Lge	FLC	FAC
Newcastle Utd	7/93	£120,000	7	·				

FA Premier Lge Record

Newcastle Utd	93/94	7			0	

PARKER Garry   Aston Villa
Full Name: PARKER, Garry Stuart   DOB: 7/9/65, Oxford
FAPL Debut: Away v Ipswich Town 15/8/92
Debut Goal: Away v Sheffield United 29/8/92

Previous Club Details			*App*			*Goals*		
Club	Signed	Fee	Lge	FLC	FAC	Lge	FLC	FAC
Luton Town	5/83	–	31+11	1+3	6+2	3	1	
Hull City	2/86	£72,000	82+2	5	4	8		
Nottingham F	3/88	£260,000	99+4	22+1	16	17	4	5
Aston Villa	11/91	£650,000	79+2	8	10	11		1

PARKER Paul   **Manchester United**
Full Name: PARKER, Paul Andrew   DOB: 4/4/64, West Ham
FAPL Debut: Home v Liverpool 18/10/92
Debut Goal: Home v Tottenham Hotspur 9/1/93
England International Debut: Home v Albania † 26/4/89

Previous Club Details			*App*			*Goals*		
Club	Signed	Fee	Lge	FLC	FAC	Lge	FLC	FAC
Fulham	4/82	–	140+13	16	11	2	1	
QPR	6/87	£300,000	121+4	14	16	1		
Manchester U	8/91	£2m	94+2	14	13	1		

FA Premier Lge Record
Manchester U   92/93   31   1

PARKINSON Joe   **Everton**
Full Name: PARKINSON, Joseph   DOB: 11/6/71, Eccles

Previous Club Details			*Apps*			*Goals*		
Club	Signed	Fee	Lge	FLC	FAC	Lge	FLC	FAC
Wigan Ath	4/89	–	115+4	11	9	6	1	
Bournemouth	7/93	£35,000	3	4	4	1	1	
Everton	3/93	£25,000						

PARLOUR Ray   **Arsenal**
Full Name: PARLOUR, Raymond   DOB: 7/3/73, Romford
FAPL Debut: Home v Sheffield Wednesday 29/8/92
Debut Goal: Home v Sheffield Wednesday 29/8/92

Previous Club Details			*App*			*Goals*		
Club	Signed	Fee	Lge	FLC	FAC	Lge	FLC	FAC
Arsenal	3/91	–	42+11	5+1	7	4	1	

FA Premier Lge Record
Arsenal   92/93-93/94   40+7   3

PEACOCK Darren   **Newcastle**
Full Name: PEACOCK, Darren   DOB: 3/2/68, Bristol
FAPL Debut: Away v Manchester City 17/8/92
Debut Goal: Home v Coventry City 20/2/93

Previous Club Details			*App*			*Goals*		
Club	Signed	Fee	Lge	FLC	FAC	Lge	FLC	FAC
Newport Co	2/86	–	24+4	2	1			
Hereford Utd	3/89	–	56+7	6	6	5	1	
QPR	12/90	£200,000	123+3	8	2	6		
Newcastle Utd	3/94	£2.7m	8					

FA Premier Lge Record
QPR   92/93/93-94   65+3   5
Newcastle Utd 93/94   9   0

PEACOCK Gavin — Chelsea

Full Name: PEACOCK, Gavin   DOB: 18/11/67 Welling, Kent

Previous Club Details			*Apps*			*Goals*		
Club	Signed	Fee	Lge	FLC	FAC	Lge	FLC	FAC
QPR	11/84		7+10		0+1	1		
Gillingham	10/87	£40,000	69+1	4	2	11		
Bournemouth	8/89	£250,000	56	6	2	8		
Newcastle Utd	11/90	£150,000	102+4	6	6	35	5	2
Chelsea	8/93	£1.25m	37	2	8	8		6
FA Premier Lge Record								
Chelsea	93/94		38			8		

PEARCE Andy — Sheffield Wednesday

Full Name: PEARCE, Andrew John   DOB: 20/4/66, Bradford on Avon
FAPL Debut: Home v Middlesbrough 15/8/92
Debut Goal: Home v Crystal Palace 3/10/92
England International Debut: Home v Brazil 19/2/87

Previous Club Details			*App*			*Goals*		
Club	Signed	Fee	Lge	FLC	FAC	Lge	FLC	FAC
Coventry City	5/90	£15,000	68+3	6	3	4		
Sheffield Wed	8/93	£500,000	28+3	6+1	3+1	3		1
FA Premier Lge Record								
Coventry City	92/93		21+3			1		
Sheffield Wed	93/94		29+3			3		

PEARCE Ian — Blackburn Rovers

Full Name: PEARCE, Ian   DOB: 7/5/74, Bury St Edmunds
FAPL Debut: Home v Liverpool † 9/5/92
Debut Goal: Away v West Ham United 27/4/94

Previous Club Details			*App*			*Goals*		
Club	Signed	Fee	Lge	FLC	FAC	Lge	FLC	FAC
Chelsea	8/91		0+4					
Blackburn Rov	10/93	£300,000	0+4	0+2	0+2	1	1	
FA Premier Lge Record								
Chelsea	92/93		0+1			0		
Blackburn Rov	93/94		0+4			1		

PEARCE Stuart — Nottingham Forest

Full Name: PEARCE, Stuart   DOB: 24/4/62, Shepherds Bush
FAPL Debut: Home v Liverpool 16/8/92
Debut Goal: Away v Oldham Athletic 22/8/92
England International Debut: Home v Brazil 8/87

Previous Club Details			*App*			*Goals*		
Club	Signed	Fee	Lge	FLC	FAC	Lge	FLC	FAC
Coventry City	10/83	£25,000	52		2	4		

Nottingham F	6/85	£200,000	301	54	30	47	7	7

FA Premier Lge Record

Nottingham F	92/93		23			2		

PEARSON Nigel   Leeds United

Full Name: PEARSON, Nigel Graham   DOB: 21/8/63, Nottingham
FAPL Debut: Away v Everton 15/8/92
Debut Goal: Away v Everton 15/8/92

Previous Club Details			*App*			*Goals*		
Club	Signed	Fee	Lge	FLC	FAC	Lge	FLC	FAC
Shrewsbury T	11/81	£5,000	153	19	6	5		
Sheffield Wed	10/87	£250,000	67+1	4	4			
Leeds United	11/93	£250,000	6+3					

FA Premier Lge Record

Sheffield Wed	92/93-93/94		17+4			1		

PEMBERTON John   Leeds United

Full Name: PEMBERTON, John Matthew   DOB: 18/11/64, Oldham
FAPL Debut: Away v Norwich City 21/11/92   Debut Goal:

Previous Club Details			*App*			*Goals*		
Club	Signed	Fee	Lge	FLC	FAC	Lge	FLC	FAC
Rochdale	9/84	–	1					
Crewe Alex	3/85	–	116+5	7	3	1	1	
Crystal Palace	3/88	£80,000	76+2	6+1	8	2		
Sheffield Utd	7/90	£300,000	67+1	4	4			
Leeds United	11/93	£250,000	6+3					

FA Premier Lge Record

Sheffield Utd	92/93-93/94		27			0		
Leeds United	93/94		7+3			0		

PENRICE Gary   Queens Park Rangers

Full Name: PENRICE, Gary Kenneth   DOB: 23/3/64, Bristol
FAPL Debut: Away v Coventry City † 26/8/92
Debut Goal: Home v Middlesbrough 19/9/92

Previous Club Details			*App*			*Goals*		
Club	Signed	Fee	Lge	FLC	FAC	Lge	FLC	FAC
Bristol Rovers	11/84	–	186+2	11	11	53	3	7
Watford	11/89	£500,000	41+2		4	17		
Aston Villa	3/91	£1m	14+6			1		
QPR	10/91	£625,000	46+13	4+1	12+1	14		1

FA Premier Lge Record

QPR	92/93-93/94		33+7			14		

PERRY Chris   Wimbledon

Full Name: PERRY, Christopher John   DOB: 25/12/75, Surrey
FAPL Debut: Home v Tottenham Hotspur † 30/4/94   Debut Goal:

Previous Club Details			*Apps*			*Goals*		
Club	Signed	Fee	Lge	FLC	FAC	Lge	FLC	FAC
Wimbledon	7/91	–	0+1					

FA Premier Lge Record

| Wimbledon | 93/94 | | 0+1 | | | 0 | | |

PHELAN Mike — Manchester United

Full Name: PHELAN, Michael Christopher   DOB: 24/9/62, Nelson
FAPL Debut: Away v Sheffield United † 15/8/92   Debut Goal:
England International Debut: Home v Italy 15/11/89

Previous Club Details			*App*			*Goals*		
Club	Signed	Fee	Lge	FLC	FAC	Lge	FLC	FAC
Burnley	7/80	–	166+2	16	16	9	2	
Norwich City	7/85	£60,000	155+1	14	11	9		1
Manchester U	6/89	£750,000	88+14	14+2	10	·2		1

FA Premier Lge Record

| Manchester U | 92/93-93/94 | | 6+7 | | | 0 | | |

PHELAN Terry — Manchester City

Full Name: PHELAN, Terence   DOB: 16/3/67, Manchester
FAPL Debut: Home v Norwich City 26/8/92
Debut Goal: Away v Chelsea 9/1/93
Eire International Debut: Away v Hungary 11/9/91

Previous Club Details			*App*			*Goals*		
Club	Signed	Fee	Lge	FLC	FAC	Lge	FLC	FAC
Leeds United	8/84	–	12+2	3				
Swansea City	7/86	–	45	4	5			
Wimbledon	7/87	£100,000	156+4	13+2	11	1		2
Manchester C	8/92	£2.5m	66	7	7	1		1

FA Premier Lge Record

| Manchester C | 92/93-93/94 | | 66 | | | 1 | | |

PHILLIPS David — Nottingham Forest

Full Name: PHILLIPS, David Owen   DOB: 29/7/63, Wegberg, Germany
FAPL Debut: Away v Arsenal 15/8/92
Debut Goal: Away v Arsenal 15/8/92
Welsh International Debut: Home v England 2/5/84

Previous Club Details			*App*			*Goals*		
Club	Signed	Fee	Lge	FLC	FAC	Lge	FLC	FAC
Plymouth Arg	8/81	–	65+8	2+1	12+1	15		
Manchester C	8/84	£65,000	81	8	5	13		
Coventry City	6/86	£150,000	93+7	8	9	8		1
Norwich City	6/89	£525,000	110	10	12	9		1
Nottingham F	8/93	£600,000	39+3	7	2	4		

FA Premier Lge Record

| Norwich City | 92/93 | | 42 | | | 9 | | |

PHILPOTT Lee
Leicester City

Full Name: PHILPOTT Lee
DOB: 21/2/70, Barnet

Previous Club Details

Club	Signed	Fee	App Lge	FLC	FAC	Goals Lge	FLC	FAC
Peterborough	7/86	–	1+3		0+1			
Cambridge U	5/89	Free	118+16	10	13	17	1	3
Leicester City	11/92	£350,000	37+9	0+1	2+1	3		

PICKERING Ally
Coventry City

Full Name: PICKERING, Albert
DOB: 22/6/67, Manchester

FAPL Debut: Away v Liverpool † 26/2/94
Debut Goal:

Previous Club Details

Club	Signed	Fee	Apps Lge	FLC	FAC	Goals Lge	FLC	FAC
Rotherham Utd	2/90	£18,500	87+1	6	9	2		
Coventry City	10/93	£80,000	1+2					

FA Premier Lge Record

Club								
Coventry City	93/94		1+2			0		

PIECHNIK Torben
Liverpool

Full Name: PIECHNIK, Torben
DOB: 21/5/63, Denmark

FAPL Debut: Away v Aston Villa 19/9/92
Debut Goal:

Danish International

Previous Club Details

Club	Signed	Fee	Apps Lge	FLC	FAC	Goals Lge	FLC	FAC
FC Copenhagen		–						
Liverpool	9/92	£500,000	16+1	5	2			

FA Premier Lge Record

Club								
Liverpool	92/93-93/94		17+1			0		

POLSTON John
Norwich City

Full Name: POLSTON, John David
DOB: 10/6/68, Walthamstow

FAPL Debut: Away v Arsenal 15/8/92
Debut Goal: Home v Aston Villa 24/3/93

Previous Club Details

Club	Signed	Fee	App Lge	FLC	FAC	Goals Lge	FLC	FAC
Tottenham H	7/85	–	17+7	3+1		1		
Norwich City	7/90	£250,000	100+3	5+1	10+1	6		

FA Premier Lge Record

Club								
Norwich City	92/93-93/94		57			1		

POOLE Kevin
Leicester City

Full Name: POOLE, Kevin
DOB: 21/7/63, Bromsgrove

Previous Club Details

Club	Signed	Fee	App Lge	FLC	FAC	Goals Lge	FLC	FAC
Aston Villa	6/81	–	28	2	1			

Northampton	11/84	Loan	3		
Middlesbrough	8/87		34	4	2
Hartlepool Utd	3/91	Loan	12		
Leicester City	7/91	£40,000	75	4	3

POTTS Steve   West Ham United
Full Name: POTTS, Steve   DOB: 7/5/67, Hartford, USA
FAPL Debut: Home v Wimbledon 14/8/93   Debut Goal:

Previous Club Details			*App*			*Goals*		
Club	Signed	Fee	Lge	FLC	FAC	Lge	FLC	FAC
West Ham Utd	7/83	–	225+10	23+1	28	1		
FA Premier Lge Record								
West Ham Utd	93/94		41			0		

POWELL Lee   Southampton
Full Name: POWELL, Lee   DOB: 2/6/73, Caerleon
FAPL Debut: Home v Wimbledon † 17/10/92   Debut Goal:

Previous Club Details			*App*			*Goals*		
Club	Signed	Fee	Lge	FLC	FAC	Lge	FLC	FAC
Southampton	5/91	–	2+5					
FA Premier Lge Record								
Southampton	92/93-93/94		1+2			0		

PRESSMAN Kevin   Sheffield Wednesday
Full Name: PRESSMAN, Kevin Paul   DOB: 6/11/67, Fareham
FAPL Debut: Home v Southampton 12/4/92   Debut Goal:

Previous Club Details			*App*			*Goals*		
Club	Signed	Fee	Lge	FLC	FAC	Lge	FLC	FAC
Sheffield Wed	11/85	–	93	14	4			
Stoke City	3/92	Loan	4					
FA Premier Lge Record								
Sheffield Wed	92/93-93/94		34			0		

PRIOR Spencer   Norwich City
Full Name: PRIOR, Spencer   DOB: 22/04/71, Hockley
FAPL Debut: Away v Sheffield Wednesday 1/9/93

Previous Club Details			*Apps*			*Goals*		
Club	Signed	Fee	Lge	FLC	FAC	Lge	FLC	FAC
Southend Utd	5/89		135	9	5	3		
Norwich City	8/93	£200,000	12	1				
FA Premier Lge Record								
Norwich City	93/94		13			0		

QUIGLEY Mike   Manchester City
Full Name: QUIGLEY, Michael Anthony   DOB: 2/10/70, Manchester
FAPL Debut: Away v Norwich City † 20/2/93 Debut Goal:

Previous Club Details   *App*   *Goals*

Club	Signed	Fee	Lge	FLC	FAC	Lge	FLC	FAC
Manchester C	7/89	–	3+9					

FA Premier Lge Record

| Manchester C | 92/93-93/94 | 3+4 | | | | 0 | | |

QUINN Mick   Coventry City

Full Name: QUINN, Mick   DOB: 2/5/62, Liverpool
FAPL Debut: Home v Manchester City 21/11/92
Debut Goal: Home v Manchester City 21/11/92

Previous Club Details   *App*   *Goals*

Club	Signed	Fee	Lge	FLC	FAC	Lge	FLC	FAC
Derby County								
Wigan Ath	9/79	–	56+13	5	3	19	1	1
Stockport Co	7/82	–	62+1	5	2	39	2	
Oldham Ath	1/84	£50,000	78+2	4	2	34	2	1
Portsmouth	3/86	–	115+6	7	7	54	6	7
Newcastle Utd	6/89	£680,000	110+5	7+2	7	59		4
Coventry City	11/92	£250,000	54+4	1+1	1+1	25	1	

FA Premier Lge Record

| Coventry City | 92/93-93/94 | 53+1 | | | | 25 | | |

QUINN Niall   Manchester City

Full Name: QUINN, Niall John   DOB: 6/10/66, Dublin
FAPL Debut: Home v QPR 17/8/92
Debut Goal: Home v Oldham Athletic 29/8/92
Eire International Debut: Away v Iceland † 25/5/86

Previous Club Details   *App*   *Goals*

Club	Signed	Fee	Lge	FLC	FAC	Lge	FLC	FAC
Arsenal	11/83	–	59+8	14+2	8+2	14	4	2
Manchester C	3/90	£800,000	135+1	13	8	50	4	2

FA Premier Lge Record

| Manchester C | 92/93-93/94 | 53+1 | | | | 14 | | |

RADOSAVIJEVIC Pedray   Everton

Full Name: RADOSAVIJEVIC, Pedray   DOB: 24/6/63 Belgrade
FAPL Debut: Away v Leeds United 26/9/92
Debut Goal: Away v Middlesbrough 10/4/93
Yugoslavia International

Previous Club Details   *App*   *Goals*

Club	Signed	Fee	Lge	FLC	FAC	Lge	FLC	FAC
St Louis (USA)								
Everton	9/92	£100,000	22+25	2+4	1	4		

FA Premier Lge Record

| Everton | 92/93-93/94 | 22+25 | | | | 4 | | |

READY Karl
Queens Park Rangers
Full Name: READY, Karl
DOB: 14/8/72, Neath
FAPL Debut: Home v Coventry City 20/2/93
Debut Goal: Away v Blackburn Rovers 24/4/94

Previous Club Details			App			Goals		
Club	Signed	Fee	Lge	FLC	FAC	Lge	FLC	FAC
QPR	8/90	–	21+4	0+1		1		
FA Premier Lge Record								
QPR	92/93-93/94		20+4			1		

REDKNAPP Jamie
Liverpool
Full Name: REDKNAPP, Jamie Frank
DOB: 25/6/73, Barton on Sea
FAPL Debut: Away v Leeds United 29/8/92
Debut Goal: Home v Chelsea 5/9/92

Previous Club Details			App			Goals		
Club	Signed	Fee	Lge	FLC	FAC	Lge	FLC	FAC
Bournemouth	6/90	–	6+7	3	3			
Liverpool	1/91	£350,000	60+9	10	5	7	1	
FA Premier Lge Record								
Liverpool	92/93-93/94		55+8			6		

RENNIE David
Coventry City
Full Name: RENNIE, David
DOB: 28/8/64, Edinburgh
FAPL Debut: Home v Arsenal 13/3/93
Debut Goal: Away v Arsenal 14/8/93

Previous Club Details			App			Goals		
Club	Signed	Fee	Lge	FLC	FAC	Lge	FLC	FAC
Leicester City	5/82	–	21	2		1		
Leeds United	1/86	£50,000	95+6	7	7	5		1
Bristol City	7/89	£175,000	103+3	8	9	8		
Birmingham C	2/92	£120,000	32+3	1		4		
Coventry City	3/93	Swap	37	3	1	1		
FA Premier Lge Record								
Coventry City	92/93-93/94		3			1		

RICHARDSON Kevin
Aston Villa
Full Name: RICHARDSON, Kevin
DOB: 4/12/62, Newcastle
FAPL Debut: Away v Ipswich Town 15/8/92
Debut Goal: Home v Chelsea 2/9/92
England International Debut: Home v Greece 17/5/94

Previous Club Details			App			Goals		
Club	Signed	Fee	Lge	FLC	FAC	Lge	FLC	FAC
Everton	12/80	–	95+14	10+3	13	16	3	1
Watford	9/86	£225,000	39	3	7	2		
Arsenal	8/87	£200,000	88+8	13+3	9	5	2	1

Real Sociedad	6/90	£750,000					
Aston Villa	8/91	£450,000	123	15	12	13	3

FA Premier Lge Record

Aston Villa	92/93-93/94	81	7

RIDEOUT Paul   Everton

Full Name: RIDEOUT, Paul D   DOB: 14/8/64, Bournemouth
FAPL Debut: Home v Sheffield Wednesday 15/8/92
Debut Goal: Away v Nottingham Forest 7/11/92

Previous Club Details			*App*			*Goals*		
Club	Signed	Fee	Lge	FLC	FAC	Lge	FLC	FAC
Swindon Town	8/81	–	90+5			38		
Aston Villa	6/83	£200,000	50+4			19		
Bari (Ita)	7/85	£400,000						
Southampton	7/88	£430,000	68+7			19		
Swindon Town	3/91	Loan	9			9		
Notts County	9/91	£250,000	9+2	2	1	3		
Rangers	1/92	£500,000						
Everton	8/92	£500,000	37+10	7	2	9	6	1

FA Premier Lge Record

Everton	92/93-93/94	37+10	9

RIPLEY Stuart   Blackburn Rovers

Full Name: RIPLEY, Stuart Edward   DOB: 20/11/67, Middlesbrough
FAPL Debut: Away v Crystal Palace 15/8/92
Debut Goal: Away v Crystal Palace 15/8/92
England International Debut: Away v San Marino 19/11/93

Previous Club Details			*App*			*Goals*		
Club	Signed	Fee	Lge	FLC	FAC	Lge	FLC	FAC
Middlesbrough	11/85	–	210+39	21+2	17+1	3	1	1
Bolton W	2/86	Loan	5					
Blackburn Rov	7/92	£1.3m	78+2	11	8	11		2

FA Premier Lge Record

Blackburn Rov	92/93-93/94	78+2	11

ROBERTS Iwan   Leicester City

Full Name: ROBERTS, Iwan   DOB: 26/8/68, Bangor
Wales International Debut: Away v Holland 11/10/89

Previous Club Details			*App*			*Goals*		
Club	Signed	Fee	Lge	FLC	FAC	Lge	FLC	FAC
Watford	7/86	–	40+23	6+2	1+6	9	3	
Huddersfield T	8/90	£275,000	142+1	13	12	51	6	4
Leicester City	11/94	£100,000	26					

ROBERTS Tony — Queens Park Rangers
Full Name: ROBERTS, Anthony Mark DOB: 4/8/69, Holyhead
FAPL Debut: Home v Southampton 19/8/92 Debut Goal:
Wales International Debut: Away v Eire †17/2/93

Previous Club Details			App			Goals		
Club	Signed	Fee	Lge	FLC	FAC	Lge	FLC	FAC
QPR	7/87	–	62	5	2+1			

FA Premier Lge Record

QPR	92/93+93/94	43				0		

ROBERTSON Sandy — Coventry City
Full Name: ROBERTSON, Alexander DOB: 26/4/71, Edinburgh
FAPL Debut: Home v QPR † 22/1/94 Debut Goal:

Previous Club Details			App			Goals		
Club	Signed	Fee	Lge	FLC	FAC	Lge	FLC	FAC
Rangers	–							
Coventry City	1/94	£250,000	0+3					

FA Premier Lge Record

Coventry City	93/94	0+3				0		

ROBINS Mark — Norwich City
Full Name: ROBINS, Mark Gordon DOB: 22/12/69, Ashton-U-Lyne
FAPL Debut: Away v Arsenal 15/8/92
Debut Goal: Away v Arsenal 15/8/92

Previous Club Details			App			Goals		
Club	Signed	Fee	Lge	FLC	FAC	Lge	FLC	FAC
Manchester U	12/86	–	19+29	0+7	4+4	11	2	3
Norwich City	8/92	£800,000	43+6	3+2		16	1	

FA Premier Lge Record

Norwich City	92/93-93/94	43+6				16		

ROBINSON Mark — Newcastle United
Full Name: ROBINSON, Mark James DOB: 21/11/68, Manchester
FAPL Debut: Home v Chelsea † 28/12/93

Previous Club Details			Apps			Goals		
Club	Signed	Fee	Lge	FLC	FAC	Lge	FLC	FAC
West Brom Alb	1/87	–	2	0+1				
Barnsley	6/87	–	117+20	7+2	7+1	5		
Newcastle Utd	3/93	£450,000	13+11			1		

FA Premier Lge Record

Newcastle Utd	93/94	11+4				0		

ROBINSON Stephen — Tottenham Hotspur
Full Name: ROBINSON, Stephen DOB: 10/12/74, Lisburn
FAPL Debut: Away v Blackburn Rovers 30/10/93 Debut Goal:

Previous Club Details			Apps			Goals		
Club	Signed	Fee	Lge	FLC	FAC	Lge	FLC	FAC
Tottenham H	1/93	–	1+1					
FA Premier Lge Record								
Tottenham H	93/94		1+1			0		

ROBSON Stewart   Coventry City
Full Name: ROBSON, Stewart Ian   DOB: 6/11/64, Billericay
FAPL Debut: Home v Middlesbrough 15/8/92   Debut Goal:

Previous Club Details			App			Goals		
Club	Signed	Fee	Lge	FLC	FAC	Lge	FLC	FAC
Arsenal	11/81	–	150+1	20	13	16	3	1
West Ham Utd	1/87	£700,000	68+1	8	6	4	1	1
Coventry City	3/91	–	55+2	2	1	3		
FA Premier Lge Record								
Coventry City	92/93 93/94		15+1			0		

ROCASTLE David   Manchester City
Full Name: ROCASTLE, David Carlyle   DOB: 2/5/67, Lewisham
FAPL Debut: Away v Ipswich Town 3/10/92
Debut Goal: Home v Manchester City 13/3/93
England International Debut: Home v Denmark 14/9/88

Previous Club Details			App			Goals		
Club	Signed	Fee	Lge	FLC	FAC	Lge	FLC	FAC
Arsenal	12/84	–	204+14	32+1	18+2	24	6	4
Leeds United	7/92	£2m	17+8	0+3	0+3	2		
Manchester C	12/93	Swap	20		2	2		
FA Premier Lge Record								
Leeds Utd	92/93-93/94		17+8			2		
Manchester C	93/94		21			2		

RODGER Simon   Crystal Palace
Full Name: RODGER, Simon   DOB: 3/10/71, Shoreham
FAPL Debut: Home v Blackburn Rovers † 15/8/92
Debut Goal: Away v Blackburn Rovers 2/2/93

Previous Club Details			Apps			Goals		
Club	Signed	Fee	Lge	FLC	FAC	Lge	FLC	FAC
Crystal Palace	7/90	£1,000	79+8	14	2+1	5		
FA Premier Lge Record								
Crystal Palace	92/93		22+1			2		

ROSARIO Robert   Nottingham Forest
Full Name: ROSARIO, Robert   DOB: 4/3/66, Hammersmith
FAPL Debut: Home v Middlesbrough 15/8/92
Debut Goal: Away v Wimbledon 22/8/92

Club	Signed	Fee	App Lge	FLC	FAC	Goals Lge	FLC	FAC
Norwich City	12/83	–	115+11	11	13+1	18	3	3
Wolves	12/85	Loan	2			1		
Coventry City	3/91	£600,000	54+5	3+1	3	8	2	
Nottingham F	3/93	£400,000	25+1	1		3		

FA Premier Lge Record

Coventry City	92/93		10			1		
Nottingham F	92/93		10			1		

ROSENTHAL Ronny   Tottenham Hotspur

Full Name: ROSENTHAL, Ronny   DOB: 4/10/63, Haifa, Israel
FAPL Debut: Away v Nottingham Forest † 16/8/92
Debut Goal: Away v Aston Villa 19/9/92
Israeli International

Previous Club Details

Club	Signed	Fee	App Lge	FLC	FAC	Goals Lge	FLC	FAC
Liverpool	3/90	£1m	32+42	2+7	5+3	21	1	1
Tottenham H	1/94	£250,000	11+4			2		

FA Premier Lge Record

Liverpool	92/93-93/94		16+14			6		
Tottenham H	93/94		11+4			2		

ROWETT Gary   Everton

Full Name: ROWETT, Gary   DOB: 6/3/74, Bromsgrove
FAPL Debut: Away v Sheffield Wednesday † 2/4/94
Debut Goal:

Previous Club Details

Club	Signed	Fee	Apps Lge	FLC	FAC	Goals Lge	FLC	FAC
Cambridge Utd	9/91	–	53+13	7	4+2	9	2	
Everton	2/94	£200,000	0+2					

FA Premier Lge Record

Everton	93/94		0+2			0		

ROWLAND Keith   West Ham United

Full Name: ROWLAND, Keith   DOB: 1/9/71, Portadown
FAPL Debut: Home v Wimbledon † 14/8/93/9   Debut Goal:
N Ireland International Debut: Home v Latvia 8/9/93

Previous Club Details

Club	Signed	Fee	Apps Lge	FLC	FAC	Goals Lge	FLC	FAC
Bournemouth	10/89	–	65+6	5	8	2		
Coventry City	1/93	Loan	0+2					
West Ham Utd	8/93	£110,000	16+7	1	4			

FA Premier Lge Record

Coventry City	92/93		0+2			0		
West Ham Utd	93/94		16+7			0		

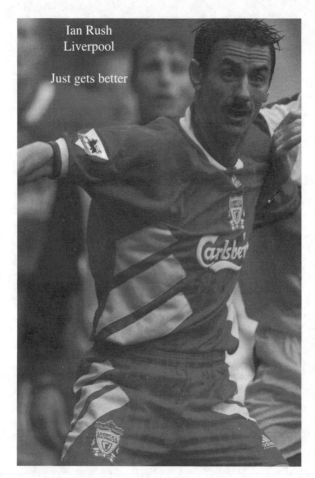

Ian Rush
Liverpool

Just gets better

RUDDOCK Neil   Liverpool
Full Name: RUDDOCK, Neil   DOB: 9/5/68, Wandsworth
FAPL Debut: Away v Southampton 15/8/92
Debut Goal: Home v Liverpool 31/10/92

Previous Club Details			*App*			*Goals*		
Club	Signed	Fee	Lge	FLC	FAC	Lge	FLC	FAC
Millwall	3/86	–						
Tottenham H	4/86	£50,000	7+2		1+1			1
Millwall	6/88	£300,000	0+2	2		1	3	
Southampton	2/89	£250,000	100+7	14+1	10	9	1	3
Tottenham H	5/92	£750,000	38	4	5	3		
Liverpool	7/93	£2.5m	38	5	2	3	1	
FA Premier Lge Record								
Tottenham H	92/93		38			3		
Liverpool	93/94		39			3		

RUSH Ian   Liverpool
Full Name: RUSH, Ian James   DOB: 20/10/61, St Asaph
FAPL Debut: Away v Nottingham Forest 16/8/92
Debut Goal: Away v Manchester United 18/10/92
Wales International Debut: Away v Scotland † 21/5/80

Previous Club Details			*App*			*Goals*		
Club	Signed	Fee	Lge	FLC	FAC	Lge	FLC	FAC
Chester City	7/79	–	33+1		5	14		3
Liverpool	4/80	£300,000	224	47	31+1	139	25	19
Juventus (Ita)	6/87	£3.8m						
Liverpool	8/88	£2.2m	176+12	22	23+2	73	14	17
FA Premier Lge Record								
Liverpool	92/93-93/94		71+2			28		

RUSH Matthew   West Ham United
Full Name: RUSH, Matthew   DOB: 6/8/71, Hackney
FAPL Debut: Home v Swindon Town † 11/9/93
Debut Goal: Home v Ipswich Town 2/4/94

Previous Club Details			*Apps*			*Goals*		
Club	Signed	Fee	Lge	FLC	FAC	Lge	FLC	FAC
West Ham Utd	3/90	–	13+11	1		3		
Cambridge Utd	3/93	Loan	4+6					
Swansea City	1/94	Loam	13					
FA Premier Lge Record								
West Ham Utd	93/94		9+1			1		

SALAKO John
Crystal Palace

Full Name: SALAKO, John   DOB: 11/2/69, Nigeria
FAPL Debut: Home v Blackburn Rovers 15/8/92   Debut Goal:

Previous Club Details			*Apps*			*Goals*		
Club	Signed	Fee	Lge	FLC	FAC	Lge	FLC	FAC
Crystal Palace	11/86		133+43	12+5	12	19	4	2
Swansea City	8/89	Loan	13			3		

FA Premier Lge Record

Crystal Palace	92/93		12+1			0		

SAMWAYS Vinny
Tottenham Hotspur

Full Name: SAMWAYS, Vincent   DOB: 27/10/67, Bethnal Green
FAPL Debut: Away v Southampton 15/8/92
Debut Goal: Home v Liverpool 18/12/93

Previous Club Details			*App*			*Goals*		
Club	Signed	Fee	Lge	FLC	FAC	Lge	FLC	FAC
Tottenham H	10/85	–	164+28	26+4	15+1	11	4	2

FA Premier Lge Record

Tottenham H	92/93-93/94		72			3		

SAUNDERS Dean
Aston Villa

Full Name: SAUNDERS, Dean Nicholas   DOB: 21/6/64, Swansea
FAPL Debut: Home v Nottingham Forest 16/8/92
Debut Goal: Home v Chelsea 5/9/92
Wales International Debut: Away v Eire † 26/3/86

Previous Club Details			*App*			*Goals*		
Club	Signed	Fee	Lge	FLC	FAC	Lge	FLC	FAC
Swansea City	6/82	–	42+7	2+1	1	12		
Cardiff City	3/85	Loan	3+1					
Brighton	8/85	–	66+6	4	7	20		5
Oxford United	3/87	£60,000	57+2	9+1	2	22	8	2
Derby County	10/88	£1m	106	12	4	42	1	
Liverpool	7/91	£2.9m	42	5	8	11	2	2
Aston Villa	9/92	£2.3m	71+1	12	7	23	6	3

FA Premier Lge Record

Liverpool	92/93		6			1		
Aston Villa	92/93-93/94		71+1			23		

SCALES John
Wimbledon

Full Name: SCALES, John Robert   DOB: 4/6/66, Harrogate
FAPL Debut: Away v Leeds United 15/8/92
Debut Goal: Home v Middlesbrough 9/3/93

Previous Club Details			*App*			*Goals*		
Club	Signed	Fee	Lge	FLC	FAC	Lge	FLC	FAC
Bristol Rovers	7/85	–	68+4	3	6	2		

Wimbledon	7/87	£70,000	231+5	18+1	18+1	11		1

FA Premier Lge Record

Wimbledon	92/93-93/94	68		1

SCHMEICHEL Peter   Manchester United

Full Name: SCHMEICHEL, Peter Boleslaw   DOB: 18/11/68, Denmark
FAPL Debut: Away v Sheffield United 15/8/92   Debut Goal:
Denmark International

Previous Club Details			*App*			*Goals*		
Club	Signed	Fee	Lge	FLC	FAC	Lge	FLC	FAC
Manchester U	8/91	£550,000	122	16	13			

FA Premier Lge Record

Manchester U	92/93-93/94	42		0

SCOTT Kevin   Newcastle United

Full Name: SCOTT, Kevin   DOB: 17/12/66 Easington
FAPL Debut: Home v Tottenham Hotspur 14/8/93
Debut Goal: Home v Sheffield Wednesday 5/3/94

Previous Club Details			*App*			*Goals*			Club
	Signed	Fee	Lge	FLC	FAC	Lge	FLC	FAC	
Newcastle Utd	12/84	–	227	18	8+1	8			1
Tottenham H	2/94	£850,000	12						

FA Premier Lge Record

Newcastle Utd	93/94	18		0
Tottenham H	93/94	12		1

SEALEY Les   Manchester United

Full Name: SEALEY, Les   DOB: 29/9/57, Bethnal Green

Previous Club Details			*App*			*Goals*		
Club	Signed	Fee	Lge	FLC	FAC	Lge	FLC	FAC
Coventry City	3/76		156	11	9			
Luton Town	8/83	£100,000	207	21	28			
Manchester U	12/89	Loan						
Manchester U	3/90	Loan	2		1			
Manchester U	6/90	Loan	31	8	3			
Aston Villa	7/91	Loan	18		4			
Coventry City	3/92	Loan	2					
Birmingham C	10/92	Loan	12					
Manchester U	1/93	Free		1	0+1			

SEAMAN David   Arsenal
Full Name: SEAMAN, David Andrew   DOB: 19/9/63, Rotherham
FAPL Debut: Home v Norwich 15/8/92   Debut Goal:
England International Debut: Away v Saudi Arabia 16/11/88

Previous Club Details

Club	Signed	Fee	App Lge	FLC	FAC	Goals Lge	FLC	FAC
Leeds United	9/81	–						
Peterborough	8/82	£4,000	91	10	5			
Birmingham C	10/84	£100,000	75	4	5			
QPR	8/86	£225,000	141	13	17			
Arsenal	5/90	£1.3m	158	21	20			

FA Premier Lge Record

Arsenal	92/93-93/94		78			0		

SEDGLEY Steve   Ipswich Town
Full Name: SEDGLEY, Stephen Philip   DOB: 26/5/68, Enfield
FAPL Debut: Home v Crystal Palace 22/8/92
Debut Goal: Home v Crystal Palace 22/8/92

Previous Club Details

Club	Signed	Fee	App Lge	FLC	FAC	Goals Lge	FLC	FAC
Coventry City	5/86	–	81+3	9	2+2	3	2	
Tottenham H	7/89	£750,000	146+17	21+1	12+2	8	1	1
Ipswich Town	6/94	£1m						

FA Premier Lge Record

Ipswich Town	92/93-93/94		61+2			8		

SEGERS Hans   Wimbledon
Full Name: SEGERS, Johannes   DOB: 30/10/61, Eindhoven
FAPL Debut: Away v Leeds United 15/8/92   Debut Goal:

Previous Club Details

Club	Signed	Fee	App Lge	FLC	FAC	Goals Lge	FLC	FAC
Nottingham F	8/84	£50,000	58	4	5			
Stoke City	2/87	Loan	1					
Sheffield Utd	11/87	Loan	10					
Dunfermline A	3/88	Loan						
Wimbledon	9/88	£180,000	230	23	18			

FA Premier Lge Record

Wimbledon	92/93-93/94		81			0		

SELLARS Scott   Newcastle United
Full Name: SELLARS, Scott   DOB: 27/11/65, Sheffield
FAPL Debut: Away v Southampton † 19/9/92
Debut Goal: Home v Ipswich Town 23/3/94

Previous Club Details

Club	Signed	Fee	App Lge	FLC	FAC	Goals Lge	FLC	FAC
Leeds United	7/83	–	72+2	4	4	12	1	

Blackburn Rov	7/86	£20,000	194+8	12	11	35	3	1
Leeds United	7/92	£800,000	6+1	1+1				
Newcastle Utd	3/93	£700,000	41+1	1+1	3	5	1	

FA Premier Lge Record

| Leeds United | 92/93 | 6+1 | 0 |
| Newcastle Utd | 93/94 | 29+1 | 3 |

SELLEY Ian   Arsenal

Full Name: SELLEY, Ian   DOB: 14/6/74, Chertsey
FAPL Debut: Home v Blackburn Rovers 12/9/92 Debut Goal:

Previous Club Details			*App*			*Goals*		
Club	Signed	Fee	Lge	FLC	FAC	Lge	FLC	FAC
Arsenal	5/92	–	24+2	2+1	3			

FA Premier Lge Record

| Arsenal | 92/93-93/94 | 24+2 | 0 |

SHARP Kevin   Leeds United

Full Name: SHARP, Kevin Phillip   DOB: 19/9/74
FAPL Debut: Away v Crystal Palace 17/4/93 Debut Goal:

Previous Club Details			*App*			*Goals*		
Club	Signed	Fee	Lge	FLC	FAC	Lge	FLC	FAC
Auxerre (Fra)		–						
Leeds United	10/92	£120,000	11+3					

FA Premier Lge Record

| Leeds United | 92/93-93/94 | 11+3 | 0 |

SHARPE Lee   Manchester United

Full Name: SHARPE, Lee Stuart   DOB: 27/5/71, Halesowen
FAPL Debut: Away v Aston Villa 7/11/92
Debut Goal: Home v Coventry City 28/12/92
England International Debut: Home v Eire † 27/3/91

Previous Club Details			*App*			*Goals*		
Club	Signed	Fee	Lge	FLC	FAC	Lge	FLC	FAC
Torquay Utd	5/88	–	9+5			3		
Manchester U	5/88	£185,000	112+21	13+6	12+4	13	9	

FA Premier Lge Record

| Manchester U | 92/93-93/94 | 52+4 | 10 |

SHAW Richard   Crystal Palace

Full Name: SHAW, Richard   DOB: 11/9/68, Brentford
FAPL Debut: Home v Blackburn Rovers 15/8/92 Debut Goal:

Previous Club Details			*Apps*			*Goals*		
Club	Signed	Fee	Lge	FLC	FAC	Lge	FLC	FAC
Crystal Palace	9/86	–	137+14	17+2	10	3		
Hull City	12/89	Loan	4					

271

Crystal Palace   92/93   32+1   0

SHEARER Alan   **Blackburn Rovers**
Full Name: SHEARER, Alan   DOB: 31/8/70, Newcastle
FAPL Debut: Away v Crystal Palace 15/8/92
Debut Goal: Away v Crystal Palace 15/8/92
England International Debut: Home v France 19/2/92

Previous Club Details			*App*			*Goals*		
Club	Signed	Fee	Lge	FLC	FAC	Lge	FLC	FAC
Southampton	4/88	–	105+13	16+2	11+3	23	11	4
Blackburn Rov	7/92	£3.3m	54+6	9	4	47	7	2

FA Premier Lge Record
Blackburn Rov   92/93-93/94   54+6   47

SHERIDAN Tony   **Coventry City**
Full Name: SHERIDAN, Anthony Joseph   DOB: 21/10/74, Dublin
FAPL Debut: Away v Leeds Utd 31/10/92   Debut Goal:

Previous Club Details			*App*			*Goals*		
Club	Signed	Fee	Lge	FLC	FAC	Lge	FLC	FAC
Coventry City	10/91	–	5+4					

FA Premier Lge Record
Coventry City   92/93-93/94   5+4   0

SHERIDAN John   **Sheffield Wednesday**
Full Name: SHERIDAN, John Joseph   DOB: 1/10/64, Manchester
FAPL Debut: Home v Blackburn Rovers 31/10/92
Debut Goal: Home v Manchester United 26/12/92
Eire International Debut: Home v Romania 23/3/88

Previous Club Details			*App*			*Goals*		
Club	Signed	Fee	Lge	FLC	FAC	Lge	FLC	FAC
Leeds United	3/82		225+5	14	11+1	47	3	1
Nottingham F	7/89	£650,000	1					
Sheffield Wed	11/89	£500,000	139+2	20	15	24	3	3

FA Premier Lge Record
Sheffield Wed   92/93-93/94   43+1   6

SHERINGHAM Teddy   **Tottenham Hotspur**
Full Name: SHERINGHAM, Edward Paul   DOB: 2/4/66, Walthamstow
FAPL Debut: Home v Liverpool 16/8/92
Debut Goal: Home v Liverpool 16/8/92
England International Debut: Away v Poland 29/5/93

Previous Club Details			*App*			*Goals*		
Club	Signed	Fee	Lge	FLC	FAC	Lge	FLC	FAC
Millwall	1/84	–	205+15	16+1	12	94	8	4
Aldershot	2/85	Loan	4+1					

Nottingham F	7/91	£2m	42	10	4	14	5	2
Tottenham H	8/92	£2.1m	54+2	6	5	34	5	4

FA Premier Lge Record

Nottingham F	92/93	3		1	
Tottenham H	93/94	54+2		34	

SHERON Mike — Manchester City

Full Name: SHERON, Michael Nigel   DOB: 11/1/72, Liverpool
FAPL Debut: Home v QPR † 17/8/92
Debut Goal: Home v Southampton 24/10/92

Previous Club Details			App			Goals		
Club	Signed	Fee	Lge	FLC	FAC	Lge	FLC	FAC
Manchester C	7/90	–	82+18	9+2	5+3	23	1	3
Bury	3/91	Loan	1+4			1		

FA Premier Lge Record

Manchester C	92/93-93/94	62+9		17	

SHERWOOD Tim — Blackburn Rovers

Full Name: SHERWOOD, Timothy Alan   DOB: 2/2/69, St Albans
FAPL Debut: Away v Crystal Palace 15/8/92
Debut Goal: Home v Norwich City 3/10/92

Previous Club Details			App			Goals		
Club	Signed	Fee	Lge	FLC	FAC	Lge	FLC	FAC
Watford	2/87	–	23+7	4+1	9	2		
Norwich City	7/87	£175,000	66+5	7	4	10	1	
Blackburn Rov	2/92	£500,000	82+5	11	7+1	5		1

FA Premier Lge Record

Blackburn Rov	92/93-93/94	75+1		5	

SHIPPERLEY Neil — Chelsea

Full Name: SHIPPERLEY, Neil   DOB: 30/10/74 Chatham
FAPL Debut: Away v Southampton 10/4/93
Debut Goal: Home v Wimbledon 12/4/93

Previous Club Details			App			Goals		
Club	Signed	Fee	Lge	FLC	FAC	Lge	FLC	FAC
Chelsea			20+7	2+1	3	5	11	

FA Premier Lge Record

Chelsea	92/93-93/94	20+7		5	

SIMPSON Fitzroy — Manchester City

Full Name: SIMPSON, Fitzroy   DOB: 26/2/70, Bradford on Avon
FAPL Debut: Home v QPR 17/8/92
Debut Goal: Home v Nottingham Forest 3/10/92

Previous Club Details			App			Goals		
Club	Signed	Fee	Lge	FLC	FAC	Lge	FLC	FAC
Swindon Town	7/88	–	78+26	9+1	2+1	9	1	

| Manchester C | 3/92 | £500,000 | 48+7 | 5+1 | 5 | 2 | | |

FA Premier Lge Record

| Manchester C | 92/93-93/94 | | 39+5 | | 1 | | | |

SINCLAIR Frank   Chelsea

Full Name: SINCLAIR, Frank Mohammed   DOB: 3/12/71, Lambeth
FAPL Debut: Away v Manchester City 20/9/92   Debut Goal:

Previous Club Details			App			Goals		
Club	Signed	Fee	Lge	FLC	FAC	Lge	FLC	FAC
Chelsea	5/90	–	77	9	9	1		
West Brom Alb	12/91	Loan	6			1		

FA Premier Lge Record

| Chelsea | 92/93-93/94 | | 65 | | | 0 | | |

SINTON Andy   Sheffield Wednesday

Full Name: SINTON, Andrew   DOB: 19/3/66, Newcastle
FAPL Debut: Away v Manchester City 17/8/92
Debut Goal: Away v Manchester City 17/8/92
England International Debut: Away v Poland 13/11/91

Previous Club Details			App			Goals		
Club	Signed	Fee	Lge	FLC	FAC	Lge	FLC	FAC
Cambridge Utd	4/83	–	90+3	6	3	13	1	
Brentford	12/85	£25,000	149	8	11	28	3	1
QPR	3/89	£350,000	124	10	11	15		2
Sheffield Wed	8/93	£2.75m	61	11	5	10		

FA Premier Lge Record

| Sheffield Wed | 92/93-93/94 | | 61 | | | 10 | | |

SKINNER Justin   Wimbledon

Full Name: SKINNER, Justin James   DOB: 17/9/72, Dorking
FAPL Debut: Away v Liverpool 26/9/92   Debut Goal:

Previous Club Details			App			Goals		
Club	Signed	Fee	Lge	FLC	FAC	Lge	FLC	FAC
Wimbledon	7/91	–	1					

FA Premier Lge Record

| Wimbledon | 92/93 | | 1 | | | 0 | | |

SLATER Stuart   Ipswich Town

Full Name: SLATER, Stuart   DOB: 27/3/69, Sudbury
FAPL Debut: Away v QPR 2/10/93
Debut Goal: Home v Sheffield United 22/9/94

Previous Club Details			App			Goals		
Club	Signed	Fee	Lge	FLC	FAC	Lge	FLC	FAC
West Ham Utd	4/87	–	134+7	16+1	16+0	11	2	3
Celtic	7/92	£1.5m						
Ipswich Town	9/93	£750,000	28	2	5	1		

274

FA Premier Lge Record
Ipswich Town 93/94   28   1

SMALL Bryan   Aston Villa
Full Name: SMALL, Bryan   DOB: 15/11/71, Birmingham
FAPL Debut: Home v Blackburn Rovers † 19/10/92   Debut Goal:

Previous Club Details		*App*			*Goals*		
Club	Signed Fee	Lge	FLC	FAC	Lge	FLC	FAC
Aston Villa	7/90 –	26+4	2	2+1			

FA Premier Lge Record
Aston Villa   92/93-93/94   18+1   0

SMITH Alan   Arsenal
Full Name: SMITH. Alan Martin   DOB: 21/11/62, Bromsgrove
FAPL Debut: Home v Norwich 15/8/92
Debut Goal: Away v Nottingham Forest 17/10/92
England International Debut: Away v Saudi Arabia – 16/11/88

Previous Club Details		*App*			*Goals*		
Club	Signed Fee	Lge	FLC	FAC	Lge	FLC	FAC
Leicester City	6/82 £22,000	190+10	8+1	8	76	4	4
Arsenal	5/87 £800,000	224+20	33+2	22+2	83	15	6

FA Premier Lge Record
Arsenal   92/93-93/94   47+8   6

SMITH David   Norwich City
Full Name: SMITH, David Christopher   DOB: 26/12/70, Liverpool
FAPL Debut: Home v Blackburn Rovers 28/2/93   Debut Goal:

Previous Club Details		*App*			*Goals*		
Club	Signed Fee	Lge	FLC	FAC	Lge	FLC	FAC
Norwich City	7/89 –	13+5		2+1			

FA Premier Lge Record
Norwich City   92/93-93/94   10+3   0

SMITH Richard   Leicester City
Full Name: SMITH. G Richard   DOB: 3/10/70, Lutterworth

Previous Club Details		*App*			*Goals*		
Club	Signed Fee	Lge	FLC	FAC	Lge	FLC	FAC
Leicester City	12/88 –	71+14	4	4	2		
Cambridge Utd	9/89 Loan	4	1				

SNODIN Ian   Everton
Full Name: SNODIN, Ian   DOB: 15/8/63, Rotherham
FAPL Debut: Home v Coventry City † 17/10/92 Debut Goal:

Previous Club Details		*App*			*Goals*		
Club	Signed Fee	Lge	FLC	FAC	Lge	FLC	FAC
Doncaster Rov	8/80 –	181+7	9	11+1	25	1	1

Leeds United	5/85	£200,000	51	3	1	6	2	
Everton	1/87	£840,000	139+5	18+3	26	3	2	2
FA Premier Lge Record								
Everton	92/93-93/94		46+2			1		

SOUTHALL Neville   Everton
Full Name: SOUTHALL, Neville   DOB: 16/9/78, Llandudno
FAPL Debut: Home *v* Sheffield Wednesday 15/8/92   Debut Goal:
Wales International Debut: Home *v* N Ireland 27/5/82

Previous Club Details			*App*			*Goals*		
Club	Signed	Fee	Lge	FLC	FAC	Lge	FLC	FAC
Bury	6/80	£6,000	39					
Everton	7/81	£150,000	452	58	58			
Port Vale	1/83	Loan	9					
FA Premier Lge Record								
Everton	92/93-93/94		81			0		

SOUTHGATE Gareth   Crystal Palace
Full Name: SOUTHGATE, Gareth   DOB: 3/9/70, Watford
FAPL Debut: Home *v* Blackburn Rovers 15/8/92
Debut Goal: Home *v* Blackburn Rovers 15/8/92

Previous Club Details			*Apps*			*Goals*		
Club	Signed	Fee	Lge	FLC	FAC	Lge	FLC	FAC
Crystal Palace	1/89	–	106+4	16+1	1	12	4	
FA Premier Lge Record								
Crystal Palace	92/93		33			3		

SPACKMAN Nigel   Chelsea
Full Name: SPACKMAN, Nigel   DOB: 2/12/60, Romsey
FAPL Debut: Home *v* Norwich City 12/9/92   Debut Goal:

Previous Club Details			*App*			*Goals*		
Club	Signed	Fee	Lge	FLC	FAC	Lge	FLC	FAC
Bournemouth	5/80	–	118+1	4	7	10		
Chelsea	6/83	£40,000	139+2	21+1	6	12		
Liverpool	2/87	£400,000	39+2	1	6			1
QPR	2/89	£500,000	27+2	2		1	1	
Rangers	11/89	£500,000						
Chelsea	8/92	£485,000	11+4	2	3			
FA Premier Lge Record								
Chelsea	92/93-93/94		11+4			0		

SPEED Gary   Leeds United
Full Name: SPEED, Gary Andrew   DOB: 8/9/69, Hawarden
FAPL Debut: Home *v* Wimbledon 15/8/92
Debut Goal: Away *v* Aston Villa 19/8/92
Wales International Debut: Home *v* Costa Rica † 20/5/90

Previous Club Details			App			Goals		
Club	Signed	Fee	Lge	FLC	FAC	Lge	FLC	FAC
Leeds United	6/88	–	163+17	16+1	13	23	2	4
FA Premier Lge Record								
Leeds United	92/93-93/94		74+1			17		

SPEEDIE David

Leicester City

Full Name: SPEEDIE, David DOB: 20/2/60, Glenrothes
FAPL Debut: Home v Tottenham Hotspur 15/8/92 Debut Goal:
Scotland International Debut: Home v England 25/5/85

Previous Club Details			App			Goals		
Club	Signed	Fee	Lge	FLC	FAC	Lge	FLC	FAC
Barnsley	10/78	–	10+13					
Darlington	6/80	Free	88	4	3	21		1
Chelsea	6/82	£65,000	155+7	23+1	12	47	7	5
Coventry City	7/87	£750,000	121+1	15	3+1	31	3	
Liverpool	2/91	£675,000	8+4		1+1	6		
Blackburn Rov	8/91	£400,000	11	1				
Southampton	7/92	£400,000	11	1				
Birmingham C	10/92	Loan	9+1					
West Brom Alb	1/93	Loan	7					
West Ham Utd	3/93	Loan	11					
Leicester City	7/93		37	3	1	12	1	
FA Premier Lge Record								
Southampton	92/93		11			0		

SPENCER John

Chelsea

Full Name: SPENCER, John DOB: 11/9/70, Glasgow
FAPL Debut: Away v Norwich City † 19/8/92
Debut Goal: Home v Manchester City 9/1/93

Previous Club Details			App			Goals		
Club	Signed	Fee	Lge	FLC	FAC	Lge	FLC	FAC
Rangers	–							
Chelsea	8/92	£450,000	25+16	0+4	5+4	12		2
FA Premier Lge Record								
Chelsea	92/93-93/94		25+16			12		

SPINK Nigel

Aston Villa

Full Name: SPINK, Nigel Philip DOB: 8/8/58, Chelmsford
FAPL Debut: Away v Ipswich Town 15/8/92 Debut Goal:
England International Debut: Away v Australia – 19/6/83

Previous Club Details			App			Goals		
Club	Signed	Fee	Lge	FLC	FAC	Lge	FLC	FAC
Aston Villa	1/77	£4,000	345+1	45	27			
FA Premier Lge Record								
Aston Villa	92/93-93/94		39+1			0		

SRNICEK Pavel — Newcastle United

Full Name: SRNICEK, Pavel   DOB: 10/3/68 Ostrava, Czech
FAPL Debut: Home v Tottenham Hotspur 14/8/93
Czechoslovakian International

Previous Club Details			Apps			Goals		
Club	Signed	Fee	Lge	FLC	FAC	Lge	FLC	FAC
Banik Ostrava								
Newcastle Utd	1/91	£350,000	74	3	5			

FA Premier Lge Record

Newcastle Utd	93/94		23			0		

STAUNTON Steve — Aston Villa

Full Name: STAUNTON, Stephen   DOB: 19/1/69, Drogheda
FAPL Debut: Away v Ipswich Town 15/8/92
Debut Goal: Home v Crystal Palace 5/9/92
Eire International Debut: Home v Tunisia 19/11/88

Previous Club Details			App			Goals		
Club	Signed	Fee	Lge	FLC	FAC	Lge	FLC	FAC
Liverpool	9/86	£20,000	55+10	6+2	14+2		4	1
Bradford City	11/87	Loan	7+1	2				
Aston Villa	8/91	£1.1m	102	12	10	7		

FA Premier Lge Record

Aston Villa	92/93-93/94		65			5		

STEIN Mark — Chelsea

Full Name: STEIN, Mark   DOB: 28/1/66, South Africa
FAPL Debut: Home v Oldham Athletic 30/10/93
Debut Goal: Away v Southampton 27/12/93

Previous Club Details			Apps			Goals		
Club	Signed	Fee	LGe	FLC	FAC	Lge	FLC	FAC
Luton Town	1/84	–	41+13	4+1	9	19		3
Aldershot	1/86	Loan	2			1		
QPR	8/88	£300,000	20+13	4	2+1	4	2	1
Oxford United	9/89	Swap	72+10	4	2+1	18		
Stoke City	9/91	£100,000	94	8	4	50	8	
Chelsea	10/93	£1.5m	18		6	11		1

FA Premier Lge Record

Chelsea	93/94		18			11		

STEJSKAL Jan — Queens Park Rangers

Full Name: STEJSKAL, Jan   DOB: 15/1/62, Czechoslovakia
FAPL Debut: Away v Manchester City 17/8/92   Debut Goal:
Czechoslovakian International

Previous Club Details			App			Goals		
Club	Signed	Fee	Lge	FLC	FAC	Lge	FLC	FAC
QPR	10/90	£600,000	107+1	8	3			

FA Premier Lge Record
QPR	92/93-93/94	40+1		0

STEWART Paul   Liverpool
Full Name: STEWART, Paul Andrew   DOB: 7/10/64, Manchester
FAPL Debut: Away v Nottingham Forest 16/8/92
Debut Goal: Home v Sheffield United 19/8/92
England International Debut: Home v Germany † 11/9/91

Previous Club Details			*App*			*Goals*		
Club	Signed	Fee	Lge	FLC	FAC	Lge	FLC	FAC
Blackpool	10/81	–	188+3	11	7	56	3	2
Manchester C	3/87	£200,000	51	6	4	27	2	1
Tottenham H	6/88	£1.7m	126+23		9	28	7	2
Liverpool	7/92	£2.3m	21+3	3	1	1		
Crystal Palace	1/94	Loan	18			3		

FA Premier Lge Record
Liverpool	92/93	21+3		1

STEWART Simon   Sheffield Wednesday
Full Name: STEWART, Simon   DOB: 1/11/73, Leeds
FAPL Debut: Away v Ipswich Town 10/3/93   Debut Goal:

Previous Club Details			*App*			*Goals*		
Club	Signed	Fee	Lge	FLC	FAC	Lge	FLC	FAC
Sheffield Wed	6/92	–	6	0+1				

FA Premier Lge Record
Sheffield Wed	92/93	6		0

STOCKWELL Mike   Ipswich Town
Full Name: STOCKWELL, Michael Thomas DOB: 14/2/65, Chelmsford
FAPL Debut: Home v Aston Villa 15/8/92
Debut Goal: Home v Wimbledon 12/8/92

Previous Club Details			*App*			*Goals*		
Club	Signed	Fee	Lge	FLC	FAC	Lge	FLC	FAC
Ipswich Town	12/82	–	284+15	23+3	18+3	20	2	1

FA Premier Lge Record
Ipswich Town	92/93-93/94	79+1		5

STONE Steve   Nottingham Forest
Full Name: STONE, Steven   DOB: 20/8/71, Gateshead
FAPL Debut: Away v Middlesbrough 10/2/92
Debut Goal: Away v Middlesbrough 10/2/92

Previous Club Details			*App*			*Goals*		
Club	Signed	Fee	Lge	FLC	FAC	Lge	FLC	FAC
Nottingham F	5/89	–	56+2	5+2	2	6		

FA Premier Lge Record
Nottingham F	92/93	11+1		1

STRACHAN Gordon   **Leeds United**

Full Name: STRACHAN, Gordon David   DOB: 9/2/57, Edinburgh
FAPL Debut: Home v Wimbledon † 15/8/92
Debut Goal: Away v QPR 24/10/92
Scotland International Debut: Away v N Ireland 16/5/80

Previous Club Details

Club	Signed	Fee	App Lge	FLC	FAC	Goals Lge	FLC	FAC
Manchester U	8/84	£500,000	155+5	12+1	22	33	1	2
Leeds United	3/89	£300,000	182+8	18	14	37	3	2

FA Premier Lge Record

Leeds United	92/93-93/94		56+7			7		

STRANDLI Frank   **Leeds United**

Full Name: STRANDLI, Frank   DOB: 16/5/72, Norway
FAPL Debut: Home v Middlesbrough † 30/1/93
Debut Goal: Home v Middlesbrough 30/1/93
Norwegian International

Previous Club Details

Club	Signed	Fee	Apps Lge	FLC	FAC	Goals Lge	FLC	FAC
IK Start								
Leeds United	1/93	£350,000	5+9	0+1	1+1	2		

FA Premier Lge Record

Leeds United	92/93-93/94		5+9			2		

STUART Graham   **Everton**

Full Name: STUART, Graham Charles   DOB: 24/10/70, Tooting
FAPL Debut: Home v Oldham Athletic 15/8/92
Debut Goal: Away v Norwich City 19/8/92

Previous Club Details

Club	Signed	Fee	App Lge	FLC	FAC	Goals Lge	FLC	FAC
Chelsea	6/89	–	70+17	11	5+2	14	2	1
Everton	8/93	25+4	2	1+1	1			

FA Premier Lge Record

Chelsea	92/93		31+8			9		
Everton	93/94		26+4					

SULLIVAN Neil   **Wimbledon**

Full Name: SULLIVAN, Neil   DOB: 24/2/70, Sutton
FAPL Debut: Away v Southampton 17/10/92   Debut Goal:

Previous Club Details

Club	Signed	Fee	App Lge	FLC	FAC	Goals Lge	FLC	FAC
Wimbledon	7/88	–	4+2					
Crystal Palace	5/92	Loan	1					

FA Premier Lge Record

Wimbledon	92/93-93/94		2+2			0		

SUMMERBEE, Nicky　　　　　　　　　Manchester City
Full Name:　　SUMMERBEE, Nicholas　DOB: 26/8/71, Altrincham
FAPL Debut: Away v Sheffield United 14/8/93
Debut Goal:　Home v Manchester City 1/9/93

Previous Club Details			App			Goals		
Club	Signed	Fee	Lge	FLC	FAC	Lge	FLC	FAC
Swindon Town	7/89	–	88+23	9+1	2+4	6	3	
Manchester C	6/94	£1.5m						
FA Premier Lge Record								
Swindon Town	93/94		35			0		

SUTCH Daryl　　　　　　　　　　　Norwich City
Full Name:　　SUTCH, Daryl　　　　　DOB: 11/9/71, Beccles
FAPL Debut: Away v Crystal Palace † 29/8/92
Debut Goal:　Home v Middlesbrough 31/10/92

Previous Club Details			App			Goals		
Club	Signed	Fee	Lge	FLC	FAC	Lge	FLC	FAC
Norwich City	7/90	–	22+16	3+2	0+1	3		
FA Premier Lge Record								
Norwich City	92/93-93/94		15+10	3		2		

SUTTON Chris　　　　　　　　　　Norwich City
Full Name:　　SUTTON, Christopher Roy　DOB: 10/3/73, Nottingham
FAPL Debut: Away v Arsenal 15/8/92
Debut Goal:　Home v QPR 17/10/92

Previous Club Details			App			Goals		
Club	Signed	Fee	Lge	FLC	FAC	Lge	FLC	FAC
Norwich City	7/91	–	88+13	8+1	10	35	3	5
FA Premier Lge Record								
Norwich City	92/93-93/94		72+6			33		

TALBOYS Steven　　　　　　　　　　Wimbledon
Full Name:　　TALBOYS, Steven John　　DOB: 18/9/66, Bristol
FAPL Debut: Away v Norwich City 5/12/92　Debut Goal:

Previous Club Details			Apps			Goals		
Club	Signed	Fee	Lge	FLC	FAC	Lge	FLC	FAC
Wimbledon	9/92	£10,000	9+5	0+1	0+1			
FA Premier Lge Record								
Wimbledon	92/93-93/94		9+5			0		

TANNER Nicky　　　　　　　　　　　Liverpool
Full Name:　　TANNER, Nicholas　　　DOB: 24/5/65, Kingswood, Bristol
FAPL Debut: Away v Nottingham Forest 16/8/92　　Debut Goal:

Previous Club Details			Apps			Goals		
Club	Signed	Fee	Lge	FLC	FAC	Lge	FLC	FAC
Bristol Rov	6/85	–	104+3	5	10	5		

Liverpool	7/88	£20,000	36+5	7+1	5
Norwich City	3/90	Loan	6		
Swindon Town	9/90	Loan	7		
FA Premier Lge Record					
Liverpool	92/93		2+2		0

TAYLOR Ian
Sheffield Wednesday

Full Name: TAYLOR, Ian V   DOB: 4/6/68, Birmingham

Previous Club Details			*Apps*			*Goals*		
Club	Signed	Fee	Lge	FLC	FAC	Lge	FLC	FAC
Port Vale	7/92	–	83	4	6	28	2	1
Sheffield Wed	6/94	£1m						

TEALE Shaun
Aston Villa

Full Name: TEALE, Shaun   DOB: 10/3/64, Southport
FAPL Debut: Away v Ipswich Town 15/8/92
Debut Goal: Home v Middlesbrough 17/1/93

Previous Club Details			*Apps*			*Goals*		
Club	Signed	Fee	Lge	FLC	FAC	Lge	FLC	FAC
Bournemouth	1/89	£50,000	99+1	8	5	4		1
Aston Villa	7/91	£300,000	118+1	13	11	2	3	
FA Premier Lge Record								
Aston Villa	92/93-93/94		76+1			2		

THOMAS Michael
Liverpool

Full Name: THOMAS, Michael   DOB: 24/8/67, Lambeth
FAPL Debut: Home v Southampton † 1/9/92
Debut Goal: Home v Norwich City 25/10/92
England International Debut: Away v Saudi Arabia 16/11/88

Previous Club Details			*Apps*			*Goals*		
Club	Signed	Fee	Lge	FLC	FAC	Lge	FLC	FAC
Arsenal	12/84	–	149+14	22+2	14+3	24	5	
Portsmouth	12/86	Loan	3					
Liverpool	12/91	£1.5m	23	1	2	1		
FA Premier Lge Record								
Liverpool	92/93-93/94		7+8			1		

THOMPSON Gary
Queens Park Rangers

Full Name: THOMPSON, Gary Lindsay   DOB: 7/10/59, Birmingham
FAPL Debut: Away v Manchester City † 17/8/92   Debut Goal:

Previous Club Details			*Apps*			*Goals*		
Club	Signed	Fee	Lge	FLC	FAC	Lge	FLC	FAC
Coventry City	6/77	–	127+7	12+1	11	38	7	4
West Brom Alb	2/83	£225,000	91	9	5	39	5	1
Sheffield Wed	3/85	£450,000	35+1	2+1	5	7	1	1
Aston Villa	6/86	£450,000	56+4	6	4	17	2	

Watford	12/88	£325,000	24+10	0+1	7+1	8	
Crystal Palace	3/90	£200,000	17+3	0+1		3	1
QPR	8/91	£125,000	10+9	3		1	3

FA Premier Lge Record

QPR	92/93-93/94	0+4	0

THOMPSON Neil   Ipswich Town
Full Name: THOMPSON, Neil   DOB: 2/10/63, Beverley
FAPL Debut: Home v Aston Villa 15/8/92
Debut Goal: Away v Oldham Athletic 19/9/92

Previous Club Details			*Apps*			*Goals*		
Club	Signed	Fee	Lge	FLC	FAC	Lge	FLC	FAC
Hull City	11/91	–	29+2					
Scarborough	8/83		87	8	4	15	1	
Ipswich Town	6/89	£100,000	184+6	14+1	17	18	1	2

FA Premier Lge Record

Ipswich Town	92/93-93/94	62	3

THOMPSON Steve   Leicester City
Full Name: THOMPSON, Steve J   DOB: 2/11/64, Oldham

Previous Club Details			*Apps*			*Goals*		
Club	Signed	Fee	Lge	FLC	FAC	Lge	FLC	FAC
Bolton W	11/82	–	329+6	27	21	49	2	4
Luton Town	8/91	£180,000	5	2				
Leicester City	10/91	swap	105+3	5	6	18	2	1

THORN Andy   Crystal Palace
Full Name: THORN, Andrew   DOB: 12/11/68, Carshalton
FAPL Debut: Home v Blackburn Rovers 15/8/92
Debut Goal: Home v Leeds United 20/12/92

Previous Club Details			*Apps*			*Goals*		
Club	Signed	Fee	Lge	FLC	FAC	Lge	FLC	FAC
Wimbledon	11/84	–	106+1	7	9	2		
Newcastle	8/88	£850,000	2					
Crystal Palace	12/89	£650,000	128	19	10	3	4	1

FA Premier Lge Record

Crystal Palace	92/93	34	1

THORNLEY Ben   Manchester United
Full Name: THORNLEY, Benjamin   DOB: 21/4/75 Bury
FAPL Debut: Away v West Ham United † 26/2/94 Debut Goal:

Previous Club Details			*Apps*			*Goals*		
Club	Signed	Fee	Lge	FLC	FAC	Lge	FLC	FAC
Manchester U			0+1					

FA Premier Record

Manchester U	93/94	0+1	0

THORSTVEDT Erik — Tottenham Hotspur

Full Name: THORSTVEDT, Erik   DOB: 28/10/62, Stavanger, Norway
FAPL Debut: Home v Coventry City † 19/8/92   Debut Goal:
Norway International Debut: v Kuwait 13/11/82

Previous Club Details

Club	Signed	Fee	Apps Lge	FLC	FAC	Goals Lge	FLC	FAC
Eik, Viking (Norway), Borussia Mönchengladback (Ger), IFK (Sweden)								
Tottenham H	12/88	£400,000	169+2	24		14		

FA Premier Lge Record

Tottenham H	92/93-93/94		56+2			0		

TILER Carl — Nottingham Forest

Full Name: TILER, Carl   DOB: 11/1/70, Sheffield
FAPL Debut: Away v Blackburn Rovers 5/9/93   Debut Goal:

Previous Club Details

Club	Signed	Fee	App Lge	FLC	FAC	Goals Lge	FLC	FAC
Barnsley	8/88	–	67+4	4	4+1	3		
Nottingham F	5/91	£1.4m	64+2	10+1	5	1		

FA Premier Lge Record

Nottingham F	92/93		37			0		

TINKLER Mark — Leeds United

Full Name: TINKLER, Mark Roland   DOB: 24/10/74, Bishop Auckland
FAPL Debut: Away v Sheffield United 6/4/93   Debut Goal:

Previous Club Details

Club	Signed	Fee	Apps Lge	FLC	FAC	Goals Lge	FLC	FAC
Leeds United	11/91	–	5+2					

FA Premier Lge Record

Leeds United	92/93		5+2			0		

TOWNSEND Andy — Aston Villa

Full Name: TOWNSEND, Andrew David   DOB: 23/7/63, Maidstone
FAPL Debut: Home v Oldham Athletic 15/8/92
Debut Goal: Home v Norwich City 12/9/92
Eire International Debut: Home v France 7/2/89

Previous Club Details

Club	Signed	Fee	Apps Lge	FLC	FAC	Goals Lge	FLC	FAC
Southampton	1/85	£35,000	77+6	7+1	2+3	5		
Norwich City	8/88	£300,000	66+5	3+1	10	8		2
Chelsea	7/90	£1.2m	108	17	7	12	7	
Aston Villa	7/93	£2.1m	31	8	3	3		

FA Premier Lge Record

Chelsea	92/93		41			4		
Aston Villa	93/94		31			3		

TURNER Andrew   Tottenham Hotspur
Full Name: TURNER, Andrew Peter   DOB: 23/3/75, Woolwich
FAPL Debut: Away v Southampton 15/8/92
Debut Goal: Home v Everton 5/9/92

Previous Club Details			*Apps*			*Goals*		
Club	Signed	Fee	Lge	FLC	FAC	Lge	FLC	FAC
Tottenham H	4/92	–	7+12	1+3	0+1	3	1	
FA Premier Lge Record								
Tottenham H	92/93-93/94		7+12			3		

ULLATHORNE Robert   Norwich City
Full Name: ULLATHORNE, Robert   DOB:
FAPL Debut: Away v Sheffield United 6/11/93
Debut Goal: Away v Manchester City 16/4/94

Previous Club Details			*Apps*			*Goals*		
Club	Signed	Fee	Lge	FLC	FAC	Lge	FLC	FAC
Norwich City	7/90	–	32+5	4	2+1	4		
FA Premier Lge Record								
Norwich City	93/94		11+5			1		

UNSWORTH David   Everton
Full Name: UNSWORTH, David   DOB: 16/10/73, Chorley
FAPL Debut: Home v Liverpool 7/12/92   Debut Goal:

Previous Club Details			*Apps*			*Goals*		
Club	Signed	Fee	Lge	FLC	FAC	Lge	FLC	FAC
Everton	5/92	–	10+2	1+1		1		
FA Premier Lge Record								
Everton	92/93-93/94		9+1			0		

VENISON Barry   Newcastle United
Full Name: VENISON, Barry   DOB: 16/8/64, Consett
FAPL Debut: Home v Tottenham Hotspur 14/8/93 Debut Goal:

Previous Club Details			*Apps*			*Goals*		
Club	Signed	Fee	Lge	FLC	FAC	Lge	FLC	FAC
Sunderland	1/82	–	169+4	21	7+1	2		
Liverpool	7/86	£200,000	13+7	14+3	16+5	1		
Newcastle Utd	7/92	£250,000	81+1	7	6			
FA Premier Lge Record								
Newcastle Utd	93/94		38+1			0		

VONK Michel   Manchester City
Full Name: VONK, Michel Christian   DOB: 28/10/68, Netherlands
FAPL Debut: Home v QPR 17/8/92
Debut Goal: Home v Oldham Athletic 29/8/92

Previous Club Details			Apps			Goals		
Club	Signed	Fee	Lge	FLC	FAC	Lge	FLC	FAC
Manchester C	3/92	£500,000	67+2	2+1	5+1	4	1	1
FA Premier Lge Record								
Manchester C	92/93-93/94		59+1			4		

WADDLE Chris   Sheffield Wednesday

Full Name: WADDLE, Christopher Roland   DOB: 14/12/60, Felling
FAPL Debut: Away v Everton 15/8/92
Debut Goal: Home v Everton 6/2/93
England International Debut: Home v Eire 26/3/85

Previous Club Details			Apps			Goals		
Club	Signed	Fee	Lge	FLC	FAC	Lge	FLC	FAC
Newcastle Utd	7/80	£1,000	169+1	8	12	46	2	4
Tottenham H	6/85	£590,000	137+1	21	14	33	4	5
Marseille (Fra)	7/89	£4.25m						
Sheffield Wed	6/92	£1m	51+1	15+1	8+1	4		2
FA Premier Lge Record								
Sheffield Wed	92/93-93/94		51+1			4		

WALKER Des   Sheffield Wednesday

Name: WALKER, Desmond Sinclair   DOB:26/11/65, Hackney
FAPL Debut: Home v Aston Villa 18/8/93   Debut Goal:
England International Debut: Home v Denmark † 14/9/88

Previous Club Details			Apps			Goals		
Club	Signed	Fee	Lge	FLC	FAC	Lge	FLC	FAC
Nottingham F	11/83	–	259+5	40	28	1		
Sampdoria (Ita)	5/92	£1.5m						
Sheffield Wed	8/93	£2.75m	42	8	4			
FA Premier Lge Record								
Sheffield Wed	92/93-93/94		42			0		

WALKER Ian   Tottenham Hotspur

Full Name: WALKER, Ian Michael   DOB: 31/10/71, Watford
FAPL Debut: Away v Southampton 15/8/92   Debut Goal:

Previous Club Details			Apps			Goals		
Club	Signed	Fee	Lge	FLC	FAC	Lge	FLC	FAC
Tottenham H	12/89	–	36+1	3				
Oxford United	9/90	Loan	2	1				
Millwall	3/93	Loan						
FA Premier Lge Record								
Tottenham H	92/93-93/94		17+1			0		

WALLACE Ray   Leeds United

Full Name: WALLACE, Raymond George   DOB: 2/10/69, Greenwich
FAPL Debut: Home v Ipswich Town 27/2/93   Debut Goal:

Previous Club Details			*Apps*			*Goals*		
Club	Signed	Fee	Lge	FLC	FAC	Lge	FLC	FAC
Southampton	4/88	–	33+2	8	2			
Leeds United	5/91	£100,000	5+1					
Swansea City	3/92	Loan	2					
Reading	3/94	Loan	3					
FA Premier Lge Record								
Leeds United	92/93-93/94		5+1			0		

WALLACE Rod   Leeds United
Full Name: WALLACE, Rodney Seymour   DOB: 2/10/69, Greenwich
FAPL Debut: Home v Wimbledon 15/8/92
Debut Goal: Home v Tottenham Hotspur 25/8/92

Previous Club Details			*Apps*			*Goals*		
Club	Signed	Fee	Lge	FLC	FAC	Lge	FLC	FAC
Southampton	4/88	–	111+17	18+1	10	44	6	3
Leeds United	5/91	£1.6m	98+4	4	2	34	2	
FA Premier Lge Record								
Leeds United	92/93-93/94		64+4			23		

WALSH Paul   Manchester City
Full Name: WALSH, Paul   DOB: 1/10/62, Plumstead
FAPL Debut: Home v Wimbledon 12/3/93
Debut Goal: Away v Ipswich Town 1/5/94

Previous Club Detail			*Apps*			*Goals*		
Club	Signed	Fee	Lge	FLC	FAC	Lge	FLC	FAC
Charlton Ath	10/79	–	85+2	9	4	24	6	1
Luton Town	7/82	£400,000	80	5	4	24	1	3
Liverpool	5/84	£700,000	63+14	10+2	6+2	25	4	3
Tottenham H	2/88	£500,000	84+44	9+6	4+4	19	2	
QPR	9/91	Loan	2					
Portsmouth	6/92	£400,000	67+6	7+1	3	13	4	
Manchester C	3/94	£750,000	10			4		
FA Premier Lge Record								
Manchester C	93/94		11			4		

WALSH Steve   Leicester City
Full Name: WALSH, Steven   DOB: 1/10/62, Plumstead

Previous Club Detail			*Apps*			*Goals*		
Club	Signed	Fee	Lge	FLC	FAC	Lge	FLC	FAC
Wigan Athletic	9/82	–	123+2	7	6	4		
Leicester City	3/92	£100,000	243+2	21	7	40	3	

WALTERS Mark   Liverpool
Full Name: WALTERS, Mark Everton   DOB: 2/6/64, Birmingham
FAPL Debut: Away v Nottingham Forest 16/8/92

Debut Goal: Home v Sheffield United 19/8/92
England International Debut: Away v New Zealand 3/6/91

Previous Club Details

Club	Signed	Fee	Apps Lge	FLC	FAC	Goals Lge	FLC	FAC
Aston Villa	5/82		168+13	21+2	11+1	39	6	1
Rangers	12/87	£500,000						
Liverpool	8/91	£1.25m	51+25	9+2	4+1	14	4	
Stoke City	3/94	Loan	9					

FA Premier Lge Record

Liverpool	92/93-93/94		33+18			11		

WARD GAVIN   Leicester City
Full Name: WARD, Gavin   DOB: 30/6/70, Sutton Coldfield

Previous Club Details

Club	Signed	Fee	Apps Lge	FLC	FAC	Goals Lge	FLC	FAC
Cardiff City	10/89	Free	58+1		1			
Leicester City	7/94	£175,000	32	3				

WARD Mark   Everton
Full Name: WARD, Mark William   DOB: 10/10/62, Huyton
FAPL Debut: Home v Sheffield Wednesday 15/8/92
Debut Goal: Away v Coventry City 7/3/93
Scotland International Debut: Away v Wales 19/5/79

Previous Club Details

Club	Signed	Fee	Apps Lge	FLC	FAC	Goals Lge	FLC	FAC
Oldham Ath	7/83	£10,000	84	5	3	12		
West Ham Utd	8/85	£250,000	163+2	20+1	17	12	2	
Manchester C	12/89	£1m	54	3	6	14		
Everton	8/91	£1.1m	82+1	6	4	6	1	
Birmingham C	3/94	Loan	9			1		

FA Premier Lge Record

Everton	92/93-93/94		45+1			2		

WARHURST Paul   Blackburn Rovers
Full Name: WARHURST, Paul   DOB: 26/9/69, Stockport
FAPL Debut: Away v Everton 15/8/92
Debut Goal: Away v Nottingham Forest 12/9/92

Previous Club Details

Club	Signed	Fee	Apps Lge	FLC	FAC	Goals Lge	FLC	FAC
Manchester C	6/88	–						
Oldham Ath	10/88	£10,000	60+7	8	5+4	2		
Sheffield Wed	7/91	£750,000	60+6	7	6+1	6	5	4
Blackburn Rov	9/93	£2.7m	4+5	1				

FA Premier Lge Record

Sheffield Wed	92/93-93/94		29+4			6		
Blackburn Rov	93/94		4+5					

WARK John   Ipswich Town
Full Name: WARK, John   DOB: 4/8/57, Glasgow
FAPL Debut: Home v Aston Villa 15/8/92
Debut Goal: Home v Tottenham Hotspur 30/8/92
Scotland International Debut: Away v Wales 19/5/79

Previous Club Details			*Apps*			*Goals*		
Club	Signed	Fee	Lge	FLC	FAC	Lge	FLC	FAC
Ipswich Town	8/74	–	295+1	4+1	36+1	94	12	10
Liverpool	3/84	£450,000	64+6	6+4	11+2	28	3	6
Ipswich Town	1/88	£100,000	87+2	4	3	23		
Middlesbrough	8/90	£50,000	31+1	5	2	3		
Ipswich Town	8/91	–	109+2	10+1	14	12		2

FA Premier Lge Record

Ipswich Town	92/93-93/94		73+1			9		

WARNER Vance   Nottingham Forest
Full Name: WARNER, Vance   DOB: 3/9/74, Leeds

Previous Club Details			*App*			*Goals*		
Club	Signed	Fee	Lge	FLC	FAC	Lge	FLC	FAC
Nottingham F		–	1	1				

WARZYCHA Robert   Everton
Full Name: WARZYCHA, Robert   DOB: 20/8/63, Wielun, Poland
FAPL Debut: Home v Sheffield Wednesday † 15/8/92
Debut Goal: Away v Manchester United 19/8/92
Polish International

Previous Club Details			*Apps*			*Goals*		
Club	Signed	Fee	Lge	FLC	FAC	Lge	FLC	FAC
Everton	3/91	£300,000	51+21	4+2	3+2	6		1

FA Premier Lge Record

Everton	92/93-93/94		18+9			1		

WATSON Dave   Everton
Full Name: WATSON, David   DOB: 20/11/61, Liverpool
FAPL Debut: Home v Sheffield Wednesday 15/8/92
Debut Goal: Away v Middlesbrough 10/4/93
England International Debut: Away v Brazil 10/6/84

Previous Club Details			*Apps*			*Goals*		
Club	Signed	Fee	Lge	FLC	FAC	Lge	FLC	FAC
Liverpool	5/79	–						
Norwich City	11/80	£100,000	212	21	18	11	3	1
Everton	8/86	£900,000	265+2	32	32	20	5	4

FA Premier Lge Record

Everton	92/93-93/94		66+1			2		

WATSON Gordon   Sheffield Wednesday
Full Name: WATSON, Gordon William George   DOB: 20/3/71, Sidcup
FAPL Debut: Away v Everton † 15/8/92
Debut Goal: Away v Oldham Athletic 7/4/93

Previous Club Details

Club	Signed Fee		Lge	FLC	FAC	Lge	FLC	FAC
			Apps			*Goals*		
Charlton Ath	4/89	–	20+11	2	0+1	7	1	
Sheffield Wed	2/91	£250,000	23+19	4+4	5+1	12	5	

FA Premier Lge Record

Sheffield Wed	92/93-93/94	18+5			12		

WATSON Kevin   Tottenham Hotspur
Full Name: WATSON, Kevin Edward   DOB: 3/1/74, Hackney
FAPL Debut: Away v Sheffield Wednesday † 27/9/92
Debut Goal: Away v Manchester City 28/11/92

Previous Club Details

Club	Signed Fee		Lge	FLC	FAC	Lge	FLC	FAC
			Apps			*Goals*		
Tottenham H	5/92	–	4+1	1+1	0+1	1	1	

FA Premier Lge Record

Tottenham H	92/93	4+1			1		

WATSON Steve   Newcastle United
Full Name: WATSON, Stephen   DOB: 1/4/74, North Shields
FAPL Debut: Home v Tottenham Hotspur 14/8/93
Debut Goal: Home v Swindon Town 12/3/94

Previous Club Details

Club	Signed Fee		Lge	FLC	FAC	Lge	FLC	FAC
			Apps			*Goals*		
Newcastle Utd	7/90	–	75+11	3	7+1	3		

FA Premier Lge Record

Newcastle Utd	93/94	30+3			2		

WATTS Julian   Sheffield Wednesday
Full Name: WATTS, Julian   DOB: 17/3/71, Sheffield
FAPL Debut: Away v Liverpool † 3/3/93   Debut Goal:

Previous Club Details

Club	Signed Fee		Lge	FLC	FAC	Lge	FLC	FAC
			Apps			*Goals*		
Rotherham Utd	7/90	–	17+3	1	4	1		
Sheffield Wed	3/92	£80,000	3+1					
Shrewsbury T	12/92	Loan	9					

FA Premier Lge Record

Sheffield Wed	92/93-93/94	3+1			0		

WEBB Neil   Nottingham Forest
Full Name: WEBB, Neil John   DOB: 30/7/63, Reading
FAPL Debut: Home v Ipswich Town † 22/8/92   Debut Goal:

Previous Club Details

Club	Signed	Fee	App Lge	FLC	FAC	Goals Lge	FLC	FAC
Reading	11/80	–	65+7	2+2	2	22		
Portsmouth	7/82	£83,000	123	9	6	34	3	1
Nottingham F	6/85	£250,000	146	21	13	47	4	2
Manchester Utd	7/89	£1.5m	70+5	14	9	8	1	1
Nottingham F	11/92	£800,000	26+4	2+3	2	3	1	2

FA Premier Lge Record

| Manchester Utd | 92/93 | | 0+1 | | | 0 | | |
| Nottingham F | 92/93 | | 9 | | | 0 | | |

WEBSTER Simon   West Ham United
Full Name: WEBSTER, Simon   DOB: 20/1/64, Earl Shilton

Previous Club Details

Club	Signed	Fee	Apps Lge	FLC	FAC	Goals Lge	FLC	FAC
Tottenham H	12/81	–	2+1					
Exeter City	11/83	Loan	26					
Huddersfield T	2/85	£15,000	118	7	7	4		
Sheffield Utd	3/88	£35,000	26+11	5	5+1	3		
Charlton Ath	9/90	£50,000	130	7	6	7		
West Ham Utd	7/93	£525,000						

WEGERLE Roy   Coventry City
Full Name: WEGERLE, Roy Connon   DOB: 19/3/64, Johannesburg, SA
FAPL Debut: Away v Coventry City † 29/8/92
Debut Goal: Home v Norwich City 3/10/92
American International

Previous Club Details

Club	Signed	Fee	Apps Lge	FLC	FAC	Goals Lge	FLC	FAC
Tampa Bay (US)								
Chelsea	6/86	£100,000	15+8		1+1	3		1
Swindon Town	3/88	Loan	7			1		
Luton Town	7/88	£75,000	39+6	10	1	10	8	
QPR	12/89	£1m	71+4	5	11	29	1	1
Blackburn Rov	3/92	£1.2m	20+14	3+3	4	6	4	2
Coventry City	3/93	£1m	25+2	3	1	6		

FA Premier Lge Record

| Blackburn Rov | 92/93 | | 11+11 | | | 4 | | |
| Coventry City | 92/93-93/94 | | 25+2 | | | 6 | | |

WETHERALL David   Leeds United
Full Name: WETHERALL, David   DOB: 14/3/71, Sheffield
FAPL Debut: Away v Southampton 19/9/92
Debut Goal: Home v Chelsea 24/3/93

Previous Club Details			Apps			Goals		
Club	Signed	Fee	Lge	FLC	FAC	Lge	FLC	FAC
Sheffield Wed	7/89	–						
Leeds United	7/91	£125,000	42+2	4	2		1	

FA Premier Lge Record

Leeds United	92/93-93/94		42+1			2		

WHELAN Noel   Leeds United

Full Name: WHELAN, Noel   DOB: 30/12/74, Leeds
FAPL Debut: Away v Sheffield Wednesday 4/5/93 Debut Goal:

Previous Club Details			Apps			Goals		
Club	Signed	Fee	Lge	FLC	FAC	Lge	FLC	FAC
Leeds United	3/93	–	7+9	1			1	

FA Premier Lge Record

Leeds United	92/93-93/94		7+10			0		

WHELAN Phil   Ipswich Town

Full Name: WHELAN, Philip James   DOB: 7/8/72, Stockport
FAPL Debut: Home v Aston Villa 15/8/92   Debut Goal:

Previous Club Details			Apps			Goals		
Club	Signed	Fee	Lge	FLC	FAC	Lge	FLC	FAC
Ipswich Town	7/90	–	64+5	6+1	2+1	2		

FA Premier Lge Record

Ipswich Town	92/93-93/94		56+5			0		

WHELAN Ronnie   Liverpool

Full Name: WHELAN, Ronald   DOB: 25/9/61, Dublin
FAPL Debut: Away v Nottingham Forest 16/8/92
Debut Goal: Away v Leeds United 29/8/92
Eire International Debut: Home v Czechoslovakia † 24/4/81

Previous Club Details			Apps			Goals		
Club	Signed	Fee	Lge	FLC	FAC	Lge	FLC	FAC
Liverpool	10/79	–	311+11	46+4	41+1	45	14	7

FA Premier Lge Record

Liverpool	92/93-93/94		40+1			2		

WHITE David   Leeds United

Full Name: WHITE, David   DOB: 30/10/67, Manchester
FAPL Debut: Home v QPR 17/8/92
Debut Goal: Home v QPR 17/8/92
England International Debut: Away v Spain 9/9/92

Previous Club Details			Apps			Goals		
Club	Signed	Fee	Lge	FLC	FAC	Lge	FLC	FAC
Manchester C	10/85	–	273+12	24+2	22	81	11	4
Leeds United	12/93	Swap	8+6		3	4		1

WHITE Devon — Queens Park Rangers

Full Name: WHITE, Devon DOB: 2/3/64, Nottingham
FAPL Debut: Home v Chelsea † 27/1/93
Debut Goal: Away v QPR 4/4/94

Previous Club Details			*Apps*			*Goals*		
Club	Signed	Fee	Lge	FLC	FAC	Lge	FLC	FAC
Lincoln City	12/84	–	21+8			4		
Bristol R	8/87		190+12	9	10	54	2	3
Cambridge Utd	3/92	£100,000	14+7			4		
QPR	1/93	£100,000	15+8	1+1		9		

FA Premier Lge Record

QPR	92/93-93/94	15+8	9

WHITLOW Michael — Leicester City

Full Name: WHITLOW, Michael DOB: 13/1/68, Liverpool

Previous Club Details			*Apps*			*Goals*		
Club	Signed	Fee	Lge	FLC	FAC	Lge	FLC	FAC
Leeds United	11/88	£10,000	62+15	4+1	1+4	4		
Leicester City	3/92	£250,000	58+2	2	3	3	1	

WHITTINGHAM Guy — Aston Villa

Name: WHITTINGHAM, Guy DOB: 10/11/64, Evesham

Previous Club Details			*Apps*			*Goals*		
Club	Signed	Fee	Lge	FLC	FAC	Lge	FLC	FAC
Portsmouth	6/89	–	149+11	7+2	7+3	88	3	10
Aston Villa	7/93	£1.2m	13+5	2		3		

FA Premier Lge Record

Aston Villa	93/94	13+5	

WHYTE David — Crystal Palace

Full Name: WHYTE , David DOB: 3/10/71, Greenwich

Previous Club Details			*Apps*			*Goals*		
Club	Signed	Fee	Lge	FLC	FAC	Lge	FLC	FAC
Crystal Palace	2/89	–	17+10	5	0+1	4	2	
Charlton Ath	3/92	Loan	7+1					

WIDDRINGTON Chris — Southampton

Full Name: WIDDRINGTON, Christopher DOB: 1/10/71, Newcastle
FAPL Debut: Away v Crystal Palace 26/9/92 Debut Goal:

Previous Club Details			*Apps*			*Goals*		
Club	Signed	Fee	Lge	FLC	FAC	Lge	FLC	FAC
Southampton	5/90	–	2+1					
Wigan Athletic	9/91	Loan	23+2	0+1	3	1		

Southampton   92/93-93/94   21+1   0

WILCOX Jason   Blackburn Rovers

Full Name: WILCOX, Jason Malcolm   DOB: 15/3/71, Farnworth
FAPL Debut: Home v Arsenal 18/8/92
Debut Goal: Away v Middlesbrough 5/12/92

Previous Club Details			Apps			Goals		
Club	Signed	Fee	Lge	FLC	FAC	Lge	FLC	FAC
Blackburn Rov	6/89	–	110+12	9+1	9	14		1

FA Premier Lge Record
Blackburn Rov	92/93-93/94	61+4			10	

WILKINS Ray   Crystal Palace

Ful Name: WILKINS, Raymond Colin   DOB: 14/9/56, Hillingdon
FAPL Debut: Away v Manchester City 17/8/92
Debut Goal: Home v Tottenham Hotspur 3/10/92
England International Debut: Away v Italy 28/5/76

Previous Club Details			Apps			Goals		
Club	Signed	Fee	Lge	FLC	FAC	Lge	FLC	FAC
Chelsea	10/73	–	176+3	6+1	11+1	30	2	2
Manchester U	8/79	£25,000	158+2	14+1	10	7	1	1
AC Milan (Ita)	7/84	£1.5m						
Paris SG (Fra)	7/87	–						
Rangers	11/87	£250,000						
QPR	11/89	–	72+1	13	12	5		2
Crystal Palace	6/94							

FA Premier Lge Record
QPR	92/93-93/94	65			3	

WILLIAMS Danny   West Ham United

Full Name: WILLIAMS, Daniel   DOB:
FAPL Debut: Away v Arsenal † 30/4/94
Debut Goal:

Previous Club Details			Apps			Goals		
Club	Signed	Fee	Lge	FLC	FAC	Lge	FLC	FAC
West Ham Utd								

FA Premier Lge Record
West Ham Utd	93/94	2+1			0	

WILLIAMS Geraint   Ipswich Town

Full Name: WILLIAMS, Geraint   DOB: 5/7/62, Treorchy
FAPL Debut: Home v Aston Villa 15/8/92   Debut Goal:
Wales International Debut: Away v Czechoslovakia 11/11/87

Previous Club Details			*Apps*			*Goals*		
Club	Signed	Fee	Lge	FLC	FAC	Lge	FLC	FAC
Bristol Rovers	1/80	–	138+3	14	9+2	8		2
Derby County	3/85	£40,000	276+1	26+3	17	9	1	
Ipswich Town	7/92	£650,000	70	7+1	9			
FA Premier Lge Record								
Ipswich Town	92/93-93/94		70			0		

WILLIAMS John Coventry City
Full Name: WILLIAMS, John DOB: 11/5/68 Birmingham
FAPL Debut: Home v Middlesbrough 15/8/92
Debut Goal: Home v Middlesbrough 15/8/92

Previous Club Details			*Apps*			*Goals*		
Club	Signed	Fee	Lge	FLC	FAC	Lge	FLC	FAC
Swansea City	8/91	£5,000	36+3	2+1	3	11		
Coventry City	7/92	£250,000	65+8	3	2	11		
FA Premier Lge Record								
Coventry City	92/93-93/94		65+8			11		

WILLIAMS Mike Sheffield Wednesday
Full Name: WILLIAMS, Michael Anthony DOB: 21/11/69, Bradford
FAPL Debut: Home v Southampton † 12/4/93 Debut Goal:

Previous Club Details			*Apps*			*Goals*		
Club	Signed	Fee	Lge	FLC	FAC	Lge	FLC	FAC
Sheffield Wed	2/91	–	6+1	1+1				
Halifax Town	12/92	Loan						
FA Premier Lge Record								
Sheffield Wed	92/93-93/94		6+1			0		

WILLIAMS Paul Coventry City
Full Name: WILLIAMS, Paul R C DOB: 11/9/69, Leicester
FAPL Debut: Home v Newcastle United † 18/8/93 Debut Goal:

Previous Club Details			Apps			Goals		
Club	Signed	Fee	Lge	FLC	FAC	Lge	FLC	FAC
Stockport Co	7/89	–	61+9	2	4	4		
Coventry City	8/93	£150,000	3+1	2+1	1			
West Brom Alb	11/93	Loan	5					
FA Premier Lge Record								
Coventry City	93/94		3+6			0		

WILLIAMS Paul Crystal Palace
Full Name: WILLIAMS, Paul DOB: 16/8/65 Stratford
FAPL Debut: Away v Everton 15/8/92 Debut Goal:

Previous Club Details			*Apps*			*Goals*		
Club	Signed	Fee	Lge	FLC	FAC	Lge	FLC	FAC
Charlton Ath	2/87	£10,000	74+8	6	6+1	23	3	3

Brentford	10/87	Loan	7			3	
Sheffield Wed	8/90	£700,000	78+15	10+3	3+2	25	3
Crystal Palace	9/92	Swap	36+6	4+1		7	

FA Premier Lge Record

Sheffield Wed	92/93	7	1
Crystal Palace	92/93	15+3	0

WILLIS Jimmy   Leicester City

Full Name: WILLIS, James   DOB: 12/7/68, Liverpool

Previous Club Details			Apps			Goals		
Club	Signed	Fee	Lge	FLC	FAC	Lge	FLC	FAC
Stockport Co	12/87	–	10					
Darlington	3/88	£12,000	78	3	5	4		
Leicester City	12/91	£100,000	32	3				
Bradford City	3/92	Loan						

WILSON Clive   Queens Park Rangers

Full Name: WILSON, Clive   DOB: 13/11/61, Manchester
FAPL Debut: Away v Manchester City 17/8/92
Debut Goal: Home v Manchester City 6/8/92

Previous Club Details			Apps			Goals		
Club	Signed	Fee	Lge	FLC	FAC	Lge	FLC	FAC
Manchester C	12/79	–	107+2	10	2	9	2	
Chester City	9/82	Loan	21			2		
Chelsea	5/87	£250,000	68+13	3+3	4	5		
QPR	7/90	£450,000	133+2	13	5	10		

FA Premier Lge Record

QPR	92/93-93/94	82	6

WINTERBURN Nigel   Arsenal

Full Name: WINTERBURN, Nigel   DOB: 11/12/63, Nuneaton
FAPL Debut: Home v Norwich City 15/8/92
Debut Goal: Home v Oldham Athletic 26/8/92
England International Debut: Home v Italy † 15/11/89

Previous Club Details			Apps			Goals		
Club	Signed	Fee	Lge	FLC	FAC	Lge	FLC	FAC
Wimbledon	8/83	–	164+1	13	12	8		
Arsenal	5/87	£407,000	231+1	30	28	5	3	

FA Premier Lge Record

Arsenal	92/93-93/94	62	1

WISE Dennis   Chelsea

Full Name: WISE, Dennis Frank   DOB: 16/12/66, Kensington
FAPL Debut: Home v Blackburn Rovers 26/8/92
Debut Goal: Away v Aston Villa 2/9/92

England International Debut: Away v Turkey 1/5/91

			Apps			Goals		
Previous Club Details								
Club	Signed	Fee	Lge	FLC	FAC	Lge	FLC	FAC
Wimbledon	3/85	–	127+8	14	11	26		3
Chelsea	7/90	£1.6m	130+1	16	7	28	3	
FA Premier Lge Record								
Chelsea	92/93-93/94		60			7		

WITTER Tony   Queens Park Rangers
Full Name: WITTER, Tony   DOB: 12/8/65, London
FAPL Debut: Away v Aston Villa 14/8/93   Debut Goal:

			Apps			Goals		
Previous Club Details								
Club	Signed	Fee	Lge	FLC	FAC	Lge	FLC	FAC
Crystal Palace	10/90	£10,000						
QPR	8/91	£125,000	1					
Plymouth Arg	1/92	Loan	3			1		
Reading	2/94	Loan	4					
FA Premier Lge Record								
QPR	93/94		1			0		

WOAN Ian   Nottingham Forest
Full Name: WOAN, Ian   DOB: 14/12/67, Heswall
FAPL Debut: Home v Liverpool 16/8/92
Debut Goal: Away v Coventry City 9/1/93

			App			Goals		
Previous Club Details								
Club	Signed	Fee	Lge	FLC	FAC	Lge	FLC	FAC
Nottingham F	3/90	£80,000	80+6	8+1	9+1	16	1	1
FA Premier Lge Record								
Nottingham F	92/93		27+1			3		

WOOD Steve   Southampton
Full Name: WOOD, Stephen Alan   DOB: 2/2/63, Bracknell
FAPL Debut: Home v Tottenham Hotspur 15/8/92 Debut Goal:

			Apps			Goals		
Previous Club Details								
Club	Signed	Fee	Lge	FLC	FAC	Lge	FLC	FAC
Reading	2/81	–	216+3	10	15	9		
Millwall	6/87	£80,000	108+2	10	10			
Southampton	10/91	£400,000	46	2+1	2			1
FA Premier Lge Record								
Southampton	92/93-93/94		31			0		

WOODS Chris   Sheffield Wednesday
Full Name: WOODS, Christopher Charles Eric   DOB: 14/11/59, Boston
FAPL Debut: Away v Everton 15/8/92   Debut Goal:
England International Debut: Away v United States 16/6/85

Previous Club Details

Club	Signed	Fee	Apps Lge	FLC	FAC	Goals Lge	FLC	FAC
Nottingham F	12/76	–		7				
QPR	7/79	£250,000	63	8	1			
Norwich City	3/81	£225,000	216	26	19			
Rangers	6/86	£600,000						
Sheffield Wed	8/91	£1.2m	90	13	10			

FA Premier Lge Record

Sheffield Wed	92/93–93/94		49			0		

WOODTHORPE Colin   Norwich City

Full Name: WOODTHORPE, Colin John   DOB: 13/1/69, Ellesmere Port
FAPL Debut: Away v Manchester City † 26/8/92   Debut Goal:

Previous Club Details

Club	Signed	Fee	Apps Lge	FLC	FAC	Goals Lge	FLC	FAC
Chester City	9/86	–	154+1	10	8+1	6		
Norwich City	7/90	£175,000	35+7	0+2	4	1		

FA Premier Lge Record

Norwich City	92/93–93/94		22+4			0		

WORTHINGTON Nigel   Sheffield Wednesday

Full Name: WORTHINGTON, Nigel   DOB: 4/11/61, Ballymena
FAPL Debut: Away v Everton 15/8/92
Debut Goal: Home v Norwich City 10/1/93
N Ireland International Debut: Away v Wales 22/5/84

Previous Club Details

Club	Signed	Fee	Apps Lge	FLC	FAC	Goals Lge	FLC	FAC
Notts County	7/81	£100,000	62+5	11	4	4		
Sheffield Wed	2/84	£125,000	333+4	41	29	12	1	

FA Premier Lge Record

Sheffield Wed	92/93+93/94		69+1			2		

WRIGHT Alan   Blackburn Rovers

Full Name: WRIGHT, Alan Geoffrey   DOB: 28/9/71, Ashton-U-Lyne
FAPL Debut: Away v Crystal Palace 15/8/92   Debut Goal:

Previous Club Details

Club	Signed	Fee	Apps Lge	FLC	FAC	Goals Lge	FLC	FAC
Blackpool	4/89	–	91+7	10+2	8			
Blackburn Rov	1091	£400,000	63+5	8	5			

FA Premier Lge Record

Blackburn Rov	92/93–93/94		31+4			0		

WRIGHT Ian   Arsenal

Full Name: WRIGHT, Ian Edward   DOB: 3/11/63, Woolwich
FAPL Debut: Home v Norwich City † 15/8/92

Debut Goal: Away *v* Liverpool 23/8/92
England International Debut: Home *v* Cameroon 6/2/91

Previous Club Details			*Apps*			*Goals*		
Club	Signed	Fee	Lge	FLC	FAC	Lge	FLC	FAC
Crystal Palace	8/85	–	206+19	19	9+2	90	9	3
Arsenal	9/91	£2.5m	98+1	15	10	62	13	11
FA Premier Lge Record								
Arsenal	92/93-93/94		68+1			38		

WRIGHT Mark   Liverpool
Full Name: WRIGHT, Mark   DOB: 1/8/63, Dorchester on Thames
FAPL Debut: Away *v* Nottingham Forest 16/8/92
Debut Goal: Home *v* Southampton 1/9/92
England International Debut: Away *v* Wales 2/5/84

Previous Club Details			*Apps*			*Goals*		
Club	Signed	Fee	Lge	FLC	FAC	Lge	FLC	FAC
Oxford United	8/80	–		1				
Southampton	3/82	£80,000	170	25	17	7	2	1
Derby County	8/87	£760,000	144	12	6	10		
Liverpool	7/91	£2.2m	84+1	8+2	9	3		
FA Premier Lge Record								
Liverpool	92/93-93/94		63+1			3		

WRIGHT Tommy   Nottingham Forest
Full Name: WRIGHT, Thomas   DOB:29/8/63, Belfast
FAPL Debut: Away *v* Coventry City † 18/8/93
N Ireland International Debut: Away *v* Malta 26/4/89

Previous Club Details			*Apps*			*Goals*		
Club	Signed	Fee	Lge	FLC	FAC	Lge	FLC	FAC
Linfield								
Newcastle Utd	3/88	£30,000	70+1	6	4			
Hull City	2/91	Loan	6					
Nottingham F	9/93	£450,000	10	2				
FA Premier Lge Record								
Newcastle Utd	93/94		0+1			1		

YALLOP Frank   Ipswich Town
Full Name: YALLOP, Frank Walter   DOB: 4/4/64, Watford
FAPL Debut: Away *v* QPR † 5/9/92
Debut Goal: Home *v* Tottenham Hotspur 27/1/93
Canadian International

Previous Club Details			*Apps*			*Goals*		
Club	Signed	Fee	Lge	FLC	FAC	Lge	FLC	FAC
Ipswich Town	1/82	–	245+23	20+2	13+3	6	1	

FA Premier Lge Record

FA Premier Lge Record
Ipswich Town   92/93-93/94   7+6   2

YATES Stephen   Queens Park Rangers
Full Name: YATES, Stephen   DOB: 29/1/70, Bristol
FAPL Debut: Home v Liverpool   Debut Goal:

| *Previous Club Details* | | | *Apps* | | | *Goals* | | |
Club	Signed	Fee	Lge	FLC	FAC	Lge	FLC	FAC
Bristol Rovers	8/93	–	195+1	9	11			
QPR	8/93	£650,000	26+2		1			

FA Premier Lge Record
QPR   93/94   27+2   0

YORKE Dwight   Aston Villa
Full Name: YORKE, Dwight   DOB: 3/11/71, Tobago, West Indies
FAPL Debut: Home v Leeds United 19/8/92
Debut Goal: Home v Crystal Palace 5/9/92
Trinidad & Tobago International

| *Previous Club Details* | | | *Apps* | | | *Goals* | | |
Club	Signed	Fee	Lge	FLC	FAC	Lge	FLC	FAC
Aston Villa	11/89	£120,000	59+31	5+2	11+2	19		2

FA Premier Lge Record
Aston Villa   92/93-93/94   24+14   6

YOUDS Eddie   Ipswich Town
Full Name: YOUDS, Edward Paul   DOB: 3/5/70, Liverpool
FAPL Debut: Home v Aston Villa † 15/8/92
Debut Goal: Home v Everton 30/10/93
Wales International Debut: Home v Costa Rica 20/5/90

| *Previous Club Details* | | | *Apps* | | | *Goals* | | |
Club	Signed	Fee	Lge	FLC	FAC	Lge	FLC	FAC
Everton	6/88	–	5+3	0+1				
Cardiff City	12/89	Loan	0+1		0+1			
Wrexham	2/90	Loan	20			2		
Ipswich Town	11/91	£250,000	29+11	1+2	5+1	1		

FA Premier Lge Record
Ipswich Town   92/93-93/94   28+11   1

YOUNG Eric   Crystal Palace
Full Name: YOUNG, Eric   DOB: 25/3/60, Singapore
FAPL Debut: Home v Blackburn Rovers 15/8/92
Debut Goal: Away v Tottenham Hotspur 22/8/92

| *Previous Club Details* | | | *Apps* | | | *Goals* | | |
Club	Signed	Fee	Lge	FLC	FAC	Lge	FLC	FAC
Brighton	11/82	£10,000	126	8	11	10		1

Wimbledon	7/87	£70,000	96+3	12	6+1	9		1
Crystal Palace	8/90	£85,000	148	24	6	15	1	
FA Premier Lge Record								
Crystal Palace	92/93		38			6		

The A-Z of Ex-FA Premier League Players 1992-94

This section contains a list of all the Premier League records of all those players who have played, at some point, in the Premiership. This might include retired players and players who have moved to clubs outside the Premiership.

Player	Club(s)	Seasons	Apps	Gls
ALLEN, Clive	West Ham Utd	93/4	7	2
ALLON, Joe	Chelsea	92/3	27+1	9
ANDERSON, Vivien	Sheffield Wed	92/3	23+2	3
ANDERSSON, Patrik	Blackburn Rov	92/3-93/4	7+5	0
BANNISTER, Gary	Nottm Forest	92/3	27+4	8
BARLOW, Andy	Oldham Ath	92/3-93/4	9+2	0
BARNES, David	Sheffield Utd	92/3-93/4	15	0
BECKFORD, Darren	Oldham Ath	92/3-93/4	18+10	9
BEESLEY, Paul	Sheffield Utd	92/3-93/4	61+3	2
BERESFORD, John	Oldham Ath	93/4	0+1	0
BERGSSON, Gudni	Tottenham H	92/3	0+5	0
BERNARD, Paul	Oldham Ath	92/3-93/4	64+1	9
BERRY, Greg	Wimbledon	92/3-93/4	6+2	1
BILLING, Peter	Coventry City	92/3	3	0
BLACKMORE, Clayton	Man Utd	92/3	12+2	0
BLAKE, Nathan	Sheffield Utd	93/4	6+5	5
BODIN, Paul	Swindon Town	93/4	27+4	7
BOZINOSKI, Vlado	Ipswich Town	92/3	3+6	0
BRADSHAW, Carl	Sheffield Utd	92/3-93/4	62+9	2
BRENNAN, Mark	Oldham Ath	92/3-93/4	24	3
BRYSON, Ian	Sheffield Utd	92/3	9+7	3
CARR, Franz	Sheffield Utd	92/3-93/4	18	4
CARRUTHERS, Martin	Aston Villa	92/3	0+1	0
CHANNING, Justin	Q P R	92/3	2	1
CHAPMAN, Lee	Leeds Utd	92/3	36+4	14
	West Ham Utd	93/4	26+3	7
CHARLES, Gary	Nottm Forest	92/3	14	0
COCKERILL, Glen	Southampton	92/3-93/4	33+4	0
COLLETT, Andrew	Middlesbrough	92/3	0+2	0
CORK, Alan	Sheffield Utd	92/3-93/4	18+28	5
COTTERILL, Steve	Wimbledon	92/3	4+3	3
COWAN, Tom	Sheffield Utd	92/3-93/4	25	0

Player	Club(s)	Seasons	Apps	Gls
COWANS, Gordon	Blackburn Rov	92/3	23+1	1
	Aston Villa	93/4	10+2	0
COX, Neil	Aston Villa	92/93-93/94	22+13	3
DALEY, Tony	Aston Villa	92/3-93/4	26+13	3
DAVISON, Ross	Sheffield Utd	93/4	8+1	0
DAY, Mervyn	Leeds Utd	92/3	2	0
DEARDEN, Kevin	Tottenham H	92/3	0+1	0
DIGBY, Fraser	Swindon Town	93/4	28	0
DIXON, Kerry	Southampton	92/3	8+1	2
DOBSON, Tony	Blackburn Rov	92/3	15+4	0
DURIE, Gordon	Tottenham H	92/3-93/4	27	4
ELLIOTT, Paul	Chelsea	92/3	7	0
EYRE, John	Oldham Ath	93/4	1+1	0
FALCONER, Willie	Middlesbrough	92/3	22+6	5
	Sheffield Utd	93/4	21+2	3
FENWICK, Terry	Tottenham H	92/3	3+2	0
	Swindon Town	93/4	23+3	0
FERGUSON, Darren	Man Utd	92/3-93/4	16+2	0
FJORTOFT, Jan Aage	Swindon Town	93/4	25+10	12
FLEMING, Craig	Oldham Ath	92/3-93/4	59+1	0
FLEMING, Terry	Coventry City	92/3	8+1	0
FLO, Jostein	Sheffield Utd	93/4	31+1	8
FOSTER, Colin	West Ham Utd	93/4	5	0
GAGE, Kevin	Sheffield Utd	92/3-93/4	43+5	0
GANNON, John	Sheffield Utd	92/3-93/4	39+1	1
GAYLE, Brian	Sheffield Utd	92/3-93/4	43	5
GERRARD, Paul	Oldham Ath	92/3-93/4	39+1	0
GIBSON, Terry	Wimbledon	92/3	6+2	1
GORDON, Dean	Middlesbrough	92/3	31+1	0
GRAHAM, Richard	Oldham Ath	93/4	4+1	0
GREENMAN, Chris	Coventry City	92/3	1+1	0
GOODEN, Ty	Swindon Town	93/4	1+2	0
GYNN, Micky	Coventry City	92/3	18+3	2
HALLE, Gunnar	Oldham Ath	92/3-93/4	63+1	6
HALLWORTH, Jon	Oldham Ath	92/3-93/4	35	0
HAMMOND, Nicky	Swindon Town	93/4	11+3	0
HARKES, John	Sheffield Wed	92/3	23+6	2
HARPER, Alan	Everton	92/3	16+2	0
HARTFIELD, Charlie	Sheffield Utd	92/3-93/4	15+7	0
HEALD, Paul	Swindon Town	93/4	0+1	0
HENDRIE, John	Crystal Palace	92/3	6+4	0
HENRY, Nick	Oldham Ath	92/3-93/4	53	6

Player	Club(s)	Seasons	Apps	Gls
HILL, Keith	Blackburn Rov	92/3	0+1	0
HODGES, Glyn	Sheffield Utd	92/3-93/4	46+15	5
HOHAN, Nicholas	Middlesbrough	92/3	17	2
HOLDEN, Rick	Man City	92/3-93/4	49+1	3
	Oldham Ath	93/4	27+1	6
HORLOCK, Kevin	Swindon Town	93/4	31+6	0
HOYLAND, Jamie	Sheffield Utd	92/3-93/4	32+7	2
HURLOCK, Terry	Southampton	92/3-93/4	32	0
IRONSIDE, Ian	Middlesbrough	92/3	11+1	0
JENKINS, Iain	Everton	92/3	1	0
JOBSON, Richard	Oldham Ath	92/3-93/4	76	5
JOHNSON, Maurice	Everton	92/3	7+6	3
KAMARA, Chris	Sheffield Utd	92/3-93/4	23+3	0
	Middlesbrough	92/3	3+2	0
KARL, Stefan	Man City	93/94	4+2	0
KEELEY, John	Oldham Ath	92/3	1	0
KEIZERWIERD, Orpheo	Oldham Ath	92/3	0+1	0
KELLY, Alan	Sheffield Utd	92/3-93/4	61+2	0
KERR, Dylan	Leeds Utd	92/3	3+2	2
KILCLINE, Brian	Newcastle Utd	93/4	1	0
	Swindon Town	93/4	10	0
KOZMA, Istvan	Liverpool	92/3	0+1	0
KRUSZYNSKI, Detzi	Coventry City	93/4	1+1	0
LAKE, Mike	Sheffield Utd	92/3	6	0
LEE, Dave	Southampton	92/3	0+1	0
LING, Martin	Swindon Town	93/4	29+4	1
LITTLEJOHN, Adrian	Sheffield Utd	92/3-93/4	30+16	11
LIVINGSTONE, Steve	Blackburn Rov	92/3	1+1	0
	Chelsea	92/3	0+1	0
MacDONALD, David	Tottenham H	92/3	2	0
MAKIN, Chris	Oldham Ath	93/4	25+1	1
MARRIOTT, Andrew	Nottm Forest	92/3	5	0
MARTIN, Lee	Man Utd	93/4	1	0
McAVENNIE, Frank	Aston Villa	92/3	0+3	0
	Swindon Town	93/4	3+4	0
McCARTHY, Sean	Oldham Ath	93/4	18+1	3
McDONALD, Neil	Oldham Ath	92/3-93/4	5+2	0
McKINNON, Raymond	Nottm Forest	92/3	5+1	1
McLAREN, Ross	Swindon Town	93/4	10+2	0
McLEARY, Alan	Wimbledon	92/3	4	0
McLEARY, Alan	Sheffield Utd	92/3	3	0
MARSDEN, Chris	Coventry City	93/94	5+2	0
MIDDLETON, Craig	Coventry City	92/3	1	0

Player	Club(s)	Seasons	Apps	Gls
MILLIGAN, Mike	Oldham Ath	92/3-93/4	81	3
MINETT, Jason	Norwich C	92/3	0+1	0
MONCUR, John	Swindon Town	93/4	40	4
MOODY, Paul	Southampton	92/3-93/4	5+3	0
MOORE, Alan	Middlesbrough	92/3	0+2	0
MORTIMER, Paul	Crystal Palace	92/3	1	0
MOULDEN, Paul	Oldham Ath	92/3	1+3	0
MUSTOE, Robin	Middlesbrough	92/3	22+1	1
MUTCH, Andy	Swindon Town	93/4	27+2	6
NAYIM	Tottenham H	92/3	15+3	3
NIJHOLT, Luc	Swindon Town	93/4	31+1	1
NILSSON, Roger	Sheffield Utd	93/4	20+1	0
O'BRIEN, Liam	Newcastle Utd	93/4	4+2	0
OLNEY, Ian	Oldham Ath	92/3-93/4	42+2	13
ORLYGSSON, Toddy	Nottm Forest	92/3	15+5	1
PARKINSON, Gary	Middlesbrough	92/3	2	0
PALMER, Roger	Oldham Ath	92/3-93/4	6+19	0
PATES, Colin	Arsenal	92/3	2+5	0
PEAKE, Andrew	Middlesbrough	92/3	33	0
PEARS, Stephen	Middlesbrough	92/3	26	0
PEDERSON, Tore	Oldham Ath	93/4	7+3	0
PENNYFATHER, Glen	Ipswich T	92/3	2+2	0
PETTERSON, Andy	Ipswich T	92/3	1	0
PEYTON, Gerry	Chelsea	92/3	0+1	0
PHILLIPS, James	Middlesbrough	92/3	42	0
POINTON, Neil	Oldham Ath	92/3-93/4	56+1	3
POLLOCK, Jamie	Middlesbrough	92/3	15+5	1
POWER, Lee	Norwich City	92/3-93/4	13+10	6
PRICE, Chris	Blackburn Rov	92/3	2+4	0
PROCTOR, Mark	Middlesbrough	92/3	5+5	0
RANSON, Ray	Man City	92/3	17	1
REDMOND, Steve	Oldham Ath	92/3-93/4	59+5	2
REGIS, Cyrille	Aston Villa	92/3	7+6	1
REID, Peter	Man City	92/3-93/4	15+9	0
	Southampton	93/4	7	0
RITCHIE, Andy	Oldham Ath	92/3-93/4	22+11	4
ROBSON, Bryan	Man Utd	92/3-93/4	14+ 14	2
ROBSON, Mark	West Ham Utd	93/4	1+2	0
RODGER, Simon	Crystal Palace	92/3	22+1	2
ROGERS, Paul	Sheffield Utd	92/3-93/4	49+2	3
ROSLER, Uwe	Man City	93/94	11	4
SANSOM, Kenny	Coventry City	92/3	21	0
	Everton	92/3	6+1	1

Player	Club(s)	Seasons	Apps	Gls
SANCHEZ, Lawrie	Wimbledon	92/3-93/4	38+4	6
	Swindon Town	93/4	6+1	0
SCOTT, Andy	Sheffield Utd	92/3-93/4	13+4	2
SCOTT, Keith	Swindon Town	93/4	21+5	4
SHARP, Graeme	Oldham Ath	92/3-93/4	51+4	16
SHEFFIELD, Jon	Swindon Town	93/4	2	0
SHIRTLIFF, Peter	Sheffield Wed	92/3	20	0
SHUTT, Carl	Leeds Utd	92/3	6+9	0
	Man City	93/4	5+1	0
SINNOTT, Lee	Crystal Palace	92/3	18+1	0
SLAVEN, Bernard	Middlesbrough	92/3	14+5	4
SMITH, David	Coventry City	92/3	6	0
STERLAND, Mel	Leeds Utd	92/93	3	0
TAYLOR, Shaun	Swindon Town	93/4	41	4
THOMAS, Geoffrey	Crystal Palace	92/3	28+1	2
TOLSON, Neil	Oldham Ath	92/3	0+3	0
TRACEY, Simon	Sheffield United	92/3-93/4	22+2	0
TUTTLE, David	Sheffield Utd	93/4	31	0
VAN DEN HAUWE, Pat	Tottenham H	92/3	13+5	0
VARADI, Imre	Leeds Utd	92/3	2+2	1
WALLACE, Danny	Man Utd	92/3	0+2	0
WARD, Mitch	Sheffield Utd	92/3-93/4	41+6	1
WATTS, Grant	Crystal Palace	92/3	2+2	0
WHITBREAD, Adam	Swindon Town	93/4	33+1	1
WHITE, Steve	Swindon Town	93/4	2+4	0
WHITEHOUSE, Dane	Sheffield United	92/3-93/4	48+3	10
WHITTON, Steve	Ipswich Town	93/4-93/4	28+8	4
WHYTE, Chris	Leeds United	92/3	34	1
WILKINSON, Paul	Middlesbrough	92/3	41	15
WILLIAMS, Brett	Nottm Forest	92/3	9	0
WILLIAMS, Paul	Coventry City	92/3	21+5	2
WILSON, Terry	Nottm Forest	92/3	5	0
WIRMOLA, Jonas	Sheffield Utd	93/4	8	0

306

Form 'n Encounter Guide

Our unique *Form 'n Encounter Guide* will allow you to plan your season's FA Carling Premiership schedule by providing you with a form guide helping you to predict what are likely to be the most exciting games to attend on a day-by-day basis. Listed are the results from the previous Premiership encounters for the matches. Please do check that the game you are looking to attend is on before you set out.

		92-93	93-94	94-95
Aug-20	Arsenal v Manchester City	1-0	0-0	
Aug-20	Chelsea v Norwich City	2-3	1-2	
Aug-20	Coventry City v Wimbledon	0-2	1-2	
Aug-20	Crystal Palace v Liverpool	1-1	–	
Aug-20	Everton v Aston Villa	1-0	0-1	
Aug-20	Ipswich Town v Nottingham Forest	2-1	–	
Aug-20	Manchester United v QPR	0-0	2-1	
Aug-20	Sheffield Wednesday v Tottenham Hotspur	2-0	1-0	
Aug-20	Southampton v Blackburn Rovers	1-1	3-1	
Aug-20	West Ham United v Leeds United	–	0-1	
Aug-21	Leicester City v Newcastle United	–	–	
Aug-22	Nottingham Forest v Manchester United	0-2	–	
Aug-23	Blackburn Rovers v Leicester City	–	–	
Aug-23	Leeds United v Arsenal	3-0	2-1	
Aug-23	Wimbledon v Ipswich Town	0-1	0-2	
Aug-24	Aston Villa v Southampton	1-1	0-2	
Aug-24	Liverpool v Chelsea	2-1	2-1	
Aug-24	Manchester City v West Ham United	–	0-0	
Aug-24	Newcastle United v Coventry City	–	4-0	
Aug-24	Norwich City v Crystal Palace	4-2	–	
Aug-24	QPR v Sheffield Wednesday	3-1	1-2	
Aug-24	Tottenham Hotspur v Everton	2-1	3-2	
Aug-27	Aston Villa v Crystal Palace	3-0	–	
Aug-27	Blackburn Rovers v Coventry City	2-5	2-1	
Aug-27	Leeds United v Chelsea	1-1	4-1	
Aug-27	Manchester City v Everton	2-5	1-0	
Aug-27	Newcastle United v Southampton	–	1-2	
Aug-27	Norwich City v West Ham United	–	0-0	
Aug-27	Nottingham Forest v Leicester City	–	–	
Aug-27	QPR v Ipswich Town	0-0	1-3	
Aug-27	Tottenham Hotspur v Manchester United	1-1	0-1	

Date	Match	92-93	93-94	94-95
Aug-27	Wimbledon v Sheffield Wednesday	1-1	2-1	
Aug-28	Liverpool v Arsenal	0-2	0-0	
Aug-29	Coventry City v Aston Villa	3-0	0-1	
Aug-30	Arsenal v Blackburn Rovers	0-1	1-0	
Aug-30	Crystal Palace v Leeds United	1-0	–	
Aug-30	Everton v Nottingham Forest	3-0	–	
Aug-30	Ipswich Town v Tottenham Hotspur	1-1	2-2	
Aug-31	Chelsea v Manchester City	2-4	0-0	
Aug-31	Leicester City v QPR	–		
Aug-31	Manchester United v Wimbledon	0-1	3-1	
Aug-31	Sheffield Wednesday v Norwich City	1-0	3-3	
Aug-31	Southampton v Liverpool	2-1	4-2	
Aug-31	West Ham United v Newcastle United	–	2-4	
Sep-10	Aston Villa v Ipswich Town	2-0	0-1	
Sep-10	Blackburn Rovers v Everton	2-3	2-0	
Sep-10	Liverpool v West Ham United	–	2-0	
Sep-10	Manchester City v Crystal Palace	0-0	–	
Sep-10	Newcastle United v Chelsea	–	0-0	
Sep-10	Norwich City v Arsenal	1-1	1-1	
Sep-10	Nottingham Forest v Sheffield Wednesday	1-2	–	
Sep-10	QPR v Coventry City	2-0	5-1	
Sep-10	Wimbledon v Leicester City	–		
Sep-11	Leeds United v Manchester United	0-0	0-2	
Sep-12	Tottenham Hotspur v Southampton	4-2	3-0	
Sep-17	Arsenal v Newcastle United	–	2-1	
Sep-17	Coventry City v Leeds United	3-3	0-2	
Sep-17	Crystal Palace v Wimbledon	2-0	–	
Sep-17	Everton v QPR	3-5	0-3	
Sep-17	Ipswich Town v Norwich City	3-1	2-1	
Sep-17	Leicester City v Tottenham Hotspur	–		
Sep-17	Manchester United v Liverpool	2-2	1-0	
Sep-17	Sheffield Wednesday v Manchester City	0-3	–	
Sep-17	Southampton v Nottingham Forest	1-2	–	
Sep-17	West Ham United v Aston Villa	–	0-0	
Sep-18	Chelsea v Blackburn Rovers	0-0	1-2	
Sep-24	Blackburn Rovers v Aston Villa	3-0	1-0	
Sep-24	Coventry City v Southampton	2-0	1-1	
Sep-24	Crystal Palace v Chelsea	1-1	–	
Sep-24	Everton v Leicester City	–		
Sep-24	Ipswich Town v Manchester United	2-1	1-2	
Sep-24	Manchester City v Norwich City	3-1	1-1	
Sep-24	Newcastle United v Liverpool	–	3-0	

		92-93	93-94	94-95
Sep-24	QPR v Wimbledon	1-2	1-0	
Sep-24	Tottenham Hotspur v Nottingham Forest	2-1	–	
Sep-25	West Ham United v Arsenal	–	0-0	
Sep-26	Sheffield Wednesday v Leeds United	1-1	3-3	
Oct-01	Arsenal v Crystal Palace	3-0	–	
Oct-01	Aston Villa v Newcastle United	–	0-2	
Oct-01	Chelsea v West Ham United	–	2-0	
Oct-01	Leeds United v Manchester City	1-0	3-2	
Oct-01	Leicester City v Coventry City	–	–	
Oct-01	Liverpool v Sheffield Wednesday	1-0	2-0	
Oct-01	Manchester United v Everton	0-3	1-0	
Oct-01	Norwich City v Blackburn Rovers	0-0	2-2	
Oct-01	Southampton v Ipswich Town	4-3	0-1	
Oct-01	Wimbledon v Tottenham Hotspur	1-1	2-1	
Oct-02	Nottingham Forest v QPR	1-0	–	
Oct-08	Chelsea v Leicester City	–	–	
Oct-08	Coventry City v Ipswich Town	2-2	1-0	
Oct-08	Liverpool v Aston Villa	1-2	2-1	
Oct-08	Manchester City v Nottingham Forest	2-2	–	
Oct-08	Norwich City v Leeds United	4-2	2-1	
Oct-08	Sheffield Wednesday v Manchester United	3-3	2-3	
Oct-08	Southampton v Everton	0-0	0-2	
Oct-08	Tottenham Hotspur v QPR	3-1	1-2	
Oct-08	Wimbledon v Arsenal	3-2	0-3	
Oct-09	Newcastle United v Blackburn Rovers	–	1-1	
Oct-10	West Ham United v Crystal Palace	–	–	
Oct-15	Arsenal v Chelsea	2-1	1-0	
Oct-15	Aston Villa v Norwich City	2-3	0-0	
Oct-15	Blackburn Rovers v Liverpool	4-1	2-0	
Oct-15	Crystal Palace v Newcastle United	–	–	
Oct-15	Everton v Coventry City	1-1	0-0	
Oct-15	Ipswich Town v Sheffield Wednesday	0-1	1-4	
Oct-15	Leeds United v Tottenham Hotspur	5-0	2-0	
Oct-15	Leicester City v Southampton	–	–	
Oct-15	Manchester United v West Ham United	–	3-0	
Oct-15	Nottingham Forest v Wimbledon	1-1	–	
Oct-15	QPR v Manchester City	1-1	1-1	
Oct-22	Arsenal v Coventry City	3-0	0-3	
Oct-22	Aston Villa v Nottingham Forest	2-1	–	
Oct-22	Blackburn Rovers v Manchester United	0-0	2-0	
Oct-22	Chelsea v Ipswich Town	2-1	1-1	
Oct-22	Crystal Palace v Everton	0-2	–	

Date	Match	92-93	93-94	94-95
Oct-22	Leeds United v Leicester City	–	–	
Oct-22	Liverpool v Wimbledon	2-3	1-1	
Oct-22	Manchester City v Tottenham Hotspur	0-1	0-2	
Oct-22	Newcastle United v Sheffield Wednesday		4-2	
Oct-22	Norwich City v QPR	2-1	3-4	
Oct-22	West Ham United v Southampton	–	3-3	
Oct-29	Coventry City v Manchester City	2-3	4-0	
Oct-29	Everton v Arsenal	0-0	1-1	
Oct-29	Ipswich Town v Liverpool	2-2	1-2	
Oct-29	Leicester City v Crystal Palace	–	–	
Oct-29	Manchester United v Newcastle United	–	1-1	
Oct-29	Nottingham Forest v Blackburn Rovers	1-3	–	
Oct-29	QPR v Aston Villa	2-1	2-2	
Oct-29	Sheffield Wednesday v Chelsea	3-3	3-1	
Oct-29	Southampton v Leeds United	1-1	0-2	
Oct-29	Tottenham Hotspur v West Ham United	–	1-4	
Oct-29	Wimbledon v Norwich City	3-0	3-1	
Nov-01	Everton v West Ham United	–	0-1	
Nov-01	Ipswich Town v Leeds United	4-2	0-0	
Nov-01	Wimbledon v Aston Villa	2-3	2-2	
Nov-02	Coventry City v Crystal Palace	2-2	–	
Nov-02	Leicester City v Arsenal	–	–	
Nov-02	Nottingham Forest v Newcastle United	–	–	
Nov-02	QPR v Liverpool	0-1	1-3	
Nov-02	Sheffield Wednesday v Blackburn Rovers	0-0	1-2	
Nov-02	Southampton v Norwich City	3-0	0-1	
Nov-02	Tottenham Hotspur v Chelsea	1-2	1-1	
Nov-05	Arsenal v Sheffield Wednesday	2-1	1-0	
Nov-05	Aston Villa v Manchester United	1-0	1-2	
Nov-05	Blackburn Rovers v Tottenham Hotspur	0-2	1-0	
Nov-05	Chelsea v Coventry City	2-1	1-2	
Nov-05	Crystal Palace v Ipswich Town	3-1	–	
Nov-05	Leeds United v Wimbledon	2-1	4-0	
Nov-05	Liverpool v Nottingham Forest	0-0	–	
Nov-05	Manchester City v Southampton	1-0	1-1	
Nov-05	Newcastle United v QPR	–	1-2	
Nov-05	Norwich City v Everton	1-1	3-0	
Nov-05	West Ham United v Leicester City	–		
Nov-09	Manchester United v Manchester City	2-1	2-0	
Nov-19	Coventry City v Norwich City	1-1	2-1	
Nov-19	Everton v Liverpool	2-1	2-0	
Nov-19	Ipswich Town v Blackburn Rovers	2-1	1-0	
Nov-19	Leicester City v Manchester City	–	–	

		92-93	93-94	94-95
Nov-19	Manchester United v Crystal Palace	1-0	–	
Nov-19	Nottingham Forest v Chelsea	3-0	–	
Nov-19	QPR v Leeds United	2-1	0-4	
Nov-19	Sheffield Wednesday v West Ham United	–	5-0	
Nov-19	Southampton v Arsenal	2-0	0-4	
Nov-19	Tottenham Hotspur v Aston Villa	0-0	1-1	
Nov-19	Wimbledon v Newcastle United	–	4-2	
Nov-26	Arsenal v Manchester United	0-1	0-0	
Nov-26	Aston Villa v Sheffield Wednesday	2-0	2-2	
Nov-26	Blackburn Rovers v QPR	1-0	1-1	
Nov-26	Chelsea v Everton	2-1	4-2	
Nov-26	Crystal Palace v Southampton	1-2	–	
Nov-26	Leeds United v Nottingham Forest	1-4	–	
Nov-26	Liverpool v Tottenham Hotspur	6-2	1-2	
Nov-26	Manchester City v Wimbledon	1-1	0-1	
Nov-26	Newcastle United v Ipswich Town	–	2-0	
Nov-26	Norwich City v Leicester City	–	–	
Nov-26	West Ham United v Coventry City	–	3-2	
Dec-03	Coventry City v Liverpool	5-1	1-0	
Dec-03	Everton v Leeds United	2-0	1-1	
Dec-03	Ipswich Town v Manchester City	3-1	2-2	
Dec-03	Leicester City v Aston Villa	–	–	
Dec-03	Manchester United v Norwich City	1-0	2-2	
Dec-03	Nottingham Forest v Arsenal	0-1	–	
Dec-03	QPR v West Ham United	–	0-0	
Dec-03	Sheffield Wednesday v Crystal Palace	2-1	–	
Dec-03	Southampton v Chelsea	1-0	3-1	
Dec-03	Tottenham Hotspur v Newcastle United	–	1-2	
Dec-03	Wimbledon v Blackburn Rovers	1-1	4-1	
Dec-10	Aston Villa v Everton	2-1	0-0	
Dec-10	Blackburn Rovers v Southampton	0-0	2-0	
Dec-10	Leeds United v West Ham United	–	1-0	
Dec-10	Liverpool v Crystal Palace	5-0	–	
Dec-10	Manchester City v Arsenal	0-1	0-0	
Dec-10	Newcastle United v Leicester City	–	–	
Dec-10	Norwich City v Chelsea	2-1	1-1	
Dec-10	Nottingham Forest v Ipswich Town	0-1	–	
Dec-10	QPR v Manchester United	1-3	2-3	
Dec-10	Tottenham Hotspur v Sheffield Wednesday	0-2	1-3	
Dec-10	Wimbledon v Coventry City	1-2	1-2	
Dec-17	Arsenal v Leeds United	0-0	2-1	
Dec-17	Chelsea v Liverpool	0-0	1-0	
Dec-17	Coventry City v Newcastle United	–	2-1	
Dec-17	Crystal Palace v Norwich City	1-2	–	

313

		92-93	93-94	94-95
Dec-17	Everton v Tottenham Hotspur	1-2	0-1	
Dec-17	Ipswich Town v Wimbledon	2-1	0-0	
Dec-17	Leicester City v Blackburn Rovers	–		
Dec-17	Manchester United v Nottingham Forest	2-0	–	
Dec-17	Sheffield Wednesday v QPR	1-0	3-1	
Dec-17	Southampton v Aston Villa	2-0	4-1	
Dec-17	West Ham United v Manchester City	–	3-1	
Dec-26	Arsenal v Aston Villa	0-1	1-2	
Dec-26	Chelsea v Manchester United	1-1	1-0	
Dec-26	Coventry City v Nottingham Forest	0-1	–	
Dec-26	Crystal Palace v QPR	1-1	–	
Dec-26	Everton v Sheffield Wednesday	1-1	0-2	
Dec-26	Leeds United v Newcastle United	–	1-1	
Dec-26	Leicester City v Liverpool	–	–	
Dec-26	Manchester City v Blackburn Rovers	3-2	0-2	
Dec-26	Norwich City v Tottenham Hotspur	3-2	1-2	
Dec-26	Southampton v Wimbledon	2-2	1-0	
Dec-26	West Ham United v Ipswich Town	–	2-1	
Dec-27	Aston Villa v Chelsea	1-3	1-0	
Dec-27	Blackburn Rovers v Leeds United	3-1	2-1	
Dec-27	Ipswich Town v Arsenal	1-2	1-5	
Dec-27	Liverpool v Manchester City	1-1	2-1	
Dec-27	Manchester United v Leicester City	–	–	
Dec-27	Newcastle United v Everton	–	1-0	
Dec-27	Nottingham Forest v Norwich City	0-3	–	
Dec-27	QPR v Southampton	3-1	2-1	
Dec-27	Sheffield Wednesday v Coventry City	1-2	0-0	
Dec-27	Tottenham Hotspur v Crystal Palace	2-2	–	
Dec-27	Wimbledon v West Ham United	–	1-2	
Dec-31	Arsenal v QPR	0-0	0-0	
Dec-31	Chelsea v Wimbledon	4-2	2-0	
Dec-31	Coventry City v Tottenham Hotspur	1-0	1-0	
Dec-31	Crystal Palace v Blackburn Rovers	3-3	–	
Dec-31	Everton v Ipswich Town	3-0	0-0	
Dec-31	Leeds United v Liverpool	2-2	2-0	
Dec-31	Leicester City v Sheffield Wednesday	–	–	
Dec-31	Manchester United v Aston Villa	1-1	3-0	
Dec-31	Norwich City v Newcastle United	–	1-2	
Dec-31	Southampton v Manchester United	0-1	1-3	
Dec-31	West Ham United v Nottingham Forest	–	–	
Jan-02	Aston Villa v Leeds United	1-1	1-0	
Jan-02	Blackburn Rovers v West Ham United	–	0-2	
Jan-02	Ipswich Town v Leicester City	–	–	
Jan-02	Liverpool v Norwich City	4-1	0-1	

Date	Match	92-93	93-94	94-95
Jan-02	Manchester United v Coventry City	5-0	0-0	
Jan-02	Newcastle United v Manchester City	–	2-0	
Jan-02	Nottingham Forest v Crystal Palace	1-1	–	
Jan-02	QPR v Chelsea	1-1	1-1	
Jan-02	Sheffield Wednesday v Southampton	5-2	2-0	
Jan-02	Tottenham Hotspur v Arsenal	1-0	0-1	
Jan-02	Wimbledon v Everton	1-3	1-1	
Jan-14	Arsenal v Everton	2-0	2-0	
Jan-14	Aston Villa v QPR	2-0	4-1	
Jan-14	Blackburn Rovers v Nottingham Forest	4-1	–	
Jan-14	Chelsea v Sheffield Wednesday	0-2	1-1	
Jan-14	Crystal Palace v Leicester City	–	–	
Jan-14	Leeds United v Southampton	2-1	0-0	
Jan-14	Liverpool v Ipswich Town	0-0	1-0	
Jan-14	Manchester City v Coventry City	1-0	1-1	
Jan-14	Newcastle United v Manchester United	–	1-1	
Jan-14	Norwich City v Wimbledon	2-1	0-1	
Jan-14	West Ham United v Tottenham Hotspur	–	1-3	
Jan-21	Coventry City v Arsenal	0-2	1-0	
Jan-21	Everton v Crystal Palace	0-2	–	
Jan-21	Ipswich Town v Chelsea	1-1	1-0	
Jan-21	Leicester City v Leeds United	–	–	
Jan-21	Manchester United v Blackburn Rovers	3-1	1-1	
Jan-21	Nottingham Forest v Aston Villa	0-1	–	
Jan-21	QPR v Norwich City	3-1	2-2	
Jan-21	Sheffield Wednesday v Newcastle United	–	0-1	
Jan-21	Southampton v West Ham United	–	0-2	
Jan-21	Tottenham Hotspur v Manchester City	3-1	1-0	
Jan-21	Wimbledon v Liverpool	2-0	1-1	
Jan-24	Arsenal v Southampton	4-3	1-0	
Jan-24	Blackburn Rovers v Ipswich Town	2-1	0-0	
Jan-24	Crystal Palace v Manchester United	0-2	–	
Jan-24	Leeds United v QPR	1-1	1-1	
Jan-25	Aston Villa v Tottenham Hotspur	0-0	1-0	
Jan-25	Chelsea v Nottingham Forest	0-0	–	
Jan-25	Liverpool v Everton	1-0	2-1	
Jan-25	Manchester City v Leicester City	–	–	
Jan-25	Newcastle United v Wimbledon	–	4-0	
Jan-25	Norwich City v Coventry City	1-1	1-0	
Jan-25	West Ham United v Sheffield Wednesday	–	2-0	
Feb-04	Coventry City v Chelsea	1-2	1-1	
Feb-04	Everton v Norwich City	0-1	1-5	
Feb-04	Ipswich Town v Crystal Palace	2-2	–	

315

		92-93	93-94	94-95
Feb-04	Leicester City v West Ham United	–	–	
Feb-04	Manchester United v Aston Villa	1-1	3-1	
Feb-04	Nottingham Forest v Liverpool	1-0	–	
Feb-04	QPR v Newcastle United	–	1-2	
Feb-04	Sheffield Wednesday v Arsenal	1-0	0-1	
Feb-04	Southampton v Manchester City	0-1	0-1	
Feb-04	Tottenham Hotspur v Blackburn Rovers	1-2	0-2	
Feb-04	Wimbledon v Leeds United	1-0	1-0	
Feb-11	Arsenal v Leicester City	–	–	
Feb-11	Aston Villa v Wimbledon	1-0	0-1	
Feb-11	Blackburn Rovers v Sheffield Wednesday	1-0	1-1	
Feb-11	Chelsea v Tottenham Hotspur	1-1	4-3	
Feb-11	Crystal Palace v Coventry City	0-0	–	
Feb-11	Leeds United v Ipswich Town	1-0	0-0	
Feb-11	Liverpool v QPR	1-0	3-2	
Feb-11	Manchester City v Manchester United	1-1	2-3	
Feb-11	Newcastle United v Nottingham Forest	–	–	
Feb-11	Norwich City v Southampton	1-0	4-5	
Feb-11	West Ham United v Everton	–	0-1	
Feb-18	Coventry City v West Ham United	–	1-1	
Feb-18	Everton v Chelsea	0-1	4-2	
Feb-18	Ipswich Town v Newcastle United	–	1-1	
Feb-18	Leicester City v Norwich City	–	–	
Feb-18	Manchester United v Arsenal	0-0	1-0	
Feb-18	Nottingham Forest v Leeds United	1-1	–	
Feb-18	QPR v Blackburn Rovers	0-3	1-0	
Feb-18	Sheffield Wednesday v Aston Villa	1-2	0-0	
Feb-18	Southampton v Crystal Palace	1-0	–	
Feb-18	Tottenham Hotspur v Liverpool	2-0	3-3	
Feb-18	Wimbledon v Manchester City	0-1	1-0	
Feb-21	Arsenal v Nottingham Forest	1-1	–	
Feb-21	Blackburn Rovers v Wimbledon	0-0	3-0	
Feb-21	Crystal Palace v Sheffield Wednesday	1-1	–	
Feb-21	Leeds United v Everton	2-0	3-0	
Feb-22	Aston Villa v Leicester City	–	–	
Feb-22	Chelsea v Southampton	1-1	2-0	
Feb-22	Liverpool v Coventry City	4-0	1-0	
Feb-22	Manchester City v Ipswich Town	3-1	2-1	
Feb-22	Newcastle United v Tottenham Hotspur	–	0-1	
Feb-22	Norwich City v Manchester United	1-3	0-2	
Feb-22	West Ham United v QPR	–	0-4	
Feb-25	Blackburn Rovers v Norwich City	7-1	2-3	
Feb-25	Coventry City v Leicester City	–	–	

316

		92-93	93-94	94-95
Feb-25	Crystal Palace v Arsenal	1-2	–	
Feb-25	Everton v Manchester United	0-2	0-1	
Feb-25	Ipswich Town v Southampton	0-0	1-0	
Feb-25	Manchester City v Leeds United	4-0	1-1	
Feb-25	Newcastle United v Aston Villa	–	5-1	
Feb-25	QPR v Nottingham Forest	4-3	–	
Feb-25	Sheffield Wednesday v Liverpool	1-1	3-1	
Feb-25	Tottenham Hotspur v Wimbledon	1-1	1-1	
Feb-25	West Ham United v Chelsea	–	1-0	
Mar-04	Arsenal v West Ham United	–	0-2	
Mar-04	Aston Villa v Blackburn Rovers	0-0	0-1	
Mar-04	Chelsea v Crystal Palace	3-1	–	
Mar-04	Leeds United v Sheffield Wednesday	3-1	2-1	
Mar-04	Leicester City v Everton	–	–	
Mar-04	Liverpool v Newcastle United	–	0-2	
Mar-04	Manchester United v Ipswich Town	1-1	0-0	
Mar-04	Norwich City v Manchester City	2-1	1-1	
Mar-04	Nottingham Forest v Tottenham Hotspur	2-1	–	
Mar-04	Southampton v Coventry City	2-2	1-0	
Mar-04	Wimbledon v QPR	1-2	1-1	
Mar-07	Blackburn Rovers v Arsenal	1-0	1-1	
Mar-07	Leeds United v Crystal Palace	0-0	–	
Mar-07	Wimbledon v Manchester United	1-2	1-0	
Mar-08	Aston Villa v Coventry City	0-0	–	
Mar-08	Liverpool v Southampton	1-1	4-2	
Mar-08	Manchester City v Chelsea	0-1	2-2	
Mar-08	Newcastle United v West Ham United	–	2-0	
Mar-08	Norwich City v Sheffield Wednesday	1-0	1-1	
Mar-08	Nottingham Forest v Everton	0-1	–	
Mar-08	QPR v Leicester City	–	–	
Mar-08	Tottenham Hotspur v Ipswich Town	0-2	1-1	
Mar-11	Arsenal v Liverpool	0-1	1-0	
Mar-11	Chelsea v Leeds United	1-0	1-1	
Mar-11	Coventry City v Blackburn Rovers	0-2	2-1	
Mar-11	Crystal Palace v Aston Villa	1-0	–	
Mar-11	Everton v Manchester City	2-3	1-0	
Mar-11	Ipswich Town v QPR	1-1	1-3	
Mar-11	Leicester City v Nottingham Forest	–	–	
Mar-11	Manchester United v Tottenham Hotspur	4-1	2-1	
Mar-11	Sheffield Wednesday v Wimbledon	1-1	2-2	
Mar-11	Southampton v Newcastle United	–	2-1	
Mar-11	West Ham United v Norwich City	–	3-3	

317

		92-93	93-94	94-95
Mar-18	Aston Villa v West Ham United	–	3-1	
Mar-18	Blackburn Rovers v Chelsea	2-0	2-0	
Mar-18	Leeds United v Coventry City	2-2	1-0	
Mar-18	Liverpool v Manchester United	1-2	3-3	
Mar-18	Manchester City v Sheffield Wednesday	1-2	1-3	
Mar-18	Newcastle United v Arsenal	–	2-0	
Mar-18	Norwich City v Ipswich Town	0-2	1-0	
Mar-18	Nottingham Forest v Southampton	1-2	–	
Mar-18	QPR v Everton	4-2	2-1	
Mar-18	Tottenham Hotspur v Leicester City	–	–	
Mar-18	Wimbledon v Crystal Palace	4-0	–	
Apr-01	Arsenal v Norwich City	2-4	0-0	
Apr-01	Chelsea v Newcastle United	–	1-0	
Apr-01	Coventry City v QPR	0-1	0-1	
Apr-01	Crystal Palace v Manchester City	0-0	–	
Apr-01	Everton v Blackburn Rovers	2-1	0-3	
Apr-01	Ipswich Town v Aston Villa	1-1	1-2	
Apr-01	Leicester City v Wimbledon	–	–	
Apr-01	Manchester United v Leeds United	2-0	0-0	
Apr-01	Sheffield Wednesday v Nottingham Forest	2-0	–	
Apr-01	Southampton v Tottenham Hotspur	0-0	1-0	
Apr-01	West Ham United v Liverpool	–	1-2	
Apr-08	Aston Villa v Manchester City	3-1	0-0	
Apr-08	Blackburn Rovers v Crystal Palace	1-2	–	
Apr-08	Ipswich Town v Everton	1-2	0-2	
Apr-08	Liverpool v Leeds United	2-0	2-0	
Apr-08	Manchester United v Southampton	2-1	2-0	
Apr-08	Newcastle United v Norwich City	–	3-0	
Apr-08	Nottingham Forest v West Ham United	–	–	
Apr-08	QPR v Arsenal	0-0	1-1	
Apr-08	Sheffield Wednesday v Leicester City	–	–	
Apr-08	Tottenham Hotspur v Coventry City	0-2	1-2	
Apr-08	Wimbledon v Chelsea	0-0	1-1	
Apr-15	Arsenal v Ipswich Town	0-0	4-0	
Apr-15	Chelsea v Aston Villa	0-1	1-1	
Apr-15	Coventry City v Sheffield Wednesday	1-0	1-1	
Apr-15	Crystal Palace v Tottenham Hotspur	1-3	–	
Apr-15	Everton v Newcastle United		0-2	
Apr-15	Leeds United v Blackburn Rovers	5-2	3-3	
Apr-15	Leicester City v Manchester United	–	–	
Apr-15	Manchester City v Liverpool	1-1	1-1	
Apr-15	Norwich City v Nottingham Forest	3-1	–	
Apr-15	Southampton v QPR	1-2	0-1	
Apr-15	West Ham United v Wimbledon	–	0-2	

		92-93	93-94	94-95
Apr-17	Aston Villa v Arsenal	1-0	1-2	
Apr-17	Blackburn Rovers v Manchester City	1-0	2-0	
Apr-17	Ipswich Town v West Ham United	–	1-1	
Apr-17	Liverpool v Leicester City	–	–	
Apr-17	Manchester United v Chelsea	3-0	0-1	
Apr-17	Newcastle United v Leeds United	–	1-1	
Apr-17	Nottingham Forest v Coventry City	1-1	–	
Apr-17	QPR v Crystal Palace	1-3	–	
Apr-17	Sheffield Wednesday v Everton	3-1	5-1	
Apr-17	Tottenham Hotspur v Norwich City	5-1	1-3	
Apr-17	Wimbledon v Southampton	1-2	1-0	
Apr-29	Arsenal v Tottenham Hotspur	1-3	1-1	
Apr-29	Chelsea v QPR	1-0	2-0	
Apr-29	Coventry City v Manchester United	0-1	0-1	
Apr-29	Crystal Palace v Nottingham Forest	1-1	–	
Apr-29	Everton v Wimbledon	0-0	3-2	
Apr-29	Leeds United v Aston Villa	1-1	2-0	
Apr-29	Leicester City v Ipswich Town	–	–	
Apr-29	Manchester City v Newcastle United	–	2-1	
Apr-29	Norwich City v Liverpool	1-0	2-2	
Apr-29	Southampton v Sheffield Wednesday	1-2	1-1	
Apr-29	West Ham United v Blackburn Rovers	–	1-2	
May-06	Arsenal v Wimbledon	0-1	1-1	
May-06	Aston Villa v Liverpool	4-2	2-1	
May-06	Blackburn Rovers v Newcastle United	–	1-0	
May-06	Crystal Palace v West Ham United	–	–	
May-06	Everton v Southampton	2-1	1-0	
May-06	Ipswich Town v Coventry City	0-0	0-2	
May-06	Leeds United v Norwich City	0-0	0-4	
May-06	Leicester City v Chelsea	–	–	
May-06	Manchester United v Sheffield Wednesday	2-1	5-0	
May-06	Nottingham Forest v Manchester City	0-2	–	
May-06	QPR v Tottenham Hotspur	4-1	1-1	
May-13	Chelsea v Arsenal	1-0	0-2	
May-13	Coventry City v Everton	0-1	2-1	
May-13	Liverpool v Blackburn Rovers	2-1	0-1	
May-13	Manchester City v QPR	1-1	3-0	
May-13	Newcastle United v Crystal Palace	–	–	
May-13	Norwich City v Aston Villa	1-0	1-2	
May-13	Sheffield Wednesday v Ipswich Town	1-1	5-0	
May-13	Southampton v Leicester City	–	–	
May-13	Tottenham Hotspur v Leeds United	4-0	1-1	
May-13	West Ham United v Manchester United	–	2-2	
May-13	Wimbledon v Nottingham Forest	1-0	–	

319

1994-95 Event Diary

August	10th	FA Charity Shield
September	7th	England International
September	14th	UEFA Champions League
		Cup-Winners' Cup 1st Round 1st leg
		UEFA Cup 1st Round 1st leg
September	28th	UEFA Champions League
		Cup-Winners' Cup 1st Round 2nd leg
		UEFA Cup 1st Round 2nd leg
October	12th	England International
October	19th	UEFA Champions League
		Cup-Winners' Cup 2nd Round 1st leg
		UEFA Cup 2nd Round 1st leg
November	2nd	UEFA Champions League
		Cup-Winners' Cup 2nd Round 2nd leg
		UEFA Cup 2nd Round 2nd leg
November	23rd	UEFA Champions League
		UEFA Cup 3rd Round 1st leg
December	7th	UEFA Champions League
		UEFA Cup 3rd Round 2nd leg
December	14th	England International
January	7th	FA Cup 3rd Round
January	28th	FA Cup 4th Round
February	18th	FA Cup 5th Round
March	1st	Champions' Cup Quarter Final 1st leg
		Cup-Winners' Cup Quarter Final 1st leg
		UEFA Cup Quarter Final 1st leg
March	11th	FA Cup 6th Round
March	15th	Champions' Cup Quarter Final 2nd leg
		Cup-Winners' Cup Quarter Final 2nd leg
		UEFA Cup Quarter Final 2nd leg
March	29th	England International
April	5th	Champions' Cup Semi Final 1st leg
		Champions' Cup Semi Final 1st leg
		Cup-Winners' Cup Semi Final 1st leg
April	9th	FA Cup semi finals
April	19th	Champions' Cup Semi Final 2nd leg
		Champions' Cup Semi Final 2nd leg
		Cup-Winners' Cup Semi Final 2nd leg
April	26th	England International
May	2nd	UEFA Cup Final 1st leg
May	10th	Cup-Winners' Cup Final
May	17th	UEFA Cup Final 2nd leg
May	20th	FA Cup Final
May	24th	Champions' Cup Final